THE CULT
OF THE
MARKET

Economic Fundamentalism
and its Discontents

THE CULT
OF THE
MARKET

**Economic Fundamentalism
and its Discontents**

DR LEE BOLDEMAN

ANU

THE AUSTRALIAN NATIONAL UNIVERSITY

E PRESS

ANU
E PRESS

Published by ANU E Press
The Australian National University
Canberra ACT 0200, Australia
Email: anuepress@anu.edu.au
This title is also available online at: http://epress.anu.edu.au/cotm_citation.html

National Library of Australia
Cataloguing-in-Publication entry

Boldeman, Lee.
The cult of the market : economic fundamentalism and its
discontents.

ISBN 9781921313530 (pbk.)
ISBN 9781921313547 (online)

1. Economics. 2. Economic policy. I. Title.

330

Cover design by Emily Boldeman

To Ken and Don

Table of Contents

Introduction

Madmen in authority, who hear voices in the air, are distilling their frenzy from some academic scribbler of a few years back.
— J. M. Keynes[1]

Let us clear from the ground the metaphysical or general principle upon which, from time to time, *laissez-faire* has been founded. It is not true that individuals possess a prescriptive 'natural liberty' in their economic activities. There is no 'compact' conferring perpetual rights on those who Have or those who Acquire. The world is *not* so governed from above that private and social interests always coincide. It is not a correct deduction from the Principles of Economics that enlightened self-interest always operates in the public interest. Nor is it true that self-interest generally *is* enlightened; more often individuals acting separately to promote their own ends are too ignorant or too weak to attain even these. Experience does *not* show that individuals, when they make up a social unit, are always less clear-sighted than when they act separately.
— J. M. Keynes[2]

There are many others who are much better equipped than I am to write this book. Many sympathetic social theorists and economists schooled in philosophy and economics could have unravelled the complex issues underpinning economic fundamentalism and its perverse influence on public policy. While there is a huge literature critiquing libertarian philosophy and mainstream economics in great depth from every possible angle, I found few texts that provided an overview that addressed my needs as a policy analyst and none that covered the field as I would have liked. I am therefore writing my own broad-ranging multi-disciplinary account to explain how we arrived at this point and what is wrong with it. I initially wrote primarily for my own benefit so as to better understand the critique that was lurking somewhere in my subconscious, and in a wide range of literature, and which underpinned the widely shared concern that mainstream economics and its derivative—economic fundamentalism—was simply 'bullshit'. In doing so, I make few claims to originality other than in respect of the selection and organisation of the material. I leave it to economic fundamentalists and mainstream economists to defend their positions.

In his paper and subsequent book *On Bullshit*,[3] leading American philosopher Harry Frankfurt has described bullshit as a form of bluffing, arguing that it is a greater threat to truth than lies. He believes that the production of bullshit is stimulated whenever a person's obligations or opportunities to speak about some topic are more extensive than his or her knowledge. This is consistent with the popular use of the term 'mumbo jumbo', in which technical language is used to enhance the authority of the user and to render his or her claims less susceptible to public scrutiny. Indeed, it has been shown recently that many healthy people confabulate routinely when pressed to talk about something they have no knowledge of, or when they try to rationalise decisions or justify opinions—that is, they invent stories that they recite with complete conviction, seeming to believe what they say.[4] Some neuroscientists believe that we confabulate all the time as we try to make sense of the world around us. Since story-telling is central to human life and intelligence, this tendency should come as no surprise.

Herein lies the danger of the compartmentalisation of knowledge and the rise of the expert economist who pronounces on public policy claiming a special relationship with the truth. As I detail in Chapter 1, this particular confabulation—economic fundamentalism—has underpinned much public policy formation throughout the world in recent decades. It is dangerous because it is diminishing our understanding of ourselves and undermining many of the institutional protections erected with such struggle to protect the vulnerable in the nineteenth and twentieth centuries.

An additional strong driver for this work is my belief, based on my own experience, that economics, as I was taught it, fails to come to grips with reality—the way the economy really functions. The idealisation of the market, which lies at the heart of neoclassical economics and the associated mathematical deductive formalism, disregards the gross imperfections of this very human activity and describes a world that does not exist and that is radically different from the one we inhabit. My work also reflects my frustration with the resultant crude policy advice provided to government ministers and with the constraint it imposes on policy options. Important policy decisions are made on the basis of a very superficial understanding of economic 'principles' and crude political theorising, rather than a detailed understanding of particular problems and their origins. In particular, policy problems are analysed in terms of 'market failure'—a concept arising out of the neoclassical idealisation of markets with its patently false assumptions. Not only do market-failure arguments have the perverse effect of reinforcing the dominant paradigm, they fail to gain policy traction in practice. I am concerned particularly with the misuse of this school of economic thought to justify the excesses of the pro-market 'reforms' and the mean-spirited social policies that are occurring throughout the world.

While critiques of neoclassical economics are common, most are highly specialised, addressing particular concerns within a Newtonian/Enlightenment framework. They are not accessible to most readers and, on the whole, they have failed to influence policy makers. This failure reflects the entrenched power of this school in policy circles. In any event, I feel that the problem lies at a more fundamental level. What is required is a change of paradigm, licensing multiple, partial perspectives, rather than a more refined dominant formalism based on stylised assumptions. Consequently, my research has been directed at trying to articulate that more fundamental critique to myself, and then to communicate it to a wider audience. While I don't expect to convince many committed economic fundamentalists and mainstream economists of the error of their ways, I do hope to persuade the rest of us to stop listening to them.

The book sets out to examine the claims of economic fundamentalism from a number of complementary perspectives, building a case for a less dogmatic and more eclectic and pragmatic approach to public policy formation. Chapter 1, 'Setting the Scene', begins our journey proper by describing the problem as I see it. It describes the strong influence of economic fundamentalism on contemporary public policy and emphasises the way in which a fundamentalist vocabulary derived from mainstream economics now dominates public policy discourse, forcing out other vocabularies.

Chapter 2, 'The Creation of Social Order is Irreducibly a Moral Project', begins the critique proper by criticising the economic fundamentalist view that the social order is based wholly on self-interest. It takes an evolutionary and constructionist approach, pointing out that we are social animals, creating our social worlds, our moral order, through language and stories. It goes on to criticise the Enlightenment optimism that human beings are perfectible, drawing on some traditional religious ideas and some recent experience to illustrate the point. Chapter 3, 'The Relationship Between the Economic System and the Social Order', continues the critique begun in Chapter 2. It draws, in particular, on *Towards a Just Social Order* by Derek L. Phillips[5] to provide a summary account of recent theoretical approaches to social order, suggesting, however, that there is no need to adopt a unicausal account of that order, or to take such speculative theoretical stories too seriously. Importantly, the chapter concludes by arguing that the moral order cannot be reduced to a social contract. Chapter 4, 'A Brief Account of the Historical Origins of Economic Fundamentalism', goes on to give a historical account of the development of the social-contract ideas that underpin economic fundamentalism. In giving this account, I have drawn on work by Charles M. A. Clark[6] and Patrick Atiyah[7] in particular.

Chapter 5, 'A Critique of the Conceptual Foundations of Economic Fundamentalism', critiques the Enlightenment and modernism and the attempt to find a foundation for certain knowledge. It points to the dissolution of the modern world-view and the false certainty that comes with it. There is no certain knowledge and such knowledge as we possess is constructed socially from a particular point of view. Chapter 6, 'The Privileged Status of "Science"', builds on the above critique of the Enlightenment to criticise the crude nineteenth-century positivist understanding of 'science' on which economic fundamentalism relies. It draws on the account given in Blaug's *Methodology of Economics*[8] in particular, supplemented by the accounts of numerous other theorists to emphasise that scientific knowledge is always constructed socially from a particular perspective, that there are no privileged perspectives and such knowledge is forever subject to revision. It concludes that the claim that science has a privileged epistemological status in virtue of its empirical basis cannot be sustained. Rather, scientific inquiry and normative theorising use much the same practical reasoning. The chapter then extends to a discussion of the social disciplines, seeing the claims of social science as being even more open to question.

Chapter 7, 'What, Then, Can We Say of the Status of Economics?', goes on to suggest that there is no such thing as a value-free social discipline. Economics should, therefore, be seen as a moral discipline, rather than as a quasi-natural science. I go on to criticise recent suggestions that economists should study moral philosophy on the basis that it is an appeal from one failed Enlightenment project to another. This is not to suggest that a morally aware economist is a bad thing, rather that moral and political theorising should have no privileged status in policy making. These are only two of the numerous sources of the stories that form the values of our society.

Chapter 8, 'The Critique of Neoclassical Economics and its Influence on Policy Decisions', provides a critique of neoclassical economics on the basis that it is largely a failed attempt to give a mechanistic account of the functioning of the economic system. What we need is not a reformed neoclassical economics—a reformed Newtonian theory—but rather a richer set of metaphors for describing economic life. While experimental, behavioural economics, information economics and new growth theory have all contributed important new insights that act as correctives to neoclassical theorising, we need to get beyond the idea that economic theorising can describe or legislate an ideal form of economic organisation. Consequently, we need to recognise that policy decisions are policy experiments, rather than deductions from well-established deterministic theory. This should take us towards a more evolutionary approach that attempts to take the complexity of economic life seriously. Nevertheless, it needs to be kept in mind that there are no privileged perspectives, only more or less useful ones, and neoclassical theorising will still have a place in particular situations. The chapter concludes by suggesting that the teaching of economics should be altered so that the core content of undergraduate courses consists of the philosophy of the social disciplines, the history of economic thought, contemporary schools of economic thought—and then, and only then, a more detailed study of particular schools.

Chapter 9, 'The Doctrine of Freedom of Contract', is intended to provide an important example of the influence of economic ideas on a fundamental legal institution: the law of contract. An extreme version of this doctrine underpins much of economic fundamentalism. The chapter gives a historical account of the attitude to contract law and fair-trading issues in the United Kingdom and the

United States in the eighteenth and nineteenth centuries—attitudes that we in Australia have inherited. Chapter 10, 'Some Normative Reflections', is a normative reflection on what has gone before. Taking something that is a good—such as economic analysis, markets, human rights, liberty or money—and turning it into an absolute is the essence of a new idolatry.

I would like to acknowledge the support and encouragement I have received from a large number of people. I owe a debt of gratitude to my close friend Ken Lees, who, while not a professional academic, is a man of deep learning who first encouraged me to resume my studies. He has been a sounding board throughout this journey. Special thanks are also due to Professor Don Lamberton, a leading information economist who has guided me through much of my studies and has tolerated my vehement criticism of his profession. Don has been generous with his friendship, knowledge, time and books, and has been a source of constant encouragement and stimulus. I am also grateful for the encouragement and friendship of the late Professor Peter Self. Numerous others have encouraged me in this task. These include Dr Evan Jones, David Hull and Harvey Anderssen, who have read, corrected and commented on numerous drafts of the chapters, and Professor Frank Stilwell, Daniel Wells, Chris Hayward, John Revesz, Janet Pagan and Professor Jim Davis. Professor Pat Troy and his colleagues at The Australian National University provided hospitality and encouragement at a crucial moment when I first resumed my studies. I am grateful also for the constant encouragement and tolerance I have received from my wife, Vicki Boldeman, and our offspring in what has been a long journey. Emily Boldeman designed the cover.

ENDNOTES

1 Keynes 1936, p. 383.
2 Keynes 1926, p. 39 (emphasis in original).
3 Frankfurt 1992.
4 Philips 2006.
5 Phillips 1986.
6 Clark 1992.
7 Atiyah 1979.
8 Blaug 1992.

Chapter 1: Setting the Scene

The life of the avaricious resembles a funeral banquet. For though it has all things requisite to a feast, yet no one present rejoices.
— Pythagoras[1]

Money, gentlemen, money! The Virus
That infects mankind with every sickness
— Sophocles[2]

Without justice, all kingdoms are but bands of robbers.
— St Augustine[3]

Justice…is the main pillar that upholds the whole edifice. If it is removed, the great, the immense fabric of human Society…must in a moment crumble into atoms.
— Adam Smith[4]

In this book, I dispute the value of the shallow, all-encompassing, dogmatic economic theories advanced by economic policy elites in recent public policy debates, along with their gross simplifications and sacred rules. Economics cannot provide a convincing overarching theory of government action or of social action more generally, and should not be used for that purpose. Nor can economics define an ideal form of social or economic organisation against which to measure our institutional and organisational arrangements.

This critique should not be taken to mean that I believe that markets, prices and property are unimportant economic institutions. Rather, these institutions perform very useful roles in the coordination of economic activity. Nor should my critique be interpreted as meaning that I think macroeconomic stability is not an important policy goal. There is, however, more to successful economic management and welfare creation than macroeconomic stability—and there is a lot more to governing a country than economic management. Rather, my critique is directed against the mainstream, dogmatic, mechanistic, imperialist and fundamentalist framework that is currently being used to analyse the economic system and to justify policy decisions. This framework has its origins in libertarian political philosophy and in neoclassical economics and the excessive faith in markets that they promote. It is simply not true that the so-called invisible hand of the market will operate unaided to maximise individual and social welfare even within the false, crude and positivist understanding of welfare used in economics. There is much more to human welfare and happiness than economic welfare. It means that we should not become slaves to these institutions.

In rejecting the false certainty of naïve, simplistic, fundamentalist economic theorising—and the dehumanising and stupid policies that flow from it—I advocate a more overtly experimental, eclectic and pragmatic approach to policy development. This is an approach that takes much more seriously the complex, interdependent, evolving nature of society and the economy, and the important roles played in our society by our traditions, our values and by political compromise. Importantly, it is an outlook that recognises the pervasive influence of asymmetries of wealth, power and information on bargaining power and prospects throughout society. As Martin Hollis and Edward Nell tell us:

> Individual incomes do not result from individual hard work but from exercises of power, political decisions, tradition and other social forces, not least the hierarchical organisation of productive work...The clear implication is that there is no natural nor any efficient allocation of incomes. A competitive scramble for incomes is simply a power struggle and there is no hope of basing an 'incomes policy' on the notion of 'productive contribution' or 'efficiency'.[5]

Mine is an outlook that also pays adequate regard to the wide diversity of economic schools and views, rather than adhering slavishly to the narrow, contentious, contemporary orthodoxy. Importantly, I believe that the value judgements that are at the heart of public policy decisions should not simply be the province of manipulative fundamentalist economic technocrats and their political allies; they are truly matters for decision by a properly informed democratic polity. We have allowed economic rationalists and economists more generally to usurp a role that rightly belongs to all of us!

Recent public policy debates throughout the world have been influenced heavily by that complex of ideas known variously as Thatcherism, Reaganism, neo-conservatism, neo-liberalism, and, in Australia, economic rationalism and, in New Zealand, Rogernomics. Like all such complexes, the terms lack precision, but they all attach to a misuse of basic economic concepts to justify a strong faith in unregulated markets and an associated distrust of governments, politics, politicians, government bureaucrats, government services and welfare provision. Some critics see this lack of precision as a fatal flaw, but in doing so reveal their ill-founded essentialist and positivist leanings.[6] Rather, definitions should not be judged as right or wrong, but only as helpful or unhelpful in delineating useful categories.[7] In this regard, Keith Webb warns us in his *Introduction to Problems in the Philosophy of Social Sciences* that the very idea that any social science can be built on shared and agreed concepts by careful definition has been lost forever.[8] Indeed, the great philosopher Ludwig Wittgenstein (1889–1951) taught us '[i]f you want to know the meaning of a word, look to its use'.[9]

John Stone, the Secretary to the Treasury from 1979 to 1984 and a prominent economic rationalist, has no such definitional problems. He says that the central proposition of economic rationalism is that 'markets will, generally speaking and over time, always provide more economically advantageous outcomes than governments'.[10] I, along with many others, view this as an extreme position that is demonstrably untrue. Long experience in Australia and overseas demonstrates that there are forms of government coordination that are welfare enhancing. Nor does the claim follow logically from mainstream economic analysis.[11] As Joseph Stiglitz—a Nobel Prize-winning economist and the former chairman of President Clinton's Council of Economic Advisers and then Senior Vice-President and Chief Economist of the World Bank—says of America's recent experience:

> No one who has watched the corporate scandals, the wasted investments of America's boom, the idle resources of America's bust, can truly believe that markets, by themselves, result in efficient outcomes...The central lesson that emerges from this story of the boom and bust—that there needs to be a balance between the role of government and of the market—is one which evidently the world has had to learn over and over again.[12]

Consequently, Stiglitz is a strong critic of 'deregulation run amok'.

Furthermore, Stone's claim assumes the existence of clear, sharp, non-problematic boundaries between markets and governments and between economic and non-economic outcomes. These boundaries are, however, different legal, political and intellectual constructs in different countries—not natural entities—and they are open to continuing question. In any event, as I will argue in Chapter 2, the economic system is a subset of a broader, evolved and complex interdependent social system in which governance in all its forms performs an enabling coordinating role. Because it is a complex system, the distribution of that coordinating role across various mechanisms cannot be determined on the basis of simplistic reductive analysis. There is unlikely to be one unique 'optimal' solution to that distribution.

Additionally, many—if not most—economists agree, on the basis of long experience and simple reasoning, that the government has a legitimate role to play in the provision of public goods such as security, law and order, emergency services, education and the creation and diffusion of new knowledge. Since economic development is heavily dependent on knowledge processes—and since it is generally conceded that knowledge has many of the properties of a public good—government involvement would appear to be central to many 'economically advantageous outcomes'. Nevertheless, no one—let alone Stone—is arguing that the Department of the Treasury should be privatised.[13] So we can take it as read that the 'generally speaking' is far less general than might appear at first sight. Herein lies the source of unending political debate. One might notice in passing that economically advantageous outcomes—interpreted as static economic efficiency—have acquired a privileged status as a criterion for policy action against other considerations.

The financial media promote the policy directions that flow from these extreme attitudes: 'as well as fiscal discipline, Australia needs continued economic reform. More competition and deregulation, further privatisation and labour market liberalisation and a smaller public sector are all imperative.'[14] And, again, more recently:

> [T]here is a harder and politically important battle awaiting the Prime Minister at home. This is the battle to maintain the momentum of economic reform…The question is not whether the government has an adequate reform agenda…it is whether it has the will to impose genuine change on reform-resistant industries, with only lukewarm support from a reform-weary parliament and public.[15]

One consequence of these attitudes in the United States is the proposal developed in Congress after Hurricane Katrina for a substantial cut in services for the poor, big tax cuts for the rich and increased budget deficits. It was the obsession with budget cuts, however, that led to the poor response of US emergency authorities to Katrina in the first place. These attitudes are reflected also in earlier madcap and anti-democratic proposals from public-choice and libertarian circles to place fiscal policy in the hands of 'independent experts', and for constitutions to be amended to limit the size of the public sector. These proposals have generated stillborn copycat proposals here from the Business Council of Australia and the Centre for Independent Studies. The latter would limit the public sector in Australia to 25 per cent of gross national product (GNP)—down from the current level of about 32 per cent, which is already at the bottom of the league table of Organisation for Economic Cooperation and Development (OECD) countries and about the same level as in the United States. In contrast, public expenditure in the 15 original European Union countries amounts to 44 per cent of gross domestic product (GDP). The effect of the proposal would be to reduce an already relatively small public sector substantially to a level significantly lower than in most other developed countries. Interestingly, the recent Australian economic 'reform' experience is now being touted as a model for European governments reluctant to undertake similar reforms in the face of voter opposition.[16]

In the above description of our subject matter, I have been content to defer to popular Australian usage and use the term 'economic rationalism'. This usage focuses attention on the inflated rationalism in economics and political theory that underpins an excessive faith in the market. Other terms have, however, been suggested. For example, Peter Self used the term 'market ideology',[17] Stiglitz[18] and George Soros[19] used 'market fundamentalism' and John Quiggin sometimes used 'free-market radicalism'.[20] Some readers could prefer one of these alternatives because they have the virtue of focusing attention directly on an uncritical and excessive adulation of markets. Such adulation is not confined to the economics profession—and the association could unfairly condemn many economists. There are many economists who are trying to untie the Gordian knot of neoclassical economics. Furthermore, there are many fine neoclassical economists—including Nobel Prize winners—who have been critics of unrestrained pro-market policies. They have, however, been voices crying in the recent economic policy wilderness.

Some could argue that there is no necessary logical connection between mainstream or neoclassical economics and such market adulation—a view that is implicit in my use of the term 'misuse' in preference to 'use'. This argument is, however, beside the point. In my long policy experience, economists and some political scientists use neoclassical economics on a daily basis as a justification for extreme pro-market policies within government, academic institutions and the media. Such attitudes seem to be a common outcome of neoclassical economic training. For my part, I want to emphasise the fundamentalist and religious nature of these beliefs and include these ideas in my title. Throughout the book, I use the shorthand term 'economic fundamentalism'—the term used normally by John Langmore and John Quiggin[21] —because it focuses attention on the leading source of these extreme ideas.

In this regard, it is important to recognise that the exaggerated claim of economic fundamentalism is a claim to moral authority: authority to determine policy directions based on an assertion of superior economic knowledge—knowledge of the way in which the economy operates and should operate. Economics constitutes the powerful thought collective, an institutionalised community providing the interpretive strategies on which this fundamentalism depends. As contemporary historian of economic ideas and economic methodologist Mark Blaug tells us, however, economics is sick, having abandoned any genuine attempt to understand how real markets work for the soporific scholasticism and empty formalism of esoteric intellectual models.[22] This reflects a bias in ancient Greek, Christian and Enlightenment thought in favour of contemplation and theory over practice. Indeed, Joseph Needham (1900–95), the famous historian of Chinese science, warns us that 'there has always been a close connection between these rationalist anti-empirical attitudes and the age-old superiority complex of administrators'.[23]

In this spirit, I argue that the idealisation—even idolisation—of markets and of the individual economic actor, which is at the heart of mainstream economics, elevates and distorts their place in the economic system. As we will see later, modelling economic processes as if they were a mechanical system is a fundamentally flawed research strategy. Inappropriate policies derived from these strategies are, however, applied every day without any recognition of their shallow foundations.

Again, such attitudes are reinforced by the triumphal and imperialist pretensions of economics as illustrated by the following recent claims by Jack Hirshleifer, which fly in the face of daily experience: 'There is only one social science...What gives economics its imperialist invasive power is that our analytical categories—scarcity, cost, preferences, opportunities, etc—are truly universal in applicability...Thus economics really does constitute the universal grammar of social science.'[24]

Consistent with the above, Hirshleifer earlier revealed social Darwinist tendencies with his adulation of the survival of the fittest when, failing to notice the fundamental importance of social cooperation in human evolution, he claimed falsely that 'the evolutionary approach suggests that self-interest is ultimately the prime motivator of humans as of all life'.[25]

Gary Becker, another Nobel Prize winner, expresses similar sentiments in his *Treatise on the Family*:

> [The] economic approach is not restricted to material goods and wants or to markets with monetary transactions, and conceptually does not distinguish between major and minor decisions or between 'emotional' and other decisions. Indeed...the economic approach provides a framework applicable to all human behaviour...all types of decisions and to persons from all walks of life.[26]

Consequently, Becker makes the wild claim that there is a market in marriages. To conceive of the social, legal institution of marriage in such terms is, however, to debase marriage into long-term prostitution, and human beings into commodities. Becker claimed that his Nobel Prize reflected an official institutional recognition within economics of the extension of the domain of microeconomic analysis to a wide range of non-market behaviours.[27] It is this overblown confidence in the capacity of economics to analyse all issues and solve all problems that leads to such policy nonsense as the following from leading American economist and legal theorist Judge Richard Posner: 'The baby shortage and the black market are the result of legal restrictions that prevent the market from operating as freely in the sale of babies as of other goods. This suggests as a possible reform simply eliminating the restrictions.'[28]

One is reminded of Jonathan Swift's (1667–1745) satirical proposal that the Irish poor breed their babies for the table. That the overwhelming majority of the population rightly regards the sale of babies as morally repugnant and utterly unacceptable seems to have passed Posner by. One wonders whether—following the same logic—he is prepared also to deregulate the market for judicial judgements, or does he somehow consider the moral and legal obligations of judicial officers to be more sacred than the moral and legal obligations of parents for their babies?

Importantly, not all prominent economists share these sentiments. For example, Joseph Schumpeter (1883–1950) told us '[n]o social system can work which is based exclusively upon a network of free contracts between [legally] equal contracting parties and in which everyone is supposed to be guided by nothing except his own [short-term] utilitarian ends'.[29] Similarly, contemporary English economist Paul Ormerod warns us: 'The ability of economists to claim omniscience, to believe that the discipline is the first to explain anything worth knowing, really is extraordinary and can only serve to irritate both students and non-economists.'[30]

In short, such intellectual arrogance rightly infuriates everyone else. Implicit in this imperialism is the positivist aspiration for economics to become the physics of the social disciplines, with the status of the overarching and privileged social theory. As we will see later, this aspiration has its roots in the Enlightenment[31] and the particular form of social and political theorising that it spawned. In addition to enhancing the self-importance of such economists, this aspiration has the added advantage of saving them from the trouble of listening to what other social theorists have to contribute to our understanding of human society. It also saves them from having to deal with a vast literature challenging their knowledge claims. A wide range of opinion from leading social scientists and philosophers will be cited throughout this book to illustrate the point. The simplistic attempts to explain the operations of our various political systems and constitutional arrangements using neoclassical economic principles are examples that give rise to particular concern. Much opposition to government coordination and regulation flows directly from these crude attempts.

While this fundamentalism involves a misuse of mainstream economic analysis, the economics profession as a whole cannot avoid some responsibility for this misuse of its analysis to undermine confidence in collective decision making and action. After all, even libertarian philosopher and economist Friedrich von Hayek (1899–1992) warns us that an 'economist who is only an economist is likely to become a nuisance if not a positive danger'.[32]

The intellectual arrogance noted above contrasts with the more usual and more modest understanding that the social sciences 'are composed of "schools", "paradigms", "research programmes", "approaches", or "theories", none of which has a monopoly on knowledge'. Consequently, 'a knowledge of social science involves acceptance of eclecticism and a multitude of ways of knowing'.[33] The very study of mainstream economics, however, involves an insidious commoditisation by which all human activity is reduced to a single motive—individual gain—with all social institutions to be derived from that motive. As Edgeworth claimed in 1881: 'The first principle of Economics is that every agent is actuated only by self-interest.'[34] As Nobel Prize-winning economist Amartya Sen has confirmed, while this attitude reflects particular formulations of certain general philosophical questions posed in the past, it survives intact in much modern economic theory.[35] Mainstream economics has failed to pay regard to the institutional frameworks that discipline self-interest and individual choice, enable economic activity and underpin society. Furthermore, such economists have failed to notice that—on their own account—we ought to conclude that their arguments reflect only their own self-interest, having no necessary relation to the truth.[36] Furthermore, if the rational-expectations theory were true there would be no need for economists at all.[37] Their own conduct gives the lie to what they are saying.

Importantly, modelling human beings only as self-interested utility maximisers is inherently debasing. This is no new objection. John Stuart Mill (1806–73), one of the heroes of liberalism, in criticising similar assumptions made by utilitarian philosopher Jeremy Bentham (1748–1832), had this to say in 1861:

> Nothing is more curious than the absence of recognition in any of his writings of the existence of conscience...Nor is it only the moral part of man's nature, in the strict sense of the term—the desire for perfection, or the feeling of an approving conscience or of an accusing conscience—that he overlooks; he but faintly recognises, as a fact in human nature, the pursuit of any other ideal end for its own sake. The sense of honour, and personal dignity—that feeling of personal exaltation and degradation which acts independently of other people's opinion, or even in defiance of it; the love of beauty, the passion of the artist; the love of order, of congruity, of consistency in all things, and conformity to their end; the love of power, not in the limited form of power over other human beings, but abstract power, the power of making our volitions effectual; the love of action, the thirst for movement and activity, a principle scarcely of less influence in human life than its opposite, the love of ease—none of these powerful constituents of human nature are thought worthy of a place among the 'Springs of Action'...Man, that most complex of being, is a very simple one in his eyes.[38]

I would go further. It is not so much that such an account of human motivation is partial but that it is grossly distorted and destructive of human sociability. It leaves out and undermines our most important qualities—the qualities that make us human and life worthwhile. In particular, it leaves out the capacity to love and care for our families, our friends and neighbours, broadly defined. It is those loving relationships that guide and nurture our developing consciousness in the first place.

When one takes a serious look at the care and attention being poured into our family, friends, colleagues and fellow citizens, the economic aspects of our lives beyond the basic level of sustenance pale into insignificance. In short, modelling human beings as essentially self-interested utility maximisers misconceives radically the nature of humankind. When have any of us attended a funeral to hear the deceased described with approval as the essential human being: 'a utility maximiser, with a healthy self-image'? To the extent that we harbour such thoughts, we are more likely to think: 'he was a selfish bastard, who won't be missed'. Much—if not most—of life is taken up with the very long-term care of those closest to us and this everyday, complex experience defies reasonable description as self-interest. When it comes to the crunch, we expect our emergency services and military personnel to place their lives at risk in the service of their communities, in their line of duty—and they do! Ordinary people rise to great heights of heroism to help and save complete strangers. We talk, write and make films endlessly about this extraordinary aspect of human life, so there is no excuse for so-called 'scientific theorists' to downplay or ignore it in the interest of their half-baked parsimonious explanations. Importantly, this modelling also leaves out of the equation the continuing conflict between that capacity to love and care and our greed and lust for power—tendencies that have to be disciplined if human society is to survive and flourish.

This social theorising, this particular form of story-telling, this attempt to make sense of particular aspects of human experience, is closely related to the question of who we are—a question that has exercised the imaginative, speculative narratives of human beings since the dawn of time. Stories of the gods, therefore, helped ancient societies to introduce a narrative unity into the diversity of observed events, simplicity into complexity and order into disorder.[39] More recently, this story-telling has been motivated in part by a general desire to find secular substitutes for the certainty and existential comfort that we derived formerly from religion and its stories[40] in the face of the mystery of existence, the fear of death, the trials of daily life and the sense of alienation we feel in our contemporary, individualistic, technological civilisation. This mystery and the attendant fears are always with us,[41] along with a pressing desire to find meaning in life and to control our destinies. This search for meaning necessarily involves reference to something or someone beyond the self[42] and seems to be the inevitable result of the development of consciousness, language and narrative, and the associated attempt to ascribe meaning and intentionality to what we perceive, including our perception of ourselves. As leading symbolic anthropologist Clifford Geertz (1926–2007) explains, the problem of meaning raises the threat of chaos, creating in us an intolerable sense of analytical, emotional and moral impotence.[43] Furthermore, as Israeli sociologist Shmuel Eisenstadt argues, the radical division that exists between the heavenly ideal world and the everyday world in the Western tradition has exacerbated the above tensions, rendering grace unattainable and spawning a this-worldly asceticism in the search for secular substitutes for grace.[44]

Similarly, American philosopher David Loy—arguing from a Buddhist perspective—suggests that in the West we have been engaged in an increasingly this-worldly search for somewhere to ground our sense of self in the face of the breakdown in traditional beliefs. He tells us: '[I]nsofar as we think we have escaped such a spiritual drive we are deceiving ourselves, for that drive…still lives on in uncanny secular forms that obsess us because we do not understand what motivates them.'[45] In particular, lacking a traditionally religious conception of sin, we are left without a means of expiating our sense of guilt and the emptiness at our core. Loy goes on to argue that many of our modern worldly values acquire their compulsiveness—and many modern institutions their authority—from this misdirected spiritual drive.

These tensions demand some response, some faith to somehow secure our network of beliefs and to justify our practices. Consequently, society remains theological because its values and institutions cannot help being based on some ultimate view about human nature. Consistent with this view, Geertz defines religion as a system of symbols that acts to establish powerful, persuasive and long-lasting moods and motivations in people by formulating conceptions of a general order of existence and clothing these conceptions with such an aura of factuality that the moods and motivations seem uniquely realistic.[46] In this sense, religious beliefs remain inescapable[47] and act to justify and sustain our socio-economic order. In pre-literate tribal life, oral and other symbolic forms were considered openly magical and complex social differentiations were employed to ensure the proper use of symbolic and oral language. In these earlier societies, religious specialists, shamans, astrologers and medicine men were the guardians of the most powerful words, symbols and stories about the conduct of social life,[48] and were, as a result, the most respected and powerful members of those societies.[49] In our society, however, it is the scientist who has displaced the priest as the moral exemplar and the person who keeps humanity in touch with something beyond us[50] —the 'really real'. This explains the desperate anxiety of numerous disciplines, including economics, to be seen as being 'scientific'. This becomes particularly dangerous when combined with intellectual and spiritual arrogance and the desire to work policy magic. This does not mean that these religious are insincere; they truly believe they are serving the greater good—but so were the Mayans as they ripped the hearts out of their sacrificial victims.

This particular economic faith—economic fundamentalism, which is an institutionalised and extreme form of secularised Calvinism—arises under the influence of the pseudo-religious beliefs of the Enlightenment and the associated erosion of traditional religious beliefs. This faith resonates in modern materialistic societies where material success is equated with moral virtue and high status.[51] The need to erect new faiths as old faiths are eroded has been compounded by modernity's misplaced confidence that science can deliver certain knowledge to produce a secularised form of religious fundamentalism based on an excessive faith in the justice, efficiency and rationality of market processes and determined to root out what it sees as the evil of excessive government. Given the extent to which other forms of fundamentalism have caught on in the United States—and the historical influence of Calvinist theology, possessive individualism and Lockean political thought in forming that country's unique understanding of itself—it is not surprising that this particular form of fundamentalism has a strong grip there. In this regard, Martin Marty and Scott Appleby describe fundamentalism as a habit of mind found within religious communities among beleaguered individuals who feel that their identities are at risk.[52] In the search for doctrinal simplicity, certainty and right behaviour, fundamentalists are driven to a selective retrieval of doctrines, beliefs and practices from a sacred past. Renewed religious identity therefore becomes the absolute basis for recreating the political and social order by an authoritarian leadership. The evangelical, proselytising nature of such fundamentalism makes a particularly powerful brew when married to the American understanding of themselves as the new Chosen People, occupying the new Promised Land with a special mission in the world sanctioned by God.[53]

Going much further than can be justified, feigning scientific objectivity and claiming certainty, the dogmatic prophets of profit behave, on the whole, like the priestly class of an exotic cult, waging holy war to create new theocratic states in which their interpretation of neoclassical economics and libertarian philosophy provides the core theology. In common with other cults, other fundamentalisms, other emotional bolt-holes, this theology involves an exotic closed system of knowledge beyond the understanding on non-initiates whose protests are dismissed arrogantly as the bleatings of the ignorant. Having erected a disciplinary edifice as elaborate as any created by medieval scholastic theology, the devotees stand fearful behind walls built on simplistic and unrealistic assumptions ready to repel all critics through obscure terminology and labyrinthine reasoning—a new Tower of Babel resplendent with intellectual pride.

Wielding significant influence over government, such economists are the new theocracy, the contemporary manifestation of Plato's guardians. Economics provides true believers with a new faith tradition complete with values, ideas of welfare[54] and of progress, which dominate public discourse and which seek to reshape our institutions and organisations.[55] Indeed, the similarity between economics and religion has often attracted comment. For example, American theologian Harvey Cox[56] recently reported that most of the concepts he came across when reading the business pages were quite familiar. He tells us that the language of those pages bears a striking resemblance to Genesis, the Epistle to the Romans and Saint Augustine's 'City of God'. Cox is not alone in detecting in such pages an entire theology, a grand narrative about the inner meaning of human history, why things went wrong and how to put them right. What he finds in the business pages—in only thin disguise—are the theologian's myths of origin, legends of fall and doctrines of sin and redemption: chronicles about the creation of wealth, the seductive temptations of statism, captivity to faceless economic cycles and, ultimately, salvation through the advent of free markets—with a small dose of ascetic belt tightening along the way. There were even sacraments to convey salvific power to the lost, a calendar of entrepreneurial saints, an evangelising group and a teaching about the end of history or what theologians call eschatology. Then there are the heretics and infidels, those who refuse to bow down before these religious beliefs and who have been cast into outer policy darkness.

The consequence has been that the market system—which is only an evolved organisational technique for coordinating a disparate set of 'economic' activities, a cultural artefact—has become an end in itself, the object of excessive devotion and the source of our identity. Economists and libertarians have helped turn a useful, if flawed, tool into a god—THE MARKET—which we all must serve. Such conduct used to be called idolatry, a demonic perversion of true religion, something that used to be considered the gravest of all human failings. This idolatry threatens to enslave us all by misleading us about what is necessary to a worthwhile life.[57] This cult is creating a vicious cycle of commoditisation, undermining other values and promoting an ever-increasing culture of production and consumption under the delusion that this is the path to true happiness, the path to a secular salvation.[58] This is, however, a spiritual need that production and consumption cannot meet. As William Barrett warns us: 'Nothing is more compelling, and more dangerous, than the idea that is all-embracing, unqualified, and so simple that it appears to settle all doubts.'[59] The result for Loy is that 'the market' cult has become the most successful religion of all time—achieving an almost universal hegemony.

This is no idle comparison. Economists in contemporary capitalist states exercise as much power as the high priests of old or as the Inquisition in Medieval Europe. Developing countries, for example, have been subjected to enormous pressure to 'liberalise' from economists in international economic institutions such as the World Bank, backed by sanctions every bit as effective as those exercised by earlier religious authorities—even if they are less overtly violent—and often with catastrophic results.

My preference for the term economic fundamentalism has the added advantage of not being as open to vicarious insult from economic fundamentalists claiming that their critics are economic irrationalist—the 'trick of charging anyone who does not agree with a particularly narrow version of French rationalism or British empiricism as an "irrationalist"'.[60] As Quiggin points out, dogmatic assertions and the claim that anyone who holds contrary views is not a real economist are standard features of economic fundamentalist rhetoric.[61] This dogmatism flows from an ill-founded belief that neoclassical economics provides us with *the* scientific explanation of economic phenomena—an explanation that aspires to the status of absolute scientific truth. As John Ralston Saul has pointed out, however, such certainty is simply a form of bullying.[62] As we will see later, it is the economic fundamentalists who are the poor economists and philosophers.

The infiltration of economic fundamentalism into public policy debates in recent decades has seen the adoption of a new radical 'conservatism'[63] and the progressive slide of Western democracies towards the political Right. In that slide, the very different terms 'democracy' and 'market economy' have been conflated in the minds of many analysts—particularly in the United States—despite the tensions between them. Words such as 'choice', 'liberty', 'freedom', 'democracy', 'reform', 'progress', 'rationality' and 'man'—symbols that have resonated powerfully in the Western tradition—have become some of the more abused terms in political discourse as a result of the attempt to appropriate them to serve these radical views. The consequence has been that a small, privileged, insulated, economic and political elite—hiding behind the claimed value neutrality of and 'scientific' status of economics—has imposed its impoverished political philosophy, values and sectional interests on the wider community under the rubric of 'economic reform'.

This slide to the Right has been assisted by the process of globalisation—a process tending to homogenise Western capitalism and cultures around what are claimed to be American models and values with the very strong support of international economic agencies and the US government. In this regard, Stiglitz forthrightly acknowledges and rejects the recent ideologically driven, self-serving hypocrisy and the bullying involved in US advocacy of deregulated markets and in US trade policies and their inconsistency with the principles of social justice and democracy.[64] Of course, those who see the United States as an exemplar have forgotten that it was only a little time ago that the US economy was performing very poorly compared with the then exemplars of Japan and Germany. In this regard, it is important to emphasise that capitalism is only a relatively recent development and that it is not a monolithic system, the same in every manifestation. There have been significant differences in the institutions, values and traditions underpinning the market systems of different countries. In particular, America's Puritan heritage and her Lockean political philosophy have involved a strong emphasis on legalistic property and individual rights. This has led to the idea of 'America' and her moral values, her distinctive civil religion, her particular construction of a collective identity, being centred on the individual and on individual instrumental reasoning, rather than in the public sphere as in some other countries. The American secularised Calvinist search for signs of 'divine election', signs of participation in a secularised 'Kingdom of God' on Earth, has become centred on individual economic status. These factors have shaped America's particular understanding of capitalism as a system with special moral status. That system has increasingly occupied the central place in the US version of modernity and has led to enormous pressure on other US institutions such as the State, the family and the Church to accommodate themselves to the logic of the market, while undermining the idea of politics as a shared search for the good of society.[65]

The United States is not, however, the Kingdom of God, or Augustine's 'City of God'; it is just another human construct with all the imperfection that this implies. For Robert Bellah, this ethic of individualistic self-interest[66] has resulted in the loss of the American vision of good. Similarly, Ann Swidler detects a depletion of America's cultural, institutional and social infrastructure.[67] They argue that US coherence as a society depends to a significant extent on its pre-modern and early modern religious inheritance—an inheritance that is eroding in the face of the competition for wealth and power and the atomising tendencies inherent in possessive individualism. Similarly, leading American theologian Stanley Hauerwas believes that the American experiment is in deep trouble.[68] In effect, THE MARKET demands devotion in all realms of life. Nevertheless, the dominant position of the United States as the most significant economic and military power in the contemporary world is playing a key role in spreading these particular individualistic values—with their anti-statist bias, their relative indifference to equity and a particular interpretation of capitalism—to other countries on the unexamined assumption that the United States and its particular institutional arrangements provide a universal model for the rest of us.

One mechanism for the dissemination of US values is the current dominance of the economics profession by Americans. As Stiglitz confirms, the basic tendency of most American economists is to presume that markets work generally by themselves and that there are just a few limited instances in which government action is needed to correct 'market failure'. He also reminds us that the economic foundations for these assumptions are weak:

> In a market economy with imperfect and asymmetric information and incomplete markets—which is to say, every market economy—the reason that Adam Smith's invisible hand is invisible is that it does not exist. Economies are not efficient on their own. This recognition inevitably leads to the conclusion that there is a potentially significant role for government.[69]

This resort by American economists to a culturally specific framework should come as no surprise, as one of the themes in the philosophy of the social disciplines is the very difficulty of stepping outside one's cultural framework. In any event, the tacit assumptions of more conventional American economists have largely shaped the creation of economic 'knowledge' and its dissemination in recent decades. There is also the particular danger that, in a world characterised by high mobility of capital, skilled labour and ideas, the neo-conservative policies and practices of the United States are inducing a competitive rush to the bottom—to the lowest common denominator—in the same way that the Great Depression was exacerbated by the beggar-thy-neighbour policies adopted throughout the world at that time.

The reality of American life, however, falls far short of its democratic ideals and its image of itself as God's own country. The United States—with its 'weak' State, its government captured by business interests, its declining public infrastructure, its large exploited underclass, its huge disparities in income and wealth, its high levels of economic insecurity, its 46 million citizens without health insurance, its high levels of crime and violence, its very high murder rate and its disproportionately high prison population—is not necessarily a country that everyone else, let alone God, wants to emulate. What's more, recent research has shown that the belief that the US system promotes a high level of social mobility is untrue.[70] This is a country awash with arms and whose popular culture glorifies violence. The consequence, as John Gray points out, is that the United States and Russia are the only advanced countries in the world to use mass incarceration as a means of social control.[71] This mass incarceration reflects the weakened condition of the other institutions on which social cohesion depends. This criticism is not intended to deny the many great achievements of US society, or the fine quality of many of its citizens and institutions, including its tradition of private philanthropy. Rather, it is to balance any excessive adulation of that society and its market system.

The danger is that the dissemination of these impoverished US values across the world will ultimately undermine the sense of social solidarity and social trust on which the continued existence of societies and nations depend. Globalisation also uproots traditional forms of work, family and community life and brings the risk of polarising communities between a small group of winners and a large group of losers.[72] Consequently, globalisation is a movement many fear as economic and cultural imperialism—a process undermining values important to particular societies while imposing other values espoused by a small imperialist elite, particularly in the United States. Ironically, while being the leading advocate of libertarianism and minimalist government, the United States does not have a purely *laissez-faire* economy. While social policy in much of the United States is mean-spirited and there is much economic exploitation, US governments are highly active when it comes to agricultural, industrial and innovation policy, heavily subsidising new business formation and industrial innovation particularly through the defence budget and through tax policy.

The slide to the Right has had the practical effect of limiting the range of political choices available to us, and of altering the range of political solutions that are viable. For example, there is a significant danger of creating a vicious cycle undermining the public provision of services. The more public services are seen as inferior social safety nets subject to arbitrary rationing—rather than the usual source of high-quality services—the more likely it is that the quality of those public services will be allowed to deteriorate, further eroding public and political support for them. There is a very real possibility of arriving at a tipping point where the public provision of such services is no longer an option. This provides a good reason to oppose the public subsidisation of private services offered in competition to publicly provided services such as we see in mixed public and private health and education systems. A cynic might see here the potential for a political strategy to undermine the public provision of health and education. That same cynic, if he or she were an Australian observer, might wonder whether we are currently witnessing the slow destruction by stealth of Australia's universal health-care system, Medicare, and our public education systems.

No wonder we see Australia as having become a meaner and trickier country in recent years. This slide to the Right has resulted already in the incremental, proximal unravelling of the class compromise achieved shortly after Federation in 1901; the post-World War II government commitment to maintaining full employment; the abolition of our unique industrial arbitration system; a significant widening of income inequalities; an erosion of political commitment to welfare provision—and to egalitarianism more generally; a reluctance to undertake public borrowing for infrastructure investment; and an excessive government focus on narrow financial considerations at the cost of broader economic and social concerns. Let us be quite clear, however, about those narrow financial considerations. No special economic virtue attaches to very low levels of public-sector borrowing. Rather, it is responsible for governments to borrow for investment in long-lived capital. What matters for macroeconomic management is the total demand on resources and the productive capacity of the economy and its growth. That management involves a balanced application of monetary and fiscal measures and not an exclusive focus on monetary measures.

Economic fundamentalism has also elevated the corporate sector to a privileged position in economic life in which private enterprise is claimed to be inherently superior to government action[73] —an elevation reflected in the absurd, but widely promoted, belief that the private sector is the source of all economic welfare. In its exaggerated admiration for efficiency, flexibility, all things private and the American way, economic fundamentalism brings with it what is known as 'managerialism'—a process in which private-sector methodologies and language have invaded the public sector, transforming the way it is organised and operates. This managerial fad, while claiming to be democratic and responsive, is in fact extremely conformist and authoritarian.[74]

Economic fundamentalism is associated also with a privileged vocabulary, which is used to frame contemporary policy debates, to provide simple, pre-constructed answers to complex questions and as clinchers to particular policy arguments: terms such as 'government intervention' (the characterisation of government activity on behalf of the community as an intrusion into the proper order, justifiable only by special economic circumstances); 'fiscal consolidation' (the advocacy of balanced government budgets at low levels of spending); 'globalisation' (close international economic integration, bringing with it the potential loss of the ability to manage our economic affairs); 'the level playing field' (the use of a trivial sporting analogy to oppose government assistance to firms or industries); 'microeconomic reform' (the wholesale scrapping of organisational arrangements developed over decades); 'privatisation' (the government's sale of the public's interests in a range of infrastructure services, sometimes at discounted prices); 'competition policy' (the unjustified assumption that unbridled competition between business entities will necessarily improve the lot of consumers and consequently general welfare, and the extension of that assumption to government business enterprises); 'deregulation' (the removal of government constraints on business activity imposed originally to serve competing values, including limiting the abuse of market power, protecting public safety and ensuring equitable treatment); 'labour-market reform' (the reduction of human labour to a commodity, a concerted attack on unionism and the dismantling of institutional protection for workers, bringing with it the potential for a resumption by business of class warfare); 'public–private partnerships' (justifying the private provision of basic infrastructure services in return for monopoly rents); and, most recently, 'mutual obligation' (a new version of the concept of the deserving poor). As such, they operate as rhetorical devices to persuade policy makers and to quieten critics.

In short, economic fundamentalism provides the dominant vocabulary, the group-think and the narrative frameworks that we use currently to legitimise public policy decisions. They operate as blinkers to close minds to other influences, other possibilities and other better worlds. In particular, these pre-digested policies relieve us of the need to attend closely to the stories of our people in their daily circumstances, rather than the speculative stories of our economists. The heroic faith in progress inherent in these latter stories also relieves us of the need to examine our past experience because, by definition, that past is incapable of challenging the present. They also encourage us to forget that, even in rich Western countries, let alone in underdeveloped countries, Lazarus still sits at our gate. We have, however, forgotten the story of Lazarus, which once challenged us to abandon the ancient self-righteous belief that material success is a sign of individual moral virtue and of God's favour.[75]

This political language has been developed in a radical attempt to redefine Australian society and its institutions, and the values that underpin them. This is because the stories we tell, and the language we use to create our understanding of who we are, how things are to be explained and how we should act. They provide the 'master narratives' or the 'master plots' by which we structure our lives, and by which 'good' and 'evil' can be identified—creating views of the world out of which it is very difficult to break.[76] They also define the communities to which we can belong. In particular, participation in contemporary policy communities involves a mastery of a particular form of language game—economic stories derived from neoclassical economics and its associated vocabulary and a willingness to use them to the exclusion of other stories and other vocabularies. Through these stories and their slogans, economic fundamentalists seek to control the ways in which we think about the human condition and how we frame questions. These slogans are, therefore, instruments of power, providing a contemporary version of George Orwell's 'Newspeak'. Like Newspeak, this is language designed to narrow the range of thought and to eliminate the possibility of expressing contrary ideas, feelings and qualities.[77] As guardians of these powerful sacred words and symbols, economic fundamentalists—like previous priestly classes—are among the most powerful members of contemporary society, obliging our politicians to invoke their sacred, magic words to justify their decisions. They have influenced heavily the trajectory of government action in many countries, including in Australia since the beginning of the Hawke government. It explains the desperate continuing need of political leaders and aspiring leaders to appear to be economically literate and fiscally conservative. Worse, much worse, they are also influencing the activities we legitimise to ourselves, and the way in which we understand ourselves.

A similar movement in the nineteenth century—which remained influential until the Great Depression of the late 1920s and 1930s utterly discredited its disastrous policy prescriptions—went under the name of *laissez-faire*. The two movements share much in common, and economic fundamentalism can be seen as a return to the values advanced by *laissez-faire*. For example, contemporary Australian sociologist Michael Pusey, in *Economic Rationalism in Canberra*, sets out to account for what he calls a 'new and minimalist *laissez-faire* state set in norms that come from a dominating neoclassical economic rationalism that is anti-statist, anti-union and either asocial or anti-social in its basic orientation to policy'.[78]

It is important to recognise, however, that economic fundamentalism arises from a number of separate, though interrelated, sources, supported by powerful interests and strong propaganda, providing 'erroneous interpretations of the past, simplistic nostrums for the present and promises of universal benefits in the future'.[79] Those sources include:

- the attempt of neoclassical economics to provide 'natural laws' of economic activity modelled on the formalisms of the classical physics of about the 1850s
- a parallel attempt of political and moral philosophy in the Enlightenment tradition, particularly in Britain and the United States, to provide a comprehensive 'rational' or 'scientific' justification of political and moral arrangements and to rebuild those arrangements
- a related exultation of a particular negative view of freedom and of rugged individualism, along with the promotion of fear of big government, by Libertarian philosophers, the extreme contemporary followers of John Locke (1632–1704), as exemplified in the writings of Friedrich Hayek (1899–1992), James Buchanan (b. 1919), Ayn Rand (1905–82) and Robert Nozick (1939–2002)
- a related application of crude social Darwinist ideas to political and social systems
- the use of these ideas as an ideological justification of the capitalist system, particularly in the face of the challenge posed by Marxism during the Cold War
- the exploitation of those writings by business and political elites as a form of self-justification for their privileges and obscene salary levels,[80] and as a means of undermining close government regulation of their activity.

Importantly, economists speak about contemporary public policy issues with an apparent authority—an authority they claim to derive from their economic expertise. Webb, however, claims that what 'the social scientist cannot do is either take over the policy-making process with a legitimacy derived from being a social scientist, or act as an *eminence grise* behind the policy-making throne while pretending to remain a social scientist'.[81]

Nevertheless, economists have been active and influential in public policy debates from the dawn of the profession—very often in opposition to social initiatives to improve the lot of the underprivileged. Such was this influence that British statesman and political philosopher Edmund Burke (1729–97) described the eighteenth century as the age of the economist.[82] Indeed, Smith's *The Wealth of Nations*, published in 1776, had a major impact on political thought and on leading politicians, including the then Prime Minister, Pitt the Younger (1759–1806). Unfortunately, the parts of Smith's thought that suited the propertied ruling class were appropriated while his concern for moral sentiments and justice for the poor were ignored.[83]

Similarly, Bentham's *Defence of Usury* of 1796 provided the intellectual foundations for later efforts to repeal usury laws in England and the United States.[84] By the end of the century, the classical economic literature was well known to the educated public and was influential in policy making generally. Given the proliferation of a wide range of technical and scientific information in the same period, it is not surprising that these speculations and the associated policy ideas took on the authority and prestige of the science and technology of the time. Paul Mantoux, writing about the same period, tells us:

> The policy of *laissez-faire* was supreme and went unchallenged in the Courts as well as in Parliament. While that policy, at first, had been purely empirical, and had not been followed in all cases, it was now supported by the peremptory formulas of political economy: there it found its theoretical justification while its actual *raison d'etre* and its practical power was derived from the interests of the capitalist class. Theory and interest, walking hand in hand, proved irresistible.[85]

The result was an intensification of economic exploitation and political oppression.[86] Edward Thompson, for example, described the enclosure movement—a movement that had been under way for a long time—as a plain case of class robbery. Stretching back into Tudor times but intensifying in the late eighteenth century, that movement occurred under rules established by a parliament of property-owners and lawyers in which new capitalist property definitions were imposed on rural villages, dispossessing the occupiers of common-right cottages of their customary rights and converting some of those rights to theft, which was severely punished. It was, however, these customary rights that had enabled the rural poor to subsist. The result was the destruction of traditional English peasant society, a radical sense of displacement and the proletarianisation of a growing army of labourers.[87] Gray calls this period a far-reaching experiment in social engineering designed to free economic life from social and political control, breaking up the socially rooted market that had existed in England for centuries.[88] It was an experiment that threatened to undermine social cohesion.

It was a harsh time for the working class and the poor in England, reflecting the very uneven distribution of power and wealth; they were generally held in contempt by an arrogant, indolent, ruling elite—the propertied class—who saw the working class as idle and depraved. Consequently, working people were denied basic political rights and their agitation for such rights was suppressed violently in the panic generated by widespread unrest and by the French Revolution.[89] Pitt the Younger, the admirer of Smith, was responsible for a series of repressive actions and legislation between 1793 and 1801.[90] For example, the *1793 Aliens Act* prevented any French Republican from coming to England. The leaders of the London Correspondence Society were arrested in 1794, questioned by the Privy Council—including Prime Minister Pitt—and charged with high treason, the penalty for which was hanging, drawing and quartering.[91] The society itself was outlawed.

In 1794, the suspension of habeas corpus also allowed the arrest and imprisonment of people 'on suspicion', without requiring charges or a trial. Local Justices of the Peace (JPs), who came from the propertied class, were ordered to investigate and prosecute leaders of the Correspondence Societies. Many were imprisoned as a result. Tom Paine's *Rights of Man* of 1791–92, which attacked the monarchy, class privilege and the barbarity of the penal code, and which advocated income tax, family allowances, public education, old-age pensions and maternity benefits, was banned as seditious libel and he was driven into exile. Similarly, the *1795 Treasonable Practices Act* made a vicious attack on personal liberties, extending the definition of 'treason' to include speaking and writing, and attacking public meetings, clubs and the publication of pamphlets. In 1795, the *Seditious Meetings Act* required public meetings of more than 50 people to be authorised by a magistrate, while JPs were given discretionary power to disperse any public meeting. In 1797, taxes on printed matter were increased vastly to price cheap periodicals out of the market. In 1799 and 1800, the *Combination Acts* forbade societies or amalgamations of people for the purpose of bringing about political reform, while interference with commerce and trade became illegal. This legislation was not repealed until 1824.

The breaking of machines in the face of widespread economic distress induced by the competitive pressures of industrialisation was made a capital offence in 1812. At least 33 men were executed as a result, including one Abraham Charlston, who was only twelve years old and who reportedly cried for his mother on the scaffold.[92] Others were transported to New South Wales. The Scottish courts were even more repressive than the English courts.[93] In summary, it can be said that not only was the working class subject to severe economic exploitation and distress, the attempt on its part to combine to obtain better wages and conditions was ruthlessly opposed. As recently as 1844, the minimum age for entering factory work was reduced to eight years of age under pressure from mill owners.[94]

Another important early economist was Thomas Malthus (1766–1834). He claimed in 1798 that economic science had found that 'man'—with his inherent self-interest—was inert, sluggish and averse to labour unless compelled by necessity to be otherwise. For Malthus, the problem of the poor was the problem of over-population. For him, there were too many poor people—they were redundant! In this view, poverty was the natural condition of life for most people.[95] He attributed this problem to the failure of the poor to restrain their sex drives, outstripping the ability of the Earth to provide sustenance, bringing in turn numerous miseries that governments were powerless to prevent. He went on to assert that the only way to eliminate pauperism was to eliminate the humanitarian reforms that permitted the poor to maintain themselves and to propagate.[96] In practice, the most potent check on over-population was high infant mortality in poor families. He went on to claim that the 'infant is, comparatively speaking, of little value to the society, as others will immediately supply its place'.[97]

To our eyes, these claims are morally bankrupt. Malthus, however, failed also to appreciate the impact that increasing productivity would have on enhancing the lives of subsequent generations and the way the birth rate would fall as a result. Nor did he appreciate the need for the poor to have numerous children to ensure that some survived to support their parents in their old age—they had large families because they were poor. Furthermore, the issue of the time probably had more to do with the distribution of the benefits of productivity growth than with population growth outstripping productivity. Nevertheless, his views were used to bolster the case for harsh treatment of the poor and unemployed.[98] This influence led William Hazlitt to say about Malthus and the poor in 1807:

> His name hangs suspended over their heads, *in terrorem*, like some baleful meteor. It is the shield behind which the archers take their stand, gall them at their leisure. He has set them up as a defenceless mark, on which both friends and foe may exercise their malice, or their wantonness, as they think proper...Their interests are at best but coldly and remotely felt by the other classes of society. Mr Malthus's book has done all that was wanting to increase this indifference and apathy.[99]

These attitudes helped fuel the belief on the part of the politically influential that relief over and above dire necessity led to an excessive rural population and to idleness. Such moralising was reflected, for example, in the invention of the distinction between the 'deserving' and 'undeserving' poor with the *Poor Law Amendment Act* of 1819. Some Malthusian crank in 1838 even proposed the infanticide of every third child to deal with the population explosion.[100]

Another famous pioneering English economist and parliamentarian David Ricardo (1772–1823) endorsed explicitly *laissez-faire* doctrines.[101] According to his 'Iron Law of Wages', all attempts to improve the real income of workers were futile: of necessity, wages remained near the subsistence level. Ricardo, like Malthus, was a strong advocate of the abolition of the Poor Laws and the abolition of outdoor relief: 'While the present laws are in force, it is quite the natural order of things that the fund for the maintenance of the poor should progressively increase till it has absorbed all the net revenues of the country.'[102]

According to Ricardo, the Poor Laws simply moved money from the workers to the idle, while Malthus claimed that they were an inhuman deceit. Not only did Ricardo believe that all contracts should be left to the freedom of the market, he believed that the law needed to facilitate exchange: 'Like all other contracts, wages should be left to the fair and free competition of the market, and should never be controlled by the interference of the legislature.'[103]

As we will see later, this attitude pays no attention to asymmetries of power and knowledge in such relationships; and those Poor Laws were very harsh. For example, some of the transactions between factory owners and the Poor Law authorities regarding the employment of pauper children resembled the slave trade.[104] The slave trade itself was abolished by Britain only in 1807 and slavery more generally only in 1833.

Ricardo also opposed the Usury Laws in 1818 and the renewal of the *Truck Act* in 1822—the latter banning payments in kind. In turn, Nassau Senior (1790–1864) was an adviser to Whig politicians in the 1830s and 1840s.[105] He was also an advocate of *laissez-faire* and was one of the commissioners responsible for the *Poor Law Amendment Act* of 1834. Senior opposed trade unionism and reductions in working hours. Influenced by these advisers, Lord Melbourne, Prime Minister for seven years in the 1830s, believed that the whole duty of government was to prevent crime and to preserve contracts.[106]

This direct influence of the major classical economists was supplemented in the early decades of the nineteenth century by economic popularisers such as James Wilson, the editor of *The Economist*, and Harriet Martineau. They convinced the general public that *laissez-faire* was the practical conclusion of orthodox political economy.[107] As John Maynard Keynes confirms, the doctrine was disseminated by the educational system.[108] One of the strongest and most influential advocates of *laissez-faire* and freedom of contract was social Darwinist Herbert Spencer (1829–1903). He saw close similarity between *laissez-faire* and Darwinism. In his *Social Statics*, Spencer idealised freedom of contract as the supreme mechanism for maintaining the social order with the minimum of coercion. His views were quite extreme—objecting, *inter alia*, to state-aided education, sanitation and public health laws and the licensing of doctors. Indeed, for Keynes, the survival of the fittest could be regarded as a vast generalisation of Ricardian economics.[109]

These attitudes had important social consequences. They contributed to the decline of equity in English common law and the rise of the doctrine of freedom of contract, and therefore to the many abuses tolerated in the name of that doctrine. Opposition to poor relief led to the English *Poor Law Amendment Act* of 1834—the new Poor Laws. The right to poor relief was the last of the rights traditionally enjoyed by the rural poor. The Poor Law Commissioners, using the language of Malthus, described the poor rate as a bounty on indolence and vice.[110] The new Poor Laws were designed to ensure more uniform and harsher treatment of those unfortunate enough to fall within its provisions in the face of more lenient treatment under the decentralised administration of the former laws. In particular, the act abolished outdoor relief, making it clear that no able-bodied person was to receive assistance from the Poor Law authorities except in a workhouse.

The conditions in the workhouses were deliberately very harsh to discourage people from seeking assistance. This treatment under the 1834 act contrasted with the treatment under the Speehamland System of 1795, 'which sought to maintain the integrity of family, village and parish centres of solidarity and the mutuality of relief and welfare'.[111] Among this harsh treatment was the splitting up of families. The workhouses themselves were little better than prisons. The conditions inspired Thomas Carlyle, in *Past and Present*, to compare the workhouses with Dante's Hell. Consequently, relief under the 1834 act involved the loss of the normal rights of citizenship and of communal ties. British Marxist historian Eric Hobsbawm argues that because the intention was to stigmatise the self-confessed failures of society—rather than helping them—there have been few more inhuman statutes.[112]

It is possible to trace the influence of these attitudes further in the response of the UK government to the potato blight-induced Irish famine of 1845–51. As acclaimed British historian Cecil Woodham-Smith (1896–1977) tells us:

> The influence of *laissez-faire* on the treatment of Ireland during the famine is impossible to exaggerate. Almost without exception, the high officials and politicians responsible for Ireland were fervent believers in non-interference by Government, and the behaviour of the British authorities only becomes explicable when their fanatical belief in private enterprise and their suspicions of any action which might be considered Government intervention are borne in mind.[113]

One million people died, half a million people were driven from their smallholdings and two million people emigrated from Ireland as a result—the total population falling by about 25 per cent. Recent British Prime Minister Tony Blair described this tragedy in the following terms:

> The famine was a defining event in the history of Ireland and of Britain. It has left deep scars. That one million people should have died in what was then part of the richest and most powerful nation in the world is something that still causes pain as we reflect on it today. Those who governed in London at the time failed their people through standing by while a crop failure turned into a massive tragedy.[114]

Blair was much too polite; it must rank as one of the worst crimes ever perpetrated by a British government—and it did this in the full knowledge of the extent of the tragedy. This led Edward Twistleton—who early on had shared the prevailing prejudices—to resign as the Chief Poor Law Commissioner in March 1849 because 'the destitution here is so horrible, and the indifference of the House of Commons to it so manifest, that he is an unfit agent of a policy that must be one of extermination'.[115]

The punitive Irish Poor Laws of 1838 were also an important contributor to the tragedy. Modelled on the English *Poor Law Amendment Act* of 1834, they are said to have been even harsher.[116]

The head of the British Treasury during the famine, Charles Trevelyan—who assumed control of the administration of the relief effort—played a major part in inhibiting greater relief efforts by the government. In his view:

> The only way to prevent people from becoming habitually dependent on the government is to bring [relief] operations to a close. The uncertainty about the new crop only makes it more necessary. Whatever may be done hereafter, these things should be stopped now, or you run the risk of paralysing all private enterprise and having this country on you for an indefinite number of years.

Furthermore, he claimed with all the compassion of an Osama bin Ladin that the 'judgment of God sent the calamity to teach the Irish a lesson, that calamity must not be too much mitigated…The real evil with which we have to contend is not the physical evil of the famine, but the moral evil of the selfish, perverse and turbulent character of the people.'

All of this happened while Ireland continued to export food guarded by British soldiers and while there was sufficient food to feed the population had it been distributed adequately.[117]

Of course, we can always respond to this record by claiming that our economists, our governments and we are innocent of a similar indifference. Before we do, however, we should listen to Stephen Lewis's 2005 Massey Lectures and his powerful condemnation of the indifference of wealthy Western countries to gross poverty and the HIV/AIDS pandemic in Africa.[118] His description of the recent policies of the International Monetary Fund (IMF) and the World Bank as capitalistic Stalinism—rending the fabric of African society under the influence of a rabid economic dialectic—has a striking resonance with the attitudes of the British government in 1848. As he tells it, 'I have spent the last four years watching people die.'[119]

We have seen more distant echoes of these morally bankrupt attitudes in many countries recently, including Australia: for example, the effective reinvention of the concept of the 'deserving poor'. This has brought with it increasing pressure on selected categories of welfare recipients, particularly sole parents and the unemployed. In this view, poverty and unemployment are again being seen as the result of individual moral failure, rather than a failure of the economic system, the structures of society and of government management to provide adequate income and employment opportunities for all people.

In 1943, prominent Australian economist Ronald Walker noted the increasing influence of economists on public policy in Australia—an influence that has continued to grow.[120] This development reflected the gradual acceptance by the Australian government of responsibility for managing the economy. It brought with it an increase in the already substantial influence of the Australian Treasury and a development of its former accountancy-based culture and expertise—a change reflected in its recruitment pattern.[121] Like treasuries everywhere, that department occupied a pivotal role in the machinery of government, having been responsible for the provision of economic advice and for the scrutiny of other departments' expenditure proposals for much of the twentieth century.[122] Its advice played a dominant role in shaping government attitudes and policy decisions for most of that period. The experience of the Great Depression and then World War II had a seminal impact on economic policy attitudes, culminating in the adoption in 1946 of the goal of full employment in Australia—a development influenced by the British *Beveridge Report* of 1942 and the resultant reforms. There was, however, a gradual shift in Treasury's advice from the early 1970s away from the maintenance of full employment through counter-cyclical policies and demand management and a rekindling of a strong faith in markets and in neoclassical economics. This shift—combined with an ingrained hostility towards government expenditure arising from its former role as the keeper of the public purse—has much to do with the growth in economic fundamentalism in Australia and the dominance of that doctrine in recent governments. This change was, perhaps, symbolised by the seminar Hayek gave to the Australian Treasury in 1976.

This increasing influence of economists and of economic fundamentalism within the Australian bureaucracy was reflected also in the progressive transformation of the Tariff Board—the body established originally to advise on tariff assistance to Australian industry—into a body ideologically opposed to such assistance. This occurred over time and in stages. It was reflected in a change of title—first to the Industry Assistance Commission in 1973, then to the Industry Commission in 1989 and, most recently, to the Productivity Commission in 1996. In the formation of the last, the Bureau of Industry Economics and the Economic Planning Advisory Committee were abolished. Both bodies had provided alternative sources of expert economic advice and had shown some capacity for independent thought, including some tendencies to depart from the economic fundamentalist orthodoxy.

The influence of economic fundamentalism in Australia was reflected also in the 1981 *Campbell Report into the Banking Industry*—a report that led ultimately to the deregulation of the Australian banking industry.[123] In this case, the members of the committee had the honesty to declare their biases in the introduction to their report, but biases they remained. A further important example is the *Hilmer*

Report of 1993 into competition policy, which has been used as a justification for the wholesale restructuring of government business enterprises at the Commonwealth and the state levels.[124] Both reports were written in Treasury. Despite its admiration for competition as a means of delivering economically 'efficient' outcomes, the *Hilmer Report*'s shallow account of competition and its benefits rests on a very uncertain conceptual base and a naïve faith in market forces. The same could be said for the *Campbell Report*. These reports should be seen as serving rhetorical political purposes rather than providing serious, historically informed analysis of policy problems.

Accounts of the growing influence of economic fundamentalism on public policy decisions in Australia often mention the influence of neo-conservative think-tanks, such as the Institute of Economic Affairs in London, the American Enterprise Institute and the Cato Institute in Washington, which have strong links with similarly minded bodies in other countries. In Australia, we have copycats in the form of the Australian Centre for Independent Studies and the Australian Institute of Public Affairs. In Canada, they have the Fraser Institute, which was founded by a disciple of Hayek and which claims pre-eminent status among Canadian public policy research organisations. The Fraser Institute boasts that it acts as an economic conscience reminding governments and their publics of the limits of governmental competence.[125] It also reminds us that its work is far from done, and that, in its view, government activity is far too extensive, strangling economic growth and impinging excessively on individual freedom.

Ian Marsh, speaking primarily about Australia, and noting the remarkable proliferation of such think-tanks, has suggested that they point to the continuing prestige and political importance of the norms of rationality in a society in which other more traditional sources of authority and legitimacy have been discredited. He tells us:

> The neo-liberal or 'new right' group of think-tanks generally cluster[s] around the strategic or agenda end of the policy process. The group has been spectacularly successful in popularising a particular public policy agenda for responding to the changed world economy—reduced public expenditure, [a] lessened role for the state, 'neutral' industry policy, weakened trade unions, etc…Some suggest this group has attained a paradigm shift in conceptions of the role of the state held by political and bureaucratic elites.[126]

More generally, political theorists have long pointed to the significant power exercised by business in all capitalist democracies because of its privileged access to policy makers and because of its capacity to finance significant research and lobbying activities. Business associations play a significant role as intermediaries in that process. The spread of these ideas has probably also been aided heavily by the influence of the transnational economic organisations such as the World

Bank and the OECD—organisations whose perverse influence over Third-World countries has been criticised so savagely.

In Canberra, another popular explanation blames the strict neoclassical approach of the Economics Faculty of The Australian National University, which has trained a large number of public service economists in the past 40 years. Of course, this is a particular example of the wider argument that it has been the very narrow training of economists in recent decades that has been responsible. For Pusey, it is the social selection and the social background of senior Australian public servants that are the keys to that understanding.[127] He claims that top public servants are the 'switchmen of history' and that when they change their minds the destinies of nations also change. He could well be right, but it could be asked whether people who get to the top in bureaucratic organisations are characterised by a capacity for deep thought—and, by the time they reach the top, their knowledge of economic discourse is usually decades out of date.

While not discounting these influences, I suggest that a number of other factors have also been important. Firstly, the impact of the Great Depression and World War II on society has largely been forgotten. Consequently, there has been an erosion of the sense of community developed through those crises, and of the appalling costs involved. In particular, there has been an erosion of the sense of gratitude due to servicemen and women and to the working classes for their sacrifices during the war. These had moderated the commitments of political elites to unregulated markets and limited the influence of the business lobby in the immediate post-war period. It is as if doctrinaire capitalism—having survived the crises of the 1930s and 1940s and their aftermath—has finally reasserted itself. Of course, the decline of class-consciousness among wage earners has contributed to this trend, as has the relative decline of the manufacturing sector with its concentrations of relatively easily organised potential union members. While business interests can still be mobilised easily, it is now much more difficult to mobilise wage earners. The decline in class-consciousness has brought with it a decline in knowledge of the long struggle involved in achieving political rights and economic security for working people in the face of vehement political and economic oppression.

The professionalisation of politics has also contributed to this trend because fewer politicians have personal experience in anything other than academic training and a political career. In the absence of a strong grounding in personal experience, they are more likely to be influenced by theoretical speculation. Furthermore, the relatively privileged lives of professional politicians and senior public servants could also have played a part in insulating policy makers from some of the harsher realities of the economic system. Here in Australia, the isolation—geographically and sociologically—of the national capital also contributes to this lack of understanding, but the cultural isolation of elites probably plays a role in all countries. As Soros argued recently in *On Globalisation*, those who believe in what he calls 'market fundamentalism' 'are reluctant to accept that the system may be fundamentally flawed when it is working so well for those who are in charge'.[128] In this vein, it has often been claimed by Marxist theorists that the state bureaucracy in capitalist societies provides a crucial element in the structure of power and privilege inherent in the capitalist system.[129]

At the end of the day, some of the responsibility for this development has to be sheeted home to our particular political leaders and our systems of government. The emerging defects in the Westminster system of government—with its recent tendency to evolve towards an elected monarchy, in which the *de facto* monarch, the prime minister, exercises excessive power, and which lacks the checks and balances of the US system—mean that ultimately the responsibility has to be sheeted home to the prime minister. Readers in the United Kingdom will have no difficulty recognising the role of Margaret Thatcher and her government in ruthlessly pursuing so-called economic reform in the face of widespread public dismay, including, it is said, on the part of the Queen. Of course, this is not to absolve the US political system and the US social and political culture from their responsibility. The US political system seems to have been peculiarly open to capture by big-business interests. Of course, for those governments lacking the will or the wit to tackle such difficult problems as unemployment, entrenched social deprivation, environmental degradation and the coordination of economic development, the cult of the market acts as a convenient smokescreen.

The increasing influence of economists in public policy development is part of a world-wide trend. Economists have come to dominate civil service recruitment in many countries,[130] with economics the essential policy science and an important entry point to a successful public service career. Certainly, this has been the case in Australia, particularly in what are now called the 'central coordinating agencies': the departments of the Treasury, Finance and Administration and Prime Minister and Cabinet. Economic fundamentalism migrated from Treasury and its offshoot, the Department of Finance, to the Department of Prime Minister and Cabinet in the 1970s and 1980s, at a time when the size and influence of that department was increasing rapidly. In part, this was a result of attempts by ministers to create alternative sources of economic advice to balance Treasury's influence. The result has been perverse: three sources of very similar, simplistic advice. Often acting in concert, these agencies have extended their power greatly in recent decades. From these centres of bureaucratic power, economic fundamentalism has colonised the senior levels of most of the Australian Public Service.[131] As a result, economic fundamentalism exercises a disproportionate influence on the government's policy agenda.

This colonisation has been facilitated by the increasing influence of managerialism and its associated 'reform' agenda on the Australian Public Service and by the top-down control exercised over the selection process for senior positions, particularly in the Senior Executive Service. One outcome has been the amendment of the *Public Service Act* to make public servants the servants of the government of the day, rather than the servants of the public. Furthermore, the formation of the elite Senior Executive Service—and the terms under which the members of that elite group are now employed—has tightened control over the advice going to ministers. The key role played by the Department of Prime Minister and Cabinet in selecting departmental secretaries—especially since the abolition of the Public Service Board—has been an important influence in that development. One consequence has been that departmental secretaries are now frequently from central agencies and, in particular, from the Department of Prime Minister and Cabinet. This process overvalues theoretical knowledge of economics and 'economic soundness' ahead of the practical knowledge of program administration or even of business affairs. Indeed, some departmental secretaries have been known to boast of their economic expertise and their 'dry' views. The loss of tenure for departmental secretaries and the curtailment of rights of appeal in respect of appointments to the more senior levels—justified on the basis of improving efficiency and responsiveness—have facilitated this development. This has had a flow-on effect at lower levels. The result has been substantial pressure for conformity, an erosion of the integrity of the service and questionable personnel practices. The erosion of these rights can only encourage risk-averse advice, sycophantic behaviour and patronage—well-recognised dangers in bureaucratic organisations. Of course, more subtle forms of social control such as social distancing also play a part in achieving conformity.[132]

Of course, those at the top of the structure do not share these negative views of recent public service reforms. For example, Dr Peter Shergold, Secretary of the Department of Prime Minister and Cabinet and Australia's top public servant, has a much more optimistic view, seeing these changes as part of a quiet revolution that has transformed the way in which the bureaucracy works and that has significantly increased its productivity.[133] Shergold, however, as Public Service Commissioner, played a leading role in promoting the legislative and administrative reforms in the Australian Public Service so he might not be the most objective of observers. At least there seems to be agreement that there has been a revolution. In my view, in the absence of adequate tenure and effective accountability for selections, the integrity and competence of the Australian Public Service is being eroded. Readers will have to judge for themselves which perspective better captures the balance of the changes; however, recent serious scandals demonstrate that all is not well.

Governments and their key advisers also exercise control over a large number of other key appointments to statutory and non-statutory bodies and to public inquiries, and this control has been an important factor in the spread of economic fundamentalism. The selection of people to head major inquiries is not left to chance. Such appointments are considered carefully in an attempt to ensure a desired outcome. Consistent with this view, Pamela Williams tells us that the legacy of the Howard government in Australia is an entrenched, hand-picked elite:

> [O]ne thing remains beyond the vagaries of chance: this is Howard's empire, and the men and women appointed to positions of power and influence across the country form a conservative river as deep as it is wide. It flows through the bureaucracy, government bodies and regulators, tribunals for refugees and industrial relations, cushy diplomatic posts, Telstra, the ABC, and arts bodies and cultural institutions…It is the fountainhead of Liberal influence for years to come.[134]

Furthermore, these economic fundamentalist views have also colonised many of the private-sector lobby groups, including those that draw their staff from the ranks of the Australian Public Service. A small number of economic consultancies are also selling specialist economic expertise to government.

What remains for this chapter is to say something about the meaning of the term 'public policy'. The term is one that will be familiar to politicians, journalists, political scientists and public servants, but it is not one that keeps the average citizen awake at night. Policy is not confined to the public sector, because even private-sector bodies engage in governance activity that attracts the term 'policy'. Consequently, the adjective 'public' is used to make it clear that it is an aspect of government activity that is being discussed. Given that the term is used during election campaigns to describe significant statements of intentions, values and aspirations, it clearly has to do with the way that we are governed, with aspects of government action.[135] It is not a term that is used with any great precision, however, and is often applied erroneously to small-scale standardised administrative procedures in the public and the private sectors to protect administrators from having to constantly justify those procedures.

Hal Colebatch notes that discussion of 'policy' usually rests on three assumed characteristics of organised action: coherence, hierarchy and instrumentality. Coherence assumes that action forms part of a coherent whole, and policy has to do with how this whole should be steered. Hierarchy assumes that the policy is about how courses of action are authorised by the people at the top—that policy rests on legitimate authority. Instrumentality assumes that policy is concerned with the pursuit of particular purposes or goals, or the solution of particular problems. Instrumentality brings with it an implied expertise, an expertise divided into functional areas, such as economic policy and educational policy, with much effort expended in trying to achieve consistency between different policy fields. Instrumentality also involves a belief that the causal relationships involved in an area of activity—and the consequences of particular actions—can be determined. Importantly, the claims of economic fundamentalism to influence government action rest on this implied expertise. Part of the arrogance of economic fundamentalism rests in its claim that neoclassical economics is the primary, or even the sole, public policy 'science'.

The usual way of talking about policy—described above—grossly over-simplifies what happens in practice. For example, the extent to which coherence can be achieved in practice across the whole ambit of government action is open to significant question. Similarly, the above discussion assumes that policy involves articulate, conscious choice, but that is also open to question. For example, it is often difficult to separate actions into clear decisions and the activities necessary to carry them out. Policy can be grounded in practice rather than an authorised decision. In any event, a formal decision is often only a stage in the policy process. A statement of intent on its own is valueless without the commitment of significant resources. Therefore, policy must not be understood simply in terms of officially proclaimed goals but in terms of the way activity is patterned among a wide range of participants. Consequently, the emphasis in the literature on policy as the exercise of legitimate authority is a non-neutral idealisation. This view needs to be amended to take account of the involvement of an extended array of people with interests in any particular policy question and of the activity of gatekeepers controlling access to decision makers. Authority is diffused to some extent throughout the system and consequently it is probably preferable to speak of the mobilisation of authority in support of programs advanced by participants in the policy community, including public officials, rather than simply the exercise of authority. Who those participants are and the vocabularies they regard as legitimate determine which policy issues are raised and how they are addressed. Like all communities, there are tacit rules about participation, a shared vocabulary and informal social controls that govern participation. Consequently, the current dominant role of economic fundamentalists as decision makers, gatekeepers and participants largely determines what is seen as a legitimate policy problem, and who is accepted as a legitimate participant in any policy community. These decisions are not neutral. What is more, central agencies are vigilant in trying to shield ministers from well-developed advice with which those agencies disagree. In the case of the present government, this process of selection is reflected in the close involvement in many policy processes of business lobby groups and the partial exclusion of unions, welfare groups and consumer representatives.

It should be clear from what has been said above that the field of public policy is a broad and confusing one, involving a gross lack of relevant information, contradictory approaches to similar problems, the neglect of others and gross uncertainty about the likely outcomes of decisions. The recent film the *Fog of War*—the autobiographical reflections of former US Secretary of Defence Robert S. McNamara—makes a similar point about the uncertainty surrounding major strategic and tactical decisions in major conflicts. In this respect, economic fundamentalism could be likened to the strategic and tactical doctrines pursued on the Western Front for most of World War I, providing the false certainty of final victory, in which the terrible cost is overlooked. In his seminal work, *On the Psychology of Military Incompetence*, Norman Dixon describes the symptoms of group-think that all too often affect large organisations and authoritarian leadership groups and which lead to such disasters:

- an illusion of invulnerability (or, more generally, the illusion of certainty)
- rationalising away information inconsistent with cherished assumptions
- an unquestioned belief in the group's morality
- the stereotyping of opponents as stupid
- a shared illusion of unanimity
- self-appointed 'mind-guards' to protect the group from adverse information.[136]

As we have seen above, all of these symptoms afflict Australia's current policy processes.

The focus of this book is not the sociology of the growing influence of economic fundamentalism but the ideas underlying it. Many contemporary policy debates involve fundamental questions bearing on the functioning of the capitalist system and the relationship between economics, ethics and the law. Frequently, those debates are impoverished by the failure of many of the participants to understand fully that a dynamic and effective civil society is a basic precondition for an effective capitalist system. This can be seen most clearly in the awful struggle of many of the countries of the former Communist bloc to transform themselves into successful capitalist societies. In their cases, the necessary civil and legal prerequisites for a successful capitalist society are simply missing and are still being created. There can be little doubt that the ill-conceived economic fundamentalist recipe has been a catastrophe for much of the Russian population. The consequence in that case appears to be a slide back towards an authoritarian state.

The next chapter will begin an examination of these underlying ideas. To capture an adequate understanding of the dependency of the capitalist system on civil society, I will consider how social order, as such, is possible. It will be argued that, in an effective civil society, the pursuit of individual and institutional choice and self-interest is constrained by internalised moral codes and by externally imposed social sanctions. In particular, I will argue that the so-called free markets of the capitalist market system are not natural types, but are complicated cultural and legal artefacts, constructed over time and relying on internal moral codes, a complex regime of legal instruments and are enforcement by governments.[137]

Subsequently, I will show how economic fundamentalists have also failed to understand the epistemological limitations of the economics discipline, the moral assumptions they employ and the implications of the existence of asymmetries of knowledge and power for the fairness of the market system. I will argue that economic fundamentalism involves the making of an organisational technique—the so-called market system—and the associated abstract knowledge narrative into a theology. An elite group of technologists, a new vanguard of economists and their allies is engaged in a utopian attempt to remake civil society in the image of their idealised technique and their instrumental rationality. It is a utopian project that has disturbing similarities with the utopian projects of the twentieth century that caused so much suffering: the communist revolutions in Russia, China and Cambodia and the fascist projects in Germany and Italy. In particular, they share an exaggerated confidence in a pseudo-scientific ideology, a determination to remake society, its institutions and humankind itself in the image of that ideology, as well as strong anti-democratic tendencies and a lack of compassion. As such, it is a logical consequence of the Enlightenment project and its peculiar instrumental understanding of human reason. In that sense, economic fundamentalists are the last of the Marxists.

My fear is not that economic fundamentalism is true, but that it might become so. It brings with it the danger of the commoditisation of everything—the turning of all values into market values, stripping the social world of love, compassion, commitment and even scholarship, for what will sell. In particular, in conjunction with ubiquitous advertising, it is promoting an excessive materialism in which we draw our only sense of identity from our consumption and our possessions. Economic fundamentalism—with its obsessive concern for easily measured economic indicators and efficiency and flexibility in the service of production—is engaged in a war on rest and leisure. It is encouraging an alienating culture of exploitation and overwork, which threatens to undermine our relationships with our spiritual needs, our families and our communities. In doing so, it is undermining the moral basis of civic society and of the capitalist system itself. In addition, it is threatening the natural ecological preconditions for the survival of our civilisation.

ENDNOTES

1 Stobæus.
2 Sophocles.
3 St Augustine 1972, p. 139.
4 Smith 1976, p. 86.
5 Hollis and Nell 1975, p. 260.
6 I will be looking at positivism—a movement in the philosophy of science—in Chapters 5 and 6.
7 Lipsey et al. 1998.
8 Webb 1995.
9 Wittgenstein 1951, cited in Barrett 1978, p. 69.
10 Stone 2000, p. 25.
11 Neville 1997.
12 Stiglitz 2003, pp. 14–26.
13 Of course, the latter might not attract much of a price.
14 Australian Financial Review 2000, p. 20.
15 Australian Financial Review 2003, p. 62.
16 Trichet 2004, cited in Australian Financial Review 2004, p. 6.
17 Self 1999.
18 Stiglitz 2002b.
19 Soros 2002.
20 Quiggin 2002.
21 Langmore and Quiggin 1994.
22 Blaug 1997.
23 Needham 1947, p. 10.
24 Hirshleifer 1985, p. 53.
25 Hirshleifer 1982, p. 52.
26 Becker 1981, p. ix.
27 Ganbmann 1998.
28 Landes and Posner 1978, p. 339.
29 Schumpeter 1976, pp. 423–4.
30 Ormerod 2001, p. 3.
31 The cultural and philosophical movement often dated from the French mathematician and philosopher Rene Descartes (1596–1650).
32 Cited in Kruskal 1982, p. 129.
33 Webb 1995, p. 2.
34 Edgeworth 1881, p. 16.
35 Sen 1977.
36 Lux 1990.
37 Hodgson 1988.
38 Mill 1962, pp. 100–1.
39 Horton 1967, pp. 50–71.
40 Ryan 1970.
41 Barrett 1978.
42 Ong 1977.
43 Geertz 1973.
44 Eisenstadt 1978.
45 Loy 2002, p. 5.
46 Geertz 1966.
47 Loy 2002.

[48] Carrithers 1992.

[49] Corcoran 1979.

[50] Rorty 1991.

[51] de Botton 2004.

[52] Marty and Appleby 1993.

[53] Carroll 2004, p. 66. See also Adam 1992.

[54] Though a non-teleological concept of welfare.

[55] This does not mean, of course, that all economists share this faith or that it is necessarily tied closely to an understanding of the discipline of economics. Nor does it mean that many economists lack high standards of integrity in their private lives or are not personally religious in the more traditional sense.

[56] Cox 1999.

[57] Hamilton and Denniss 2005.

[58] Loy 1997.

[59] Barrett 1978, p. 323.

[60] McCloskey 1994, p. 30.

[61] Quiggin 1999.

[62] Saul 2001.

[63] This is something of a contradiction in terms given the radical nature of the agenda.

[64] Stiglitz 2005.

[65] Madsen et al. 2002.

[66] Bellah 1975.

[67] Swidler 2002.

[68] Hauerwas 2002.

[69] Stiglitz 2005, p. 10.

[70] Crook 2007, p. 12.

[71] Gray 1998.

[72] Cox 2002.

[73] Quiggin 1999.

[74] McKenna 2005.

[75] Luke 16:19–31.

[76] Abbott 2002.

[77] Corcoran 1979.

[78] Pusey 1991, p. 6.

[79] Jones 2000, p. 1.

[80] Kirrily Jordan and Frank Stilwell (2007) reported that the cash remuneration of the chief executives in the top 51 companies who were members of the Business Council of Australia was 63 times the average annual earnings of full-time Australian workers in 2005. It had been only 19 times the average wage in 1990.

[81] Webb 1995, p. 6.

[82] Lux 1990.

[83] Rothschild 2001.

[84] Horwitz 1977a.

[85] Mantoux 1961, cited in Kanth 1986, p. 10. Kanth goes on to argue that the revisionist attempt to distance economics from *laissez-faire* policies cannot be sustained.

[86] Thompson 1963.

[87] Ibid.

[88] Gray 1998.

[89] Thompson 1963.

[90] http://dspace.dial.pipex.com/town/terrace/adw03/c-eight/pitt/repress.htm#comb

[91] Fortunately, juries refused to find them guilty.

[92] www.spartacus.schoolnet.co.uk/PKluddites.htm

93 Rothschild 2001.

94 Bromley 2005.

95 Loy 1997.

96 See Malthus 1973, p. 260; and Lux 1990.

97 Cited in Lux 1990, p. 35.

98 Malthus was not completely identified with *laissez-faire* as he subsequently went on to oppose the abolition of the Corn Laws and to advocate counter-cyclical economic policies.

99 Cited in Lux 1990, p. 37.

100 http://dspace.dial.pipex.com/town/terrace/adw03/peel/poorlaw/attacks.htm

101 Lux (1990, p. 42) citing Kanth 1986, p. 88.

102 To be fair to Ricardo, it should be noted that he was talking about the incentive then existing for employers to underpay their employees in the expectation that the Poor Laws would supplement their wages so as to provide those employees with the minimum for subsistence. Cowherd (1977), however, showed that the increased costs of relief that were the source of these concerns were the result of increased unemployment after the end of the Napoleonic Wars and not the Poor Laws themselves.

103 Atiyah 1979, p. 314.

104 Mokyr 2002.

105 John Stuart Mill (1994, p. 163) was the only classical economist to point out that the enforcement of contracts was itself a form of government activity and that this necessarily imposed on the State a duty to determine which contracts should be enforced.

106 Atiyah 1979.

107 Ibid. and Keynes 1926.

108 Keynes 1926.

109 Ibid.

110 Thomson 1963.

111 Seligman 1992, p. 116.

112 Hobsbawm 1990.

113 Woodham-Smith 1992, pp. 54–5.

114 Blair 1997, cited in Kinealy 2002, p. 1.

115 Cited at http://www.rootsweb.com/~irlker/famemig.html and again at http://www.vincentpeters.nl/triskelle/history/greatfaminepolitics.php?index=060.090.010

116 Kinealy 2002.

117 See http://www.historyplace.com/worldhistory/famine/hunger.htm

118 www.cbc.ca/ideas/massey.html

119 One should acknowledge, however, the more recent and much more generous response of Western countries and in particular that of the George W. Bush administration.

120 Walker 1943, Ch. 1.

121 Whitwell 1986.

122 The Department of Finance was split from Treasury in 1976, but the departments have continued to operate in tandem, despite the occasional family spat. Both departments operate in close cooperation with the Department of Prime Minister and Cabinet.

123 Campbell 1981.

124 Hilmer et al. 1993.

125 Fraser Institute year?.

126 Marsh 1994.

127 Pusey 1991.

128 Soros 2002, p. 2.

129 Miliband 1969.

130 Markoff and Montecinos 1993, pp. 37–68.

131 Pusey (1991) points to social selection and social background as key mechanisms. The author emphasises the top-down control exercised over the selection process for SES officers, and the tendency

for senior bureaucrats to 'clone' themselves and their views in making selections for such positions. This has a flow-on effect at lower levels. The result is substantial pressure for conformity.

[132] See, for example, Westphal and Khanna (forthcoming); Zippelius 1986, pp. 159–66; Coleman 1990.

[133] Shergold 2003.

[134] Williams 2004, p. 1.

[135] Colebatch 1998.

[136] Dixon 1976.

[137] Howell 2000.

Chapter 2: The Creation of Social Order is Irreducibly a Moral Project

The wise and virtuous man is at all times willing that his own private interests should be sacrificed to the public interest.
— Adam Smith[1]

Assumptions Underlying Contemporary Public Policy Debates

In the first chapter, I argued that recent public policy debates have been impoverished by the failure of policy makers—under the influence of economic fundamentalism—to appreciate the extent to which the market system depends on, and is a sub-system of, the broader social system. Famously, it was Margaret Thatcher who claimed that there was no such thing as society. She had failed to notice that, by the very same peculiar logic, there was no such thing as a nation, an economy or a market, either. Rather, civil society, the political system, the market system and the broader culture are all involved in a complex mosaic of interlocking, mutually supporting structures and activities that provide the system of relationships, the social system within which we live.[2] The interactions between these elements resemble a complex, interdependent ecological system. Importantly, the complex system of moral, social and legal constraints that underpins our social order is an essential part of that ecological system. Threats to that social order are, therefore, threats to the whole system. Because of this interdependency, I argue that a healthy, just society that promotes human flourishing and actively mediates commercial relationships is an essential prerequisite to an effective, developed market system.

In contrast, economic fundamentalism tacitly assumes that social relationships are reducible to transactions between self-interested individuals—that is, economic relationships are the fundamental social relationships. It is this assumption and the reductionist tendency in Western thought that has allowed a particular economic methodology to become the dominant methodology for the evaluation of public policy choices in our society. Implicit in this assumption is the demeaning proposition that self-interest is the fundamental motivation of human beings. Contrary to popular belief, however, Smith, the father of economics, did not share this view, as the above quotation makes quite clear. Similarly, leading positivist economist and sociologist Vilfredo Pareto (1848–1923) acknowledged that 'real men governed by purely economic motives do not exist'.[3]

Nevertheless, the vocabulary of mainstream economics and its values now provide the dominant vocabulary and values for policy evaluation, crowding out other vocabularies and other values. Furthermore, within that economic vocabulary, 'economic efficiency'—the shorthand description of Pareto-optimality—has become the dominant value to be served by government policy. This has been true of most recent Australian policy debates, including the Australian fair-trading debate to which I will turn in the discussion on the doctrine of freedom of contract in Chapter 9. That debate raises in a direct fashion the relationship between the economic system and the social system, and the role of the State in supporting economic activity. It provides a good example of the influence of economic ideas on a fundamental legal institution that is backed by the coercive powers of the State, and which facilitates complex and longer-term economic exchanges.

How is Social Order Possible?

Cooperative behaviour is a fundamental, ubiquitous feature of human life. Let me say that again with emphasis in case you missed it: *cooperative behaviour is a fundamental, ubiquitous feature of human life!* Our day-to-day relationships are subject to a pervasive structuring of which we are largely unconscious. The excessive contemporary focus on the role of competition in market economies has concealed the fundamental significance of this cooperative behaviour. Without it, no human behaviour—social or economic—of any significance is possible. Let me emphasise the point again with an added twist: competition is not *the* fundamental *force* in human affairs—social or economic. For the moment, we will concentrate on how this cooperative behaviour, this structuring, this social order, is to be explained, with that word 'force' to be the focus of some attention in Chapters 5 and 8. The quest for such an explanation has long been at the centre of religious, philosophical, sociological and anthropological speculation. It is also related closely to the central questions of political life, namely: how should society be organised? How should the resources of society be distributed? What is the extent of our responsibility for others? Should individual freedom be restricted, to what extent, and in what ways? In so far as these questions ask what *ought to be*, they are moral ones: they ask about what is good, what is bad, and involve the fundamental questions about who we think we are.

Much academic discourse directed at these questions since the Enlightenment has emphasised the primacy of the individual, contrasting a methodological individualism with more corporatist notions. It has been something of an academic fashion in Western circles in recent centuries. Contemporary research has, however, shown that individuals are complex entities with internal states,[4] and if a reductionist strategy is thought essential to scientific investigation then, for consistency, one should not stop at the individual. This is not a position I take. Rather, I start from a position that sees the individual as embedded in society—an embedding that takes place through a continuing enculturation.

Consequently, I see the extensive theoretical discourse focused on whether the 'individual' is 'prior' to society or vice versa as a sterile waste of time—the product of obsessive Western dichotomous thinking. It seems clear to me that individuals constitute—and are constituted by—society. Putting it another way, the human 'I' discovers himself or herself only in encountering another 'I' and achieves identity and maturity only as a person in community.[5] In short, there is and can be no 'I', except in relationship and in contrast with others. The very idea of individuality is nonsense in the absence of comparison.[6] Furthermore, it is now clear that the evolutionary emergence of *Homo sapiens* is inseparable from the emergence of society. As sociologist Werner Stark (1909–85) argues, 'Here we are challenged to realise that the self and society are also coequal and coeval; that they are…twin-born.'[7] And again, 'Think society away, and *Homo sapiens* disappear; what is left is a speechless, mindless beast.'[8]

What this means is that there is no pre-social, fixed human nature on which to base discourse about human behaviour. Social life is not an optional extra;[9] it lies at the core of what it is to be human. Consequently, it is not possible to strip culture away in order to get to a more *essential* human nature in the way that many reductionist theories since the Enlightenment have tried to do.[10] This is an insight that renders the idea of the autonomous individual—so beloved of economics and much recent political philosophy—a dangerous falsehood.

Even the contemporary Western concept of the self, which seems so natural and self-evident to contemporary Western thinkers, is an artefact of a long social discourse.[11] This Western liberal notion of the human person as a free, independent, inquiring, rational and maximising individual is a masculine, Enlightenment view,[12] derived from a long Western Christian tradition, as mediated by John Calvin (1509–64) and René Descartes (1596–1650). To Buddhists, this view is a delusion and the source of human unhappiness. Indeed, other societies have held very different ideas of who we are, connected closely also to their particular forms of social organisation. For example, Homeric culture barely conceived of a self outside of social roles. Similarly, Geertz (1926–2006) writes of Balinese culture:

> [There is] a persistent and systematic attempt to stylise all aspects of personal expression to the point where anything idiosyncratic, anything characteristic of the individual…is muted in favour of his assigned place in the continuing, and so it is thought, never-changing pageant of Balinese life. It is *dramatis personae*, not actors, that endure; indeed it is *dramatis personae*, not actors, that in the proper sense really exist. Physically men come and go—mere incidents in a happenstance history of no genuine importance, even to themselves. But the masks they wear, the stage they occupy, the parts they play, and most important, the

spectacle they mount, remain and constitute not the façade but the substance of things, not least the self.[13]

Geertz therefore concludes:

> [T]he Western conception of a person as a bounded, unique, more or less integrated motivational and cognitive universe, a dynamic centre of awareness, emotion, judgment, and action organised into a distinctive whole and set contrastively both against other such wholes and against a social and natural background is, however incorrigible it may seem to us, a rather peculiar idea within the context of the world's cultures.[14]

Importantly, these different views of the self are not just different they are incommensurable. This means that it is not possible to synthesise these understandings to obtain a genetic concept of the self.[15] This insight poses a fundamental challenge to the positivist view of the social sciences, on which economic fundamentalism is based. That discredited positivist view presupposes that there are 'sheer facts' to be discovered about human interactions and about the world more generally. Consequently, it ignores the social process through which these 'sheer facts'—and the conceptual frameworks on which they are based—are established. Now these are not new ideas, however much they have been ignored in positivist discourse. Even Sir Francis Bacon (1561–1626), one of the fathers of empiricism and the scientific method, described four kinds of barriers—'Idols of the Tribe, Cave, Market Place, and Theatre'—that act against the achievement of objective knowledge and shape perception and thought. These were the limitations of human nature in general, the preconceptions of individuals, the fashions of day-to-day discourse and the dogmas of philosophies and science. Of course, Bacon hoped that the empirical method would provide a way out of these problems. Now, however, we can be far less sure that this is possible.

It is now clear that our taken-for-granted 'reality', our everyday understanding of the world, of our scientific knowledge and of ourselves is socially constructed. Importantly, language is now seen as the social medium into which we are born and within which we live, rather than simply being a tool we use to describe a pre-existing reality.[16] Consequently, the extent of our ability to get beyond language is problematic. The only reality we can know anything about is the reality we encounter through our language[17] and our stories. As Peter Berger and Thomas Luckmann tell us:

> I apprehend the reality of everyday life as an ordered reality. Its phenomena are prearranged in patterns that seem independent of my apprehension of them and that impose themselves upon the latter...The language used in everyday life continuously provides me with the necessary objectifications and posits the order within which these make

sense and within which everyday life has meaning for me...In this manner language marks the coordinates of my life in society and fills that life with meaningful objects.

And again: 'Everyday life is, above all, life with and by means of the language I share with my fellow men. An understanding of language is thus essential for any understanding of the reality of everyday life.'[18]

Consequently, for bacteriologist and philosopher of science Ludwik Fleck (1896–1961), 'Cognition is the most socially conditioned activity of man, and knowledge is the paramount social creation. The very structure of language presents a compelling philosophy characteristic of that community, and even a single word can represent a complex theory.'[19]

The idea that language, as a sign of something else, was always removed from reality was a cornerstone of the ancient rhetorical tradition that held sway over Western societies for many centuries.[20] This does not mean, however, that the natural and social worlds do not play a role in constraining our conceptual system, or that there is no order in those worlds. Rather, it can play this role only through our experience of it, and that experience is constructed socially through language and stories. Consequently, American philosopher Nelson Goodman (1906–98) goes so far as to argue that it is not meaningful to talk about the way the world is.[21] In this vein, Wittgenstein has pointed out that concepts must necessarily presuppose the existence of—and operate according to—the public rules of a social milieu, and presuppose a shared public domain of discourse.[22] The very language of that discourse is itself a product of a language community, a culture.

American linguist Benjamin Whorf (1897–1941) put it this way:

> Thinking also follows a network of tracks laid down in a given language, an organisation which may concentrate systematically upon certain phrases of reality, certain aspects of intelligence, and may systematically discard others featured in other languages. The individual is utterly unaware of this organisation and is constrained completely within its unbreakable bonds.[23]

Furthermore, Whorf tells us, on the basis of his studies of other cultures and languages, the 'various grand generalisations of the Western world, such as time, velocity, and matter, are not essential to the construction of a consistent picture of the universe'.[24]

Wittgenstein goes further:

> Language disguises thought. So much so, that from the outward form of the clothing it is impossible to infer the form of the thought beneath it, because the outward form of the clothing is not designed to reveal the

form of the body, but for entirely different purposes. The tacit conventions on which the understanding of everyday language depends are enormously complicated.[25]

In this same spirit, contemporary linguists Lakoff and Johnson have drawn attention to the pervasiveness of metaphor in everyday life, and, in the process, spelt out in part the mechanism by which language structures reality. The terms in which we think and act—our conceptual system—are fundamentally metaphorical in nature, reflecting the dominant historical and social order.[26] Similarly, many other theorists have argued that the way in which social phenomena are labelled serves as a device for social control. Accordingly, the leading sociologist of science, Karl Mannheim (1893–1947), claimed that almost no human thought was immune to the ideologising influences of its social context; that knowledge must always be knowledge from a certain position.[27] This view applies with particular force to knowledge of society itself. Consequently, the extent to which our accounts of social phenomena are a product of those phenomena—or of the process by which they are derived—is always problematic. John Shotter bluntly sums all of this up:

> [O]ur understanding and our experience of reality is constituted for us, very largely, by the ways in which we *must* talk in our attempt…to account for it…In accounting for ourselves we must always meet the demands placed upon us by our status as responsible members of our society, that is, we must talk in ways that are both intelligible and legitimate to others, in ways that make sense to them and relate to interests in which they can share.[28]

As we saw earlier, there is an important circularity here. We tend to become what we say we are.

Culture is something we learn as children growing up in a society and discovering how our parents and those around us interpret the world.[29] This process of enculturation is a process of sharing knowledge[30] —the knowledge by which people design their own actions and interpret the behaviour of others. This knowledge provides us with the standards we use for deciding what is, for deciding what can be, for deciding how one feels about it, for deciding what to do about it and for deciding how to go about doing it.[31] The creation and sustainment of such shared meanings is itself a social process in which moral knowledge is incorporated into a society's moral vocabulary and its social discourse.

This is often described as a process of institutionalisation. The development of language is itself considered the paradigm case of that institutionalisation, the basis of intelligence and the mechanism by which knowledge can be transmitted through time and space. Therefore, William Noble and Iain Davidson argue that 'mindedness'—that human conduct that exhibits signs of awareness, interpretation, understanding, planning, foresight or judgement—cannot occur independently of language. 'Mindedness' and language are learned through years of socialisation through interactions with others.[32] For Berger and Luckmann:

> Language now constructs immense edifices of symbolic representations that appear to tower over the reality of everyday life like gigantic presences from another world…In this manner, symbolism and symbolic language become essential constituents of the reality of everyday life and of the common-sense apprehension of this reality…Language builds up semantic fields or zones of meaning that are linguistically circumscribed. Vocabulary, grammar and syntax are geared to the organisation of these semantic fields. Thus language builds up classification schemes to differentiate objects…forms to make statements of action as against statements of being; modes of indicating degrees of social intimacy, and so on.[33]

In particular, the acquisition of language is an integral part of personality development. In this regard, George Mead argues that the hearing of one's own speech—and observing the response of others—is central to the recognition of the self as an object and agent.[34] Among that reality is our understanding of our own lives in the context of the passage of time. Consequently, Jerome Bruner argues that because we have no way of describing lived time other than in the form of narrative, we construct our understanding of ourselves as an autographical narrative: '[I]t is only through narrative that we know ourselves as active entities that operate through time.'[35] For his part, Jean-Paul Sartre tells us that 'a man is always a teller of stories, he lives surrounded by his own stories and those of other people, he sees everything that happens to him in terms of these stories and he tries to live his life as if he were recounting it'.[36] We construct our understanding of the causal relationships involved in happenings in the natural world in the same way—as knowledge narratives.

Accordingly, it seems clear that the contemporary liberal concept of the human person is the product of a particular tradition, a particular social discourse and a cultural artefact. To be a person in contemporary Western society is not to be a certain kind of being—'a self'—but to have internalised a particular socially transmitted and approved moral story, which is then used to structure that Western individual's sense of identity. Consequently, it is a story that is used to organise one's knowledge, experience and behaviour.[37] It follows immediately from the above insights that, at most, individuals—even Western individuals—can be only partially sovereign and autonomous, and it is a deceit to pretend otherwise. The formation of our values, and even of our consumer preferences, is a social process and cannot sensibly be separated from them.

My starting position is at odds with the starting point of the dominant school of economics—neoclassical economics. As the basis of its discourse, that school adopts the reductionist strategy characteristic of most science since the Enlightenment: an extreme methodological individualism, the assumption that human beings are essentially self-interested and an impoverished account of human reason. This 'presumes a deeply utilitarian understanding of social life...severed from connections to any concrete sense of identity, purpose, or meaning. Morality, religion, and the whole normative dimension of social life get either pushed out of sight or explained away as resultants of more important, or more real factors.'[38]

It is a starting point that makes it difficult for economists and economic fundamentalists to understand how economic action is constrained and shaped by the structures of social relations in which we are embedded.[39] Furthermore, its methodological individualism is not a morally neutral stance, but an ideological conviction—one that is confined largely to the Western world. Not only does it contain within it a view as to how societies are formed and how they function, it contains a strong distinction between the 'me' and 'you', which brings with it a strong distinction between 'mine' and 'yours'. While economists seek to tell us how our society should be organised, their methodological assumptions undermine their ability to engage adequately with the values that underpin our society.

Of course, some might argue that there is no necessary logical connection between the acceptance, or rejection, of individualism as a methodological principle and one's attitude towards individualism and individual liberty as moral and political ideals. Nevertheless, there is a close connection between these ideas historically and they come together in the context of welfare economics, which attempts to account for welfare improvements in terms of the subjective preferences of individuals. Martin Hollis has, however, warned us that the atomised individuals of neoclassical economics are entirely reactive to the environment, with no freedom of movement.[40] The consequence is that neoclassical economics denies human agency. It is therefore inconsistent with Libertarian political philosophies that stress human autonomy. It follows that there is a fundamental inconsistency at the heart of economic fundamentalism. We will turn to a more detailed discussion of those relationships in Chapter 8. In any event, contemporary economic fundamentalists claim to hold to individualism as a fundamental value as well as a methodological principle. It is, however, an individualism shorn of any compassion for real people in their daily circumstances as opposed to a claimed—and highly qualified—concern for their right to make their own decisions. It does not, for example, extend to a genuine concern for the autonomy of those who have no money or no job.

This qualified adulation of individual autonomy is itself deeply flawed. It seeks to gauge our individual worth in terms of our ability to 'distance ourselves from commitment to society'[41] and elevates selfishness from the status of a 'deadly sin'—the equivalent of idolatry—to the status of the essential human characteristic. In sharp contrast, most of our religious traditions teach us that to be authentically human, and even to find ourselves, we have to lose ourselves in the service of others and in the contemplation of the divine—a contemplation that is said to extinguish the sense of self and to promote a sense of the unity of all existence. Of course, this selfish view of humanity is also untrue as a scientific, psychological description of real human beings. The truly autonomous human being—*Homo economicus*, 'economic man'—is autistic, incapable of entering into normal human life with its continuous emotional engagement with others—engagement that is essential to normal human development. Indeed, that emotional responsiveness to others is more basic than symbolic thought, providing the basis for the acquisition of language and the development of symbolic thought.[42]

One important consequence of this adherence to methodological individualism has been a stubborn refusal on the part of economists to examine the formation of preferences—the basis of our choices. They do so on the grounds of what is called the doctrine of consumer sovereignty—the idea that we are all free to form our own preferences without having to justify them. As such, it is simply a restatement of the economic profession's commitment to individualism. It privileges so-called individual preferences—as opposed to social institutions and collective rules of behaviour—on the assumption that preferences have been chosen individually. This view ignores the extent to which our choices are conditioned by our positions in the social system—positions that involve normative obligations and power relationships enforced by society. It ignores the fact that we justify our choices to ourselves in the language of contemporary culture and the social construction of that language and culture. It also assumes that we know what alternatives are open to us and that we know what we want. So it simply refuses to examine the great extent to which preferences are learned and not chosen. It also ignores the particular influence that others have on those preferences, the extent to which they depend on previous choices and the extent to which they are either incomplete or inconsistent. What is more, it ignores the highly manipulative nature of much advertising. Furthermore, the economists' assumption that preferences are consistent has been proven to be false[43] —a finding that undercuts rational choice theory, which, in turn, underpins the theory of demand.

In this regard, Ormorod argues that the assumption that tastes and preferences are fixed is one of the most restrictive assumptions of orthodoxy, severely limiting the capacity of economics to illuminate real-world problems. This is because the alteration of tastes and preferences—particularly under the influence of others, including advertising—is pervasive in the real world.[44] We might note in passing that this obsession with individual preferences and individual autonomy does not extend to our treatment of children—and no economist is arguing that it should. It follows that they are accepting tacitly that there is a legitimate social role in the shaping of individual preferences: consumer sovereignty does not extend to children, or to the mentally disturbed, or to some aboriginals—that is, that there are other values to be served that override their autonomy. What, then, about the merely confused, or the poorly informed, or the badly misled? To label concerns for such people as simply paternalistic is not to mount a cogent argument but to make a questionable moral judgement.

Importantly, such preferences are said to include our internalised values and roles, with action and role-playing seen as being always instrumental and gratifying.[45] That is, they believe that human motivations are universally reducible to the competitive maximising of personal gain. Of course, such an account renders the words 'preferences' and 'choice' empty of meaning. Nevertheless, as contemporary critic and economist Michael McPherson[46] tells us, mainstream economics has been defined by the principle that the nature and origins of tastes and preferences lie outside the proper domain of economic inquiry. It provides the entry point into neoclassical economics—'the essence of all properly scientific economic thinking'[47] —and consequently excludes other forms of economic analysis. American pacifist and economist Kenneth Boulding (1910–93) jokingly referred to the immaculate conception of the indifference curve.[48] These boundaries are essential to the deterministic, reductionist and mechanical systems thinking that constitutes the neoclassical method. Of course, the constructionist perspective outlined above involves a quite fundamental challenge to this impoverished theorising, because it directs attention towards the social processes through which our choices are legitimised to us and to each other and away from what are wrongly assumed to be individual psychological processes.

Importantly, this refusal to examine seriously the formation of preferences is an ideological stance and an *ad hoc* strategy designed to protect the structure and methodology of economic thought from a fatally destructive criticism. If the consumer is not entirely sovereign, the ideological use of the concept of Pareto-optimality in welfare economics collapses. This untenable stance flows directly from economic theory's commitment to Cartesianism—the philosophical movement at the heart of the Enlightenment—and to a Newtonian cosmology. We will explore the consequences of those commitments in some detail in subsequent chapters. For the moment, it is sufficient to note that economics does not want to explore the complex of motives or feelings that lies behind real human choices. Rather, it renames people as economic actors and sets out to explore the so-called 'rational choices' of these 'idealised' actors. In this unreal, idealised, rationalist, but impoverished world, instrumental calculation is enthroned as the distinctive quality of human reason while the emotions are repudiated.[49] This is a debased, impoverished rationalism that is remote from the original Greek conception of reason as humankind's highest faculty—a sharing in the divine nature conceived of as pure mind[50] —and from the more modest concept that arose with humanism and is again being explored in contemporary thought.

A further fundamental objection can be raised to this focus on preferences and the optimisation of choices. It privileges the role of consumption in human affairs compared with the role of production. *Homo economicus* is a consumer, rather than a producer. It is quite clear, however, that for most people, their roles in the workforce are a crucial part of their sense of identity.

Social Order is an Evolved Complex Moral Order

Philosophers and theologians in the Western tradition have tended to draw a strong distinction between humankind and other animals, believing—at least in earlier times—that humankind alone shared in the divine nature and that this set us apart radically from other animals. It is now quite clear, however, that we are descended from other social animals. Even our earliest hominoid ancestors lived as members of structured social groups. Our closest contemporary relatives—the other primate species—also live in social groups that exhibit cooperative behaviour involving parental care, cooperative foraging, mutual protection, self-denial and reciprocal kindness.[51] This social behaviour among primates appears to extend back millions of years. Therefore, it seems fair to assume that human cooperation is partly a legacy of our primate origins.[52] Indeed, contemporary research is attributing a central role to collaboration and trust in human evolution and, in particular, to the evolution of language. It is, therefore, simply not true that we are born entirely selfish.

Humans have an unusually long period of infantile and juvenile dependency on adults and this fact alone should put paid to any excessive adulation of individualism. The basic ability to intensively attend to and respond to others is present at birth.[53] New-born human babies imitate the expressions of others and enter into an exchange of feelings. By twelve months, they show a specific need to share purposes and meanings and to learn how to denote common ideas by means of symbolic expression. It is also clear that the life chances of a person—and the lifelong sense of his or her own worth—is heavily dependent on the experience of being loved as a child.

Human nurture and cooperation more generally are not simply a result of biological inheritance. Even among other primates, behaviour is not determined purely genetically; social learning is also important. Primate behaviour is a consequence of a complex mix of genetic, cultural and environmental factors with some recent research tending to emphasise the significance of the cultural element. Cultural learning is even more important to humans because human cooperation involves a much more complex range of behaviours and far wider networks than does cooperation among other primates. It is our ability to fashion more complex and more varied forms of social life that distinguishes us from them—an ability that depends on language and story-telling.

It is, therefore, now generally considered that humans are distinguished uniquely from other animals by our capacity for—and possession of—complex cultures and language. The possession of culture played an active role in shaping the final stages of human development.[54] The evolution of the human race—and particularly the emergence of intelligence and symbolic capacity—entailed a complex in which the organised hunting of large animals, life in organised social groups and the making and the use of tools were interconnected.[55] As contemporary anthropologist Roger Keesing (b. 1935) puts it: '[T]he whole pattern evolves together; changes in physical structures and changes in behaviour, both genetically and socially transmitted, are tied together.'[56] Michael Carrithers emphasises the evolution of social intelligence as playing the key role in this development[57] —a position consistent with the social function of intellectual hypothesis advanced by British psychologist Nicholas K. Humphrey.[58] Similarly, Philip Lieberman believes that our ability to talk is one of the keys to understanding the evolutionary process that made us human.[59]

It also appears that there is no necessary opposition between the influence of instinct and of learning in this evolutionary process. Among recent commentators, anthropologist Peter Reynolds[60] rejects explicitly the proposition that human evolution has been characterised by the replacement of instinct by culture. Rather, human behaviour and animal behaviour more generally appear to involve a complex interaction between instinct and experience. He argues that there is a great deal of behavioural continuity and that the instinctive systems that function in animals have parallels among humans. There appears to be a 'progressive' development of social behaviour, particularly among primates. We also appear to share much of the same emotional equipment. Reynolds concludes that a theory of human evolution that presupposes the development of reason at the expense of emotion, or of learning at the expense of instinct, conflicts with the evidence. Importantly, he argues that the relationship between reason and emotion is not one of hierarchy, but of specialisation by function—the brain integrating different kinds of information into a unified course of action. Consequently, the progressive evolution of primate cognition did not depend on the replacement of innate behaviour by learned behaviour, but on the selection and control of innate behaviour by conceptually stored information. The comparative evidence also supports progressive changes in the capacity for conceptualisation, in instrumental skills and in the volitional control of behaviour during the course of human evolution.

Keesing argues that our behavioural potential appears to be many-sided, complex, culturally shaped and socially expressed:

> [T]he human behavioural repertoire entails countervailing tendencies. Humans probably do have behavioural tendencies to dominate, to compete, to be aggressive (though probably not to be territorial in a strict sense). But they also have tendencies to share, to cooperate, to be altruistic. Institutions and customs may intensify competition, reinforce dominance, or express aggression in warfare and combat; but they may reinforce our propensities to share, cooperate, be egalitarian and peaceful.[61]

Similarly, Mary Midgley argues that there is no need to choose between explanations based exclusively on social or innate human tendencies, because she believes that such causes do not compete; they supplement each other.[62] For example, she suggests that such innate tendencies as fear and anger are necessary motives and elements in a good life. Further, she points to the complexity of human motives and of the states labelled as aggression, spite, resentment, envy, avarice, cruelty, meanness and hatred and the complex activities they produce. Importantly, she argues that we are capable of these vices because we are capable of their opposites—the virtues. The capacity to form long-term relationships necessarily involves the possibility of rejecting or abusing that relationship. Aggression is only one among many motives that can lead to wickedness. Nor is it true that all aggressive behaviour is evil. She argues that we need to think of wickedness not primarily as a positive, definite tendency such as aggression—which needs special explanation—but rather as a negative, as a general kind of failure to live as we are capable of living. This, she suggests, involves recognising a whole range of natural motives associated with power: aggression, territoriality, possessiveness and competitiveness. The positive motives that move people to evil conduct are often quite decent ones such as prudence, loyalty, self-fulfilment and professional conscientiousness. The appalling element for Midgley lies in the lack of other motives, which ought to balance these—in particular, a proper regard for other people and a proper priority system that would enforce it.

It should be quite clear from the above that it would be a mistake to devalue the critical influence of cultural evolution in trying to correct the excessive distinction made between nature and nurture in earlier accounts of human evolution. It is also important to note that an evolutionary account of human development does not involve any necessary acceptance of the biological determinism connected with such contemporary theorists as Edward O. Wilson (*Sociobiology: The New Synthesis*) and Richard Dawkins (*The Selfish Gene*). The more extreme pronouncements of these theorists are simply wrong. Their story is simply another attempt—in a long line of attempts in the Enlightenment tradition—to find a deterministic, mechanical explanation of human behaviour. Their selfish-gene metaphor is simply not helpful. Genes are not selfish; they lack the agency that would enable them to be described appropriately in that way. Nor are living organisms reducible to their genes, as recent research into the human genome has shown.

Contemporary biologist Brian Goodwin says it quite bluntly: organisms cannot be reduced to the properties of their genes and have to be understood as dynamic systems with distinctive properties. He argues that a more dynamic comprehensive theory of life focused on the dynamics of emergent processes would reinstate organisms as the fundamental units of life. In this view, organisms are not simply survival machines for genes. Organisms assume intrinsic value, having worth in and of themselves.[63] For Goodwin, such a realisation arises from an understanding of organisms as centres of autonomous action and creativity, connected with a causal agency that cannot be described as mechanical. It is the relational order that matters. Of course, this applies with particular strength to humans, and Goodwin extends this conclusion to social structures where relationships, creativity and values are of primary significance.

As should be clear from the above, this social order is acknowledged to be a moral order; it determines how we *should* act. As pioneering French sociologist Emile Durkheim (1858–1917) pointed out:

> [W]e are involved in a complex of obligations from which we have no right to free ourselves...Thus, altruism is not destined to become, as Spencer desires, a sort of agreeable ornament to social life, but it will forever be its fundamental basis. How can we ever really dispense with it? Men cannot live together without acknowledging, and, consequently, making mutual sacrifices, without tying themselves to one another with strong, durable bonds. Every society is a moral society.[64]

The study of social life is therefore a study of social norms, the institutions in which they are embodied and the stories we tell about them. It involves not simply regularities in conduct, but regulated conduct.[65] It is the shared values embedded in those stories that act as the mortar that binds together the structure of each human community, with rewards and punishments based on those commonly held values. It is also the pervasiveness of these values and rules that gives each person a sense of belonging, a sense of community.[66] Our very survival depends on such conformity. For the most part, conformity is a result of the internalisation of values and conceptions of what is desirable. These provide security and contribute to personal and social identity. Such cultural knowledge is, however, often tacit; it is so regular and routine that it lies below a conscious level. Michael Polanyi tells us that paying express attention to such knowledge can impede the skilful application of it in much the same way as giving express attention to a motor skill can impede the application of that skill.[67] Such skills are not exercised by following the rules explicitly. The aim of training is to free us from the need to follow such rules consciously.[68]

Sociability, then, is not simply a natural trait. Rather, social phenomena are due to nature and nurture. What is distinctive about human beings is our capacity to control our behaviour—what Stark calls our 'animality'—a capacity that other species on the whole lack.[69] The process of nurture, the process of socialisation, is a process of moralisation.[70] The survival of sociality requires a system of discipline that sets limits to, and works against, the drives that we have inherited. It is this control that makes human civilisation possible and it is only then that higher values can influence human conduct. American cultural anthropologist Marshall Sahlins (b. 1930) puts it this way:

> It is an extraordinary fact that primate urges often become, not the secure foundation of human social life, but a source of weakness in it...In selective adaptation to the perils of the Stone Age, human society overcame or subordinated such primate propensities as selfishness, indiscriminate sexuality, dominance and brutal competition. It substituted kinship and cooperation for conflict, placed solidarity over sex [and] morality over might.[71]

Scottish philosopher David Hume (1711–76) made a similar argument: 'It is certain that self-love, when it acts at its liberty, instead of engaging us to honest action, is the source of all injustice and violence...We must allow that the sense of justice and injustice is not derived from nature, but arises artificially, though necessarily, from education and human conventions.'[72]

For Stark, it is the control of greed exercised by the social norms that, in particular, constitutes a crucial victory of culture over animality.[73] He sees what he calls society's primary laws as emerging out of these social norms. These norms—a society's *ethos*—are not only taught to us by our parents, as indicated above, we learn them from our stories, our popular music, our fairy-tales, fables, sagas and legends, symbolism and ceremony, and from popular, artistic and educational literature. In the contemporary world, radio, television, film and the Internet provide much of the medium for this learning. These norms always operate in conjunction with ethical and religious teachings.

Importantly, for Stark, religion lies behind the other ethos-building institutions, filling the gaps left by custom and law—a view consistent with that of Geertz cited in Chapter 1. Because only crude offenders are detected, the pressures encouraging obedience to the law cannot be fully effective. They leave inner dispositions largely unaltered and cannot enforce the performance of good deeds. In these circumstances, the belief that our moral conduct will ultimately be rewarded or punished by some transcendent judge provides a powerful incentive for moral conformity. Stark, drawing on the work of French philosopher Henri Bergson (1858–1941), doubts whether society and culture could survive without a metaphysical prop of some kind. As indicated in the previous chapter, even in our partly secularised society, religious conceptions have not been eliminated. Not only do traditional religious views survive in a significant proportion of the population, powerful religion substitutes such as the deification of nature and of history have a similar influence.

The evolution of social norms and institutions has involved a long process of moral search and experimentation. Stark, drawing on the work of American social evolutionist William Sumner (1840–1910), describes it as follows:

> What Sumner saw at work, in the lap of society, was a process of selection separating by way of trial and error, useful and disappointing expedients, and leading to the adoption of the former and the discarding of the latter. The guide in this never resting and never ending stream of experimentation is not pure but practical reason, not ratiocination, but, rather, common sense. General principles of action may and do in the end emerge, but they are merely abstract formulations, summings up, of concrete experiences.[74]

The conviction that humans have themselves created the social system within which they have their being is central to this point of view. For Stark, the self-creation of society is the greatest of all social phenomena. What have been selected in this historical process of evolution are ways of behaving that mitigate the war of all against all. Hayek, the darling of economic rationalists, also described a historical, evolutionary process of trial and error for the development of social rules.[75] Successful action results in the rule being selected, whereas unsuccessful action results in the rule being discarded.

Importantly, if humankind has made society in the process of its own evolution, it is not the pure product of 'nature'. In the words of Berger and Luckmann, '[s]ocial order is not part of the "nature of things" and it cannot be derived from the "laws of nature". Social order exists *only* as a product of human activity.'[76] Equally, if humankind has made society, it has also made the economic system.

These insights have considerable significance for the study of human behaviour itself. The social and economic systems and their constituents are not natural types or entities such as sodium chloride—exhibiting natural regularities to be described by the natural sciences—they are social artefacts. It is also clear from the above that culture is not a once-for-all influence; it is a continuing process constructed and reconstructed during human interaction.[77] Consequently, contemporary anthropologist Bruce Knauft tells us: 'Culture is now best seen not as an entity, tied to a fixed group of people, but as a shifting and contested process of constructing collective identity…This is as true in New Guinea as it is in New York.'[78] The entire cultural and institutional environment within which the institutions of governance are embedded is the product of history and is subject to a path of dependency to at least some extent.[79] Consequently, history matters.

In their account, Berger and Luckmann explain that institutionalisation arises out of the habitualisation of actions that tend to be repeated frequently and their associated typifications.[80] These actions can then be reproduced with an economy of effort, making it unnecessary for each situation to be defined anew. Institutions control conduct by setting up predefined patterns of conduct, and are experienced as possessing a reality of their own that confronts members of the group as an external and coercive fact. The objectivity of this created world of meaning hardens as those patterns are passed on to children, and are experienced by them as an objective reality and an authoritative claim. Among groups, it ensures predicability of behaviour, stabilising actions, interactions and routines, which are then taken for granted. As such, they make possible a division of roles and labour in the widest sense.

Such an institutional world, and its associated roles, requires ways in which it can be explained and justified—that is, it requires legitimisation, giving rise to legitimising formulae. These legitimisations, these stories, are also learned during socialisation. In the evolution of human society, a widening canopy of legitimisations has been created, backed by the mechanisms of social control. For Berger and Luckmann, this edifice of legitimisation uses language as its principal instrument, with the fundamental legitimising explanations being built into the vocabulary. Importantly, society, identity and reality are each crystallised in the human subject in the process of internalising the language, which provides the means and the content of socialisation.

Language also provides the means for objectifying new experiences, allowing their incorporation into the existing stock of knowledge and the means by which these sedimentations are transmitted in the tradition of a collective. In this way, legitimisations can be adapted so as to reinterpret experience without necessarily upsetting the institutional order. Berger and Luckmann stress that this process of legitimisation does not primarily involve a preoccupation with complex theoretical systems because 'the primary knowledge about the institutional order is the sum total of "what everybody knows" about the social world, an assemblage of maxims, morals, proverbial nuggets of wisdom, values and beliefs, myths [and] so forth'.[81] With the evolving complexity of a society, however, there similarly arose specialised bodies of 'theoretical' knowledge providing a stable canopy of meaning for the society and ultimately creating symbolic universes in which all sectors of the institutional order were integrated in an all-embracing frame of reference. In the process, they attained a measure of autonomy capable of modifying, as well as reflecting, institutional processes.

As more complex forms of knowledge arose—and as an economic surplus developed—there also arose specialist legitimisers, who devoted themselves full-time to integrating the meanings attached to disparate institutional processes. In the process, they became increasingly removed from the necessities of everyday life, claimed a novel status and claimed knowledge of the ultimate status of what everyone did. These legitimisers, these story-tellers, these 'priests', form part of the system of social control, justifying the institutional order and giving normative dignity to its practices. The symbolic universe provides order for the subjective understanding of biographical experience and the history of society more generally—our sense of who we are.

> The entire society now makes sense. Particular institutions and roles are legitimised by locating them in a comprehensively meaningful world. For example, the political order is legitimated by reference to a cosmicThe entire so order of power and justice, and political roles are legitimated as representatives of these cosmic principles.[82]

This human projection of meanings onto reality creates the world in which we live, but these symbolic universes are social products with a history. Of course, no symbolic universe is entirely taken for granted, with variation in the way in which the universe is conceived, with competition between rival groups of experts, the repression of dissent and the evolution of the tradition to ward off heretical groups. Importantly, an ideology develops when a particular definition of reality comes to be attached to a concrete power interest. So it has been with our society and with our market system. Of course, in modern pluralist societies, there tends to be a taken-for-granted shared universe and different partial universes existing in mutual accommodation and tension.

Berger and Luckmann go on to give an account of what they call the conceptual machineries of universe maintenance, pointing to the role of mythology, theology, philosophy and science in creating and maintaining the symbolic universe. For them:

> Modern science is an extreme step in this development, and in the secularisation and sophistication of universe-maintenance. Science not only completes the removal of the sacred from the world of everyday life, but removes universe-maintaining knowledge as such from that world. Everyday life becomes bereft of both sacred legitimation and the sort of theoretical intelligibility that would link it with the symbolic universe in its intended totality. Put more simply, the 'lay' member of society no longer knows how his universe is to be conceptually

maintained, although, of course, he still knows who the specialists of universe-maintenance are presumed to be.[83]

In summary, social life is made possible only through the disciplining of what Stark calls our animal nature or our animality.[84] Not only have our instincts been tamed, they have been transformed into factors making for social cohesion. Nevertheless, underneath human culture, animal nature is still present and needs permanent discipline. At best, the average socialised person is only semi-moralised up to a moderate standard of law-abidingness. We adjust to social life by internalising and operating its norms and by internalising and manipulating them. We learn how to seem social as well as how to be social—not only how to serve, but how to hold our own, to manipulate and how to exploit. Of course, we often also lie to ourselves about our own motives. Consequently, there is often a deep discrepancy between human ideals and real conduct. Every society must therefore guard against antisocial conduct; it must have and apply sanctions, to deter as far as possible criminal behaviour in the widest sense of the word.

It is important to note before we move on that the above evolutionary account of the development of human society and of culture does not involve any acceptance of the social Darwinism that is identified with Spencer or Sumner in the late nineteenth century, and which attempted to justify the dominant social hierarchies of Victorian society.

The Maintenance of Social Order Also Involves the Creation of Moral Institutions

Clearly, punishment—or the threat of punishment—is necessary for a general climate of obedience to social norms. What is more, there is an element of force in all forms of property, marriage and religion. In smaller and simpler communities, unorganised social pressure could have been sufficient to maintain the social control necessary to guard against a war of all against all,[85] though some genetically based sense of hierarchy could also have been important. What is perhaps more certain is that, in its early days, law was barely differentiated from other forms of social pressure.[86] The evolution of larger, more complex and more anonymous societies involved splitting the social code into two parts—custom and law—with organised law enforcement by people forming part of a governmental apparatus.

This perspective sees the State as having grown out of a basic social need for a coordinating mechanism especially to ensure safety and order, with the State as the guardian and enforcer of the key norms.[87] Plato (427–347 BC), Aristotle (384–22 BC), the Stoics[88] and the Epicureans[89] all thought of the State as coterminous with society itself. Much more recently, Stark argued that society solved one of its most difficult problems by placing a monopoly of the means of compulsion in the hands of the State.[90] For his part, Norbert Elias[91] also sees the advancing division of functions involved in the civilising process—including the division of labour—as going hand in hand with the monopolisation of physical force and the growing stability of the central organs of society. It is the monopolisation of force—this narrowing of free competition—in conjunction with increasing pressures for self-constraint that create the pacified social spaces in which the functional dependencies between people can grow, the social fabric can become more intricate and economic activity can flourish.

In his account of the origins of the State and civilisation, based on the study of the six original civilisations of which we have knowledge, Elman Service specifically denies the class-conflict theory of the origin of either the State or of civilisation. He agrees that the creation of culture was *the* human achievement, the means by which societies tamed and governed their members and created and maintained complex social organisations. This depends on the ability of the political aspects of a culture to integrate and protect the society. Some societies, however, have done more than perpetuate themselves, having found political–cultural solutions that enable them to grow to ever-greater size and complexity. Service argued that the origins of government lay essentially in the institutionalisation of centralised leadership, which in developing its further administrative functions grew into a hereditary aristocracy.[92] Primal government worked to protect and legitimise itself in its role of maintaining the whole society. In this view, political power organised the economy rather than the reverse.

Despite all claims and appearances to the contrary, the law is really a liberator not an oppressor, and so is the State as the ultimate enforcer of the law. These moral functions can, however, easily be subverted so that the State becomes an oppressor. This experience provides the motivation for much political philosophy, and for political programs aimed at regulating the role of the State itself.

Unorganised social pressure in support of key norms and the organised enforcement of law is not enough to ensure social order. We cannot do without a sense of guilt—the guilt flowing from the breach of internalised norms.[93] The survival of a community depends on its moral cohesion and the coercive force of the law cannot maintain that moral cohesion alone: secular restraints are not enough to deter evil, antisocial or merely illegal acts. The healthier the society, the less it relies directly on legal sanctions. Ideally, life in society should be lived above the law, not by it. Australian theologian Bruce Kaye, in particular, emphasises that social interaction degenerates when it is construed narrowly in terms of legal obligations.[94] The law is a framework and a guide as to the character of the civic system, but is not an adequate dynamic for the civil community. Similarly, within organisations, an effective dynamic goes beyond narrow legal definitions. The *ethos* or culture of such organisations is a vital motivating and shaping factor in the civil community that the organisation exists to create and serve. Kaye argues that, if a company interprets its place in the civil and market systems in narrow legalistic terms, it will not create the civil community within its own life, or in its relationships with the host society, which will enable it to fulfil its basic purposes. More prosaically, much contemporary management literature points to the role that goals, values and missions perform in maintaining organisational efficiency.[95]

Voluntary efforts to behave morally and to uphold the law are necessary for complex social organisations; otherwise law enforcement would become impossible as well as tyrannical. These inward voluntary limitations—so necessary for corporate life—are the product of conscience, conviction and inward persuasion and belief, and cannot be imposed directly from outside. Convention is therefore society's strongest defence against anarchy and the tyranny of an all-pervading disciplinary and coercive law. G. R. Dunstan's account emphasises the role of institutions as the means by which moral insights are given stability and permanence.[96] Without such institutions, moral insights would be lost in times of need. This emphasis on conventions places a primary emphasis on morality as a common possession rather than as a matter of individual choice or decision.

For Dunstan, such conventions incorporate expectations as well as imposing limitations. We take the predictability necessary for social life for granted because we assume that we know what to expect of one another in roughly comparable situations. We can do so because a large part of our socialisation—our elementary social and moral education—involves training in the meeting of such mutual expectations. Such expectations involve a prescriptive element because social situations are understood as relationships in which certain conduct is expected as appropriate to the roles of the people involved.[97] Fidelity, in this context, means meeting the expectations appropriate to one's role. Simply following the moral rules—including obeying the law—is not enough. Personal integrity requires one to be on guard against formalism and to be conscious of the live, human, ethical reality behind such obligations. In times of rapid social change, such expectations can be fluid or imperfectly understood, but there is a recognisable continuity and cohesion in them. Frequently, there are conflicts between these roles and their accompanying obligations and consequently the need for moral judgement cannot be avoided.[98] Such role behaviour—and the mutual support of people in their groups—is a significant part of everyday life, bound up with our awareness of ourselves as agents. Consequently, Mead believed that a person was built up of internalised roles, so that the expectations of others became the self-expectations of a self-steering person.[99]

These conventions are very demanding because they flow from what the community believes to be of worth. They include specific beliefs about the worth of people regardless of their specific characteristics. These include beliefs about the value of human relationships and the common interest in the truths on which they stand. Such beliefs have a history and, in the case of Western societies, can be traced in the twin roots of our culture: Greek culture and Judaeo-Christian religion. A mature religious ethic, such as the Judaeo-Christian tradition, makes demands well beyond mere utilitarian considerations to the supreme worth of sacrifice, in the transcendence of self in subordination and service to the other.

These learned moral traditions are complex and usually tacit. Such moral judgements are neither simple deductions from principles nor simply calculation of consequences; but, as I pointed out earlier, they have been built into our vocabulary and our stories. Such moral judgements involve a skilled performance.[100] Even the moral abstractions of our legitimisers express general aims, which cannot be made operational in a straightforward way through clear-cut 'means-to-ends' calculation, though such abstractions supply a general orientation for living. Also, as we have already seen, there are conflicts in the roles we perform and there also conflicts between the abstractions we use. What this means for American philosopher Hubert Dreyfus is that skilled social behaviour transcends the analytical application of universal rules in a way of thinking that is rapid, intuitive, holistic, interpretative, experientially based and context dependent.[101] Importantly, for Cambridge economist Tony Lawson, the social system is an inherently dynamic process, which emerges from and depends on human practice, but which is not reducible to individual human agency. In short, it is an emergent evolutionary system.[102]

Consistent with the account given earlier, British moral philosopher Robert Downie emphasises the emotional element in social morality: the ties generated by kinship, common religion, custom, language, traditional ways of earning a living, traditional loyalties of all kinds and, more generally, shared broad cultural traditions.[103] Nevertheless, there are limits to the degree of variability in social rules. Social moralities must have certain structural features in common. Downie lists a number of obvious truths as limiting the scope for variety: our lack of self-sufficiency, our limited benevolence, our approximately equal power, our limited understanding and skills and limitations imposed by the environment and scarcity.[104] Consequently, we require means of limiting violence, exploitation and competition and means for encouraging cooperation. All of this implies that there is necessarily a strong element of consequentialism in social morality. This does not mean that social morality is, or must be, limited to an examination of the consequences of action. The beliefs on which we act extend our moral values well beyond such consequentialism.

Not only are there social rules and expectations, there are said to be social rules about social rules. Downie describes second-order rules of recognition, of change and of empowerment and procedure. For their part, Australian public-choice philosopher Geoffrey Brennan and American Nobel Prize-winning economist

James Buchanan[105] emphasise the importance of rules at the constitutional level. They argue optimistically that the natural tendency for conflict in the interests of individuals is moderated substantially in the choice of rules. In their view, it is these second-order rules and moral principles that help us determine the moral legitimacy of government action. This view presupposes the existence of sufficient social capital and freedom from violence to enable discourse about such rules. It also ignores the extent to which there are real conflicts of interest involved in those constitutional rules. Additionally, there is no reason to believe that these add up to a coherent, consistent system. Nor, as Brennan and Buchanan point out, is there any reason to believe that the forces of social evolution will always ensure the selection of the best rules.

In summary, while there is wide range of views about the basis of our moral and legal principles, there is strong support for the proposition that the moral and legal principles, along with a sense of community, provide crucial elements in the governance structures of our societies.

The Maintenance of Social Order Involves Moral Choice and Struggle

The maintenance of social order involves a struggle within the individual, a struggle to control our behavioural tendencies to dominate, to compete, to be aggressive—those behavioural tendencies that Stark reduces to greed and lust. That this is consistent with our daily experience is acknowledged widely, but this is not a new intuition. Various religious traditions have been talking about such issues for as long as we have written records. For example, for the Hebrew prophets, the existence of evil in the world was a consequence of humankind's overreaching pride, of human freedom reaching beyond its limits, leading to alienation from God. For Zarathustra of Balkh (c. 626–551 BC), the potential for good and evil was born in all of us—a consequence of what he saw as a cosmic battle between good and evil, the battle between the supreme god, Ahura Mazda, and the evil god, Ahriman. This teaching points to the prevalence and strength of evil in the world, and of the resulting conflicts within us.[106]

The *Bhagavadadgita* (*Song of the Lord*), a popular Indian religious poem forming part of the *Mahabharata* (*The Great Epic of the Bharata Dynasty*), dating from the fifth century BC, teaches that human beings are distinguished from animals by the knowledge of right and wrong. The world is the field of righteousness and the battleground for mortal struggle between the good and evil in each of us. Drawing on this Indian tradition, Sidharta Gautama (the Buddha, 563–483 BC) taught that all life was suffering and that human suffering could be transcended only by seeing through the illusions of worldly reality and the individual self—and by cultivating a personality that was free from the deluded desires and passions that caused suffering.[107] In this view, suffering arises out of selfish cravings and such cravings can be overcome by following the eightfold path of Buddhism. About the same time, in China, Confucius (Kong Fuzi, 551–479 BC), drawing on the idea of the interdependence of all things, was concerned to define and help cultivate the way to a harmonious society. His teachings were concerned with the avoidance of vice and the cultivation of personal virtue, proper government, the values of family and community.

The ancient Greek conception of hubris—the human bent towards self-aggrandisement, pride and all associated forms of egotism—has similarities with the Judaeo-Christian conception of the Fall.[108] In this view, a shadow lies over every human being because we do not have the ethical stamina we need. This Greek concept emphasised the tragic dimension of this darker side of human beings. Hubris, in this sense, is not pride but the self-elevation of the great beyond the limits of its finitude.[109] In this tradition, Socrates (c. 470–399 BC) was concerned to explore the concepts of the good life and of virtue. While there is some difference of emphasis, the moral metaphysics of ancient Athens is similar to the fundamental moral stance of the Christian Church.

For the Christian Church also, moral evil is omnipresent. As Saint Paul (10–67), some time in the middle of the first century AD, said:

> I have been sold as a slave to sin. I cannot understand my own behaviour. I fail to carry out the things I want to do, and I find myself doing the very things I hate…for though the will to do what is good is in me, the performance is not, with the result that instead of doing the good things I want to do, I carry out the sinful things I do not want.[110]

Again, contemporary Christian theology talks about humankind's 'torn' or 'broken' condition[111] in alluding to what has more traditionally been called original sin. The Fall involves strong claims about how the human world is, rather than simply a mythological story of how it came to be that way. As contemporary Anglican theologian David Tracey would have it: 'The one piece of Christian doctrine that is empirically demonstrable is that there is something awry with the world.'[112] The Christian tradition goes on to suggest that an effective social order is possible only through a covenant relationship with God—a relationship that is corporate and individual.[113] Importantly, mainstream contemporary Christian theologians see the myth of the Fall as incorporating a profound insight into the human condition—a fall to moral responsibility—and not as a historical account of the origin of evil. Balancing this negative view of the human condition, the somewhat dualistic Christian tradition also sees humankind as having being made in the likeness of God, and as having been saved by Christ, who initiated the Kingdom of God, within which we can experience our true calling as children of God, open to love and the possibility of radical goodness.

It is largely the doctrine of original sin as developed by Saint Augustine of Hippo (354–430) and transmitted through the Protestant reformers that found philosophical expression in English philosopher Thomas Hobbes' (1588–1679) 'war of all on all'.[114] Hobbes believed that we were all motivated by a restless desire for power, which we required to assure us of the means to live well. In Hobbes' view, in a 'state of nature',

> there is no place for industry; because the fruits thereof is [sic] uncertain: and consequently no culture of the earth; no navigation, nor use of commodities that may be imported by sea; no commodious buildings; no instruments of moving and removing such things as require much force; no knowledge of the face of the earth; no account of time; no Arts; no Letters; no society; and which is worst of all, continuous fear, and danger of violent death; and the life of man, solitary, poor, nasty, brutish and short.[115]

This is simply a secularised version of Calvin's natural man.[116] For Hobbes, it was only as a consequence of the discipline enforced by government that a civilised life was possible.

The more optimistic Enlightenment view that humankind and human structures are perfectible is found in the works of Swiss philosopher Jean-Jacques Rousseau (1712–78). This optimism—that humankind was basically good—was condemned by a number of councils of the Christian Church as the Pelagian heresy in the fifth century, by the Catholic Council of Trent in the sixteenth century and by a number of Protestant councils about the same time. Rousseau thought that human beings were endowed by nature with compassion for their fellow humans—a view he derived from Smith and Hume. He also believed, however, that human life in a 'state of nature' was one of solitude: 'Having no fixed habitation and no need of one another's assistance, the same persons hardly meet twice in their lives, and perhaps then without knowing one another or speaking together…They maintained no kind of intercourse with one another, and were consequently strangers to vanity, deference, esteem and contempt.'[117]

It is now clear that this individualistic anthropology is nonsense. Our primate ancestors lived in social groups and we evolved as social animals. Nevertheless, while generally holding that humankind in this mythical 'state of nature' was inherently good, Rousseau conceded that the weight of human experience demonstrated that human beings were wicked. He claimed that it was human society that induced people to hate each other and to inflict every imaginable evil on one another. He also disputed that private interests were linked to the public interest; rather, they excluded each other. The laws of society were a yoke that everybody wished to impose on others, but not themselves.[118]

The point of this account for current purposes is not theological but empirical. It is not intended to promote particular religious beliefs or a particular or masculine image of God, or to encourage an orgy of guilt feelings.[119] Rather, this account is intended to encourage a more realistic understanding of the human condition. These traditional theological concerns about human sinfulness have been absorbed into secular discourse and then—under the influence of Enlightenment optimism—forgotten. Worse, economic orthodoxy has been dominated by the claim that self-interest provides an adequate basis for modelling human behaviour and, in the process, is legitimising selfishness.

Human moral finitude is, however, alive and active in the world. These traditional religious concerns incorporate a profound insight into the human condition, an insight pointing to the fragility of our social order and an insight that we ignore to our peril. Certainly, in our daily life we do not, and cannot, ignore the fact that to be human is *inter alia* to be proud, to be vain, to want to dominate others, to become angry, to be vindictive, violent, vengeful, greedy, dishonest, untruthful, weak-willed, easily lead, self-destructive, frightened, confused and to become discouraged.

Of course, we find it easy to see these faults and failings in others. What is frequently overlooked is the insidious and ever-present influence of these tendencies on our own actions and values and on social values more generally. We need to protect ourselves from our own dark side and we should not ignore this particular reality in our institutional arrangements. One consequence is that even our moral vocabulary—and our moral, religious, political and legal institutions—can be subverted into instruments of immoral conduct.

The whole Enlightenment project has been based on a much more optimistic view of the human condition through a secular appropriation of the Christian eschatological hope. It involves a strong belief in the power of rationality to lead to moral and technological progress and greater human happiness. This is despite a human history that includes countless wars, massacres, tortures, cruelty, exploitation and abuses of every kind. Surely the history of the twentieth century demonstrates conclusively that such optimism is misplaced and that we live always on the edge of chaos. Rather than being assured, a peaceful, just social order is something that has to be striven for constantly. The twentieth century saw human viciousness and barbarism on a scale that is hard to imagine. For example, William Eckhardt estimates that in the period 1900–89, 86 million people were killed in war.[120] The Soviet regime alone killed about 62 million people in the 70 years after 1917, with 9.5 million of those killed in the 1930s.[121] These are only some of the grosser statistics. There are other incidents of inhuman treatment of our fellows without number. In Sigmund Freud's (1856–1939) judgement: '[T]he tendency to aggression is an innate, independent, instinctual disposition in man…constituting the most powerful obstacle to culture…there is no likelihood of our being able to suppress humanity's aggressive tendencies.'[122]

One response to this catalogue of violence might be to argue that it reinforces suspicion of government. This is not, however, an adequate response. While governments—even nominally democratic governments—can behave very badly, not everything they do is bad. Also, in the above cases, government leaders found ready accomplices for their crimes among ordinary citizens. Similarly, while business does great good, it also does much evil—including such things as the design and manufacture of gas chambers, the manufacture and distribution of weapons, assisting the proliferation of nuclear weapons, the corruption of governments, the sale of addictive substances known to cause vast numbers of premature deaths, the sale of unsafe and shoddy products more generally, the pollution of the environment, the evasion of taxation, the exploitation of workers and the systematic deception of customers and shareholders.

Taking cigarettes as an example, Simon Chapman, Professor of Public Health at the University of Sydney, has estimated that 4.9 million people world-wide are killed by smoking every year—19,000 of them in Australia. This is a rate of death rivalling the worst examples of twentieth-century tyranny. The number of Australian smoking deaths is larger than the deaths caused by breast, cervical and skin cancer, AIDS, suicide, alcohol and road crashes combined.[123] There is well-confirmed scientific evidence for these estimates and the cigarette companies have known about the adverse effects and the addictive properties of their products for many years. Indeed, they have manipulated these addictive properties. Consequently, there is no way that cigarette producers and their distributors—including the local supermarket and corner store—can avoid some moral responsibility for these horrible premature deaths. While we have a war on terrorism, however, we do not have a war on cigarette production and distribution—presumably because this mass killing occurs as a part of everyday economic transactions, because of the superficial acquiescence of the victims and the political power of the perpetrators.

Worse still, we do not have a real war on poverty, hunger or disease. Our tolerance of these particular continuing evils involves the premature deaths of vast numbers of people in Third-World countries.

If these historical insights are not enough evidence to convince the reader of the capacity of human beings—just like us—to engage in the grossest evil in the pursuit of power and economic gain, let us now turn briefly to slavery—one of the cruellest institutions in human history. Slavery apparently first appeared in subsistence pastoral economies, but the transition to a semi-market economy brought a significant expansion in the number of slaves and much harsher treatment of them.[124] Slavery played a dominant role in production in early semi-market economies. For example, plantation slavery was common in ancient Greece and in the Roman Empire, while slaves were also used in mining, industry, commerce, domestic service and brothels and in harems. As a consequence, slavery was accepted as normal for a significant proportion of the population. In ancient Athens—the exemplar of the democratic *polis*—slaves made up about one-third of the population. Warfare, slave raiding, kidnapping, punishment, debt, the sale of children and birth to a slave mother provided the supply. Aristotle even argued that some people lacked the higher qualities of the soul necessary for freedom and were born to be slaves. To its shame, the Christian Church for most of its history did not condemn this base institution, even if it advised slave owners to be kind to their slaves. Islam took a similar view.

In relatively recent times, the European colonisation of the Americas exploited a pre-existing African slave trade to provide slaves to exploit the lands stolen from the indigenous populations to produce goods for export to Europe. This obscene trade to the West Indies and South America began in 1517, growing rapidly by the end of the seventeenth century. In British North America, the trade started in 1619 and developed slowly until new arrivals totalled about 260,000 in 1754. Overall, it is estimated that more than 15 million African slaves were transported to the Western Hemisphere before the suppression of the trade. It is thought that approximately one-third of the African slaves shipped—usually in appalling conditions—died as a consequence of their treatment on the voyage and in the 'hardening' process of their exposure to European diseases. While slaves in the Americas and throughout the Western world were emancipated in the eighteenth and nineteenth centuries, the institution lingers on in some underdeveloped states and in some hidden ways.

It has been estimated recently that there are currently as many as 20 million sex slaves throughout the world, including some in Australia. This tendency towards the exploitation of others—which allowed this evil institution to persist for so long—is still with us. Furthermore, the International Labour Organisation (ILO) estimates that 8.4 million children work as slave labourers, prostitutes or soldiers world-wide. Of these, 1.2 million are kidnapped, sold or smuggled each year.[125] The United Nations Children's Fund, UNICEF, describes the trafficking of children into prostitution and slavery as a billion-dollar business. Importantly also, the descendants of emancipated slaves have struggled throughout the Americas to free themselves from the low socio-economic status to which they were condemned by the ruthless exploitation of their ancestors.

The conclusion is obvious. We are all capable of unspeakable acts and an extraordinary indifference to the suffering of others. Before we get carried away, therefore, about the perfectibility of modern humans, or even about labour-market deregulation, it would be wise to remember that within every person there exists the capacity to be a slave driver, a slave owner, a death-camp guard, a camp commandant, a torturer and a tyrant—writ large or in the minutia of everyday life.

This is the reason why people have long sought to put in place structures to inhibit the accumulation of excessive power and its abuse. It has been one of the primary justifications advanced for liberalism and the market system in the past two centuries. There has also, however, been a recent strong tendency to overlook the exploitation and the abuse of power that occurs within the market system itself. It is not simply governments that are capable of tyranny. With the passing of the Soviet Union, we might have been better served if we had looked more closely at the warts within our own system, rather than giving ourselves over to triumphal gloating at the collapse of the utopian socialist dream.

Summary

This chapter started off by pointing to the influence of the economics profession and economic fundamentalism on public policy and expressing concern at that influence. I suggested that economic fundamentalism assumed that social relationships were reducible to transactions between self-interested individuals—that is, that economic relationships were the fundamental social relationships. It has been argued that as a consequence, the vocabulary of economics with all its entailments now provides the dominant vocabulary for the evaluation of public policy choices.

My more detailed analysis began with an examination of the basis of the social order, starting from a position that saw the individual as embedded in society. I pointed out that there is no such thing as a pre-social human nature and that the formation of our values—and even of our consumer preferences—is a thoroughly social process. In support, I pointed to our earliest hominoid ancestors as having lived as members of social groups. Our evolution involved a complex in which the organised hunting of large animals, life in organised social groups and the making and use of tools were interconnected. That evolution is inseparable from the evolution of human culture. That culture is something we learn as children—discovering how our parents and those around us interpret the world. This evolved social order is acknowledged widely to be a moral order—an order that determines how we should act. The study of social life is, therefore, the study of social norms, institutions and the stories in which they are embodied—not simply regularities in conduct, but regulated conduct. These regulations set limits to, work against and channel the drives we have inherited. It is the control of greed, broadly defined, which constitutes a crucial victory of culture against animality—a victory that permitted complex organisations to emerge. Central to this view is the idea that human beings as they have evolved created the social system in which they have their being. This evolution of human culture is not a once-and-for-all process; it is a continuing process.

The maintenance of any social order involves, then, a moral struggle within and between individuals—a struggle to control our behavioural tendencies to dominate, to compete and to be aggressive. There are severe limits to our successful control of these tendencies. This fact has been acknowledged widely throughout human history and in different cultures, particularly in the context of religious teachings. In particular, it is reflected in the Christian doctrine of original sin—a doctrine secularised by Hobbes in his war of all on all—and then largely forgotten. It is a doctrine that incorporates a profound insight into the human condition—an insight that we ignore to our peril, particularly in the design of our institutional and organisational arrangements. It is unorganised social pressure, organised enforcement of law and our own sense of guilt flowing from any breach of internalised norms that provide the moral coercion that permits the social system to survive.

It is also clear that no society can survive without stable moral traditions backed up by effective means of coercion. Leading moral philosopher Alasdair MacIntyre tells us, however, that our day-to-day moral vocabulary derives from several different and incompatible moral traditions.[126] Consequently, the moral foundations of modern society are incoherent and fragmented. This would seem to pose a significant threat to that social system and some commentators have sensed deterioration in the social, intellectual and philosophical capital of the Western civil order.

Having concluded that human civilisation is always under threat from what used to be called human sinfulness—including human greed—in the next chapter, we will go on to examine the relationship between the economic system and the social order. It will suggest that the economic system, like society itself, is a social artefact and, far from being autonomous, is dependent on the systems of social control discussed above.

ENDNOTES

[1] Smith 1757, Part VI, Section III, Ch. 1.

[2] Shotter 1985.

[3] In his mature work, he added the qualification 'always'. Pareto 1896, cited in Guala 1998.

[4] Secord 1986.

[5] von Bruck 1986.

[6] Saul 2001.

[7] Stark 1978, p. 66.

[8] Stark 1983, p. 191.

[9] Simons 1995.

[10] Rabinow 1983.

[11] Carrithers et al. 1985.

[12] Midgley 1984.

[13] Geertz 1975, p. 50.

[14] Geertz 1979, p. 229.

[15] Bernstein 1983.

[16] Ibid. and Crotty 1998.

[17] Brown 1988.

[18] Berger and Luckmann 1971, pp. 36, 51–2.

[19] Fleck 1979, p. 42.

[20] Carruthers 1990.

[21] Goodman 1968.

[22] Wittgenstein 1951.

[23] Whorf 1967, p. 256.

[24] Ibid., p. 216.

[25] Wittgenstein 1978.

[26] Lakoff and Johnson 1980.

[27] Mannheim 1936. Mannheim also believed that while idealogising influences could not be eradicated entirely, they could be mitigated by the systematic analysis of as many of the varying socially grounded positions as possible. It is a view that should encourage us to resist strongly the imperialist pretensions of economics.

[28] Shotter 1985, p. 168.

[29] Fortes 1983.

[30] Spradley and McCurdy 1994.

[31] Ibid., p. 69.

[32] Noble and Davidson 1996.

[33] Berger and Luckmann 1971, p. 55.

[34] Cited in Goody 1995.

[35] Abbott 2002.

[36] Sartre 1964, cited in Bruner 1987, p. 5.

[37] Harre 1985.

[38] Madsen et al. 2002.

[39] Granovetter 1991.

[40] Hollis 1977.

[41] Saul 2001, p. 23.

[42] Hobson 2002.

[43] Cherniak 1986.

[44] Ormerod 2001.

[45] Hollis 1985.

[46] McPherson 1983.

47 Amariglio et al. 1990, p. 126.
48 Boulding 1970.
49 Toulmin 1990.
50 Tarnas 1991.
51 Midgley 1994.
52 Key and Aiello 1999.
53 Carrithers 1992.
54 Fortes 1983.
55 Keesing 1981.
56 Ibid., p. 16.
57 Carrithers 1992.
58 Humphrey 1976.
59 Lieberman 1998.
60 Reynolds 1981.
61 Keesing 1981, p. 21.
62 Midgley 1984.
63 Goodwin 1997.
64 Durkheim 1993, pp. 227–8.
65 Emmet 1966.
66 Spradley and McCurdy 1994.
67 Polanyi 1958.
68 Brown 1988.
69 Stark 1976.
70 Stark 1983.
71 Sahlins 1960.
72 Hume 1966, pp. 187–205.
73 Stark 1983.
74 Stark 1978, p. 198.
75 Frowen 1997.
76 Berger and Luckmann 1971, p. 70.
77 Williamson 1994.
78 Knauft 1996, p. 44.
79 Williamson 1994.
80 Berger and Luckmann 1971.
81 Ibid., p. 82.
82 Ibid., p. 121.
83 Ibid., p. 130.
84 Stark 1976.
85 Stark 1978, p. 124.
86 Llewellyn 1931–32.
87 Stark 1978, p. 201.
88 Stoicism was a school of Hellenistic philosophy, founded by Zeno of Citium (333–264 BC) in Athens, which became popular throughout Greece and the Roman Empire.
89 Epicureanism was a system of philosophy based on the teachings of Epicurus (340–270 BC), founded about 307 BC. Epicurus was an atomic materialist.
90 Stark and Sumner believe that class dividedness and even class warfare can be accommodated fully within the framework of their analysis. Stark agrees that each class or group in society has its own mores and that the upper strata tend to force their own customs on the lower strata. Indeed, he acknowledges that chiefs, kings, priests, warriors, statesmen and other functionaries have often used their authority to promote their own interests. In any event, there is no need for us to deny the possibility that dominance played a role in the historical processes that created societies and states. Of course, it

would also be entirely consistent with Stark—and with the liberal tradition—to argue that our desire to acquire such dominance requires control. Indeed, the coercive nature of social control necessarily raises the question of the legitimate limits of such cohesion—a question of central concern for this analysis.

91 Elias 1994.

92 Service 1975.

93 Dunstan 1974.

94 Kaye 1994.

95 See, for example, Senge 1992b.

96 Dunstan 1974.

97 Ibid.

98 Emmet 1966.

99 Cited in Gerth and Mills 1954.

100 See Dunstan 1974; Emmet 1966.

101 Cited in Flyvbjerg 2001.

102 Lawson 2003.

103 Downie 1972.

104 Ibid.

105 Brennan and Buchanan 1985.

106 Midgley 1984.

107 Solomon and Higgins 1996.

108 Of course, mainstream contemporary Christianity would interpret the story of the Fall as myth rather than as history. The story of the Fall in 'Genesis' is not a historical account of the origin of human sinfulness; rather, it is an expression of the insight that sin originates in human pride and self-will.

109 Tillich 1963, p. 93.

110 Romans 7:14–20.

111 von Bruck 1986.

112 Tracey 1976, as reported by Edwin Byford, personal communication.

113 Of course, the traditional Christian view sees this human brokenness not simply in terms of one's alienation from one's fellows, but, more importantly, in terms of humankind's alienation from God and consequently from the rest of creation. In this view, evil is the result of a human turning from God. Receptivity to the presence of God is replaced by ego projections. Consequently, every human is apt to fail when put to the test. This tragic flaw is seen as the cause of humankind's inability to build a truly satisfactory society and a truly integrated social whole. As Pope John Paul II said in *Centesimus Annus*:

> A man is alienated if he refuses to transcend himself and to live the experience of self-giving and of the formation of an authentic human community...A society is alienated if its forms of social organization, production and consumption make it more difficult to offer this gift of self and to establish this solidarity between people.

114 Simons 1995.

115 Hobbes 1651, p. 186.

116 Loy 2002.

117 Rousseau 1935, p. 188.

118 Ibid.

119 In particular, I do not intend to be interpreted as endorsing Christianity's traditional ambivalence towards human sexuality. That ambivalence places an undue emphasis on only one aspect of human behaviour, it reflects an individualistic bias and down plays the corporate, structural nature of much evil in the world. Neither is the above account intended to support fundamentalist interpretations of religious doctrines, creationism or the political program of the so-called religious right. Neither is it intended to condone the innumerable evils—large and small—done in the name of organised religion throughout history—from human sacrifices and religious wars to mass killings, the burning of witches, the torture and murder of 'heretics', the exploitation of guilt as a source of institutional and personal power, the abusive indoctrination of young children in the service of long-term dependency and the

toleration of the physical and sexual abuse of children by the clergy. Our spiritual yearnings are open to the grossest of abuses by leaders claiming to speak on behalf of God. Furthermore, history has demonstrated that spiritual pride is among the worst of human failings. If God is truly the Abba of the New Testament, there is no place for fear in any relationship with such an intimate, loving parent.

[120] Eckhardt 1989.

[121] Glover 1999.

[122] Freud 1932, cited in Webb 1995, p. 15.

[123] Chapman 2004.

[124] Encyclopaedia Britannica 1981.

[125] Bita 2002, p. 9.

[126] MacIntyre 1966.

Chapter 3: The Relationship Between the Economic System and the Social Order

Is society mainly a market place, in which self-serving individuals compete with one another—at work, in politics, and in courtship—enhancing the general welfare in the process? Or do we typically seek to do both what is right and what is pleasurable, and find ourselves frequently in conflict when moral values and happiness are incompatible? Are we, first of all, 'normative-effective' beings, whose deliberations and decisions are deeply affected by our values and emotions?
— Amitai Etzioni[1]

In brief, the principle of self-interest is incomplete as a social organising principle. It operates effectively only in tandem with some supporting social principle. This fundamental characteristic of economic liberalism, which was largely taken for granted by Adam Smith and John Stuart Mill in their different ways, has been lost sight of by its modern protagonists…The attempt has been made to erect an increasingly explicit social organisation without a supporting social morality…In this way, the foundations of the market system have been weakened.
— Fred Hirsch[2]

Introduction

The previous chapter began an examination of two key, but buried assumptions, which have underpinned much recent public policy formulation: the ideas that the economic system is autonomous and that the economic system has priority over the social system. These two assumptions have allowed economics to become the dominant methodology and vocabulary for the evaluation of public policy choices in our society. As a consequence, 'economic efficiency'—defined in neoclassical terms—has become the dominant value to be served by government policy.

The discussion so far has centred on the question of how social order originates. It has been shown that there is broad consensus that the social order is a moral order that developed with the social evolution of the human race. It was concluded that there was no pre-social human nature, and consequently the study of social life involved the study of regulated conduct, not simply the study of regularities. It is our shared values that act as the mortar that binds our communities together and these are backed by formal and informal means of coercion and our own sense of guilt. Importantly, it is the control of our greed that constitutes one of the prime victories of culture over our 'animality'. That victory is, however, incomplete and the maintenance of a peaceful society involves constant struggle. I concluded that, in an effective civil society, the pursuit of individual and organisational choice and 'self-interest' were heavily constrained by internalised moral codes and by externally imposed social sanctions. The resulting order was constantly under threat from what used to be called human sinfulness, particularly human greed.

This chapter will give an account of the various contemporary theories that are used to account for that social order before focusing on the relationship of dependence between the economic and social systems, pointing to the neglect of this relationship by economic fundamentalists. In addition, the chapter will provide a brief historical overview of this debate as it arose after the breakdown of the medieval hierarchical world-view, particularly under the influence of the Reformation.

Current Theories Explaining the Existence of Social Order

Chapter 2 provided an evolutionary account of the development of social order supplemented by a discussion of some of the elements that make up that social order. Among many theorists, however, my evolutionary account will not seem satisfactory as an explanation of our social order, however much the theorist agrees that something like that described really took place. What will often be sought is a satisfying 'theoretical' story providing a causal explanation that is necessarily ahistorical, which attempts to tease out what is 'really' going on in society and what are the 'laws' that determine the way things are. This involves making a distinction between occurrences that are not necessarily associated—that is, contingent—and occurrences that occur closely together, and which are taken to involve some causal relationship. Consequently, such an attempt at causal explanation involves a belief in the existence of some underlying influence or structure or law that creates an objective order, which our culture obliges us to observe and which can be abstracted from historical reality with all its contingent elements in a way analogous to theoretical accounts in the physical sciences. As we will see later, the extent to which there are such underlying structures that are accessible to us is problematic given that this level of abstraction cannot be subject to empirical falsification, as in the physical sciences. The value of such theoretical stories as a means of explanation is, therefore, problematic. The danger is that dialectic is simply substituted for 'proof'.

Such theorising is often distinguished from theoretical accounts that provide a justification for what exists or what is thought to be desirable. The latter does not usually involve an examination of the moral judgements we really make and the values that underlie them, but rather an appeal to some single, plausible fundamental principle in an attempt to legislate what those moral judgements should be. Often these genuine attempts at explanation and judgement are associated with the theorist's desire to legislate particular judgements about fundamental political and social institutions. The progression of such ideas often involves the attempt by particular theorists to differentiate their stories from those of others. As a consequence, these stories appear to exhibit a developmental trajectory similar to those found in the natural sciences and in industrial development. To me, this Enlightenment project—important though it is claimed to be in providing a justification for our social arrangements—is tainted by an unrealistic apriorism, uni-causal explanations and tenuous and tedious distinctions.

No single dominant story has emerged from these efforts to explain the existence of social order and of our political and moral institutions. Phillips tells us that there are, however, four primary theoretical approaches to the problem:

- the private-interest doctrine
- situational analysis
- the consensus doctrine
- the conflict approach.[3]

The private-interest story assumes that individuals are guided entirely by considerations of self-interest—a view held by economic fundamentalists. Spencer, the most prominent of the *laissez-faire* advocates, is usually cited as a holder of an extreme version of this approach, believing that the pursuit of self-interest formed a self-regulating mechanism in society. Hobbes and Weber are also self-interest theorists who emphasise the inevitability of conflict. In contrast with Hobbes, for Weber, competitive struggles often generate social regularities. George Homans, a well-known contemporary exponent of a private-interest approach, works explicitly with an exchange model based on free-market principles. According to Homans, social interaction is social exchange involving such rewards as esteem, admiration and respect and such costs as boredom, embarrassment and expenditure of time. It is the informal rules governing these exchanges that provide for social order. The problem with such private-interest stories is that they are unable to explain how there could be sufficient similarities among individuals and enough continuity through time to have created organised societies. Nor, as is argued shortly, is it possible to explain all obedience to rules and laws by the calculation of benefits derived from them, or from fear of punishment. The existence of shared social norms is ignored. Such theories have no room for moral notions such as right and wrong. Consequently, they omit the moral dimension in human relations and moral discourse is not even possible.

Erving Goffman, a situational analyst, also sees people as narrowly self-interested, acting out their roles as public means to private ends. For Goffman, society is a pseudo-moral system in which everyone is engaged busily in the exchange of impressions. Situational morality more generally stresses the importance of the properties and structures of situations in influencing social conduct. Goffman, however, lacks an adequate account of what it is to be human and of human beings possessing a sense of personal identity. Also missing is any commitment to moral standards other than those found in social situations. Nor can he account for moral rules opposed to any derived from those social situations.

The majority of sociologists, including Durkheim and Talcott Parsons, are described as consensus theorists. For these theorists, social order is made possible by a consensus about shared values and meanings. For Parsons, 'institutions or institutional patterns' are defined as '[n]ormative patterns, which define what are felt to be, in the given society, proper, legitimate, or expected modes of action or of social relationship…They are patterns supported by common moral sentiments.'[4]

People are motivated to observe these normative standards through socialisation and social control and through the feelings of self-respect, guilt and shame. Phillips argues that such models are unable to account for social conflict, making too much of control mechanisms and too little of human spontaneity and inner conflict. It is also criticised as a tacit commitment to the *status quo*. More importantly, it is argued that such theorists are not committed to morality as such, only to a moral system that yields order. Such theories can say nothing, therefore, about the moral status of a particular society. Consequently, fears about moral relativism are raised to dispute this tradition. Despite theses criticisms, there is much in the consensus approach that is useful. In particular, Phillips agrees with Durkheim, Parsons and most other sociologists that individuals are motivated to act in accordance with normative standards. As argued in Chapter 2, the internalisation of these standards helps provide much of the restraining control necessary for social order. Social order is made possible by consensus within a social system about normative standards; and motivation to observe these standards can best be assured by the mechanisms of socialisation and social control. Phillips, however, is concerned that consensus theorists never consider the possibility of justifying rationally these dominant moral standards. I will argue later that this Enlightenment aspiration for a 'rational' justification of our moral values is unattainable.

Conflict theorists such as Louis Coser and Randall Collins place a strong emphasis on power relationships, coercion, competition and the mechanisms of political allocation. They point to constraint and conflict about values and coercion. For Coser, such conflicts are functional in that they help to structure the larger social environment by assigning positions to the various subgroups within the system and by helping to define the power relations between them. For Collins, however, social life is mainly a fight over the control of resources. What ought to concern us, according to Collins, is how various factors of power, coercion, control of resources and the like produce particular moral values and beliefs in the first place. For Collins, ethics are ultimately arbitrary—simply a device for dominating others. In the process, Collins assumes that moral principles have only instrumental value. His doctrine makes it impossible to treat one another as moral beings. Phillips goes on to give an account of Alvin Goulder's critique of the functionalist concern with social order. Phillips reduces this to a criticism of the functionalist concern for quiet values such as temperance, wisdom, knowledge, goodness, cooperation or trust and faith in the goodness of God. Nowhere does Goulder formulate and defend his own values.

Similarly, Alan Gewirth attempts to provide a rational justification for moral principles and institutions, avoiding some of the weaknesses of earlier theories, including hypothetical people, hypothetical situations and states of nature. His approach involves trying to deduce these principles from the nature of human action and the web of social relations in which we are embedded. He sees the control of actions for worthwhile ends as inherently social and inter-subjective. He conceives of voluntariness and purposiveness as the most general features of all actions encompassing the effectual, traditional, value-rational and means–ends actions considered by Max Weber. He considers that all actions have a normative structure involving evaluative judgements of the goodness of their purposes, that every agent implicitly makes claims to freedom and well-being as being intrinsically good and accepts logically that all agents have the same prudential generic rights. It follows for Gewirth that every agent must acknowledge certain generic obligations and this leads to his supreme moral principle to act in accordance with the generic rights of your recipients as well as yourself, not just restraining from action damaging to others but contributing positively to their well-being. This obligation extends to social rules and institutions. As Phillips tells us, however, the most influential of contemporary sociological theories of action is that advanced by Parsons. Importantly, however, Parsons does not set out to provide a rational justification for any particular set of moral values—believing that to be impossible. He starts from the concept of an actor whose actions are goal oriented, are involved in situations, are regulated normatively and involve motivation. Because any such actor is involved in interactions with other actors, the outcome of any action is contingent on the response of others. Because the possibility of instability in this situation exceeds the possibility of stability, such actions must be integrated by a shared institutionalised normative order. Of course, this is what was argued in Chapter 2. Without such a normative order, we would be left with the war of all on all.

Summarising the above, there seems to be broad agreement that normative values are significant to human society, though there is less agreement on the positive role they play. Some theories, in stressing their capacity for manipulation in favour of the powerful, invoke effectively a dark account of the human condition and the doctrine of original sin unmediated by any recognition of the positive contribution of such values to human emancipation—a major theme of Jurgen Habermas's theory of justice, to which we will turn in Chapter 7. My sympathy, along with Phillips', lies with the consensus theories represented by the sociological tradition, and particularly the account given by Parsons. There is, however, no need to reject in their entirety the other perspectives outlined. Clearly, there is some truth in the transactions view of human society; it simply fails to provide anything like a complete account. Indeed, from the perspective developed earlier, it leaves out the bits that are most important. Similarly, there is clearly much conflict in social life and no account should ignore that conflict. Power relationships and coercion are ever-present features of social life and this is one of the main reasons why one should fear an unrestrained market system—as we should fear unrestrained government power. The Christian tradition, with its emphasis on original sin, points to the possibility of abuse of power relations and of moral rules themselves. In summary, there is no need to adopt a uni-causal theory. What does concern me, however, is the attempt by some of these theorists to reconstruct rationally our moral values in accordance with their pet theories and, as a result, to legislate how we should all behave. The evolved social world is much too complex for such reductionism. This was the reason why Aristotle warned us that the good had no universal form and consequently was not reducible to any single principle. So it is much more realistic to acknowledge that the emergence of social order and its maintenance involves a complex of influences over a long period of time.

One important theorist not quite fitting the above is the rational-choice theorist Jon Elster.[5] He does not believe that social norms can be reduced to any single principle—a view given empirical support by the historical account of MacIntyre. In particular, Elster insists that social norms cannot be reduced to rationality or to any other form of optimising mechanism. He argues that such a view cannot deal with the problem of free riding and the voluntary provision of public goods. The rational self-interest of individuals can lead them to behave in ways that are collectively disastrous. He even suggests that a form of irrationality—what he calls magical thinking—plays an important role in many decisions to cooperate. Consequently, Elster entertains briefly the idea that civilisation owes its existence to a fortunate coincidence. He goes on to argue that altruism, envy, social norms and self-interest all contribute in complex, interacting ways to order, stability and cooperation, and provide the cement of society: 'Every society and each community will be glued together, for better and for worse, by a particular, idiosyncratic mix of these motives.'[6]

As already noted, the trouble with nearly all such stories is that—remote from the possibility of empirical falsification—they remain, at the end of the day, speculation. While ideas might be refined and inconsistencies in particular arguments eliminated, conflicting ideas cannot finally be resolved. In addition, we slip so easily and unconsciously between causal explanations and justification. Explanations advanced as causal rapidly take on normative power. Clearly, it is important to have a vision of who we are to provide some grounding for our decisions, but there is a danger that we can become trapped in a fundamentalist implementation of a particular vision—to the exclusion of other perspectives. Karl Marx is instructive in this regard:

> Hitherto men have constantly made up for themselves a false conception about themselves, about what they are and what they ought to be. They have arranged their relationships according to their ideas of God, or normal man, etc. The phantoms of their brains have gained the mastery over them. They, the creators, have bowed down before their creatures. Let us liberate them from the chimeras, the ideas, dogmas, imaginary beings under the yoke of which they are pining away.[7]

Such images are unavoidable if we are to have any discourse at all; and Marx's criticism can be applied with particular potency to his own thinking. The lesson is not to abandon all such visions—an untenable position—but to hold them lightly with some humility, open to other forms of explanation, while acknowledging that the complexity of human society rules out any simple explanatory scheme.

Another approach to explaining the existence of social order seeks an empirical grounding and involves an examination of the development of moral values in growing children. In particular, French developmental psychologist Jean Piaget (1896–1980) conceived of morality as a system of rules for social behaviour, and the essence of morality as the respect that individuals acquired for those rules. Piaget's account of moral development in children up to the age of twelve focuses primarily on its cognitive aspects, though it is not purely a cognitive process. Rather, it is an interactive process during which children's understanding of rules changes. Piaget's account involves a three-stage progression in a child's moral understanding: constraint, followed by cooperation, giving rise to generosity. Piaget sees generosity as a refinement of justice manifest in the concept of equity, which he considers a fusion of justice and love. Piaget noted that altruism, empathy and sharing were all evident in the behaviour of very young children, but he also noted that the legal sense was far less developed in young girls than in boys. In contrast, girls showed a greater capacity for tolerance and innovation in their play. Indeed, Carol Gilligan, a contemporary developmental psychologist, suggests that girls avoid conflict rather than develop rules for limiting its extent, and that Piaget was influenced unduly by his study of boys.[8] There is also good reason to believe that Piaget's account is culturally specific. According to Piaget, five- to six-year-old Swiss children conjecture that nature is just, and he goes on to say that belief in immanent justice wanes with age and experience. Such a development is not, however, true of many in

South-East Asia for whom the natural order is a moral order in which events happen for a moral purpose. Piaget's developmental hypothesis does not hold for Indian children—even if it does hold for Swiss children, something that has also been questioned. Belief in immanent justice does not wane with age among such people.[9]

Lawrence Kohlberg extended Piaget's study of moral development in children into adolescence, modifying Piaget's theory in the process. His is also an interactive theory with three levels of development:

- the pre-conventional, where rules and social expectations are external to the self
- the conventional, where the self has internalised the expectations of others
- the post-conventional, where the self is differentiated from the rules and expectations of others, and values are defined in terms of self-chosen principles. These are further subdivided into two stages. Importantly, he sees the post-conventional level as involving, firstly, a contractual-legalistic orientation and, then, a universal-ethical principle orientation. He suggests that very few people develop to such a stage.

His is a unitary conception of morality as justice, by which he means equality in a democratic society. His account emphasises the role of social institutions in which the basic values of a society are embodied, downplaying the influence of direct teaching. This could be seen as running counter to Freud and the sociological tradition with their emphasis on the internalisation of social values, but there is no necessary opposition between these accounts: they involve a difference of emphasis towards the role of conscious moral reasoning and away from the unconscious—and from tacit moral knowledge. In commenting on Kohlberg's theory, Phillips concludes that cognitive moral development at every stage of moral reasoning is influenced inescapably by unconscious mechanisms, by moral precepts that are acquired earlier and are available consciously and by the moral values and norms of the group and of the wider society.[10] This is demonstrated clearly by the example of Indian children given above.

This difference in emphasis reflects Kohlberg's own commitment to a particular cultural tradition involving a particular type of moral story, which we have already questioned: a rational, unitary account of a morality, based on the concepts of justice and rights in which the rational individual standing alone is the ideal moral agent, entering with rights into fair contracts with others. His interview methodology, however, required his subjects to talk like moral philosophers. This realisation undermines the force of his argument.

Furthermore, rights are only one way of talking about morality. There are other types of moral stories involving fundamentally different starting points in the conception of the self, society and nature, and these do not necessarily take the form of formal arguments. The latter are very much in the minority.[11] For example, in the Christian tradition, the story of the Good Samaritan carries a particular, powerful moral message, but it is not couched as a formal argument. The similar duty-based theories, however, are another formal way of talking about morality and are concerned with the conformity of individual action to a code of conduct. In the case of India, a duty-based ethical code is combined with a role-based conception of society. Moreover, Kohlberg fails to present any persuasive evidence linking moral reasoning to real behaviour. There is no reason to assume that a capacity to engage in higher levels of moral reasoning leads to moral conduct. If this were so, we would expect there to be a disproportionate percentage of academic moral philosophers among those who engage in heroic good works and who we canonise.

Gilligan argues that Kohlberg's perspective reflects the concern of adolescents justifying by reason their separation from those to whom they were formerly bound. Its limitation lies in its failure to see a world of relationship, compassion and care. Whereas justice emphasises the autonomy of the person, care underlines the primacy of relationship. Kohlberg's theory involves a general neglect of the emotional and behavioural aspects of moral development. In opposition to Kohlberg, Gilligan suggests that moral development proceeds along two different but intersecting paths that run through different modes of experience and give rise to different forms of thought: 'Whereas the analytic logic of justice is consonant with rational social and ethical theories and can be traced through the resolution of hypothetical dilemmas, the ethic of care depends on the contextual understanding of relationship.'[12]

This ethic of care develops through relationships that give rise to an understanding of interdependence and is sustained by the ability to discern connection. The fundamental tension in human psychology between the experience of separation and the experience of connection is reflected in the age-old dialogue between justice and love, reason and compassion, fairness and forgiveness. This tension underlies the conflicting conceptions of the human with which I began this chapter. Gilligan argues that these discrete experiences give rise to two different moral languages: a language of rights that justifies separation, and a language of responsibility that sustains relationships. A focus on the first language at the cost of the second opens the way to manipulation, exploitation and the rationalisation of hurt.

Gilligan's account provides a timely reminder of the dual nature of our Christian inheritance, especially since the Reformation. In Christian language, the life of faith is both corporate and individual. The Christian life is to be lived in community, but it is a life to which individuals as well as communities are called and in which individual conscience is respected. Clearly, there is a tension between these two pillars. The individualistic aspect of Christian belief—including belief in an individual soul—has been translated into our current secular emphasis on individualism, as an explanatory mechanism and as a normative ideal, through the Enlightenment and its liberal discourse. In Anglo-Saxon countries, however, in contrast with Continental countries, we have lost sight of the communal aspects of the tradition.

Importantly, current work in developmental psychology influenced by Russian developmental psychologist Lev Semenovich Vygotsky (1896–1934) and Russian neuropsychologist Alexander Luria (1902–77) on the social origin of higher mental processes and in particular on the role of spoken language in the shaping of a child's capacity to think and act, also undermines Kohlberg's Platonist aspirations.[13] Instead of children's mental equipment being part of a permanent 'human nature' with which all humans alike confront experience, the internalisation of speech is now seen as the means by which children acquire their native culture, their moral values and even their capacity to think. This is consistent with the comparative research on the acquisition of cultural conceptions of the person conducted by social psychologist Joan Miller[14] and, this is consistent with the constructionist view outlined earlier. We have, therefore, come full circle. Our moral values are embedded in the language we are taught as a child and that language is itself a social construct and a social tradition.

I reject Kohlberg's account, but his emphasis on the role of moral reasoning serves to remind us that social norms are subject to reflection, criticism and revision. Moral philosophers play a role in that reflection, criticism and revision, but their speculations are based also on the ideas and circumstances of their societies. Moral philosophers—economists included—are not the only participants in such moral discourse; it can be seen, heard or read in the media every hour of every day. Nonetheless, moral philosophers help crystallise those ideas.[15]

Despite these long debates—particularly in the sociological discipline—neoclassical economists have neglected to discuss the relationship between the economic system and the broader social system. As contemporary economists Brennan and Buchanan tell us, 'These economists have tended to neglect the importance of rules under the sometimes naïve presumption that the "market will out", regardless of institutional constraints.'[16]

In effect, neoclassical economists have endorsed tacitly Margaret Thatcher's claim that there is no such thing as society and along with it a particularly contentious moral theory. In the process, they are effectively imposing that particular tenuous moral theory on the rest of us, without any moral authority to do so. This conduct reflects the imperialist pretentiousness of neoclassical economics in seeking to explain all social phenomena in defiance of the rest of the social disciplines and the humanities.

Any complex exchange economy needs, and presupposes, an already existing state of general pacification in order to function. Such an economy and its associated institutions are not natural phenomena and they do not arise spontaneously.[17] They are social, historical artefacts. Indeed, the dichotomy between the social system and the economic system is itself a social artefact and is a product largely of the Scottish Enlightenment.

These imperialist tendencies appear even among economists well disposed towards the importance of social norms. For example, contemporary economists Avner Ben-Ner and Louis Putterman[18] label religious prophets as 'moral entrepreneurs', presumably on the basis that the language of economic explanation is more 'scientific' and more privileged than the traditional religious description. Similarly, these tendencies can be seen in the recent attempts of economists to include our moral concerns within the framework of preferences and consequently within the framework of instrumental and maximising calculation. As argued earlier, however, an economic approach to our moral values—based on the traditional self-interest model—is simplistic and misleading not simply because of the neglect of altruistic behaviour. Among economists, Albert Hirschman (b. 1915) argues against the use of such a simplistic model of human behaviour: 'What is needed is for economists to incorporate into their analyses, wherever that is pertinent, such basic traits and emotions as the desire for power and for sacrifice, the fear of boredom, pleasure in both commitment and unpredictability, the search for meaning and community, and so on.'[19]

Certainly, minor revisions to the neoclassical model such as allowing bounded rationality or allowing individuals to have altruistic preferences will not be enough to correct this form of modelling.[20] This is because it is simply not true that society consists of a set of independent individuals, each of whom acts to achieve goals that are arrived at independently, and that the functioning of the social system consists of the combination of these independent actions of independent individuals.[21] This billiard-ball view is derived crudely from a number of interrelated influences. Firstly, the only perceptible actors in society are individuals.[22] Secondly, as we will see in subsequent chapters, the political and moral philosophers of the seventeenth and eighteenth centuries—influenced by a mechanical cosmology—built such a view from the Reformation's emphasis on individual conscience. Thirdly—and largely as a consequence of the first two—individuals are more isolated in modern society than they were in the past. Nevertheless, in modern societies, individuals still do not act independently or set their goals independently; and their interests are still not wholly selfish. The contemporary account of the individual used in much moral and political philosophy and in economics simply does not give us a rich enough account.

The standard response to this critique is the claim that moral values are incorporated into individual preferences; however, this effectively denies the pervasive, conflicting and regulatory influences of culture. It does so in an attempt to preserve the methodological individualism essential to neoclassical modelling and the primacy of voluntariness essential to its normative use. As I have argued already in Chapter 2, morals are a community construct. It is the assumed conventional dichotomy between the individual and the group that is misleading. It eliminates the tacit, interactive, dynamic relationship between individuals and between those individuals and the cultures within which they are embedded. Treating values as a kind of preference is simply an *ad hoc* strategy to insulate that theory from falsification by eliminating its predictive power and rendering it empty. It also eliminates the distinction embedded in our languages between selfish and unselfish behaviour.[23] The neglect of these considerations is, however, central to the whole neoclassical research program. That program is committed strongly to explanation in terms of methodological individualism, reductionism, instrumental rationality, the Newtonian metaphor and its associated mathematic modelling and self-interest as the fundamental social force. Indeed, the Newtonian metaphor, which is associated with a natural-law outlook, is the dominant metaphor and the master narrative in contemporary economics. These constitute the neoclassical image of what it is to be properly 'scientific'. These commitments are fundamentally normative and misleading rather than positively scientific. Inherent in that commitment is a view of society as a social contract. This is not simply a result of the positivist movement in economics and philosophy for the best part of the twentieth century; it has deeper roots in the whole Enlightenment program, about which more will be said in the next chapter. It provides a particularly good example of how a particular intellectual paradigm or tradition locks us into a particular way of looking and discussing.

While contemporary neoclassical economists have largely neglected the relationship between the economic and social systems, this is not true more generally. It is to the discussion of that relationship by prominent theorists to which we now turn.

The neglect noted above is surprising given the extent of the discussion of the relationship between the social and economic systems since the time of Smith (1723–90). Smith was well aware of the dependency of the economic system on legal rules and institutions; it is a common misrepresentation to regard Smith as the prophet of economic fundamentalism. Sen puts it this way:

> While many admirers of Smith do not seem to have gone beyond this bit about the butcher and the brewer, a reading of even this passage would indicate what Smith is doing here is to specify why and how normal transactions in the market are carried out, and why and how division of labour works, which is the subject of the chapter in which the quoted passage occurs. But the fact that Smith noted that mutually advantageous trades are very common does not indicate that he thought

that self-love...could be adequate for a good society. Indeed, he maintained precisely the opposite.[24]

Furthermore, in his best-known work, *The Wealth of Nations*, Smith echoes Hobbes when he says it is 'only under the shelter of the civil magistrate that the owner of that valuable property which is acquired by the labour of many years or perhaps of many successive generations, can sleep a single night in security'.[25]

Earlier, in the *Theory of Moral Sentiments*, he wrote that

> in the race for wealth and honours and preferments...[the individual] may run as hard as he can, and strain every nerve and muscle, in order to outstrip his competitors. But if he should jostle or throw down any of them, the indulgence of the spectators is entirely at an end. It is a violation of fair-play, which they cannot admit of.[26]

Importantly, Smith recognised that justice was more a precondition for human interaction, interchange and cooperation than a product of that interaction. What is more, in the *Theory of Moral Sentiments*, Smith argues that economic activity is rooted in the non-economic need for sympathy and appreciation.[27] Economist Lionel Robbins, in talking about Smith's views, suggested that the 'invisible hand' was 'the hand of the law-giver, the hand which withdraws from the sphere of the pursuit of self-interest those possibilities which do not harmonise with the public good'.[28] It is quite clear that for Smith the 'invisible hand' is the hand of God:

> [T]he ancient Stoics were of the opinion, that as the world was governed by the all-ruling providence of a wise, powerful, and good God, every single event ought to be regarded as making a necessary part of the plan of the universe, and as tending to promote the general order and happiness of the whole: that the vices and follies of mankind, therefore, made as necessary a part of this plan as their wisdom or their virtue; and by that eternal art which educes good from ill, were made to tend equally to the prosperity and perfection of the great system of nature.[29]

As the above makes clear, Smith was also a Newtonian, seeing the economic system and the social order as a mechanical, equilibrium system involving two fundamental balancing social forces—self-interest and sympathy—and that that balancing was the product of divine providence. Smith, therefore, under the influence of his friend Hume, could be seen as the father of the application of the Newtonian metaphor to economic analysis, just as earlier Hobbes was the father of the application of the Newtonian metaphor to political theory.

This issue of the relationship between society and the economy was central to the work of Karl Marx. He claimed that all distinctively human activity had a social dimension and was made possible only as a result of membership in society.

Cooperation and compassion were more human attitudes than selfish indifference or hostility. He also pointed out that commodities did not go to the market and make exchanges on their own account. Value was not inherent in a commodity; rather, it was a relationship between people expressed as a relationship between things. Consequently, Marx emphasised that the market consisted of social relationships; however, he also told us in his preface to *Contribution to the Critique of Political Economy*:

> The totality of these relations constitute[s] the economic structure of society—the real foundation, on which legal and political superstructures arise and to which definite forms of social consciousness correspond. The mode of production of material life determines the general character of the social, political, and spiritual processes of life. It is not the consciousness of men that determines their being, but on the contrary, their social being determines their consciousness.[30]

This is interpreted usually as meaning that the economy constitutes the 'real foundation' of society, and on this foundation 'the legal and political superstructure' is based.[31] In other words, the moral superstructure of a society is adapted to its socio-technical or economic substructure. This should not, however, be interpreted as meaning that Marx thought that the superstructure was unimportant.[32] Indeed, Berger and Luckmann tell us that the mechanical determinism inherent in the above interpretation misrepresents the dialectical character of Marx's thought and his real understanding.[33] For Marx, realities were never isolated entities standing in a linear relationship. Rather, reality could be understood only as multifaceted interaction.[34] Nevertheless, he was concerned that human thought was founded in human activity—labour in the widest sense—and in the social relations brought about by this activity. Consequently, Berger and Luckmann suggest that substructure and superstructure should be understood as human activity and the world produced by that activity respectively. Inherent in these views is the belief that there is no such thing as an immutable human nature and that peoples' wants are largely a function of how society is organised. One consequence is that the various societal forms found in human history are reflected in human self-understanding—a view not inconsistent with the constructionist ideas outlined in Chapter 2. A further consequence for Marx was that the economic elite shaped the perceptions and ideas of the working population, permeating their entire existence: 'The ideas of the ruling class are, in every age, the ruling ideas: ie, the class which is the dominant material force in society is at the same time its dominant intellectual force.'[35] This is a form of oppression, the source of a false consciousness and of alienation. Of course, these ideas strike at the heart of the idea of individual autonomy and of consumer sovereignty.

In *Capital*, Marx claimed to disclose the 'natural laws' of capitalist production and was perhaps guilty of the same error as the bourgeois economists he criticised: the reification of economic categories and their elevation into universal laws. It was on the basis of these so-called universal laws that he claimed that socialism was a vastly superior form of social organisation to capitalism and that socialism was destined to replace capitalism.[36] Central to these claims was the belief that capitalism debases human beings, reducing them to a state of alienation—an appendage of a machine. Capitalism was a form of society in which the social bond was mutual self-interest, dissolving the social world into atomised individuals confronting each other. It was a system based on the exploitation of the majority—who earned their living by the sale of their labour—by a small minority, who owned the means of production. It was this exploitation that produced class warfare. Nothing less than communism—true democracy—would do away with class antagonisms and enable human beings to live fully human lives. The selfishness and egoism inherent in capitalism were morally reprehensible—the very antithesis of true humanity—and the State and private property were impoverishing human creations, defending the interests of the rich. In particular, the only rights protected in liberal states were those of the egotistical man. Marx believed further that capitalism was incapable of maintaining the full use of the resources of advanced societies, while communism would do so. In addition, communism would produce members of society with better wants and superior accomplishments.

Of course, history has now moved past the Soviet experiment with its problematic connection to Marx's thought and its massive casualty list. Nevertheless, it is no longer possible to maintain a utopian confidence in a socialist alternative to the capitalist system, however much we might decry the failings of the latter. Importantly, that experience has also discredited Marxist thought. In the process, the shared roots in the Enlightenment of Marx's utopianism and that of capitalism are rarely noticed.

The economic sociology tradition dating from Weber regards the economic process as an organic part of society, constantly interacting with other forces.[37] Weber saw economic action as social and emphasised the autonomy of the social orders, law, politics and religion *vis-a-vis* the economy. In opposition to Marx, he argued that it was not the underlying economic forces that created cultural products such as religion and ideology; rather it was culture that produced certain forms of economic behaviour.[38] This emphasis on culture as distinct from economics is said to have been characteristic of Western Marxism and of the Frankfurt school in particular. For example, Habermas argues that people constitute their reality and organise their experience in terms of knowledge-guiding interests, and that Marx's focus on production provides an inadequate base on which to ground a socially and historically developing rationality.[39]

In *The Protestant Ethic and the Spirit of Capitalism*,[40] Weber argued that the early Puritans, in seeking to glorify God alone and in renouncing the acquisition of material goods as an end in itself, developed certain virtues such as honesty and thrift that were extremely helpful to the accumulation of capital. Weber went on to argue that the reinforcement of social virtues such as honesty, reliability, cooperativeness and a sense of duty to others had the effect of heightening the capacity of adherents to cohere in new communities.[41] This was helpful to economic development because small sectarian communities created natural networks through which businessmen could hire employees, find customers, open lines of credit and the like. Nevertheless, Weber saw market exchange as exceptional in that it represented the most instrumental and calculating type of social action that was possible between human beings. For Dorothy Emmet,[42] the fruitful way of interpreting Weber's views is in terms of the mutual conditioning of one by the other, and this is consistent with the organic outlook of contemporary economic sociology.

For Durkheim, the division of labour serves a much broader function than the creation of wealth and efficiency.[43] For him, it is the principal vehicle for creating cohesion and solidarity in modern society. As the division of labour advances, people cease to bond together on the basis of their similarities (what he called mechanical solidarity) but on the basis of the duties and rights arising out of the interdependency produced by the division of labour (organic solidarity). It is these duties and rights that hold society together. Consequently, morality was central to the whole cohesion of society. Durkheim went on to argue that a whole structure of norms and regulations surrounded economic exchanges and made them possible. In particular, without some generally shared feelings about honest dealings, contracts would be unenforceable.

Durkheim insisted that even a well-functioning exchange economy was in constant danger of being hollowed out by fraud and force. Indeed, Durkheim, in his preface to the second edition of *The Division of Labor in Society*, published in 1902, was concerned about the state of juridical and moral anomie—lawlessness or disconnectedness—which attended economic life in his day:

> The most blameworthy acts are so often absolved by success that the boundary between what is permitted and what is prohibited, what is just and what is unjust, has nothing fixed about it, but seems susceptible to almost arbitrary change by individuals. An ethic so unprecise and inconsistent cannot constitute a discipline...
>
> That such anarchy is an unhealthy phenomenon is quite evident, since it runs counter to the aim of society, which is to suppress, or at least to

moderate, war among men, subordinating the law of the strongest to a higher law. To justify this chaotic state, we vainly praise its encouragement of individual liberty. Nothing is falser than this antagonism too often presented between legal authority and individual liberty. Quite on the contrary, liberty (we mean genuine liberty, which it is society's duty to have respected) is itself the product of regulation. I can be free only to the extent that others are forbidden to profit from their physical, economic, or other superiority to the detriment of my liberty. But only social rules can prevent abuses of power. It is now known what complicated regulation is needed to assure individuals the economic independence without which liberty is only nominal.

If in the task that occupies almost all our time we follow no other rule than that of our well-understood interest, how can we learn to depend upon disinterestedness, on self-forgetfulness, on sacrifice? In this way, the absence of all economic discipline cannot fail to extend its effects beyond the economic world, and consequently weaken public morality.[44]

Karl Polanyi takes up much the same theme. For him, the human economy was embedded and enmeshed in institutions—economic and non-economic. The latter were vital.[45] Consequently, Polanyi objected to what he called the economistic fallacy of equating the whole of the economy with the market. By doing so, the true nature of the economy was distorted. In *The Great Transformation*,[46] Polanyi disputed Smith's claim that humans had a natural propensity to truck and barter. In *The Economy as an Instituted Process*,[47] he argued that historically there were several different ways of organising an economy: through reciprocity, redistribution and exchange or a combination of all three. Even within markets, prices that fluctuate frequently—due to competition—represent a fairly late stage of development

The market economy as an institutional structure was insignificant until relatively recent times. Nevertheless, the division of labour was a phenomenon as old as society and sprang from differences inherent in the facts of sex, geography and individual endowment. Polanyi believed that historical and anthropological research justified the view that the economy was, as a rule, submerged in social relationships. Economic actors do not act to safeguard their individual interests in the possession of material goods but to safeguard their social standing, claims and assets. Material goods are valued only in so far as they serve this end. In tribal society, an individual's economic interest is rarely paramount as the community keeps its members from starving. It is the maintenance of social ties, on the other hand, that is crucial. Disregarding the accepted code of behaviour would involve cutting oneself off from one's community. In any event, in the long run, all social obligations are reciprocal and serve the individual's long-term interests. In a society characterised by reciprocity, the idea of profit is barred and haggling is decried, while giving freely is acclaimed as a virtue. As Polanyi said:

> Broadly, the proposition holds that all economic systems known to us up to the end of feudalism in Western Europe were organised either on the principles of reciprocity or redistribution, or householding, or some combination of the three. These principles were institutionalised with the help of a social organisation which, *inter alia*, made use of the patterns of symmetry, centricity, and autarchy. In this framework, the orderly production and distribution of goods was secured through a great variety of individual motives disciplined by general principles of behaviour. Among these motives gain was not prominent. Custom and law, magic and religion co-operated in inducing the individual to comply with rules of behaviour which, eventually, ensured his functioning in the economic system.[48]

Consequently, Polanyi believed that what economists saw as the typical market was just one of many possible forms of organised exchange. To Polanyi, two watershed events in European history were responsible for the emergence of the modern market economy: the creation by the mercantilist state of 'internal markets' and the radical elimination of all market regulation beginning in the early nineteenth century in England. To him, the result was unspeakable misery for the common people until actions were finally taken to protect society from 'the self-regulating market'. Consequently, he traces many of the key tragic political events of the twentieth century to the radically utopian attempt in mid-nineteenth century England to transform all of society into one giant market.

For Polanyi, the control of the economic system by the market has overwhelming consequences for the organisation of society: it means no less than the running of society as an adjunct to the market. Instead of the economy being embedded in social relations, social relations are embedded in the social system. A self-regulating market demands nothing less than the institutional separation of society into an economic and a political sphere. To include human beings (labour) and their natural surroundings in the market system is to subordinate the substance of society itself to the market. Consequently for Polanyi, a market economy can exist only in a market society. The very idea of a self-adjusting market implied a stark utopia. He believed that such an institution could not exist for any length of time without annihilating the human and natural substance of society.[49]

The dominant school of economics in the late nineteenth and early twentieth centuries was institutional economics and was associated with such figures as Thorstein Veblen, Wesley Mitchell and John Commons. It was devoted to the investigation of the institutions that underpinned the market economy. It rejected the reductionism of the marginalist school while emphasising the importance of the legal foundations of an economy and the evolutionary, habituated and volitional processes by which institutions were created and changed.[50] This perspective was not open to mathematical formalism and was eclipsed by neoclassical economics.

Interestingly, Hayek, a strong supporter of market processes and a minimalist state in his later writings, made it clear that what he had called the 'spontaneous' order of the market was dependent on the system of abstract rules, deep-rooted convictions and moral rules, which was the product of civilisation and which represented the institutional infrastructure of the economic system.[51] For Hayek, informal rules such as custom and conventions are probably even more important in daily economic life than the formal ones. Hayek was conscious of the complexity of that social system, arguing that no 'single human intelligence is capable of inventing the most appropriate abstract rules because those rules which have evolved in the process of growth of society embody the experience of many more trials and errors than any individual mind could acquire'.[52]

Another more recent theorist to write on the issue is sociologist Mark Granovetter. He also argues that economic institutions—like all institutions—do not arise automatically in some form made inevitable by external circumstances; they are constructed socially.[53] They are constructed by individuals whose action is facilitated by and constrained by the structure and resources available in the social networks in which they are embedded. Just as for firms and economic groups, how industries are organised is a social construction that often might have been otherwise. He also reminds us that economic action—like all action—is socially situated and cannot be explained by individual motives alone; it is embedded in continuing networks of personal relations rather than carried out by atomised actors. Like Polanyi, he points out that the pursuit of economic goals is accompanied by such non-economic goals as sociability, approval, status and power.

While some economic literature focuses attention on the role of our moral codes in permitting the exchanges involved in any complex division of labour, we would do well to remind ourselves that most economic activity occurs in groups and, without an effective social order, no large-scale group activity would be possible. Indeed, collectives are the important decision-making units in contemporary society. Consequently, Herbert A. Simon (1916–2001) found it puzzling that neoclassical economics placed markets at the centre of the stage with all economic phenomena and all social phenomena to be explained by translating them into, or deriving them from, market transactions based on negotiated contracts.[54] In criticising this approach, Simon pointed to the absence of adequate empirical testing and an absence of an adequate consideration of the literature on organisations and decision making. Because organisations are the dominant feature of the economic landscape, Simon suggests that the term 'organisational economy' might be a more appropriate description than 'market economy'.[55] He also points out that the boundary between markets and organisations varies greatly from one society to another and from one time to another, and argues that these variations need to be explained. Further, he argues that we should begin with empirically valid postulates about what motivates real people in real organisations, and points to four well-documented organisational phenomena: authority, rewards, identification and coordination. Consequently, for Simon, prices are only one of the mechanisms for the coordination of behaviour, either between organisations or within them.

Douglass North (b. 1920) approaches this issue from the perspective of an economic historian interested in explaining economic growth and the differential performances of economies. In *Institutions, Institutional Change and Economic Performance*,[56] he argues that a proper understanding of the nature of human coordination and cooperation has been missing from economic analysis. While many economic historians emphasise the role of technological innovation in the development of human society and in economic growth, North places his emphasis on the development of institutions. He defines those institutions as the humanly devised constraints that shape human interaction and this brings us back into the sociological stream discussed earlier. North sees human cooperation as a fundamental theoretical problem that needs to be explained because complex, impersonal exchange is the antithesis of the condition under which cooperation arises from rational self-interest in game theory. In particular, he sees a vast gap between the relatively clean, precise and simple world of game theory and the complex, imprecise and fumbling way by which human beings have gone about structuring human interaction. He also disputes that evolutionary pressures will lead to institutions that are 'efficient' in the neoclassical sense. He also points out that historically the growth of economies has occurred within the institutional framework of well-developed coercive polities because it is difficult to sustain complex exchange without a third party to enforce agreements.

The difficulty in enforcing agreements has always been the critical obstacle to increasing specialisation and the division of labour. Enforcement poses no problem when it is in the interests of parties to live up to an agreement. Without institutional constraints, however, self-interested behaviour will foreclose complex impersonal exchange because of the uncertainty that either party will find it in their interest to live up to an agreement. Transaction costs will reflect this uncertainty by including a risk premium, the magnitude of which will turn on the likelihood of defection. North argued that throughout history the size of this premium had been too large to allow complex impersonal exchange and therefore limited the possibilities for economic growth.

For North, it has been the evolution of institutions that has limited these costs and in the process created a hospitable environment for the complex exchange necessary for economic growth. Uncertainties surround such complex exchange. They arise as a consequence of the complexity of the problems to be solved and our limited problem-solving abilities. In all societies—from the most primitive to the most advanced—people impose constraints on themselves to give a structure to their relations with others. In these circumstances, history matters because the past, the present and the future are connected to the past by the continuity of a society's institutions. Consequently, today's and tomorrow's choices are shaped by the past.

Such institutions include formal rules and informal constraints such as convention and codes of behaviour. Institutional constraints include what individuals are prohibited from doing and under what conditions some individuals are permitted to undertake certain activities. The rules and informal codes are sometimes violated and punishment is enacted. Therefore, an essential part of the functioning of institutions is the costliness of detecting violations and the severity of punishment. Taken together, the formal and informal rules and the type and effectiveness of enforcement shape the whole character of the social and economic system. Institutions affect the performance of the economy by their effect on the costs of exchange and production. Together with the technology employed, they determine the transaction and transformation costs that make up total costs.

In the course of his analysis, North makes a crucial distinction between institutions and organisations. While organisations—like institutions—provide a structure to human interactions, he differentiates the rules from the players. The institutional framework influences fundamentally what organisations come into existence and how they evolve. In turn, they influence how the institutional framework evolves. Such institutions—from conventions, codes of conduct and norms of behaviour to statute and common law and contracts between individuals—are evolving and are continually altering the choices available to us. Such evolution is a complicated process usually involving incremental change. Even discontinuous changes—such as revolution and conquest—are never completely discontinuous because of the embeddedness of informal constraints in societies. Although formal rules can change overnight as the result of political or judicial decisions, informal constraints embodied in customs, traditions and codes of conduct are much more impervious to deliberate policies. These cultural constraints connect the past with the present and the future and provide a key to explaining the path of historical change.

The institutions necessary to accomplish economic exchange vary in their complexity, from those that solve simple exchange problems to ones that extend across space and time and numerous individuals. The greater the specialisation and the number and variability of valuable attributes associated with a good or service, the more weight must be put on reliable institutions that allow individuals to engage in complex contracting with a minimum of uncertainty. Exchange in modern economies consisting of many variable attributes extending over long periods of time necessitates institutional reliability, which has emerged only gradually in Western economies. North believes that formal rules make up only a small, although very important, part of the constraints that shape choices in these economies. In our daily interaction with others, whether within the family, in external social relations or in business activities, the governing structure is defined overwhelmingly by codes of conduct, norms of behaviour and conventions. Underlying these informal constraints are formal rules, but these are seldom the obvious and immediate source of choice in daily interactions.

It is clear that exchange is not simple in tribal societies. In the absence of the State and formal rules, a dense social network leads to the development of informal structures with substantial stability. Informal constraints are pervasive features of modern economies as well. These informal constraints involve extensions, elaborations and modifications of formal rules, socially sanctioned norms of behaviour and internally enforced standards of conduct. Cooperative frameworks of economic and political impersonal exchange are at the heart of social, political and economic performance. While formal rules can help, it is the informal constraints embodied in norms and internally imposed codes of conduct that are critical. In short, North[57] does not believe that the rational choice paradigm can explain the historical and contemporary record of economic growth.

In a complementary account, Francis Fukuyama[58] also sees what he calls spontaneous sociability as critical to economic life. His view of the role of moral values in promoting organisational innovation and economic development owes much to the earlier work of Weber and Polanyi. Communities of shared values, whose members are willing to subordinate their private interests for the sake of the larger goals of the community, can alone generate the kind of social trust that is critical to organisational efficiency. Consequently, the ability to create large, private business organisations in such societies as Germany, Japan and the United States is related to the fact that they are high-trust societies with abundant social capital.

Echoing North's[59] and Williamson's[60] focus on transaction costs, Fukuyama argues that widespread distrust imposes a kind of tax on all forms of economic activity—a tax that high-trust societies do not have to pay. Justified expectations of honest conduct in transactions reduce costs incurred finding a buyer or seller, negotiating a contract, complying with government regulations and enforcing that contract in the event of dispute or fraud. There is less need to spell things out in lengthy contracts, less need to hedge against unexpected contingencies, fewer disputes and less need to litigate if disputes arise. In some high-trust relationships, parties do not even have to worry about maximising profits in the short run, because they know that the other party will make a deficit in one period good later. Importantly, a high-trust society can organise its workplace on a more flexible and group-oriented basis, with more responsibility delegated to lower levels of the organisation. Such a society will be better able to engage in organisational innovation, since the high degree of trust will permit a wide variety of social relationships to emerge. Workers usually find their workplaces more satisfying if they are treated like adults who can be trusted to contribute to their community rather than like small cogs in a large industrial machine designed by someone else. On the other hand, low-trust societies must fence in and isolate their workers with a series of bureaucratic rules. Consequently, the ability of companies to move from large hierarchies to flexible networks of smaller firms will depend on the degree of trust and social capital present in the broader society. This is important in contemporary discussions of the development of electronic commerce and the associated possibility of creating virtual organisations using new communications technology. A low-trust society might never be able to take full advantage of the efficiencies that these developments offer.

Fukuyama argues that the most effective organisations are based on communities of shared ethical values.[61] Such communities do not require extensive contracts and legal regulation of their relations because prior moral consensus gives members of the group a basis for mutual trust. In this regard, Williamson warns us against seeing trust in purely calculative terms, as to do so can have corrosive effects on the relationships involved.[62] Groups can enter into a downward spiral of distrust when trust is repaid with what is perceived as betrayal or exploitation.

Fukuyama, like Stark and Weber, points out that traditional religions—or ethical systems such as Confucianism—constitute the major institutionalised sources of such culturally determined behaviour because their shared moral languages give their members a common moral life. To some extent, any moral community, regardless of the specific ethical rules involved, will create a degree of trust among its members. Certain ethical codes tend to promote a wider radius of trust than others do by emphasising the imperatives of honesty, charity and benevolence towards the community at large.

Fukuyama continues his discussion in terms of social capital, which he defines as a capability that arises from the prevalence of trust in a society or in certain parts of it. Social capital differs from other forms of human capital in so far as it is usually created and transmitted through cultural mechanisms such as religion, tradition or historical habit. The social capital needed to create this kind of moral community cannot be acquired—as in the case of other forms of human capital—through a rational investment decision. Rather, it requires habituation to the moral norms of a community and the acquisition of virtues such as loyalty, honesty and dependability. The group, moreover, has to adopt common norms as a whole before trust can become generalised among its members. In other words, individuals simply acting on their own cannot acquire social capital. Social capital is based on the prevalence of social rather than individual virtues.

Fukuyama also argues that those societies with a high degree of communal solidarity and shared moral values should be more economically efficient than more individualistic ones. The larger organisations become, the greater the tendency is for individual members to become free riders. The stronger the social solidarity, the more likely it is that members will identify their own well-being with that of the group and the more likely it is that they will put the group's interests ahead of their own. In the words of eminent American Nobel Prize-winning economist Kenneth Arrow:

> Now trust has a very important pragmatic value, if nothing else. Trust is an important lubricant of a social system. It is extremely efficient; it saves a lot of trouble to have a fair degree of reliance on other people's word. Unfortunately this is not a commodity that can be bought very easily. If you have to buy it, you already have some doubts about what you've bought. Trust and similar values, loyalty or truth-telling, are examples of what the economist would call 'externalities'. They are goods, they are commodities; they have real, practical, economic value; they increase the efficiency of the system, enable you to produce more goods or more of whatever values you hold in high esteem. But they are not commodities for which trade on the open market is technically possible or even meaningful.[63]

Arrow went on to argue that the whole economic system would break down if it were not for reinforcement agents and incentives based on morality. Elster, however, specifically rejects this as an adequate account of all social norms on the grounds that not all norms are Pareto improvements,[64] some norms that would make everybody better off are missing and the fact that a norm does make everybody better off does not explain why it exists.[65] The last of these would require the demonstration of a feedback mechanism in which the benefits of the norm contribute to its maintenance. In this regard, Elster suggests that a form of social—as opposed to individual—selection could provide an adequate feedback mechanism. Similarly, American sociologist James Coleman[66] (1926–95) concluded that rational-choice theory could not explain the process by which norms were internalised. Furthermore, social psychologist Daniel Batson[67] conducted a series of experiments that went a long way towards disproving that all altruistic behaviour could be explained by the desire to avoid unpleasant feelings or self-punishment or to gain social approval, a sense of efficacy or shared pleasure—a conclusion supported by field research.

In the light of the above, I would argue that our moral, as well as our legal, institutions provide essential infrastructure for the social system in general and the economic system in particular. Although it has long been recognised that infrastructure is an essential part of the economic system, discussion of that infrastructure is limited mostly to physical infrastructure—a limitation associated with a very poor understanding of the concept of capital. Coleman[68] points to the properties of social capital that distinguish it from the private, divisible, alienable goods treated by neoclassical economic theory. Importantly, while it is a resource that has value in use, it cannot be exchanged easily. Social capital is not the private property of any of the people who benefit from it; it is an attribute of the social structure in which a person is embedded. Social capital does not benefit primarily those whose efforts bring it into existence, but those who are part of the particular structure. The result is that most social capital is created or destroyed as a by-product of other activities. It also means that the importance of social capital is frequently unrecognised.

Of course, the comprehensive legal framework for economic organisation—including property rights and contracts—developed by complex societies also forms an essential part of that apparatus of social control and as such is an essential precondition to any complex division of labour; no one would argue that trust or moral obligation alone could take its place. These institutions are an essential part of any complex market system, but they rest on a bedrock of ethical habits. As Durkheim argues, contracts—which appear to be voluntary, calculated deals among uncommitted individuals—draw effectively on prior shared bonds that are not subject to negotiation, and of which the parties are often unaware.[69]

Conclusion

Earlier it was argued that two key assumptions had been introduced into contemporary public policy debates by economic fundamentalists. These were the autonomy of the market and the primacy of the market over the social. It has been argued that the complex exchange necessary to a highly specialised division of labour requires a pre-existing state of social peace. That state of peace is dependent on our evolved cultural systems with their informal norms and formal rules backed by formal and informal means of coercion and by our own sense of guilt at the breach of internalised norms. Consequently, the market is a sub-system nestled within a more encompassing societal context. Of course, these systems are not independent of each other: they interact and condition each other. Indeed, social and economic institutions cannot be distinguished clearly.[70] Nevertheless, the process of economic competition is not self-sustaining; its very existence, as well as the scope of transactions organised by it, is dependent to a significant extent on the societal 'capsule' within which that competition takes place.[71]

It has been noted in passing that an evolutionary account of the existence of the social order will not seem to be a satisfactory account to some theorists, who will be looking for an ahistorical account analogous to the theoretical accounts given in the physical sciences. While doubts are entertained about the value of such accounts, and no dominant theory has emerged, a brief overview has been given of the types of theories being advanced in contemporary discourse. It is concluded, however, that there is no need to adopt a uni-causal approach and that all of the accounts discussed provide some insight into the human condition. Of particular importance is the account given by Elster, who concluded that social norms could not be reduced to any single principle and, in particular, could not be reduced to rationality or any other form of optimising mechanism. This brief survey of competing theories ends with an account of the approaches of prominent development psychologists, who have attempted a more empirical approach based on the moral development of children. In particular, Kohlberg's unitary, rationalist conception of morality as justice is discussed and discounted as not providing a convincing account. Gilligan's alternative account of the moral development of children suggests that moral development proceeds along two different but intersecting paths that run through different modes of experience and give rise to different forms of thought: an analytical logic of justice and an ethic of care.

The advocates of social-contract theory, however, work with a model of society that is a replica of the market. Their attempt to model society's moral infrastructure as a social contract is an attempt to reduce all social phenomena to what is itself a particular social phenomenon. It is a contract that takes the simplest of transactions as its paradigmatic example,[72] but a simple exchange transaction provides only a poor model for complex long-term contracts. By trying to generate the rules of economic life internally and by viewing them as having emerged from rational, self-maximising individuals, such theorists have effectively assumed what they set out to explain.

Such a view argues that our long-term interests require the capacity to discipline our appetites—the suppression of our animality—but this argument does no more than incorporate some of our moral values within the concept of self-interest. While it highlights the frequent presence of considerable tension between our immediate desires and our long-term interests, these long-term interests incorporate only some of our moral values. In any event, this concept of self-interest is not descriptive of the real behaviour of real individuals, amounting to no more than idealisations of individuals and of their self-interest—idealisations that fly in the face of daily experience. In any event, as argued earlier, there is no historical basis for the view that fully formed individuals preceded communities and their shared rules, roles and beliefs. Indeed, contemporary society could not exist without the complex of social and religious norms that sustain it. The development of that society—indeed, the formation of complex communities generally, along with their associated norms and institutions—has been a long process of social evolution along with the development of supporting religious and philosophical beliefs. Of course, it could be said that this process of social evolution produced what amounts to a tacit social contact, but such an assertion would be mere sophistry, devoid of content.

The competition process itself is constrained and sustained by social and legal rules. The complex division of labour in modern societies involves a complex of relationships and institutions, which cannot be reduced to transactions. Rather state, 'law and society are entwined in mutually reinforcing virtuous connection; rather than mutually reinforcing vicious competition. Or so it is when we are in luck.'[73]

The next chapter will focus first on the history of the concept of the social contract and the associated doctrine of freedom of contract as the central paradigms in economic fundamentalism. It will also point to the growing difficulty encountered in trying to justify these theoretical ideas as the original divine basis of natural law was secularised and attempts were made to naturalise it. This leads readily into the question of how economists perceive their own enterprise and how that enterprise fits in with the Enlightenment project.

ENDNOTES

[1] Etzioni 1988, p. ix.

[2] Hirsch 1977.

[3] Phillips 1986. I have drawn heavily on Phillips for this account.

[4] Parsons 1949, p. 203.

[5] Elster 1989.

[6] Ibid., p. 285.

[7] Marx and Engels 1970, Preface.

[8] Gilligan 1982.

[9] Shweder and Miller 1985.

[10] Phillips 1986.

[11] Shweder 1986.

[12] Gilligan 1983.

[13] Phillips 1986.

[14] Miller 1984.

[15] Downie 1972.

[16] Brennan and Buchanan 1985, pp. 13–14.

[17] Polanyi ???

[18] Ben-Ner and Putterman 1998.

[19] Hirschman 1983, p. 29.

[20] Sugden 1998.

[21] Coleman 1990.

[22] Ibid.

[23] Mansbridge1998.

[24] Sen 1987, p. 24.

[25] Smith 1776, Book V, Ch. 1, cited in Atiyah 1979, p. 327.

[26] Smith 1757, Part II, Section II, Ch. 11, cited in Atiyah 1979, p. 327.

[27] Seligman 1992.

[28] Robbins ????, p. 56, cited in Atiyah 1979, p. 327. We might note in passing that the use of sporting analogies in describing economic competition remains popular to this day. We might also note that it is the controlling set of rules and the mechanism of enforcement that makes such contests possible.

[29] Meek 1977, p. 10.

[30] Marx 1961, p. 67.

[31] Smelser and Swedberg 1994. This brief account of the views of the Economic Sociology School draws primarily on this reference.

[32] Crotty 1998.

[33] Berger and Luckmann 1967.

[34] Crotty 1998.

[35] Marx 1961, p. 93.

[36] Conway 1987.

[37] Smelser and Swedberg 1994.

[38] Fukuyama 1995.

[39] Crotty 1998.

[40] Weber 1930.

[41] Weber 1978.

[42] 'In the long run, however, the consequences of the accumulation of wealth by ascetically minded business men made for an erosion of asceticism.' (Emmet 1966, p. 129)

[43] Durkheim 1993, p. 3.

[44] Ibid., pp. 2–4.

[45] Smelser and Swedberg 1994, p. 15.

[46] Polanyi 1944.

[47] Polanyi 1957.

[48] Polanyi 1944, pp. 54–5.

[49] Ibid., p. 73.

[50] See http://en.wikipedia.org/wiki/Institutional_economics

[51] Frowen 1997.

[52] Cited in ibid., p. 43.

[53] Granovetter 1992.

[54] Simon 1991.

[55] Simon suggests that the choice of name could matter a great deal, and could strongly affect the choice of variables that are important enough to be included in any first-order theory of the phenomena.

[56] North 1990.

[57] North 1998.

[58] Fukuyama 1995.

[59] North 1990.

[60] Williamson 1994.

[61] Stark defines trust as the expectation that arises within a community of regular, honest and cooperative behaviour—based on commonly shared norms—on the part of other members of that community.

[62] Williamson 1994.

[63] Cited in Fukuyama 1995, pp. 151–2.

[64] See Chapter 8.

[65] Elster 1989.

[66] Coleman 1990.

[67] Cited in Mansbridge 1998.

[68] Coleman 1990.

[69] Durkheim 1993.

[70] Ben-Ner and Putterman 1998.

[71] Etzioni 1988.

[72] Atiyah 1979.

[73] Krygier 1996, p. 17.

Chapter 4: A Brief Account of the Historical Origins of Economic Fundamentalism

> How selfish soever man may be supposed, there are evidently some principles in his nature, which interest him in the fortune of others, and render their happiness to him, though he derives nothing from it except the pleasure of seeing it.
> — Adam Smith[1]

Introduction

At the conclusion of Chapter 3, it was argued that the proposition that self-interest was the fundamental ordering principle operating in society could not be sustained. This conclusion is inconsistent with the beliefs of many economists, who claim that the existence of social groups and of social order can be explained by voluntary contracts between individuals who have made the rational calculation that cooperation is in their long-term self-interest. This view begs the question of whether real individuals are capable of determining what is in their long-term self-interest—a question that, in practice, has often been settled in the negative. In contrast, I argue that civilisation requires the suppression of self-interest through social norms and that, in practice, our decisions are deeply affected by socially inculcated values and by our emotions. Consequently, the complex of relationships and institutions that make the division of labour possible cannot be reduced to voluntary transactions between individuals.

I also argued in Chapter 3 that our moral codes and our legal system provide the infrastructure and the institutional basis essential for the social system in general and the economic system in particular. While it has long been recognised that infrastructure is essential to the functioning of the economic system, economists generally have taken that social infrastructure for granted, limiting their consideration to physical things. This limitation involves even a very narrow understanding of the economic concept of 'capital'—a limited understanding that is breaking down. This has led to recognition among some economists of the importance of 'human capital' to the functioning of the economic system. That concept is, however, confined too frequently to embodied marketable knowledge and skills. This is far too narrow a view of the abilities and attributes required for successful human interaction—economic and social. The development of that human capital involves the process of socialisation and moral education, but the content of that socialisation has been invented in the process of social evolution and involves some vision—or visions—of the 'good society'.

It is clear that religious and intellectual speculation has played an important part in the development of such visions. This intellectual speculation involves the attempt to see beyond the historical to what—in the rationalist, classical scientific tradition—are conceived of as more radically fundamental, underlying forces, which are seen as fixed natural laws. As such, it incorporates a conception of natural laws as mathematical, eternal and absolute—a reflection of some perfect mathematical form—derived from ancient Greek philosophers Pythagoras (569–500 BC) and Plato, and reinvigorated by the Enlightenment. Such a vision—and its associated speculative reasoning—attempts also to lay down the form that moral justification *should* take. I will critique this tradition in more detail in the next chapter.

As indicated in Chapter 2, these are not new questions. Rather, they are as old as philosophy and its fascination with deductive political and moral stories. Even the idea of the 'invisible hand'—beloved of economists—was old in 1759 when Smith first used the phrase.[2] Just how old could come as something of a surprise, even though Smith tells us. In his *Theory of Moral Sentiments*, Smith says:

> [T]hat the ancient Stoics were of [the] opinion, that as the world was governed by the all-ruling providence of a wise, powerful, and good God, every single event ought to be regarded, as making a necessary part of the plan of the universe, and as tending to promote the general order and happiness of the whole: that the vices and follies of mankind, therefore, made as necessary a part of this plan as their wisdom or their virtue; and by that eternal art which educes good from ill, were made to tend equally to the prosperity and perfection of the great system of nature.[3]

The idea could have originated with Hesiod, one of the earliest Greek epic poets, in the seventh century BC—though he might have just been reporting an idea with wide currency within his culture.[4]

In Chapters 2 and 3, I provided an evolutionary account of the emergence of social order along with a brief summary of the various ahistorical theories that have been used to account for social order. These ahistorical approaches have not led to—nor are they likely to lead to—any consensus. Rather, the history of the social sciences has been dominated by three competing opinions:

- society is merely a collection of individuals
- society is an integrated whole; the term 'society' stands for a reality
- society is neither a fiction nor a fact; it is an entity ever in the making, a process.[5]

The first view is based on a mechanical, atomistic metaphor. In this view, atoms are conceived of as the solid fundamental particles in nature interacting in a mechanical fashion like billiard balls. Consequently, this view leads to the use of mechanical analogies and to social theories in which supra-individual forces must be explained in terms of individual behaviour. It also sees the social system as an equilibrium system modelled on the equilibrium system of classical mechanics and of Newtonian cosmology. As we will see in the next chapter, this is the fundamental idea—the paradigm, the cosmology—that underpins the Enlightenment. It is this view that underpins neoclassical economics, which models human beings and their interactions as if they were mechanical, equilibrium systems. This perspective, however, in denying the existence of a super-individual entity, still has to account for our understanding of the existence of such entities. To suggest simply that such understandings are mistaken—as Margaret Thatcher did—is inconsistent with that perspective's own methodological individualism. This is because it denies the primacy of the meanings and intentions of individuals when they use the word 'society' to describe a collective entity with a pervasive influence on our lives.[6] The second view, which is based on an organic metaphor, is the way ancient Greek and medieval philosophers viewed society—the view that was overthrown by the Enlightenment. In this view, society is conceived of as an organism similar to the human body—a view lending itself to biological analogies. Important historically is the view of God as the head and society as the body.

Both of these views exclude essential elements of the social order and cannot, therefore, provide an adequate account. There is a tension between these views and an associated tension between the public and private spheres. These tensions—which remain unresolved to this day—have been central to Western political speculation. The boundaries to be placed between the public and private spheres and the limits on individual liberties are the stuff of day-to-day politics and the defining themes to which I drew attention in the opening paragraphs of Chapter 1. The third view of nature as process—or as evolution—arises primarily out of the relatively recent experience of change in social and economic life within the lifetime of reflective commentators. As a result, change came to be seen as a fundamental factor that had to be explained. This process view better accounts for the integration of the social order and the independence of the individuals that comprise it.[7]

What is clear, however, is that we are heirs to a dominant tradition of moral and social argument, arising out of the Enlightenment and based on atomism and a mechanical, Newtonian metaphor that continues to influence our policy development processes. The broad philosophical and scientific foundations of this tradition in the Enlightenment will be discussed in Chapter 5. For the moment, we will focus on a more detailed account of the origins of the various social doctrines that flow from this tradition—doctrines that influence contemporary economic and policy thought, including social contract theory.

A Brief History

The city-state—the *polis*—began to emerge as a new form of social and political organisation in Greece in the eighth century BC out of that culture's religious, military and economic history. The *polis* was a complex hierarchical society built on an organic metaphor around the notion of citizenship. The *polis* provided ancient Greece with an intellectual model of how society was constituted.[8] Only in the *polis* was real human existence conceived of as being possible. Plato and Aristotle agreed that to be a member of a *polis* involved a life of collective involvement, transcending private interests. Plato argued that political power existed to serve the welfare of the *polis* and its citizens and that this required greed and ambition to be constrained by philosopher-kings guided by the power of reason. For Aristotle, politics was the moral consummation of all other levels of human activity and the State expressed the common moral life of the community.[9]

In medieval times, Thomas Aquinas provided the dominant Christianised Aristotelian version of this organic model: a hierarchical cosmos created and maintained by God, in which everything had its ordained place and humans served God's ends.[10] This organic model did not postulate—nor would it have allowed—the strong separation between the public and private spheres that characterises some modern societies. Of course, this account is not intended to endorse the rigid and authoritarian nature of this model. Nor is it intended to excuse the often-exploitative relationships it permitted in practice. Nevertheless, in this model, a set of fundamental principles of justice, based in the cosmic order itself, was seen as the foundation of the social order and of all enacted law. In this view, one should cultivate moral virtues rather than merely keep the moral law. In consequence, people were seen as owing a wide range of duties to God, to the Church, to their feudal lord and to other people. It involved an appreciation of the interdependency of society and of the debt owed to the lower classes. It also involved the consolation of the promise of immortal life to those at the bottom of the hierarchy.[11] In addition, the possession of property by the elite involved temporary custodianship, not ownership. Such custodianship carried duties as well as rights. Among other things, it was the duty of those in authority to stamp out usury and to ensure that prices and wages were just.

This hierarchical view played a crucial role in a developing natural-law tradition from John of Salisbury in the twelfth century, St Thomas Aquinas in the thirteenth, Nicholas of Cusa in the fifteenth, the *Vindiciae Contra Tyrannos* (attributed to Philippe Duplessis-Mornay and Hubert Languet) in the sixteenth and Hugo Grotius in the seventeenth.[12]

Calvin provided a later ethical vision of the social world as a holy community of saints participating voluntarily in an unmediated relationship with Christ—the source of transcendent power and authority. This vision drew on the Pauline and Augustinian theological tradition, Calvin's particular theology and a literal reading of the Old and New Testaments. In stressing the sovereignty of God, Calvin and Calvinists sought to remake society in the image of a religious community. In this vision, leadership in church and state fell to men pre-ordained for salvation by God. Importantly, the individual was imbued with a new autonomy while the nature of the social ties between these individuals was redefined. The Reformation had more broadly articulated a new idea of authority within the Church and within society. In particular, it brought with it a new conception of ministry based on consent, collective agreement and the fundamental equality of believers and ministers before God. Furthermore, it sanctified secular life, giving religious legitimisation to secular callings. This Calvinist vision was attractive to the prosperous mercantile classes of the sixteenth and early seventeenth centuries for whom material wealth and business success were signs of God's grace and their membership among the elect. In this way, Calvinism helped create a climate favourable to capitalism. In the US colonies in particular, Puritan settlers attempted to start afresh and organise a Christian commonwealth that would serve as a model for the rest of the world. As a result, the US culture remains Calvinist in some form or other to this day.

All of these theories involved an account of social existence in terms of a vision of an ultimate good or divine purpose. What is particularly important for my account is the fact that the medieval concept of 'man' as a political and social being—necessarily involved in a network of social relations—which was derived from Aristotle—gradually waned. This decline brought with it a need for a new explanation. This waning was associated also with the decline of the moral and secular authority of the Western Christian Church, partly as a result of the struggle for power between religious and secular authorities in medieval Europe, and partly as a result of the Reformation and the religious and political strife that followed.

Progressively, the intellectual climate came to be defined by deism and an associated distancing of God from human affairs.[13] Under this deist view, while God had actively created the Universe and was the final cause of the physical and social order, He had then turned His back, leaving it to operate automatically by laws built in at the outset. This involved a vision of God different from that of the Judaeo-Christian revelation, that of the Stoics: a God fitting the Enlightenment's new cosmology and the Newtonian mechanical world-view, a clock-maker God who started the cosmic clock and who filled in the gaps between the rapidly expanding natural forms of explanation and social and physical reality. Over time, the Enlightenment rejected Christianity's claim of a historical revelation that was the source of truth and value.[14] It thus progressively brought into question the idea that the source of social order was to be found outside society. It also progressively disengaged moral discourse from direct theological discourse and in the process strengthened the distinction between the public and private realms. In this disengagement, the magisterium of the Church—its claimed authority to teach on faith and morals on the basis of a commission from God—passed imperceptibly from ecclesiastical authorities and their theologian advisers to natural and moral philosophers, who claimed an authority to teach on social and political arrangements because of their special knowledge of the truth and of natural laws. What remained in deism, as a remnant of God's presence in the world, were the facility of reason and the holiness of rationality.[15] We hear this echo still in our own day in the continued adulation of human rationality. Of course, the growing strength of capitalist market relations—with its distinction between public and private—reinforced this need for a new conception of the social order.

This deist view was still a vision of a benevolent God in which natural laws were seen as having been created to ensure human happiness. Consequently, the discovery of and obedience to such laws was essential to human happiness. It also imputes a purpose to social phenomena. This trend was also directly associated with the development of science and a desire to find a scientific and increasingly more natural explanation of the social order. This established the intellectual climate that determined what was accepted as a valid explanation. In this climate, the transcendent grounding of the social order was no longer seen as providing an adequate explanation. While not yet totally abandoning belief in and a reliance on the benevolence of God, human attributes or 'human nature' were seen increasingly as the ultimate determinants of the regularities and uniformities in social life and the vision of the social good. It was a process that progressively divinised nature and human reason, providing a secular source of meaning and justification as comprehensive and as dogmatic as that provided by the religion it replaced. Clark calls this Enlightenment project 'the Natural Law Outlook'. It was a project with three essential elements: a belief in social physics, naturalism and the derivation of a natural universal moral theory.[16]

For example, Hobbes, the first of the major contract theorists, had a strong interest in the new philosophy and in the science of the seventeenth century, having been Francis Bacon's secretary.[17] His was a materialistic, reductionist and mechanistic theory and he used the Newtonian metaphor in his theorising even before Sir Isaac Newton (1643–1727) had put the finishing touches to that paradigm. He aimed to develop a science of politics comprising universal propositions proven conclusively as the propositions of Euclid. This new type of political theorising, which became typical of modernity, incorporated a new and distinctive view of the way in which people should relate to the world. The individual is conceived of as an isolated mind and will with a vocation to bring the world under the control of reason—a way of thinking that privileges the rational, wilful subject.[18]

Hobbes' theory involved a mechanics of the mind and a mechanics of society in which strivings within our bodies determined our actions in our relationships with each other. For Hobbes, the unceasing pursuit of power and pleasure was the sociological counterpart to the concept of gravity. This theme reappeared later in Bentham's utilitarian account of morality. As indicated above, this tradition breaks with Aristotle and Aquinas and their view of humans as inherently social and political animals. Rather, this tradition postulates theories that are highly individualistic and pre-social, and that are voluntaristic, consensual and rationalist.[19] Nevertheless, they are theories with roots in earlier political theorising in which the idea of contract was used to undermine the quasi-divine pretensions of kings and emperors.[20]

This use of the idea of contract can be traced to the Old Testament, to Roman law and the political practice of medieval Europe, where kings were often elected and ruled in accordance with pre-existing laws and customs.[21] In particular, among the Germanic peoples, the idea of a *pactum* governing their monarchy was derived from the idea of a covenant, which in turn was derived from the social and religious history of the ancient Middle East as recorded in the Old Testament. In such a covenant, divine authority was invoked as a witness to morally binding agreements. These agreements were often in the form of a suzerain treaty between a stronger political leader and a weaker one, but they also covered mutual pledges between more equal partners. The Old Testament relates how this 'basic, "mutual", oath-bound creation of responsible relationships' is recognised to be a close analogy of the way in which God relates to humanity and a model of how we should relate to each other under God.[22] It involves also a revelation of the nature of a just, merciful God who engages directly in the creation and sustaining of righteous living in community.

This progressive secularisation of covenant, through the development of social contract theories, was also associated closely with the religious, social and political developments in the surrounding societies. In particular, contract ideas provided radical Protestants with a means of justifying their political dissent. It also suited the new merchant classes and their allies in challenging the monopoly on political power of the established oligarchies.[23] In particular, these ideas were congenial to Calvinists engaged in struggle against ruling state authorities opposed to their religious beliefs. For example, the *Vindiciae Contra Tyrannos*, which appeared in 1579, attributed the obligations of a ruler to his vocation or divine calling. Consequently, the covenant between ruler and people was not simply between ruler and people, it was between ruler, subjects and God, and expressed the will of God.[24] It was the influence of Calvinism, with its propensity to think of obligations in terms of covenants, combined with the importance of Calvinism in the political conflicts in sixteenth and seventeenth-century Europe, which first raised contract theory to a central position in Western political theory.[25]

In particular, the popularity of the contractual ideas in seventeenth-century Britain is attributable directly to the influence of Puritanism—the English brand of Calvinism. Contractual ideas were used by politicians and propagandists to justify rebellion during the English Civil War (1642–51)—a war that was provoked by the religious policies of Charles I and by his claims to absolute political power founded on divine will. This Puritan contractualism is reflected also in *The Agreement of the People*, a proposed contract drawn up between 1648 and 1649 by the Levellers, the radical democratic party in the English Civil War, and in their demands for a popular franchise.[26]

Covenant and social contract ideas—particularly those developed by John Locke—were used to justify the second expulsion of the restored Stuarts in 1688, and became part of the prevailing ideology. Changing ideas about the nature of property rights came to a head at the same time, with the ownership of property tending to become more 'absolute'. In these struggles, the Whigs also wrested from the Crown a new freedom of property.[27] While in medieval times the relationship between the Crown and its tenants combined rent and taxes, the ideas of rent and taxes had gradually become separated. The abolition of feudal tenures in 1660 and the creation of new excise taxes marked this fundamental shift in ideas about land as private property. The great lords ceased to be tenants of the Crown and became owners, while freeholders also began to see themselves as owners. In the process, the rural poor were progressively dispossessed of their customary land rights. As we saw earlier, the England of the period has been described as a property owners' association with the landless classes excluded from the political process. It was against the landless classes that the property owners sought government protection.[28] These changing ideas and the associated theories of Hobbes and Locke were related also to the emerging market society.[29] The consequence was that the logic of capitalism, rationalisation and the Enlightenment's faith in material and moral progress became intertwined.[30]

Consequently, the propertied elite found it easy to conceive of civil society as based on a social contract, not on socially defined moral obligations backed by divine law.[31] As a result, the concept of contract gradually replaced custom as the source of law and social obligations, including the obligations associated with commercial contracts. There was an ambiguity in this theorising.[32] It is not entirely clear whether Hobbes and Locke were discussing the origins of political society or criteria for judging it. It does seem that both believed that theirs was a historical account. It is now clear that their accounts were not. Subsequent contract theorising—such as that of Immanuel Kant (1724–1804) and John Rawls (1921–2002)—is defended as an analogy in which contract is used to try to deduce the ideal form of political organisation.[33] As such, they are clearly normative theories. We might note in passing that the standard criticism of such theories is that they presuppose a universal human nature that determines the distinguishing characteristics of the 'state of nature' that lead to a need for a universal contract. Social-contract theorists have not relied on an account of human nature based on empirical evidence, but on an arbitrary, idealised model that assumes that human beings are motivated by self-interest and that they are rational in their pursuit of that self-interest. As we have already seen, these are the assumptions under which neoclassical economics operates; however, the account I gave earlier of the social construction of reality—and of the wide differences in values and practices that have been observed in practice—undermines belief in such a universal human nature.

What was new in this theorising was the idea that contractual relationships were created by the free choice of the individuals involved, not the idea that such relationships involved mutual rights and duties. It followed that for Hobbes , and many later theorists, a price agreed by the parties was a just price merely by virtue of the agreement. Importantly for our account, for Hobbes, the obligation to abide by one's promises—a cornerstone of all social contract theory—is an obligation of natural law corresponding with the self-interest and common interest of all men.[34] For Hobbes, men acting freely created civil society, even when it was imposed on them by conquest. The overriding requirement for law meant that rational men would and did assent to surrender their 'natural liberty' even to a conqueror. This aspect of Hobbes' doctrine appears to reflect his commitment to peace—a commitment reflected in his submission to Cromwell in 1651 after the defeat of the Royalists. This aspect of Hobbes' doctrine was, however, unattractive to his English contemporaries as it brought into question the legitimacy of the execution of King Charles I.

Locke's ideas were much more acceptable, as he modified Hobbes' account to provide a justification for resistance to tyrants in the name of individual rights, liberty and property. Locke was associated closely with the Whig cause, being the philosophical spokesman of the great Whig landowners, the landowning classes and the rising bourgeoisie. Locke owed his influence to his defence of their property rights.[35] In Locke's state of nature, people are naturally free and equal and are not in a constant state of war. Rather, they are acquiring property. They own their own person and their labour. It was through this labour that the common property of mankind was appropriated to individual use; and it was the hard-working who, Locke claimed, acquired the most property. While in the state of nature there were severe limits to the unequal division of property, the invention of money made it possible for great inequalities of wealth to develop. In using money, people agreed tacitly to such an unequal distribution. In establishing civil society, individuals agreed to surrender some of their right to protect that property. Consequently, for Locke, the principal role of government was to protect property rights—rights that he claimed predated government itself. Since it is transparently obvious that no one had, in fact, assented to such a contract, Locke relies on the notion of tacit consent to support his contractual views.

This theory drew heavily on the concept of natural law—a law deriving from divine law—to explain, in particular, the limits on the powers of government and the obligation to keep promises and agreements. Locke drew specifically on the work of Anglican theologian Richard Hooker (1554–1600), the creator of the distinctive Anglican theology the *via media*. For Hooker, society did not occur spontaneously but resulted from the deliberate seeking of communion and fellowship in political societies. Government and laws were also the result of agreement.[36] For Hooker, the universe was ruled by natural laws appointed by God , governing the physical universe and moral questions. They were discovered by reason and were not to be found solely in scriptures or in church teaching. It is a vision that draws also on the Calvinist vision of a community of individuals under God's dominion in which man is God's workmanship and His property. This provided the necessary transcendental underpinnings for Locke's theory of civil society. This vaguely religious justification of property also helped to make Locke's ideas more attractive to the English governing classes.[37] Nevertheless, in time, this concept of natural law came to be stripped of its associations with divine laws and nature ultimately came to denote human appetites.

Locke and Newton were strong influences on the Scottish Enlightenment and on Smith (1723–90), one of its leading figures. Newton, the seminal figure in the science of the seventeenth century, gave this natural-law outlook widespread scientific credibility. Newton emphasised the independence of scientific discoveries from theology and metaphysics, even though the belief in a divine order was central to his beliefs.[38] He believed that the rational and the natural were synonymous. Consequently, the structure of nature—God's design—could be discovered by reasoning, particularly mathematical reasoning, applied to observation and experimentation. He also believed that this method was important for moral philosophy and for salvation for that also was part of God's design.

Important to this account is the influence of the dominant Protestant natural-law philosophers, Hugo Grotius (1583–1645) and Samuel Pufendorf (1632–94). It was through these influences that the natural-law outlook was transmitted to Smith. As indicated above, their philosophy involved a continuation and an extension of certain strains in scholasticism and, in particular, the distinction between positive law and natural law. Natural law was seen as the earthly manifestation of divine law, revealed through nature and reason, while humans created positive law.[39] Grotius and Pufendorf were also leading contract theorists in their own right. With Grotius—who was seen as the founder of modern natural-law theory—natural law was founded on reason and rational axioms similar to mathematical axioms that could be intuited by everyone. This marks a major break in the natural-law tradition. Grotius saw that instead of natural law relying on revelation, it was seen as working through a social instinct implanted in humans by God. It was a theme picked up by Smith. Indeed, the tradition of moral philosophy associated with the Scottish Enlightenment and out of which the modern ideas of civil society emerged was steeped in natural-law speculation.[40]

Another influence was Bernard Mandeville's (1670–1733) *Fable of the Bees*, first published in 1714, which argued, amid much scandal, that the pursuit of self-interest—when managed properly within an appropriate institutional framework and under the direction of wise statesmen—could be transformed into public benefits with good consequences. Hume and Smith, leading lights in the Scottish Enlightenment, picked Mandeville's view that vanity motivated people to conform to social norms.[41] The Scottish Enlightenment's idea of civil society was an attempt to develop an individualistic theory of society that could cope with the disparate and contradictory human motivations—which were described usually as altruism and egoism—and with the weaknesses of Locke's account.[42] What was new in this vision of civil society was its understanding of human interaction as a moral sphere in which moral attributes were derived by reason from the nature of humans themselves, and not from a transcendent reality. The concept of moral affections and natural sympathy now provided the grounding that had previously been provided by God.

As argued above, this interweaving of natural law and Calvinist principles was particularly influential in the seventeenth and eighteenth centuries in the Puritan communities of North America, which saw themselves as a new chosen people, and where there was a conscious effort to establish a new social and political order—a holy commonwealth—based on these principles. Of course, this utopianism had ultimately to accommodate the failure of some members of the new settlements to join the Church and the breakdown of community solidarity as the settlements expanded. This provoked a major crisis in American Puritanism, leading to a redefinition of the normative order. That order, which had been identified with the Church, came to be seen as residing within each individual conscience. As Adam Seligman tells us, the result is that the moral order is seen as resting not on grace but on the personal moral behaviour of the individual.[43] The evolution of the American polity involved a confluence of influences connecting the integration of an increasingly secularised Puritan tradition with Lockean political philosophy, a rationalised natural-law tradition and the Enlightenment's belief in the perfectibility of 'mankind'. It was these principles—this civil religion[44]—that the American revolutionaries invoked in their quest for political independence and they remain central to the unique American understanding of themselves. In Britain and Europe, different traditions militated against the very strong emphasis on individualism, natural rights and anti-statism that characterises America.

In his *Treatise on Human Nature* and again in an essay *Of the Original Contract*, Hume attacked Locke's social-contract ideas.[45] Nevertheless, he believed in a constant human nature, which history could illuminate and which could provide the basis of a scientific moral philosophy. Hume agreed that, at first, government was founded on contract because men were so equal in physical ability that they could be subject to authority only by their own agreement. Hume, however, rejected the social contract account of legitimate political authority. There was no state of nature. It was a mere philosophical fiction. Nor was society formed by a social contract constituted by promises. Rather, societies evolved and formed gradually. Even if there had been some initial agreement, the subsequent obligations of its citizens were not and could not be derived from any original agreement to which they were not parties, or from any renewed agreement of their own. Similarly, he rejected the notion of tacit consent.

For Hume, the duty of allegiance owed to a state and the obligation to perform contracts were based on self-interest and neither was derived from the other. Similarly, Hume rejected the idea that society was founded to protect property rights. The concept of a property right is itself an artificial concept depending on morality and justice and these are notions created and recognised by society. Property rights cannot pre-date society . For Hume, the whole contractual edifice of political theory was unnecessary. Justice in general, rights of property in particular and the obligation to perform a promise derive from convention in the same way that the use of money or language is derived. Nevertheless, for Hume, the stability of possessions, their transfer by consent and the performance of promises are fundamental to the working of society. These rules are not, however, rooted in any historical, mythical, logical or transcendental status.[46]

What was to stop this individualistic, self-interested society from degenerating into a Hobbesian war of all on all?[47] Hume thought it was enlightened self-interest—not unbridled licence—that would do the trick. Hume assumed that most of the educated population would realise that it was in their interests not to pursue short-term advantage at the expense of longer-term interest. Those who did not would be dealt with by the law and would adjust their behaviour. Obligations that originated from self-interest came to be generalised until they were seen as general moral obligation, independent of particular cases.

A second answer is associated with Smith and his attempt to create a science of morals and society. Contrary to popular belief, Smith was no admirer of mere selfishness:

> The wise and virtuous man is at all times willing that his own private interests should be sacrificed to the public interest of his own particular order or society. He is at all times willing too, that the interest of this order or society should be sacrificed to the greater interest of the state or sovereignty, of which it is only a subordinate part. He should, therefore, be equally willing that all those inferior interests should be sacrificed to the greater interest of the universe, to the interest of that great society of all sensible and intelligent beings, of which God Himself is the immediate administrator and director.[48]

Consequently, it is clear that Smith did not believe that society was based simply on selfishness and greed . On the contrary, in *The Theory of Moral Sentiments*, Smith discussed the basis of moral feelings or sentiments and their relationship with justice. Smith argues that though men have natural sympathy for each other—and are led by that sympathy to act with benevolence—these motives are insufficient to curb men's natural propensity to act in their own interests. Thus, for Smith, justice is the supreme virtue as it counteracts human selfishness. Importantly, for Smith, the 'invisible hand' was a consequence of divine design, of a benevolent providence that had so arranged human nature as to produce this outcome.

Smith further elaborated his views on economic affairs in *The Wealth of Nations*. In the process, he also drew on the natural-law outlook described above to provide what he thought were constant universal natural laws. For Smith, moral sentiment balanced any attempt to describe rational self-interest in terms of reason disengaged from the 'passions' or from the self freed from the eyes of others. In particular, for Smith, the motivating force of economic activity was the desire for recognition by others. Therefore, the individual self could never be totally disengaged from society, nor could reasoned self-interest be abstracted from those passions, which, through the moral sentiment, rooted man in society.[49] Consequently, Smith recognised the interdependence of individuals and the social embedding of individual existence. Furthermore, this civil-society tradition was inconsistent with any restriction of reason to what we would now call instrumental rationality .

Despite his popular identification with *laissez-faire* ideas, Smith took no crude minimal view of the functions of government. In his view, the State had three principal purposes: to protect citizens from external enemies; to protect citizens from force and fraud; and to erect public works and institutions that were in the public interest but were too costly to be carried out by individuals. Importantly for this account, Smith also rejected any dogmatic prohibition on state interference with contracts:

> Such regulations may, no doubt, be considered as in some respect a violation of natural liberty. But those exertions of the natural liberty of

a few individuals, which might endanger the security of the whole, are, and ought to be restrained by the laws of all governments...The obligation of building party walls, in order to prevent the communication of fire, is a violation of natural liberty, exactly of the same kind with the regulations of the banking trade here proposed.[50]

As Seligman points out, Hume's undermining of the unity of reason and moral sentiments ultimately subverted the Scottish Enlightenment's civil society ideas and encouraged still further the growth of liberal individualism while further undermining the concept of a common good. Kant tried to rebuild that link, claiming the existence of universal natural laws of human action and a determined plan of nature.[51] In doing so, he reasserted the Enlightenment ambition drawing on the idea of moral personhood, the tradition of ascetic Protestantism and the transcendental qualities of universal reason, which he saw as creating a secular version of the autonomous individual conscience. Thus, in Kant, reason replaced God as the source of universal values and moral injunctions. With Kant, however, the State is no longer viewed as coterminous with civil society, and morality is now separated from legality and privatised so as to reside within the conscience only of the morally and economically autonomous individual. This individualistic moral and political theorising involved a further erosion of the idea of citizenship and the communal nature of political life, undermining still further the status of the public sphere and the idea of a common good.

In the early nineteenth century, the desire to create a science of morals and politics became centred on utilitarianism—a development of elements of Hume's thought.[52] By attributing to human beings certain universal, constant, fundamental and opposed natural inclinations, the search for pleasure and the avoidance of pain, utilitarians claimed to have given morals and politics an empirical scientific foundation. These tendencies provided a substitute for the fictional natural rights on which Locke and some earlier theorists had relied. In the process, utilitarians claim to provide an ahistorical, universal and allegedly scientific account of moral and political theory based on a form of social physics and a mechanical Newtonian model in a somewhat similar way to Locke. Importantly, Bentham aspired to be the Newton of the moral world and thought he had found in the above the single unifying principle akin to gravity that regulates the social world.[53] Bentham starts from his particular view of human nature and deduces all institutions and legal arrangements from these properties. While Bentham made random use of historical examples to bolster his claims, it was doubtful that utilitarian theorists provided an account of the process by which society was formed.[54] This utilitarianism was attached pragmatically to classical political economy and subsequently formed the basis for neoclassical economics and its particular failed attempt at Newtonian scientific theorising about human beings and their economic activities.

Bentham provided an alternative legal philosophy to social contractualism, though he did not extricate himself from the natural-law outlook. In particular, he used the idea of a state of nature in a similar way to Locke and retained his individualism. There was, however, a change of emphasis because, for Bentham, it was the role of the lawmaker to create and adjust laws to create an artificial harmony of interests between individual action and the public good. Of course, there was great dissatisfaction with the initial utilitarian account. In particular, support for utilitarianism was undermined by a refusal to accept that pleasure and pain were the only sources of human action—a belief that contradicted everyday experience. Nor can it explain why people find pleasure in different things.[55] Nevertheless, Mill was a utilitarian continuing the Enlightenment's search for a science of society.

While he tried to broaden Bentham's understanding of happiness in terms of pleasure and pain, Mill never shook off his utilitarian beliefs. In *Utilitarianism*, Mill argues that there is no natural harmony of interests between individuals and that it is the lawmaker's role to create such harmony.[56] For Mill, the principles of justice are principles of long-term expediency. This view was mirrored in the growth of legal positivism whereby law was not the result of a social contract but of a hierarchical power relationship. The source of authority was customary obedience. It reflected also a growing scepticism with universal principles of human nature—a scepticism many contemporary economists seem to have overlooked. Mill had an exceptionally strong belief in freedom combined with the possibility of progress, particularly in terms of his positive conception of freedom.[57]

Mill thought that progress was to do with self-realisation or self-improvement—living in accordance with an ideal chosen by the individual, with virtue—rather than the growth of happiness, as with Bentham. Like Locke and Bentham, Mill was an individualist in that all ends were individual ends and the function of government was to facilitate the attainment of those ends. For Mill, however, civilised society helped those individuals to form those ends. Consequently, he believed in education and voluntary cooperation in self-government as a means of moral improvement. Despite his basic utilitarian beliefs, Mill nevertheless saw morality as a product of social life composed of such things as love, fear, self-esteem and religious emotions. As John Plamenatz tells us, Mill believed that we could not live for ourselves alone.[58] Somewhat inconsistently, he also held that virtue became a good in itself.

Mill went on to support representative government because it improved the quality of life of those who enjoyed it, rather than because it created a harmony of selfish interests. Nevertheless, he did not believe that it was suited to all people all of the time because people were made fit for such freedom only by social discipline. While a strong supporter of the market economy, Mill was unhappy with the practical consequences of that system for the poor of his day and he sought moral and political limits to its operation.[59] He saw that the poor had no opportunity to enjoy freedom as he conceived it and he saw excessive wealth as inimical to that liberty. Consequently, he supported such things as inheritance tax, guaranteed minimum incomes and industrial democracy .

At this point, we reach a major cleavage in this tradition, between political economy increasingly conceived of as a positive, deductive science and political and moral philosophy, which continues with its rationalist speculation about political and moral principles but which gradually shed its claims to be a scientific enterprise. We will resume our examination of the scientific claims of economics in subsequent chapters, concentrating for the moment on the continued development of political speculation.

Peter Self (1919–99) describes a further major cleavage opening up within the liberal tradition between positive and negative liberals after Mill—a cleavage remaining to this day—with economic fundamentalists and most libertarians members of the negative school. In contrast, the positive liberals such as Thomas Green, John Hobson and Leonard Hobhouse were strong supporters of social reform to improve the lot of the poor and, along with the socialists, they were highly influential in the growth of social legislation in the late nineteenth century. Their successors in Australia are the small 'l' liberals and many on the left of politics.

The negative 'liberals' were opposed to the growth of social legislation, holding that freedom meant merely the absence of government coercion. Of course, in conceiving of government action solely in terms of coercion—rather than in terms of communal decision making and coordination—the negative liberals take a very narrow view of the nature of governmental action and its contribution to welfare. Within the negative school, the social evolutionists sought to provide an alternative account that was scientific and historical while remaining staunchly individualistic. In the process, they abandoned the psychological reductionism that had characterised Hobbes and Locke and many subsequent theorists. For Spencer , the leading social evolutionist,[60] the principle of utility was no rule but the articulation of the problem to be solved.[61] The theory of evolution undermined the notion of a universal human nature on which deductive utilitarianism depended. Spencer drew on the increasingly secularised natural-law tradition—a secularisation that reflected the increasing rejection of earlier religious certainties. For Spencer, therefore, the universality of natural causation provided a substitute for the Puritanism of his childhood, with progress a substitute for the eschatological promises of Christianity. In fact, in much nineteenth-century thought, the uniformity of nature had acquired a logical status and a numinous aura that made it a substitute for the idea of God. In the process, moral qualities were bestowed on the universe.

Spencer saw the idea of evolution from the simple to the complex as a process deriving from the fundamental laws of matter and motion, to manifestations of force. Only classical mechanics—the Newtonian metaphor—provided an adequate scientific understanding of reality. In this, Spencer was typical of his age—the age immediately before the rise of relativity and quantum mechanics in physics. He attempted to apply evolution to all phenomena in the universe, particularly to the social world. Consequently, he was an evolutionary determinist who believed that progress occurred through inevitable stages according to inflexible laws: 'Either society has laws, or it has not. If it has not, there can be no order, no certainty, no system in its phenomena. If it has, then, are they like the other laws of the universe—sure, inflexible, ever active, and having no exceptions?'[62]

He saw social life as a struggle similar to the struggle for survival in the natural world. Consequently, he saw social competition as part of the process of evolution. Importantly, nothing could be done in the long term to stop the process of competition and the attempt to do so—to alleviate social conditions—merely assured the short-term survival of the unfit. This doctrine had much in common with Malthus 's belief that the poor were redundant.[63] The survival of the fittest was justified as if it were a natural scientific law. This elevation of competition served to justify Spencer's strong opposition to social legislation—a function it continues to serve. In this view, a lack of success is associated with a lack of virtue. There was some ambiguity, however, as to whether the fittest meant the best, or merely an adaptation to existing circumstances. Of course, this ambiguity goes to the heart of the difficulty with this type of theorising: if it is the best, why? The answer to that question adds another layer of moral theorising. If it is merely adaptation to existing circumstances, why is that adaptation moral?

Freedom of contract was a necessary part of Spencer's theory. It was the supreme mechanism for maintaining social order with the absolute minimum of compulsion and coercion. Spencer's views can therefore be seen as an extreme version of contractualism in which the State is nothing more than a large partnership.[64] Restriction on the freedom of contract interfered with the natural order of things and enabled the unfit to survive longer than they would otherwise. Importantly, Spencer regarded the claims of social institutions other than economic institutions as alien to the human personality, from which they would ultimately free themselves. Consequently, Spencer opposed a wide range of social reforms on the ground that it constituted an interference with the freedom of contract. Surprisingly, Spencer saw his views as being consistent with the utilitarian formulae of the greatest happiness of the greatest number. This pseudo-science was not particularly influential in England. It was, however, very popular in the United States for a long time and had a formidable influence on American thinking and law.[65] As John Murphy writes,

119

Spencer's influence on American thought in the second half of the nineteenth century was particularly strong. He formulated his *laissez-faire* philosophy in such a way that it appealed 'at once to the traditional individualism and the acquisitive instincts of Americans, who were able without too great inconsistency to regard whatever they did, individually, as in harmony with evolution and whatever government or society did, collectively, as contrary to natural law'.[66]

Vestiges of this doctrine remain in some extreme justifications of the market system and of its social inequality that are met in economic fundamentalism.

Hayek, the author of *The Road to Serfdom*, a polemical defence of *laissez-faire*, was similarly a social evolutionist. To a large extent, the whole of Hayek's work was a reaction to the rise of Nazi tyranny, with its adulation of the State and the 'will to power'. This led to his obsessive focus on 'negative freedom'—the avoidance of government coercion—and the neglect of other meanings of the term 'freedom'. It followed that he was a strong critic of Keynes and his counter-cyclical policy prescriptions. Similarly, he was opposed to social security legislation, which he saw as special provision for the needy, arguing that the pursuit of social justice was a mirage.[67] For Hayek, the economic system was a self-regulating system too complex to understand fully and consequently there were limits to what reason and economics could achieve. In particular, he was opposed to any government interference in price signals, which he saw as a mechanism for conveying information arising out of a spontaneous, decentralised market process that was too complex to be understood by the social planner, and too dangerous to interfere with. Consequently, he was also a vehement critic of socialist central planning. Indeed, he felt that the economics profession more broadly had made a mess of things as a result of its attempt to imitate the procedures of the physical sciences.[68] Hayek's view ignores the imperfect nature of price signals as an information source and the fact that the social institutions on which the market system rests are themselves human creations built over many centuries and subject to constant change on the basis of experience. Hayek's own economic work was neglected in the enthusiasm for Keynes' work and, from the 1950s onwards, Hayek concentrated on philosophy, politics and psychology. It follows that while Hayek could give some comfort to the economic fundamentalists in his opposition to government, in the cause of his understanding of freedom he gives no comfort to the contemporary neoclassical economist.

Summary

We saw with Hobbes and Locke the beginnings of a new type of political and moral theorising, which sought its grounding in the natural world, individualism and the so-called scientific perspective. While the various theories that have been recounted do not, of necessity, make a coherent whole, they nevertheless reflect the same Enlightenment ambition to produce a secular, naturalist and rational justification for our moral allegiances and social arrangements. As such, they represent a tradition of thought sharing certain presuppositions and ways of conceptualising, and in which the participants frame their thoughts in relationship to earlier thinkers in the same tradition.[69] This Enlightenment ambition has failed for reasons that will be explored shortly.[70]

This tradition, nevertheless, constitutes the complex of ideas—the background mood—on which market ideology and economic fundamentalism rely. With Locke, therefore, we have a view of property rights as being prior to society—a natural right, but one based on divine law. We also see the contract metaphor used to explain the existence of society. With such theorists as Mandeville, Hume and Smith , we see the gradual transformation of self-interest from being a source of moral failure to a source of public good, albeit moderated by competition and by a dash of sympathy for others. In the process, the divine, deistic underpinnings were removed gradually and replaced with nature and reason—concepts that were increasingly deified or reified. Through the alchemy of the Newtonian metaphor, these naturalist justifications of self-interest are turned into a formal moral theory in the form of utilitarianism. Of course, it is this utilitarianism that underlies much economic theory. With Spencer, the moderation—which was in Smith—was removed and instead the attempt was made to justify naked self-interest under the rubric of the survival of the fittest. They all share what Richard Rorty (1931–2007) calls Locke's unfortunate desire to privilege the language of natural science over other vocabularies.[71] While Hayek wished to avoid that privilege, in seeing the market as a self-regulating system, he was ruling out government coordination and social risk sharing on a priori grounds; and it was reasoning that would enslave us to the economic system.

More recently, we have seen a major revival in contract thought as a consequence of Rawls' *A Theory of Justice*.[72] Interestingly, Rawls' idea of a reflective equilibrium as a way of evaluating our sense of justice—and as a theory of moral sentiments—is a deliberate echo of Smith.[73] It has already been argued that the concept of social relationships as contractual is taken for granted by economic fundamentalists and by economists generally and this is probably one reason why Rawls' ideas have been so attractive. Indeed, David Gauthier claims that such a view lies at the core of the ideology of Western capitalism.[74] This ideology—this metaphor, this claim to conceptual priority—is now part of the deep, pre-reflective tacit structure of self-consciousness and the symbolic universe, the way in which we conceive of ourselves as human, the way we relate to each other, to structures and institutions and to the natural world. In this view, society is conceived of as merely instrumental, meeting no fundamental human need.[75] It also involves a view of ourselves as insatiable appropriators engaged in a competitive search for power, with rationality understood as being related instrumentally to the satisfaction of individual interests. Gauthier sums up the historical development of this ideology in the following terms:

> What is to be appropriated is first thought of as real property, land or real estate. The distinction between land and other forms of property is then denied, and what is to be appropriated becomes the universal measure of property, money. Finally, in a triumph of abstraction, money as a particular object is replaced by the purely formal notion of utility, an object conveniently divested of all content. The rational man is...simply the man who seeks *more*. Thus it follows that not only the individualistic instrumental conception of rationality, but more precisely the individualistic utility-maximising conception, is part of the ideology of the social contract.[76]

The maximising conception of rationality entailed by contractualism and the natural-law outlook precludes the very possibility of rational agreement, because it undercuts the internal constraints necessary to maintain contractual relationships. In the past, radical self-interest was usually considered a primary threat to society, to be repressed by religion , law, morality and tradition. As has been argued in Chapter 3, the contractual tradition, contemporary economics and more especially economic fundamentalism have failed to understand the extent to which the social, political and economic orders have been sustained by motives different from those contained in the contractual conception of human nature. The faith that is placed in this contract tradition, and this form of theorising, cannot be sustained.

This chapter has provided a historical account of the intellectual tradition on which economic fundamentalism rests. Along the way, it has provided some criticism of this tradition, pointing in particular to the way in which it initially served the interests of wealthy British landowners. In the next chapter, I will deepen this critique by relating this tradition to the Enlightenment and criticising the intellectual arrogance that has flowed from that project.

ENDNOTES

[1] Smith 1757.

[2] The phrase was used only once in Adam Smith's *Wealth of Nations* and is usually misquoted by leaving out its social context:

> As every individual, therefore, endeavours as much as he can both to employ his capital in the support of domestic industry, and so to direct that industry that its produce may be of the greatest value; every individual necessarily labours to render the annual revenue of the society as great as he can. He generally, indeed, neither intends to promote the public interest, nor knows how much he is promoting it. By preferring the support of domestic to that of foreign industry, he intends only his own security; and by directing that industry in such a manner as its produce may be of the greatest value, he intends only his own gain, and he is in this, as in many other cases, led by an invisible hand to promote an end which was no part of his intention. Nor is it always the worse for the society that it was no part of it. By pursuing his own interest he frequently promotes that of the society more effectually than when he really intends to promote it. (Smith 1776, Chapter II of Book IV)

[3] Smith 1757, p. 36.

[4] Passmore, John 1994, personal communication.

[5] Stark 1962.

[6] Frisby and Sayer 1986.

[7] Stark 1962.

[8] Seligman 1992. The account in this chapter draws in particular on this reference and on Clark (1992).

[9] Loy 2002.

[10] Ibid.

[11] Botton 2004.

[12] Seligman 1992.

[13] Ibid.

[14] Gascoigne 1994b.

[15] Seligman 1992.

[16] Clark 1992.

[17] Lessnoff 1986.

[18] White 1991.

[19] Lessnoff 1986.

[20] Ibid.

[21] Gough 1936. Gough points to the possible influence of the sophists of ancient Greece among whom social-contract views—which were highly individualistic and made use of the concept of a state of nature—had some currency. Gough tells us that much of the political philosophy of Plato and Aristotle was concerned to combat these subversive views. For Plato, therefore, every man has his station and duties, while for Aristotle man is by nature a political animal. The State for Aristotle is not a mere living together in one place for mutual protection and economic exchange but a moral association to develop man's highest faculties and enable him to live the good life.

[22] Stackhouse 1999a.

[23] Gorski 2002.

[24] Lessnoff 1986.

[25] Ibid.

[26] Gough 1936.

[27] Atiyah 1979.

[28] Ibid.

[29] Macpherson 1964.

[30] White 1991.

[31] The relationships between the rulers and the ruled and between the people themselves were treated under the general heading of the social contract.

[32] Burrow 1966.

[33] Lessnoff 1986.

[34] Ibid.

[35] Ibid.

[36] Gough 1936.

[37] Atiyah 1979.

[38] Clark 1992.

[39] Ibid.

[40] Seligman 1992.

[41] Voorhoeve 2003.

[42] Seligman 1992, p. 26.

[43] Ibid.

[44] See Bellah 1967 and 1975.

[45] See Hume 1878 and 1980.

[46] Seligman 1992, p. 38.

[47] Atiyah 1979.

[48] Heilbroner 1986, p. 141.

[49] Seligman 1992.

[50] Smith (1776, Book II, Chapter II), cited in Atiyah 1979, p. 303.

[51] Clark 1992.

[52] Burrow 1966.

[53] Clark 1992.

[54] Burrow 1966, pp. 62–3.

[55] Ibid., p. 70.

[56] Atiyah 1979, p. 328.

[57] Plamenatz 1963.

[58] Ibid.

[59] Self 1999.

[60] Bannister insists that many so-called social Darwinists such as Spencer were not Darwinists. He cites with approval Howard Gruber, who argues that it is in harmony with Darwin's thinking that the struggle for survival must enhance cooperation and rational long-term planning for collective ends rather than short-sighted individualistic efforts for private gain. He goes on to say that there seems to be little grounds for assuming that Darwinism gives support to unbridled individualism, unregulated competition and *laissez-faire* or brutality and force in social affairs. (Bannister 1979, pp. 15–33.)

[61] Burrow 1966, p. 216.

[62] Ibid., p. 208.

[63] Atiyah 1979. Indeed, Malthus had written his *Essay* in opposition to William Godwin's advocacy of an egalitarian society and his view that poverty was caused by the maldistribution of society's wealth.

[64] Gough 1936.

[65] Atiyah 1979, p. 285.

[66] Murphy 1990, p. 17.

[67] Self 1999.

[68] Hayek 1974.

[69] MacIntyre 1988.

[70] MacIntyre 1981.

[71] Murphy 1990.

[72] Rawls 1971.

[73] Rengger 1995.

[74] Gauthier 1977.

[75] Ibid.

[76] Ibid., p. 152.

Chapter 5: A Critique of the Conceptual Foundations of Economic Fundamentalism

'I perceive,' said the Countess, 'Philosophy is now become Mechanical.'
'So Mechanical,' said I, 'that I fear we shall quickly be asham'd of it;
they will have the World to be in great, what a watch is in little; which
is very regular, and depends only upon the just disposing of the several
parts of the movement. But pray tell me, Madam, had you not formerly
a more sublime Idea of the Universe?'
— Bernard le Bovier de Fontenelle[1]

The word Reason, and the epithets connected with it—'Rational' and
'Reasonable'—have enjoyed a long history which has bequeathed to
them a legacy of ambiguity and confusion.
— Michael Oakeshott[2]

Introduction: The Contemporary Epochal Transformation in the Western Mind

In the previous chapter, I provided a brief historical account of the social-contract
tradition on which economic fundamentalism rests. In the next three chapters,
I propose to extend that critique by looking at the epistemological foundations
of that tradition in the cultural and philosophical movement called 'the
Enlightenment'. I will criticise its belief that reason and the scientific method
can provide us with certain geometric knowledge of the natural and social world,
concentrating in particular on the grossly exaggerated claims of rationalism and
its tools. In the next chapter, I will extend that critique to positivist scientific
beliefs, pointing out that science and social inquiry are only fallible human
activities always subject to revision. I will then move in Chapter 7 to a discussion
of the normative nature of social inquiry and to criticise claims to normative
expertise. The effect of these three chapters taken together is to undermine the
claims of social science and political and moral philosophy to a privileged position
in the determination of government action.

The Enlightenment was central to the breakdown of the synthesised
Ptolemaic–Aristotelian conception of the world. That particular synthesis—that
paradigm, that intellectual trajectory—had not only provided the master
narrative and the conceptual basis of the medieval world, it had informed
Western philosophical, religious and scientific understanding for about 15
centuries.[3] Let me emphasise that influence again, lest its significance passes us
by. The synthesised Ptolemaic–Aristotelian conception of the world provided

the very basis of the medieval experience of reality. Incredible though it might seem now, that medieval Christian experience of reality was not only different from our understanding, it was as tangible, complete and self-evident as our modern experience of an impersonal and material objective reality, or as the ancient Greek experience of an even more 'mythical' reality.[4]

The Enlightenment, then, involved a radical cultural change, sweeping away what was said to be superstition and tradition and promising progress, equality, freedom and justice. This involved the formation of a new cosmology, which provided a new explanatory archetypal story and a different reality. This is the reality formed by the Newtonian world-view in which the universe is viewed as a machine—a self-sufficient mechanism involving the interaction of matter and forces—lacking purpose and meaning. It was only with Enlightenment thinkers such as Bacon, Descartes and Newton that the idea first emerged clearly that there were laws governing the natural world and that it was the role of natural philosophers or what we now call scientists to discover them. The earlier theory of scientific explanation developed by Aristotle was essentialist and had no room for such a concept.[5] As we will see later, this mechanical world-view still lies at the heart of contemporary economic thought, which seeks to model human beings and their interactions as a mechanical system.

We might note in passing that the fact that such different conceptions of fundamental realities have been held in all seriousness by people every bit as intelligent as us, should warn us against placing excessive confidence in our current intellectual constructs and the stories we tell about them. While we might have better institutions for checking knowledge claims, these cannot guarantee freedom from error.

Habermas, in his qualified defence of the Enlightenment, describes the project of modernity as

> the effort to develop objective science, universal morality and law, and autonomous art, according to their inner logic. At the same time, this project intended to release the cognitive potentials of each of these domains to set them free from their esoteric forms. The Enlightenment philosophers wanted to utilise this accumulation of specialised culture for the enrichment of everyday life, that is to say, for the rational organization of everyday social life.[6]

Habermas believes that this project has unrealised potential for increasing social rationality, justice and morality. Contrary to Habermas—and as we will see below—many contemporary theorists see the Enlightenment story as having greatly diminished the apparent significance of humanity itself, its rational and volitional freedom and the emotional, aesthetic, sensory, imaginative and intentional qualities that had seemed most constitutive of the human experience until that time.[7] While the Enlightenment story placed rationality on a pinnacle, the conception of reason itself was narrowed. The classical notion of reason as a divine gift involving a normative dimension was displaced and reason was reduced to instrumentality and deductive logic. Indeed, human decision making was reduced to a mechanical system. In this scheme, the life of the imagination and the emotions was discounted along with judgement, experience and wisdom.

A substantial literature has now developed questioning many of the claims of this Enlightenment tradition, which leading contemporary French philosopher Jean-François Lyotard (1924–98) calls the mood of modernity, and its associated grand narratives—the grand, large-scale theories and philosophies of the world, science, history, progress and freedom. These narratives are the stories our culture tells itself to legitimise its practices and beliefs, and which purport to grasp the truth, including the truth about society and—drawing on Wittgenstein—its language games.[8] In his critique, Lyotard tells us: 'In contemporary society and culture—postindustrial society, postmodern culture—the question of the legitimation of knowledge is formulated in different terms. The grand narrative has lost its credibility, regardless of what mode of unification it uses, regardless of whether it is a speculative narrative or a narrative of emancipation.'[9]

These grand narratives are unable to contain our diversity, our incommensurable beliefs and us. Hence, for example, Lyotard rejects totalising social theories that are reductionist, simplistic and even 'terroristic'.[10]

Similarly, American sociologist Richard Madsen and his colleagues warn us that:

> There is a painful contradiction between what modernity promises and what it delivers. It promises—indeed demands—intellectual, moral, and political emancipation. Yet it delivers an iron cage…Morality, religion, and the whole normative dimension of social life get either pushed away or explained away…What goes typically unnoticed and unremarked [on] is how this apparent straightforward approach locks its adherents into a closed universe of diminished meaning and possibility.[11]

Of particular concern to this account is the extent to which the attempt by libertarian philosophers in the Enlightenment tradition to legislate a particular negative interpretation of individual freedom and their adulation of markets are threatening to again enslave us all.

Importantly, one of the defining moments of recent consciousness has been the recognition that the social and religious order is a human construction for which we ultimately have to take responsibility. This recognition prompted leading thinkers such as Friedrich Nietzsche (1844–1900), Michel Foucault (1926–84), Jacques Derrida (1930–2004) and Pierre Bourdieu (1930–2002) to attempt to dismantle the values defining modernity itself: reason, freedom and the autonomous self. Nietzsche—perhaps the first of the existentialist philosophers—was highly critical of contemporary German culture, dogmatic systems in philosophy including those of Plato and Kant, claims to truth and God as a single, ultimate, judgemental authority. In this spirit of questioning, he challenged the foundations of Christianity and traditional morality. He saw these dogmatic systems as inventions and conventions providing repose, security and consistency.[12] Foucault challenges the ability of the human sciences to offer universal scientific truths about human nature. He sees those claims as often being mere expressions of ethical and political commitments of a particular society—the outcome of contingent historical forces rather than scientifically grounded truths.[13] Foucault has, therefore, undermined the claims of the human sciences to neutrality by showing how the drive towards freedom and autonomy is an extension and deepening of practices of power.[14] Derrida, for his part, questioned the self-evident, logic and non-judgemental character of the dichotomies by which we live, such as legitimate/illegitimate, rational/irrational, fact/fiction or observation/imagination.[15] He sees these dichotomies as being defined culturally and historically and even reliant on one another, rather than being conceptual absolutes with stable meanings. Similarly, Bourdieu attempts to show that the things that are sacred to modern elites are social constructions and he tries to expose the hidden means by which the powerful and wealthy assert superiority[16] and reproduce themselves.

In summary, this questioning has discredited the story that has been told about knowledge since the Enlightenment. This is not to deny the achievements of the past few centuries in increasing our understanding of the natural world and in freeing us from some of the grosser superstitions that worried the medieval mind and which provided the justification for many unspeakable crimes—particularly at the hands of the Christian Church. Neither is it intended to diminish the enormous contribution of liberal and socialist thinkers and activists in the Enlightenment tradition in advancing the emancipation of ordinary citizens—a hope Habermas continues to entertain. Nor is it intended to deny the enormous improvement in average living standards in recent centuries. Nevertheless, and paradoxically, the Enlightenment, in its advocacy of radical scepticism in the cause of human emancipation, is seen increasingly as being bankrupt,[17] as having undermined its own story[18] and as having created a Kafka–Beckett-like state of absurdity and existential isolation.[19] Having undermined belief in God, society and tradition, radical scepticism has undermined belief in belief itself, including belief in reason.

In the process, most contemporary philosophers have rejected the views of Descartes, the father of modern philosophy, and his quest for an Archimedean fixed and immovable point on which to ground our knowledge—a grounding he thought he had found in his existence and his ability to think, certified by a non-deceiving God.[20] This just wouldn't do in the absence of a non-deceiving God and in the face of the realisation that the language of argument presupposed what he was trying to prove. What is more, that language is a continuing social construct. Nor will it do to erect reason or nature as God substitutes. The moment one admits God, again, one also admits revelation as the source of knowledge superior to reason.

In relatively recent times, the search for absolute knowledge manifested itself in an extreme form in logical positivism, which viewed science as the ultimate arbiter of truth in a heroic struggle against ignorance and superstition.[21] As such, it was a utopian attempt to legislate what constituted scientific knowledge. Such scientific truth, it was claimed, was discoverable only by the enlightened mind cleansed of metaphysical beliefs. It could then set us free from the shackles of tradition and its associated institutions and build a new and better world. As we saw earlier, this optimism reflected a strong faith in progress and the perfectibility of humankind.

French philosopher Claude Saint-Simon (1760–1825), writing in the Cartesian tradition, had great faith in science and in industrialisation and advocated the reorganisation of society on positive scientific lines. Nevertheless, Auguste Comte (1798–1857), his secretary, is usually seen as the father of positivism. Comte had a similar faith in the power of science, particularly sociology, to advance human civilisation. He built his philosophy of positivism as a universal system around that faith. The logical positivists centred on the Vienna Circle of the 1920s and 1930s, building on Comte's ideas, sought, in particular, to differentiate science from other thinking. They claimed that it was only through positivist scientific thought that a true view of the social and physical world was possible. This is truly a foundational project in the Enlightenment tradition.[22] This story involved four main beliefs:

- the only things that are real are the things that are observable
- all general names are only summary abbreviations for the numerous objects in reality
- it is possible to distinguish between facts and values and consequently to have a social science that is factual and devoid of values
- there is a unity of method between the natural and social sciences.[23]

These claims exercised a profound influence on philosophy and the philosophy of science from the 1920s to the 1950s and in the associated idealisation of formal theory. Most contemporary philosophers have, however, rejected logical positivism. In the words of leading contemporary Australian philosopher John Passmore, 'Logical Positivism…is dead, or as dead as a philosophical movement ever becomes.'[24]

Philosopher of science Karl Popper (1902–94) even claimed to have done the killing:[25]

> [T]hroughout my life I have combated positivist epistemology, under the name of 'positivism'...I have fought against the aping of the natural sciences by the social sciences, and I have fought for the doctrine that positivist epistemological is inadequate even in its analysis of the natural sciences which, in fact, are not 'careful generalisations from observations', as it is usually believed, but are essentially speculative and daring; moreover, I have taught, for more than thirty-eight years, that all observations are theory-impregnated, and that their main function is to check and refute, rather than to prove, our theories. Finally I have not only stressed the meaningfulness of metaphysical assertions and the fact that I am myself a metaphysical realist, but I have also analysed the important historical role played by metaphysics in the formation of scientific theories.[26]

Two other leading philosophers, Willard Quine (1908–2000) and Thomas Kuhn (1922–96), are often also given the credit for killing positivism; and the foundational idea that philosophy can determine on a priori grounds the standards for scientific knowledge died with it. Indeed, the positivist ideal of a universal and substantive 'logic of science' was simply misguided.[27] Similarly, positivism's attempt to divorce science from metaphysical beliefs—beliefs that attempt to describe the ultimate nature of reality—has failed. We will go into this is in a little more detail shortly.

This turning away from the Enlightenment and modernity involves a rejection of the claimed privileged status of science and of rationality, the belief in universals—absolute truths, universal values and a common human nature—and in progress and in the perfectibility of humankind. In particular, there can be no final appeal from an objective viewpoint to an attainable ultimate truth.[28]

Importantly, respected American cultural historian Richard Tarnas believes a great epochal transformation comparable with that of the Enlightenment is occurring in the Western mind in reaction to the dissolution of the foundations of the modern world-view, which has left us bereft of certainties.[29] Contemporary Australian theologian Duncan Reid sums up this dissolution very well.[30] For Reid, this paradigm shift has two interrelated aspects. The first involves a shift away from Western political, cultural and economic predominance. The realisation that other cultures—which are also enjoying rapid improvements in material welfare—have fundamentally different perspectives on the human condition has led to a questioning of our fundamental cultural assumptions. This shift is accompanied by a change within the Western scientific world-view and a sense of disillusionment with the technology it has given us. In particular, the Newtonian mechanistic world-view has been undermined because Newtonian physics has been discredited completely as an answer to any fundamental question about the nature of the world.[31] That view is not just limited as an explanation of physical reality; it is fundamentally flawed, however much it might continue to serve as a convenient fiction in describing the behaviour of relatively large objects—the sorts of objects that we perceive around us.

At a deeper level, physics has come to understand reality, not in terms of atomism—discrete particles that can be described independently of all others—but as a complete network, the most basic elements of which are not entities or substances, but relationships:

> All entities, even inanimate entities, constituted as they were by their 'experiences' of being in relationship, could now be understood as subjects which adapt to their environment. Reality was no longer to be 'grasped' solely by analysis and reduction to component parts. Understanding had to be reinterpreted in a less dominating, more participatory way, as the perception of parts interacting in the context of an indivisible totality.[32]

No longer are the properties of things seen as being fixed absolutely with respect to some unchanging background, rather they arise from interactions and relationships.[33] As renowned mathematical physicist Roger Penrose (b. 1931) confirms, the fundamental entities in physics are not events in space and time but rather processes, and space and time emerge only at a secondary level.[34] Thus the idea that 'science' can view the world from outside—as a disembodied observer—has been discredited. Similarly, the reductionist method—in which phenomena are simplified until they can be described by simple mathematical equations—is undermined. Even the Platonic view of natural laws as eternal and absolute has been questioned, along with any simple idea of causality.[35]

The second aspect of this paradigm shift has been a crisis of meaning in Western epistemology:

> The whole Western philosophical tradition had worked on the assumption that knowledge...was accessible through language. But now the word...has been unseated from its place of honour. Language, rather than an inadequate but in principle perfectible attempt to refer to some intelligible metaphysical reality beyond itself, has come to be seen as a self-contained system in which reference is to the system itself.[36]

The common thread in these two crises is the loss of any sense of objective certainty in the physical sciences or in political–cultural matters. As a consequence, we have to deal with a new and profound sense of historical relativism and the belief that there can be no overarching 'absolute' or unifying principle that can reconcile all the relativities of human thought and experience.

Additionally, we are shifting from a particular privileged explanatory paradigm—the Newtonian world-view—to a world in which there is no privileged perspective and no privileged archetypal story, a world full potentially of existential uncertainty, even terror.

More optimistically, for American pragmatist Richard Bernstein, these crises are creating a public space in which basic questions about the human condition can be raised anew.[37] Specifically, Bernstein believes that there is something wrong with the ways in which questions in relation to rationality have been posed in the past, and he points to a need for the conversation to move beyond objectivism and relativism. He believes that what he calls the attacks on the tyranny of method open the way to a new conversation on rationality and to 'a more historically situated, non algorithmic, flexible understanding of human rationality, one which highlights the tacit dimension of human judgment and imagination and is sensitive to the unsuspected contingencies and genuine novelties encountered in particular situations'.[38]

Similarly, Tarnas tells us that the dissolving of old assumptions and categories could permit the emergence of entirely new prospects for conceptual and existential reintegration with richer interpretive vocabularies and more profound narrative coherencies.[39] He warns us, however, that in the absence of any viable, embracing cultural vision, the old assumptions remain in force, providing an increasingly unworkable and dangerous blueprint for human thought and activity.

The Excessive Western Faith in Objectivism

What we have arrived at is not some minor esoteric quibble but a fundamental attack on the foundation of our fundamental beliefs: the Enlightenment tradition and its world-view. The belief that we have access to absolute and unconditional truths about the world, *epistēmē*, has been a fundamental belief of much Western philosophy since the ancient Greeks. This belief—this myth, this passion, this story—could have originated with Pythagoras (569–475 BC) and Parmenides (b. 510 BC). Plato (427–347 BC) and Aristotle (384–22 BC) elaborated this belief in different ways. It has been shared by the rationalist and empirical traditions until recently. These traditions differ only in their account of how we arrive at such truths.[40] The rationalists—the followers of Plato—believe that only our innate capacity to reason can give us knowledge of things as they really are, whereas for the followers of Aristotle—the empiricists—all knowledge of the world arises from our sensory perceptions. As we will see shortly, however, Aristotle did not extend that idea to moral beliefs.

Nevertheless, Western art, literature and philosophy have all shared the idea that, beyond the empirical, mundane realm lies a greater reality—some version of Plato's forms—independent, immovable, permanent and absolute. This transcendentalism—a synthesis of Greek and Christian thought—has shaped the reality in which Westerners live. Even for Aristotle with his strong empirical bent, human beings could apprehend infallible truth because, he believed—along with Plato—that we shared in the divine mind. One consequence is that institutionalised authority structures in the West are always legitimised by invoking abstract transcendental justifications: God or, more lately, natural law, reason, method, a generalised will of the people or human rights.[41]

This transcendentalism lies at the heart of the Enlightenment project and its search for a certain, ahistorical foundation for knowledge, truth, rationality and morality. In the Christian tradition, the transcendental absolute—the source of certainty—was the decree of an anthropomorphised God. Through the Enlightenment, however, God was gradually secularised,[42] to be replaced with nature, natural laws, reason and method, which continued to occupy a transcendental level, governing the way things should be and providing us with access to absolute truth.[43] As the following account will make clear, however, there are no Platonic forms of truth, law, reason and method or, indeed, of the market, to which we can appeal. Nevertheless, for most contemporary Westerners, this Enlightenment tradition continues to provide their fundamental understanding of the world and their vocabulary of legitimation. Similarly, the right to teach is still defined by the teacher's special knowledge of a universal message.[44] Since the Enlightenment, however, the guardian of truth and justice is no longer the priest, but the intellectual claiming special insight into reason and the world—and a special right to speak for humanity. Plato and his disciples rather than God certified this new magisterium. Tragically, Plato's totalitarian vision has promoted the very intellectual arrogance that his teacher, Socrates (469–399 BC), sought to deflate at the cost of his life.

In contrast with the West, the Confucian civilisations of South-East Asia do not conceptualise a meaningful level of human action and causation beyond the world of experience.[45] This is because Chinese cosmology lacked monotheism and a transcendental level.[46] The Chinese even lack a word for God. Instead, there was a cosmological ordering of the world, represented by the harmonious hierarchical interrelations of the heavens, earth and mankind—a notion of order that excluded the Western notion of law. In the Chinese world-view, the harmonious cooperation of all beings arose from the fact that they were all parts in a hierarchy of wholes, forming a cosmic pattern. What they obeyed were the internal dictates of their own natures, not the orders of a superior authority external to themselves. In the Chinese tradition, there is no God, or God-given laws, and no transcendental level that leaders can use to justify their claims to power. Consequently, a different vocabulary of legitimation was developed—a vocabulary in which justifications for power were based on the requirements for natural harmonies in this world. Power over another was justified in terms of one's obedience to one's position in a universal relational order.

One of the leading philosophical critics of modernity, Stephen Toulmin,[47] links the origins of the Enlightenment and its obsession with foundations for objective knowledge to the rise of the nation-state and to the general state of crisis in seventeenth-century Europe. He explained that between the fourteenth and the sixteenth centuries, Europe experienced a rebirth—'the Renaissance'—in which the classical learning of the Greeks and Romans was rediscovered, substantially expanding the horizons of the Western medieval world. In particular, this learning increased understanding of the wide diversity and contextual dependence of human life and brought recognition that theoretical inquiries needed to be balanced against discussions of concrete practical issues.

In this regard, Tarnas reminds us that the Renaissance built on an earlier scholastic awakening that was stimulated in part by increased contact with Byzantine and Islamic centres of leaning and the rediscovery of a large body of Aristotle's writings. This awakening was aided by technological innovations, which had increased productivity and had highlighted the value of human intelligence in mastering the forces of nature and acquiring useful knowledge. These scholastics prepared the way in the late medieval universities for the Enlightenment and the scientific revolution. Aquinas, in particular, drawing on Aristotle, denied the capacity of the human intellect to know directly Plato's forms—believing instead that we needed sensory experience to acquire an imperfect but meaningful understanding of things in terms of such eternal archetypes. In turn, Franciscan philosopher William of Ockham (1288–1348) contributed to the further breakdown of the medieval view by denying the reality of such Platonic universals outside the human mind and human language and claiming that speculative reason and metaphysics lacked any real foundations.[48]

These trends tended to undermine the claims of Christian revelation, as they had been understood, and, importantly, the Church's spiritual authority. These trends were helped further by the expansion of the universities, the invention of printing and an associated enormous increase in literacy and learning, eroding the monopoly on learning that had long been held by the clergy. Importantly, it also eroded the claimed authority of the Christian Church to interpret scripture. About the same time, Nicholas Copernicus (1473–1543) undermined the Ptolemaic image of the physical universe with his heliocentric theory. Galileo Galilei (1564–1642), Johannes Kepler (1571–1630) and Newton built on this work to create the new cosmology—the Newtonian cosmology that is at the centre of the modern world-view.

One result of the rediscovery of classical learning and the associated intellectual ferment was that religious Renaissance humanists such as Michel de Montaigne

(1533–92) and Desiderius Erasmus (c. 1469–1536) came to believe that we could claim certainty about nothing and that philosophical speculation reached beyond the scope of experience in ways that could not be defended.[49] This acute awareness of the limits of our practical and intellectual powers—in particular of our ability to reach unquestioned 'truth' or unqualified 'certainty'—discouraged dogmatism. Accordingly, Montaigne warns us that 'it is to place a very high value on your surmises to roast a man alive for them'.[50]

Consequently, these philosophers showed a new, open-minded, sceptical tolerance along with practical doubt about the value of theory in such fields as theology, natural philosophy, metaphysics and ethics. Toulmin tells us that this uncertainty reflected the attitude of Aristotle for whom the good had no universal form, and for whom moral, sound judgement always respected the detailed circumstances of specific kinds of cases.[51] For Aristotle, ethics was not a field for theoretical analysis but for practical wisdom: *phronēsis* . This humility was part of the price of our being human and not gods. As a result, throughout the Middle Ages and the Renaissance, it had been understood that problems in social ethics were not to be resolved by appeal to any single and universal tradition. Rather, multiple considerations and coexisting traditions need to be weighed against one another using all the available resources of moral thought and social tradition.

In contrast, the dream of the Enlightenment—of seventeenth-century philosophy and science—was Plato's demand for *epistēmē* , or theoretical grasp. This Platonic dream remains at the heart of our contemporary over-valuation of theoretical speculative stories in public policy formation. The Renaissance brought with it an increased understanding of the Platonic tradition and a neo-Platonic revival not unlike the earlier rediscovery of Aristotle. In particular, it brought with it a renewed interest in the Pythagorean vision of a universe ordered in accordance with transcendent mathematical forms.[52] Galileo believed that God—'the great Geometer'—had written the book of nature in mathematical symbols. Descartes—a considerable mathematician as well as a scientist and philosopher—similarly conceived of the universe as an atomistic system governed by a few mechanistic rules. He set himself the task of discovering an irrefutable basis for certain knowledge. This he sought to do by scrapping inherited concepts and starting again, using rationally validated methods having the necessity of geometrical proofs. In this Cartesian program, logical analysis was separated from—and elevated far above—the study of rhetoric, discourse and argumentation: 'In Descartes' vision, science, progress, reason, epistemological certainty, and human identity were all inextricably connected with each other and with the conception of an objective, mechanistic universe; and upon this synthesis was founded the paradigmatic character of the modern mind.'[53]

Importantly, as Toulmin explains, such certainty was attractive given the general state of spiritual, intellectual and political crisis in seventeenth-century Europe, in reaction to such events as the assassination of the tolerant King Henri IV of France in 1610 and the Thirty-Years War (1618–48) between most of the major European continental powers.[54] Loy emphasises the viciousness of this war and of the underlying religious conflict over what was seen as humankind's eternal destiny.[55] The increased emphasis on biblical teaching and the ensuing conflict over interpretation undermined biblical authority as a source of political ideas and promoted a resort to reason as an alternative source of authority. Similarly, Tarnas draws our attention to the chaos in the cultural and intellectual life of Europe resulting from the violent disputes between ever-multiplying religious sects over whose conception of absolute truth would prevail. These events undermined tolerance as a way of defusing denominational rivalry, led to an active distrust of unbelievers and to a belief in belief itself. In this climate, it became urgent to discover some rational method of demonstrating the truth of philosophical, scientific or theological doctrines, particularly the theological doctrines.

Interestingly, Loy, drawing on Arnold Toynbee (1889–1975), links the concurrent growth of nationalism—which he sees as the worship of the deified community—with this sense of crisis. He believes nationalism provides one unconscious secular alternative religion after the breakdown in the authority of the Christian Church and the ensuing growth in the sense of insecurity.[56] Furthermore, he believes that the modern nation-state continues to derive its power over us from our need to identify with and ground ourselves in something greater than ourselves.

In the event, as Toulmin tells us, Galileo in physics, Descartes in epistemology and science and Hobbes in political theory committed Western society to new and 'scientific' ways and to the use of more 'rational' ways of dealing with the problems of life and society. They assumed that there were uniquely rational procedures for handling the intellectual and practical problems of any field of study—procedures that involved setting aside superstition, mythology, authority and tradition, and attacking problems free of local prejudice and transient fashion, on the authority of reason itself. In this hope to bring all subjects into formal theory, the Enlightenment philosophers also altered the language of reason itself in subtle ways. In particular, they became committed increasingly to abstract universal, timeless theories, setting aside serious interest in the different kinds of practical knowledge: the oral, the particular, the local and the timely (and, I would add, the personal).

In particular, moral philosophy followed the theoretical road of natural philosophy, relegating practical ethics to second place. It set about clarifying and distinguishing the concepts of ethics and formulating the universal, timeless axioms that it assumed must lie at the base of any rational system of ethics. As a result, dogma acquired an imperative sense, with moral questions having unique, simple and authoritative answers. Similarly, academic jurisprudence developed formal and theoretical goals. In political theory too, a new style emerged, of which Hobbes' theory was paradigmatic. This flight from the particular, concrete, transitory and practical aspects of human experience became a feature of cultural life in general. From this perspective, the essence of humanity was seen as the capacity for rational thought and action while the emotions were seen as frustrating or distorting reason. This distrust of emotions is still current and reinforces the Cartesian, or calculative, idea of 'rationality'.

Interestingly, Descartes himself acknowledged our fallibility and thus a need for some other agency to certify the truth of human reasoning. There has to be some fixed foundation for our knowledge or we cannot escape intellectual and moral chaos—and this fear continues to worry some philosophers. Descartes found his escape in his belief in a beneficent, infinite and infallible God, who was no deceiver and who underpinned our reason and the procedural certainty of mathematical reasoning.[57] In this, he was following Plato and Aristotle. It is therefore ironic that his vision—combined with the empirical vision of Francis Bacon—became the basis of the West's new faith: a faith in science, scientific rationalism and human progress—the last being a secularisation of the Christian hope in the coming of the Kingdom of God.

Rorty provides a complementary account pointing to 300 years of Enlightenment rhetoric about the importance of distinguishing sharply between science and religion, science and politics, science and art and science and philosophy. According to Rorty, the paradigm of human activity has been that of 'knowing'—possessing justified true belief, or beliefs so intrinsically persuasive as to make justification unnecessary.[58] It follows from the Greek belief that what differentiates humans from other animals is our ability to *know* universal truths, numbers, essences and the eternal—in short, to acquire *epistēmē* .

Similarly, Rorty explains that Western philosophy has attempted to underwrite or debunk knowledge claims on the basis of its special understanding of the nature of knowledge and of the mind.[59] Consequently, the central concern of Western philosophy has been to construct a general theory of representation in which the mind is seen to represent faithfully an independent external reality. The Enlightenment contributed the very idea of an autonomous philosophical discipline, separate from and sitting in judgement on religion and science. Rorty, however, rejects this attempt to set philosophy as the foundational discipline of culture and the judge and jury of other disciplines. He claims that the attempt since the Greeks to explain 'rationality' and 'objectivity' in terms of the conditions of representation is a self-deceptive effort to eternalise the normal discourse of the day. He further denied the existence of an 'Archimedean point' in human understanding that would provide a foundation to all knowledge, and which would provide the source of certainty that the Enlightenment desired.

In particular, he denies the concept of knowledge as mental representation or that we can find within the 'mirror of the mind' a special privileged class of representations so compelling that their accuracy cannot be doubted. This metaphor of the human being whose mind is an unclouded mirror, and who knows, is the image of God. It follows that the human aspiration for objective truth is an attempt to become god-like in the absence of a belief in God. For Rorty, the whole project of establishing a theory of knowledge for the purpose of passing judgement on particular knowledge claims is misconceived. He simply denies that philosophy can adjudicate such claims.[60]

In the same spirit, American philosopher of science Alexander Rosenberg tells us that a purely epistemological exploration of alternative theories of knowledge will not come to any philosophical consensus—nor will it advance science. Rosenberg argues that far from having priority, such philosophy depends on science rather than the other way around. Importantly, he argues that philosophy is nothing more or less than extremely general and abstract theory, on a cognitive par with the natural and social sciences with no demarcation principle between them.[61] Any distinction between the two relies on the discredited positivist distinction between analytical statements—true in virtue of the meanings of their terms—and synthetic statements that have empirical content. As we will see in greater detail in Chapter 7, this distinction cannot be sustained and, as a consequence, we cannot draw lines between philosophy and science.

As we saw with Descartes, underlying these Enlightenment aspirations is an assumption that geometry, mathematics and logic provide *the* paradigm of rationality and that that 'provides a comprehensive standard of incorrigible certainty against which all other claims to knowledge must be judged'.[62] It assumes that there are definite rule-governed, algorithmic procedures—timeless universal principles—for arriving at that solution from information that is taken as given.[63] These rules were seen as freeing us from arbitrariness, as providing the certainty and the reliability sought by the Enlightenment. This algorithmic view, however, reduces human rationality and judgement to a crude mechanical system. As such, it reflects the Enlightenment's mechanical cosmology and its attempt to locate explanation in that mythological archetype, that master narrative. This mechanistic objectivism seeks to relieve us of responsibility for our beliefs.[64] In this tradition—influenced by Hume—inductive arguments were thought suspect because they could not provide such certainty. Consequently, solutions based on experience do not have the 'necessity' that is thought to characterise reasoned results.

It is these beliefs that are used to justify the distinction made frequently between the context of discovery and the context of justification. In this view, the way in which some truth is discovered is to be distinguished from the justification of that truth and it is the latter that is important, not the process by which we come to believe. These beliefs also provide the basis of the contrasts made between reason and faith and reason and authority. This view, however, opens up two questions central to this faith in reason: firstly, on what basis are we to select the rules of argumentation and of reason? And secondly, on what basis are we to select the assumptions from which to begin? These questions indicate a need for foundational rules and foundational propositions. In respect of the latter, we can ask the further question, how am I to know that I have a correct understanding of any of the concepts involved in my assumptions—including the concepts involved in my foundational rules—or that there is such a correct understanding? Indeed, it is unlikely that such a 'correct' understanding is possible, because such correctness assumes that concepts are fully determined, ideal and timeless entities—Plato's forms again. As we have already seen, however, concepts are only the tools we create to classify things and events as we interact with the world. Consequently, it is extremely unlikely that they involve complete sets of necessary and sufficient conditions. It is extremely unlikely that our language can reflect adequately such exacting standards or that the resulting concepts can be applied consistently.

In this regard, American academic psychologist Kenneth Gergen—following Wittgenstein and Quine—tells us that the meaning of words and sentences derives from the context in which they are used and that these contexts are so many and varied that there is no means of securing word-object identities.[65] Additionally, the ways in which we categorise the natural and social worlds are to some extent tradition bound, because the acquisition of concepts is tied to the learning and use of language and reflects the ways of life and understandings current in society.[66] Furthermore, German social philosopher and critical theorist Theodor Adorno (1903–69) warns us against the domination exercised by concepts, their rigidity and their poverty—their inability to ever capture the richness of reality.[67] Consequently, our concepts are always an imperfect work in progress. We also have to ask from what source are these variable concepts to derive their intellectual authority other than from tradition itself—something the Enlightenment has rejected?

These questions are not finally resolvable because they threaten either an infinite regress of justifications, vicious cycles or recourse to dogma.[68] The conventional solution to them invokes so-called 'self-evident' or 'self-justifying' propositions, intuitions, inductions or perceptions. Such propositions or observational reports cannot, however, provide an indisputable, self-evident foundation for knowledge because they already presuppose a learned vocabulary and grammar. As we have already seen, these are themselves social constructs belonging to a particular linguistic group. To repeat the point made in Chapter 2, there is no world that we can 'know', experience or argue about independently of our language.

Importantly, Chomsky's solution to this problem—the claim that we are all born knowing a universal grammar—simply does not stack up against the evidence. It is inconsistent with what we know of the under-organised, flexible nature of the brains of the new-born, as well as the role of spoken language in shaping children's capacity to think—to which we drew attention in Chapter 3. Rather than being born with an innate grammar specified by a genetic blueprint, we have a capacity to induce the conventions of language use from exposure to that language.[69] This capacity derives from the manner in which the neural networks in our brains function, develop and structure experience. I would go further, believing that this innate capacity to induce patterns from exposure to relatively small numbers of examples is an important part of human intelligence, even if it fails to provide the formal certainty sought by rationalists. Even if Chomsky's claim of an innate grammar were true, it would still not tell us that arguments from true premises that used that grammar were true in the sense in which the rationalists used the word true. We are forced, therefore, to agree with eminent Catholic theologian Hans Kung when he concluded:

> People often do not realise that in all their thinking and doing they for all practical purpose constantly presuppose the rationality of reason and so rely upon the ambivalent reality of the world and humanity. That means, in all our doubting and thinking, in our intuitions and deductions there is a priori, a prior act of trust, that is in charge.[70]

These problems are compounded by the insight that metaphors are pervasive in everyday language, thought and action.[71] They are not purely a linguistic construction but are essential to the development of thought. This is because the ordinary unconscious conceptual systems embodied in our language, culture and religion—by which we live on a day-to-day basis—are fundamentally metaphorical in nature. Let me say that again for emphasis: the way in which we think and structure experience involves an imaginative understanding of thing in terms of others—metaphors that tend to form coherent systems. Only purely physical reality is describable in non-metaphorical language, while many of our important concepts are either abstract or not clearly delineated in experience. The greater the abstraction, the more layers of metaphor required. For example, the concept of 'argument' and the language used about it is partially structured, understood, performed and talked about in terms of the concept of 'war'. This metaphorical structuring includes our language about language and our language about reasoning. In particular, we typically conceptualise the non-physical in terms of the physical. It follows, as Lakoff and Johnson confirm, that it is simply not true that 'what is real is wholly external to, and independent of, how human beings conceptualise the world'.[72]

Importantly, the systematic character of such metaphors necessarily conceals other aspects of the concept or experience because there can never be an exact fit between the metaphor and the reality it seeks to describe. In particular, they can prevent us from focusing on aspects inconsistent with the metaphor. Furthermore, this metaphorical structuring is partial. It can be extended in some ways but not in others. Consequently, this structuring can provide only a partial understanding of experience. These metaphors can vary from culture to culture and need not fit together—being based on different kinds of experience. For example, not all cultures give the priority that we do to an up–down orientation; some cultures give a much more important role to balance or centrality.

Our experience of physical objects and substances provides an additional basis for understanding that goes beyond orientation. Understanding our experience in terms of objects and substances allows us to pick out parts and to treat them as discrete entities or substances of a uniform kind. This enables us to refer to them, categorise them and quantify them, and consequently to tell stories and to reason about them. In particular, our experience with physical objects provides a basis for a very wide variety of ontological metaphors. Such ontological metaphors are so natural and pervasive in our language and thoughts that they are usually taken as self-evident direct descriptions. Ontological metaphors in which a physical object is specified as being a person allow us to understand a wide variety of experiences in terms of human motivations, characteristics and activities. Because concepts are structured metaphorically in a systematic way, it is possible to use expressions from one domain to talk about corresponding concepts in the metaphorically defined domain. For example, the idea of knowledge having a 'foundation' (used above) has been taken from the metaphor of theories as buildings. Lakoff and Johnson argue that the idea that basic concepts are primitives that cannot be decomposed is mistaken. Rather, we experience some things as a complex of properties occurring together, as an experiential gestalt—that is, the experience of them occurring together is more basic than their separate occurrence. The consequence is that these complexes of experiences cannot reasonably be reduced to a more basic set of properties. We therefore classify particular experiences in terms of the experiential gestalts in our conceptual system. Metaphorical entailments also play an essential role, linking the metaphorical structuring of a concept. Additionally, there are often many overlapping metaphors that partially structure a concept. Consequently, our understanding takes place in terms of entire domains of experience and not in terms of isolated concepts.

This has an important implication for the understanding of definitions. The standard, objective view assumes that experiences and objects have inherent properties and that we understand and define them in terms of these properties. An objective view involves saying what those inherent properties are, by giving necessary and sufficient conditions for the application of a concept. It follows from Lakoff and Johnson's account that we understand concepts only in part in terms of such inherent properties. For the most part, we understand concepts primarily in terms of concepts from other natural kinds of experience, in terms of what Lakoff and Johnson call their interactional properties, having to do with such things as perception, motor activity, purpose and function. Our concepts of objects—like our concepts of events and activities—are characterisable as multi-dimensional structured gestalts, whose dimensions emerge from our experience of the world. It appears that we categorise things in terms of prototypes and that members are admitted to a category because they have a sufficient family resemblance to the prototype. Consequently, Lakoff and Johnson argue along with Wittgenstein that there need be no fixed core of properties of prototypes that are shared by members of the category. Interactive properties are important in determining what counts as a sufficient family resemblance. Categories can be extended in various ways for various purposes and are open ended. Further, we conceptualise sentences metaphorically in spatial terms. These spatial metaphors automatically structure relationships between form and content. The regularities of linguistic form cannot be explained in formal terms alone. The consequence is that syntax is not independent of meaning. Rather, the logic of a language is based on the coherence between the spatialised form of the language and the metaphorical aspects of the conceptual system. It also follows that many of the similarities that we see are a result of the conventional metaphors that are part of our conceptual system, rather than being inherent in the entities themselves.

The fact that our normal conceptual system is structured metaphorically has an important consequence for us. There is no such thing as a direct physical experience—something emphasised in Chapter 2. Every experience takes place within a vast background of cultural presuppositions. Cultural assumptions, values and attitudes are not a conceptual overlay that we can choose to place or not place on an experience; rather, all experience is cultural through and through. Consequently, there is no such thing as objective truth. Rather, truth is always relative to a conceptual system that is defined in part by metaphor. Importantly, such truth is always partial. We have no access to the whole truth or to any definitive account of reality. Importantly, metaphors play a central role in the construction of social and political realities. Additionally, we have the capacity to create new metaphors, giving us the capacity to give new understandings of experience, to create a new reality and to create a new truth. All of this has a profound implication for our understanding, in particular, of the social disciplines. In these disciplines, we cannot talk truthfully about objective reality, but only about our particular understanding of it, which is itself a social artefact. As we saw in Chapter 2, the people in power are often in a position to impose their metaphors on the rest of us and consequently their understandings of the social and natural worlds. Because most people in our society have been sold the idea of objective truth, those who do so define what is then believed to be absolutely true. The upshot of all of this is that there is no ground for supposing that that there exists a body of self-evident propositions that would allow us to justify substantive beliefs.

Nor can we simply assume that we have discovered the appropriate rules of argumentation. In this regard, American philosopher Harold Brown tells us that 'there are trade-offs between accepting certain rules of inference and achieving other cognitive goals, and once this is recognised, we can no longer accept the claim that familiar inferences require no justification'.[73] It is such problems as these that led Popper, a contemporary champion of rationalism, to depart from traditional epistemology and to accept that it is not possible to establish a priori foundations for knowledge and to accept that there can be no certain knowledge.

It is quite clear from the above that the entire structure of rational analysis rests on a non-rational basis. At the heart of the rationalist claim to provide a foundation for knowledge are acts of faith in the rationality of reason itself and its rules—the 'reasonableness' of the assumptions underlying any particular argument and of the language in which it is expressed. More than this, for Hungarian –British polymath Michael Polanyi (1891–1976), the decisive issue for the theory of knowledge is that 'into every act of knowing there enters a tacit and passionate contribution of the person knowing what is being known, and that this coefficient is no mere imperfection, but a necessary component of all knowledge'.[74] He also confirms that our believing is conditioned at its source by our belonging to a society and its cultural machinery and is therefore influenced by the forces holding on to social privilege.

In any event, these particular forms of reasoning have themselves come under sustained attack. With the realisation that alternative, useful geometries were possible, mathematicians and geometers recognised that geometries were formal logical systems, based on arbitrary assumptions with no necessary connection to reality. In particular, the existence of alternative geometries undermined the view that Euclidean geometry was a body of a priori necessary propositions.[75] There is no a priori method by which we can decide which geometry to apply. It is also possible to conceive of different logics and different arithmetic. There are even doubts about the consistency of conventional arithmetic. To make matters worse for the logicians, Gödel demonstrated that it was theoretically impossible to produce any final solution to the problem of the foundations of mathematical logic. As English–Australian theoretical physicist Paul Davies reports:

> [T]he grand and elaborate edifice of mathematics was built on sand. Mathematical systems rich enough to contain arithmetic are shot through with logical contradictions…[H]owever elaborate mathematics becomes, there will always exist *some* statements…that can *never* be proved true or false. They are fundamentally undecidable. Hence mathematics will always be incomplete and in a sense uncertain.[76]

Similarly, leading American mathematician Morris Kline confirms this loss of certainty: '[T]he present state of mathematics is anomalous and deplorable. The light of truth no longer illuminates the road to follow…The loss of truth [is]…a tragedy of the first magnitude [in which] the concept of a universally accepted, infallible body of reasoning…is a grand illusion…The age of Reason is gone.'[77]

Furthermore, it was not possible for such an axiomatic system to be self-contained.[78] Consequently, Penrose tells us that mathematical understanding is not something that can be formulated in terms of rules. Consistent with the claims made here, Penrose goes on to say that there is something in our understanding that is not computational.[79]

One consequence of the indeterminacy of mathematics is that all physical theories are also uncertain because they are cast in the language of mathematics. The same applies to all social theories cast in the same language. Not only does this mean that there are limits to rational inquiry, it precludes us from ever developing a complete theory of everything in the grand manner sought by some physicists—an impossibility acknowledged recently by leading contemporary theoretical physicist Stephen Hawking.[80] Mathematics is simply a tool created by the human mind and it has no necessary connection to any metaphysical or theological absolutes.[81] Consequently, for American logician Clarence Lewis (1883–1964),

> There are no 'laws of logic' which can be attributed to the universe or to human reason in the traditional fashion…Rather all logical systems and 'laws' were human conventions honoured only for their utility…Logical truth could not possibly serve as an ultimate criterion since the nature and form of that truth necessarily depended upon the prior choice of a particular logical system.[82]

This critique undercuts all pretensions to a priori and absolute knowledge.[83] For Edward Purcell, summarising American pragmatists John Dewey (1859–1952), William James (1842–1910) and Charles Sanders Peirce (1839–1914), truth 'was not to be found in the abstract logic of ideas, but in their practical consequences. There were no absolute or a priori truths, only workable and unworkable hypotheses.'[84]

Indeed, Toulmin believes that an exclusive preoccupation with what he calls logical systematicity in science and philosophy has been destructive of historical understanding and rational criticism.[85] He believes further that people demonstrate their rationality not by ordering their concepts and beliefs into tidy formal structures but by a willingness to respond to novel situations, acknowledging the shortcomings of their former procedures and moving beyond them. Consequently, he attacks the logicians' claim to exceptional insight into the nature of argument and their erection of a special class of argument—the class of unequivocal, analytical, formally valid argument with a universal statement as a major premise—as the paradigmatic case of sound argument and rationality. He sees this idealisation as an extreme view, a vast over-simplification that is unrepresentative and misleading:

> The over-simplified categories of formal logic have an attraction, not only on account of their simplicity, but also because they fit in nicely with some other influential prejudices. From the time of Aristotle logicians have found the mathematical model enticing, and a logic which modelled itself on jurisprudence rather than geometry could not hope to maintain the mathematical elegance of their ideal. Unfortunately, an idealised logic, such as the mathematical model leads us to, cannot keep in serious contact with its practical application. Rational demonstration is not a suitable subject for a timeless, axiomatic science; and if that is what we try to make of logic, we are in danger of ending up with a theory whose connection with argument-criticism is as slight as that between medieval theory of rational fractions and the 'music' from which it took its name.[86]

Acceptance of these idealisations in practice would radically constrain our reasoning abilities, because they make impossible demands on our intelligence. They also stop us from asking when rational inquiry is useful.[87] Further, they inhibit us from examining the techniques of argument that we use in practice, and which techniques are best for which purpose. It is also clear that it is not possible to reduce all decisions to the application of algorithms. The development of cognitive skills is closely analogous to the development of physical skills—involving skilful performance.[88] In particular, the human capacity for judgement, for selecting the information most relevant to the situation or question at hand and for balancing competing priorities or perspectives is not a mechanical skill and is not reducible to rule-following. As Brown says, 'The classical model of rationality takes rule-following to be a fundamental cognitive ability and attempts to capture skills in sets of rules, but this has things backwards since the ability to act in accordance with a set of rules is itself a skill.'

The exaggerated claims for deductive reasoning disguise the moral or political choices that are inevitable between possible inferences in long chains of reasoning. Likewise, deductive reasoning—by using contradictory assumptions—can produce radically different ethical systems and geometrical forms of argumentation give us no means of choosing between those assumptions.

For Rorty also, it is a mistake to believe that there are ahistorical standards of rationality by which we can discover who is rational and who is not. This is not to abandon all standards, but simply to recognise our fallibility and finitude. Consequently, justified true belief can be no more than conformity to the norms of the day. Words take their meanings from other words—not their representative character—and vocabularies acquire their privilege from the people who use them not because they are transparent to the real. As a result, we must give up our desire for a uniform and normalised sense of truth while maintaining a sense of the transience of ideas along with the realisation that the latest vocabulary could just be one of the potentially limitless vocabularies in which the world can be described. Every culture is entitled to judge matters of rationality by its own lights. Similarly, MacIntyre requires us to look behind questions of abstract rationality and ask whose conception of rationality is being used in any situation.[89]

It follows from the above that there can be no all-encompassing discipline that legitimises the others.[90] Rather, justification is a social phenomenon—a conversation—and not a transaction between a knowing subject and reality. Consequently, words such as 'rational', 'objective' and 'cognitive' are simply marks of distinction applied to matters about which there is agreement. This conversational justification is naturally holistic, in contrast with the reductive and atomistic habits of the epistemological tradition. It is also associated with the dissolution of the philosophical dualisms that have characterised theoretical debate since the Enlightenment. This attempt to devise mutually exclusive categories seems less and less convincing.[91]

This conversational view of truth and knowledge does not devalue human knowledge. Rather, it sees us as finite, historical, dialogical beings, always in conversation and always in search of understanding and who must accept responsibility for our decisions. Importantly, it is a view that employs a more realistic concept of truth—that is, that which can be justified to a community of interpreters open to tradition, according to the standards and practices that have been developed in the course of history. It recognises that nothing can count as justification except by reference to what is already accepted—and that there is no way to get outside our language and beliefs to find better tests. These 'prejudices' should not be seen as a contamination of what would otherwise be a pure and objective view, because there is no such thing.[92] This view therefore attacks what the decisive figure in twentieth-century hermeneutics, Hans-Georg Gadamer (1900–2002), called 'the peculiar falsehood of modern consciousness the idolatry of scientific method and the anonymous authority of the sciences'.[93]

This metaphor of culture as a conversation, rather than a structure erected on foundations, is central to the hermeneutical tradition. This European philosophical tradition—which is concerned with human understanding and the interpretation of texts—throws further light on the questions raised above and occupies a central role in contemporary philosophical discourse. This tradition arose from biblical and literacy criticism, which sought understanding of a text in the context of its production. It was then extended into the study of history and the nature of historical knowledge. Subsequently, it has developed into the understanding of understanding itself, in which understanding is conceived of as universal and underlying all activities: 'Understanding must be conceived as a part of the process of the coming into being of meaning, in which the significance of all statements…is formed and made complete.'[94]

Meaning and understanding are essentially and intrinsically linguistic and not psychological processes.[95] Like Rorty's approach, this approach does not provide another kind of epistemological theory, but discards epistemological and foundational concerns altogether.[96] Its key insight is that the interpretation of a text involves a dialogue between the author and the text and the text and the reader. Consequently, there is no definitive interpretation of a text. Rather, the meaning of a text changes over time according to how it is read and received. Similarly, the meanings of the concepts with which we try to make sense of the world are subject to continuous negotiation.[97] Consequently, the determination of specific meanings is a matter for practical judgement and not a priori theory and scientific proof. Indeed, understanding involves a circular, iterative, dialectic process—a hermeneutical circle.

Bergstein describes hermeneutics as a defensive reaction against the universalistic and reductive claims made in the name of science—that it is science alone that is the measure of reality, knowledge and truth. It abandons the belief that all contributions to a discourse are commensurable—that is, can be brought under a set of rules that tell us how to reach 'rational' agreement. This is a reason that is conceived of as being a technical instrument, the means to manipulation and control. Further, it emphasises the historicity of all understanding and interpretation, and criticises the basic dichotomy between the subjective and the objective. In consequence, it attacks the Cartesian belief that it is possible to free human reason completely of bias, prejudice and tradition. Rather, reason gains its power within a living tradition. Consequently, in *Truth and Method*,[98] Gadamer rejects the dichotomies between reason and tradition, reason and prejudice and reason and authority that have been entrenched since the Enlightenment. This is the essence of reason rooted in human finitude, rather than a deficiency.[99]

For Gadamer, these limits can be transcended through exposure to other discourses and cultural traditions. He places language at the centre of understanding, stressing its role in opening the interpreter to other subjectivities. Importantly, for Gadamer, understanding does not involve reconstructing a speaker's intention, but instead mediates between the interpreter's immediate and emerging horizons. Understanding is bound and embedded in history, employing the interpreter's personal experience and cultural traditions to assimilate new experiences. As John Mallery et al. tell us: 'This purely subjective and continual unfolding interacts with and is conditioned by experience, particularly the experience of language, which tends to mould the developing subject in conformity with the traditions encoded in linguistic utterances and in the language itself.'[100]

Nevertheless, an interpreter's imagination can carry the understanding of a text beyond her or his initial understanding. Even so, interpretations are constrained by the questions posed. Similarly for Habermas, truth and meaning do not await discovery, but are negotiated by actors through social discourse.[101]

Within this approach to knowledge, Rorty suggests a distinction between normal discourse and abnormal discourse, generalising Kuhn's normal and revolutionary science, which we will discuss shortly. Normal discourse is that which is conducted within agreed conventions, while abnormal discourse involves ignorance of—or the setting aside of—these conventions. No discipline can explain such abnormal discourse.

It is important to note that this view—that we can have no certain knowledge—is now conventional wisdom. Its acceptance entails a rejection of intellectual arrogance and dogmatism, particularly the lack of intellectual humility that seems to have infested the entire Western intellectual tradition, particularly since the Enlightenment. As with the Reformation, the lack of a convincing theoretical base—and the radical disagreement it engenders—undermines the magisterium of the theorist. Indeed, we need to take seriously the possibility that the total social environment is too complex, and the human mind too limited, for us to understand[102] —a view with echoes in Hayek,[103] Niebuhr[104] (1882–1971) and, more recently, Brian Arthur.[105]

The next chapter will explore the implications of this critique for the status of science and the social disciplines.

ENDNOTES

1 de Fontenelle 1686, cited in Cox 1984, p. 38.

2 Oakeshott 1962.

3 Tarnas 1991.

4 Ibid.

5 Milton 1998.

6 Habermas 1981, p. 9.

7 Tarnas 1991.

8 Lyotard 1984.

9 Ibid., p. 37.

10 Kellner 1988.

11 Madsen et al. 2002.

12 Wicks 2004.

13 Gutting 2003.

14 Madsen et al. 2002.

15 Rawlings 1999.

16 Madsen et al. 2002.

17 Kellner 1988.

18 Knodt 1995.

19 Tarnas 1991.

20 Bernstein 1983.

21 McIntyre 2005.

22 Kincaid 1996.

23 Webb 1995.

24 Passmore 1967.

25 Popper 1974.

26 Adorno et al. 1976, p. 298ff.

27 Kincaid 1996.

28 Brown 1991.

29 Tarnas 1991.

30 Reid 1993.

31 Smolin 1998, p. 29.

32 Reid 1993, p. 10.

33 Smolin 1998.

34 Penrose 1995.

35 See http://en.wikipedia.org/wiki/Causality for a contemporary discussion of causality.

36 Reid 1993, p. 9.

37 Bernstein 1983.

38 Ibid., p. xi.

39 Tarnas 1991.

40 Lakoff and Johnson 1980.

41 Hamilton 1994.

42 Swartz 1995.

43 Hamilton 1994.

44 Rabinow 1983.

45 Hamilton 1994.

46 This is too simple a view, which is subject to challenge, but that challenge will not be taken up here. That challenge does not undermine Hamilton's fundamental point. The Eastern view does not lead to a belief that everything is explainable by rational means or, indeed, to a drive for understanding of

causes in that mode, but in a search for harmony with the origin of meaning: the '*Dao*'—the 'Way'—that mystery that we in the West call God.

[47] Toulmin 1990.

[48] Tarnas 1991.

[49] Toulmin 1990.

[50] Levack 1987, p. 21.

[51] Toulmin 1990.

[52] Tarnas 1991.

[53] Ibid., p. 280.

[54] Toulmin 1990.

[55] Loy 2002.

[56] Ibid.

[57] Bernstein 1983; Tarnas 1991.

[58] Rorty 1979.

[59] Ibid.

[60] Backhouse 1992.

[61] Rosenberg 1986.

[62] Toulmin 1972, p. 14.

[63] Brown 1988.

[64] Polanyi 1958.

[65] Gergen 1986, p. 2.

[66] Toulmin 1972.

[67] Crotty 1998.

[68] Albert 1987.

[69] Lieberman 1998; Churchland 1995.

[70] Kung 1988, p. 201.

[71] Lakoff and Johnson 1980.

[72] Ibid., p. 146.

[73] Brown 1988, p. 75.

[74] Polanyi 1958.

[75] Rosenberg 1986.

[76] Davies 2004c.

[77] Kline 1980, cited in Clark 1992, p. 172.

[78] See Nagel and Newman 1959.

[79] Penrose 1995.

[80] Davies 2004a.

[81] Purcell 1973.

[82] Lewis 1932, p. 505.

[83] Purcell 1973.

[84] Ibid., p. 6.

[85] Toulmin 1972.

[86] Toulmin 1958, p. 147.

[87] Berkson 1987.

[88] Brown 1988.

[89] MacIntyre 1988.

[90] Rorty 1979.

[91] Horwitz 1992.

[92] de Lavoie 1990.

[93] Gadamer 1975b, pp. 310–25.

[94] Ibid., p. 157.

[95] Bernstein 1983.
[96] de Lavoie 1990.
[97] Ibid.
[98] Gadamer 1975b.
[99] Bernstein 1983.
[100] Mallery et al. 1986.
[101] Ibid.
[102] Purcell 1973.
[103] Frowen 1997.
[104] Niebuhr 1944, pp. 70–1.
[105] Waldrop 1992.

Chapter 6: The Privileged Status of 'Science'

Plato is dear to me, but dearer still is truth.
— Aristotle[1]

If we see knowing not as having an essence, to be described by scientists or philosophers, but rather as a right, by current standards, to believe, then we are well on the way to seeing conversation as the ultimate context within which knowledge is to be understood.
— Michael Oakeshott[2]

Introduction: Science and Rationality

In the previous chapter, I critiqued the Enlightenment and the more extreme claims made for human reason in that tradition. In particular, I rejected the proposition that it was possible for human beings to possess certain objective knowledge. This chapter explores the implications of those insights, looking in particular at the status of those activities going together under the rubric of 'science' and of the knowledge they produce. The chapter is not intended to decry the enormous achievements of scientists in the past several centuries in throwing light on the natural world and the contribution that those achievements has made to our standard of living. Clearly, the institutionalised search for new scientific knowledge is a very important part of contemporary civilisation. What is intended in this chapter is a critique of the story told about the nature of that search in the past century and a half.

Rorty reminds us that in our culture the ideas of 'science', 'rationality', 'objectivity' and 'truth' are bound up with each other, where 'truth' is conceived of as correspondence with reality.[3] It has been usual to claim that 'science' is the very paradigm of rationality. The meaning of this claim is, however, uncertain as it is now quite clear that there is no logic of science as such—no certain single mechanical rubric for choosing and evaluating scientific hypotheses. Indeed, American philosopher of science Harold Kincaid tells us that the attempts to identify the defining features of science have a long and disappointing history.[4] The claim is a throw-back to the discredited positivism discussed in the previous chapter and to the hypothetical-deductive view of science associated with it. Such claims are part of the rhetoric surrounding the Enlightenment's search for absolute knowledge—a knowledge that enjoys a privileged status over commonsense perceptions and understandings.[5] The critique outlined in Chapter 5, however, undermines the epistemological claims on which Western science has been based since the Enlightenment. Furthermore, as physical chemist and philosopher of science Michael Polanyi tells us, the rules of rational inquiry can be of little practical importance to the scientist: '[D]iscovery, far from representing a definite mental operation, is an extremely delicate and personal art which can be but little assisted by any formulated precepts.'[6]

In the same spirit, philosopher of science Ernest Nagel (1901–85) described science as an institutionalised art of inquiry and, as we will see shortly, that is a far better description.[7] It should also be clear from Chapter 5 that the particular Enlightenment view of rationality—which sees science as the paradigm—misrepresents the nature of human intelligence itself. Therefore, British philosopher of social sciences Peter Winch (1926–97) writes:

> Now it is of course true that the role played by such [scientific] work in the culture of [W]estern industrialised societies is an enormously important one and...[it had] a very far-reaching influence on what we are and what we are not prepared to call instances of 'rational thought'. But it was an essential part of my argument...to urge that our own conception of what it is to be rational is certainly not exhausted by the practices of science.[8]

Rorty challenges this identification of 'rational' with a special method; rather, he suggests it names a moral virtue: the virtue of being reasonable, encompassing tolerance, respect for the opinions of others, a willingness to listen, reliance on persuasion rather than force and eschewing dogmatism, defensiveness and righteous indignation.

Furthermore, it might be more appropriate to consider scientific investigations as being a response to our limited cognitive abilities—an attempt to create closed systems of belief to enable us to get by in the world—rather than an expression of a God-like capacity for generating understanding through 'rationality'. As social psychologist Paul Secord tells us, such closed systems rarely occur in the world, and only then in the laboratory.[9]

The above claim also assumes that Newtonian physics is the exemplar of a single archetypal scientific method whose laws are valid universally. Not only has this admiration for Newtonian physics faded, physicists are speculating that the so-called fundamental natural laws of physics are not immutable and transcendent but could be no more than local by-laws—valid only in our particular patch of the cosmos.[10] Davies reminded us only recently that conventional physics had no idea of what the external source of these laws might be.[11] Some theorists are speculating that they emerged as part of the evolution of the universe itself and our observation of it.

The assumption that there was a single scientific method was reflected in the work of Comte, who asserted that there was a hierarchy of knowledge in which 'science' was the pinnacle. Consequently, Comte argued that even sociology could be a positive science modelled after physics[12] —an ambition that sociology has long since abandoned, but one to which economics clings. Implicit in this belief is the proposition that the generalisations in physics are somehow more basic than those of the other sciences and certainly more basic than in the social disciplines, and that somehow everything can be reduced ultimately to physical generalisations. Reductionism in the spirit of Greek atomism lies at the heart of this assertion. This reductionism, this reification, this scientism, is, however, inconsistent with the wide range of real scientific practices and theories that are not reducible to physics. This inconsistency suggests that changes in belief and terminology are required. What is more, American philosopher Norman Swartz—drawing on Wittgenstein's model of family resemblances in which there is no core property shared by all members of a family—tells us that it is exceedingly difficult to tell precisely what a scientific law is. Like all concepts, there is no single defining set of necessary and sufficient conditions for a statement being a scientific law. While we would all accept that there is considerable order in the natural and social worlds, the generalisations we use to describe that order are social artefacts that are not literally true—being at best approximations, idealised reconstructions or instrumental tools going beyond the evidence available to us.[13]

Similarly, from the Enlightenment, we have inherited a cultural image of the scientist as a hero overcoming ignorance and bringing reality under control. The effect is to privilege particular types of inquiry, particular social practices and their associated stories over other forms of inquiry. It is not so much that one should necessarily object to the use of a general term such as 'science' to encompass the wide range of systematic inquiries carried out into the character of the physical and social worlds; rather, it is that 'science' now carries too many misleading entailments, implying a privilege and a unity of method that cannot be sustained.

Blaug reports that in the mid-nineteenth century, the usual story told about scientific investigations was that they started with the free and unprejudiced observation of facts. Such investigations were then supposed to progress by inductive inference to the formulation of universal laws and theories about those facts. The induced laws and theories were then to be checked by comparing their empirical consequences with all the observed 'facts'—including those with which they began.[14] In this context, scientific progress was seen as a linear process with the inclusion of more and more kinds of phenomena under laws of greater and greater generality—a reflection of the Enlightenment's faith in reductionism and in progress.

This image of science reflects the ideas of Bacon—one of the fathers of empiricism referred to in Chapter 2. This story has, however, been discredited. All perception and language is theory impregnated. Only those sensory impressions that are significant from some particular perspective become 'perceptions'.[15] Similarly, the positivist claim that only the statements that are verifiable by observation are meaningful is contradicted by positivists' own claims and by the large numbers of scientific theories that are based on far more than direct conclusions from sensory data—on ideas that are not observable directly.[16] Since Hume pointed to the inability of induction to establish logical certainty, the idea that induction formed the basis of a rational scientific method has been problematic.[17] Importantly, it is now said that these images of science give a distorted picture of the way in which scientific investigations have been conducted. In particular, the belief that it is possible to verify scientific theories has had to be discarded because rival theories can always be developed to fit the data in any particular case and there is no formal method that allows us to choose between such competing theories.[18] It is also clear that the picture of science as a cumulative linear process cannot be sustained. As positivist Donald Fiske (1917–2003) and cultural psychologist Richard Shweder tell us, '[T]he criteria for progress in the sciences are task-specific, diverse, ambiguous, and shifting. No criterion has served as a general standard or a universal ideal.'[19] Furthermore, not all science is concerned with a search for general laws. Indeed, political scientist Phillip Converse argues that each science has its own texture; while educational psychologist Lee Cronbach (1916–2001) claims that the social disciplines are progressive because they possess an ever-richer repertoire of questions—not because they have ever more refined answers about fixed questions.[20] Nor does the above image take adequate account of the institutionalisation of scientific investigations in the modern world.

So let us be quite clear: this story, this legitimising mythology—the legacy of the Enlightenment—has been discredited. A fundamental change in our understanding of scientific investigations has resulted from the work of recent philosophers of science[21] —an understanding that is not positivist and that makes far humbler claims. In particular, as we have already seen, the foundationalist claim that philosophy can describe on a priori grounds the standards for scientific knowledge has been discredited.[22] As a result, the late Australian philosopher of qualitative research, Michael Crotty, advises us to hold all our understandings of the natural and social worlds lightly, tentatively and far less dogmatically—'seeing them as historically and culturally affected interpretations rather than eternal truths'.[23]

It is now clear that scientific inquiry cannot provide us with the certain knowledge sought by the Enlightenment. That has proven to be a utopian dream. There is no certain truth to be found through method or technique. All knowledge is tentative and subject to revision. At best, all we can have is 'justified' belief, wherein the criteria for justification are themselves contestable. It is also agreed generally that all scientific knowledge is constructed socially—the work of an interpretive community. Furthermore, Descartes' method of radical scepticism has very little attraction for real scientists. The majority of scientific knowledge—including knowledge of the appropriate methods—is accepted on authority, as an act of trust in a particular scientific tradition with its corpus of knowledge, norms, ideals, heroes and heroic stories, as passed on by teachers and colleagues either through direct instruction or by example. Any individual scientist does not build her or his field anew, but lays down new deposits on the theoretical sediments already in place.[24] Importantly, critical theory warns us that these inherited constructed meanings can serve particular hegemonic interests and power structures in a world in which there are strong disparities in the distribution of power.[25]

According to Kincaid, there is a common thread to nearly all contemporary philosophy of science: it is not positivist.[26] Also, many of the differences between the above theorists are matters of emphasis.[27] It is questionable whether a strong differentiation is possible or desirable. Bernstein sums up this new perspective in the following terms:

> Awareness has been growing that attempts to state what are or ought to be the criteria for evaluating and validating scientific hypotheses and theories that are abstracted from existing social practice are threatened with a false rigidity or pious vacuity and that existing criteria are always open to conflicting interpretations and applications and can be weighed in different ways. The effective standards and norms that are operative in scientific inquiry are subject to change and modification in the course of scientific inquiry. We are now aware that it is not only important to understand the role of tradition in science as mediated through research programs or research traditions but that we must understand how such traditions arise, develop, and become progressive and fertile, as well as the ways in which they can degenerate.[28]

The Contemporary Philosophy of Science

Let us look at these issues in a little more detail. Physicist and philosopher of science Pierre Duhem (1861–1916) taught us that there were no critical experiments in physics that could establish that a hypothesis was true. Theories face experimental refutation collectively. An experiment that refutes a hypothesis refutes a network of interconnected ideas—rather than a single idea—pointing to a problem within that network rather than pinpointing the problem. This is because predictions that are tested are deduced from theoretical hypotheses, auxiliary hypotheses and other knowledge. Consequently, it is always possible for the scientist to save a hypothesis by adjusting the auxiliary hypotheses. Duhem pointed out further that the choice of hypotheses to test is governed by considerations of order, symmetry and elegance rather than by their ability to describe the world accurately. Quine extended Duhem's idea to take in the whole of science, suggesting that it was an entire web of belief—even a world-view—that faced refutation as a whole. He also points out that it is possible to save any belief if we are prepared to make the necessary adjustments elsewhere. This is a phenomenon that is widespread and has been well documented by anthropologists in the case of beliefs in such things as magic. Norwood Hanson (1924–67) taught us that what we took to be facts depended on our conceptual system.[29]

Consistent with the above body of criticism, Popper rejected the nineteenth-century attempt to prescribe a method of discovery or of verification. He tells us:

> Science is not a system of certain, or well-established, statements; nor is it a system which steadily advances towards a state of finality…The old scientific idea of *epistēmē*—of absolute certain, demonstrable knowledge—has proved to be an idol…It may indeed be corroborated, but every corroboration is relative to other statements which, again, are tentative. Only in our subjective experience of conviction, in our subjective faith, can we be 'absolutely certain'.[30]

Popper does not provide us with a logic of science, nor does he believe that such logic is possible. He also rejected the positivist attempts to distinguish the meaningful from the meaningless along the lines proposed by the positivists. Instead, he sought to divide all human knowledge into two categories: science and non-science. In his view, science is distinguished from non-science by its method of formulating and testing propositions, not by its subject matter and not by a claim to certainty of knowledge. Nevertheless, Popper draws no absolute line between science and non-science, as falsifiability and testability are matters of degrees. All 'true' theories are merely provisionally true—having so far defied falsification. Because no individual scientific hypothesis was ever falsified conclusively, Popper suggested certain normative limits on the methods that could be used to safeguard theories against falsification based on what he believed to be sound practice. Let me emphasise the point: there exists no formal method to rule out *ad hoc* assumptions to save a hypothesis, and Popper has to employ normative rules to save his conjecture–falsification approach from such tinkering.

> The empirical basis of objective science has thus nothing 'absolute' about it. Science does not rest upon solid bedrock. The bold structure of its theories rises, as it were, above a swamp. It is like a building erected on piles. The piles are driven down from above into the swamp, but not down to any natural or 'given' base; and if we stop driving the piles deeper, it is not because we have reached firm ground. We simply stop, when we are satisfied that the piles are firm enough to carry the structure, at least for the time being.[31]

This does not mean, however, that falsification thereby ceases to be a valuable practical scientific tool—though there will be occasions when a hypothesis fails a test because of the inadequacy of auxiliary assumptions. Importantly, for Popper, a theory is scientific only if it gives rise to a known set of conditions that are testable and which will falsify that theory if they do not occur. This was the basis of his critique of Marxism: that it could not be subjected to empirical test and therefore was not scientific. A similar criticism is often made about the core of the neoclassical economic program. Blaug complains—with considerable justification—that mainstream economics preaches falsification but does not practise it. He sees this as a problem all through the social disciplines and even in the natural sciences.[32]

Hungarian Imr Lakatos (1922–74) followed in Popper's footsteps but talked about progressive and degenerating research programs, suggesting that it was a research program as a whole as it developed over time that should be the focus of attention, rather than its state at a particular point in time. He sees research programs as comprising a hard core, which is essentially untestable, and auxiliary hypotheses, which are testable. He suggests that a research program is theoretically progressive if it predicts some novel, hitherto unexpected fact, and empirically progressive if each new theory leads to the discovery of some new fact. He also cautions about being too hasty in assessing a program, while acknowledging that it is possible to persist with a degenerating research program for too long. This approach, however, while apparently reflecting real practice, weakens the normative significance of Popper's message. It also gives little practical guidance to a researcher or observer evaluating such a program at any particular point in time.

Importantly, Thomas Kuhn (1922–96), the most influential modern philosopher of science, argues that the appeal to falsification is misleading, because in practice scientists seem to be trying to verify rather than to falsify theories, and because theories that are falsified by particular experiments are rarely abandoned. His seminal work, *The Structure of Scientific Revolutions*, looked at the history of scientific practice and concluded that all science was based on an agreed framework of unprovable assumptions about the nature of the universe, rather than simply on empirical facts. These assumptions—a paradigm—comprise a constellation of beliefs, values and techniques that are shared by a given scientific community, which legitimise their practices and set the boundaries of their research.[33] Importantly, this view undermines directly the claimed objectivity and value-free neutrality of scientific investigations.[34] Kuhn argues that what he calls 'normal science' 'aims to elucidate the scientific tradition in which [the scientist] was raised rather than to change it'.[35] It uses the same methods that the rest of us use in everyday life. He suggests, therefore, that examples are checked against criteria, data are fudged to avoid the need for new models and guesses—formulated within the current jargon—are tried out in the search for something that covers the cases that cannot be fudged.[36] He goes on to argue that radically new theories arise not as a result of falsification but by the replacement of a hitherto explanatory model—or paradigm—with a new one. Such revolutionary science—the overthrow of a paradigm as a result of repeated refutations and anomalies—is the exception in the history of science. Implicit in this view is the idea that science does not advance in a steady, linear process.

Normal science is a thoroughly social process in which the problems to be examined and the general form the solutions should take are the result of agreement among a scientific community. It is a self-sustaining, cumulative process of problem solving within the context of a common analytical framework. The breakdown of normal science is marked by a proliferation of theories and by methodological controversy. In this climate, a new framework can appear offering a decisive solution to hitherto neglected problems. Conversion to the new approach takes on the nature of an identity crisis or a religious experience. Importantly, Kuhn tells us that there is no neutral algorithm or systematic decision procedure that will determine choice between competing paradigms. He claims that new paradigms are not only incompatible with their predecessors, they are incommensurable. This is because there is no third, neutral language within which rival paradigms can be expressed in full.[37]

Importantly, Bernstein likens this decision process to Aristotle's practical reasoning—the type of reasoning in which there is a mediation between general principles and a concrete situation that requires wit, imagination, interpretation and the judicious weighing of alternatives—reasoning that is shaped by the social practices of the relevant community. Resolution does not take place by an appeal to the canon of deductive logic or by any straightforward appeal to observation, verification or falsification. Rather, 'the cumulative weight of the complex arguments advanced in favour of a given paradigm theory, together with its successes, persuade the community of scientists'.[38]

Kuhn subsequently listed five criteria for choice—accuracy, consistency, scope, simplicity and fullness—stressing that these criteria, which functioned as values, were imprecise and were frequently in conflict. He explains that this does not involve a total abandonment of rationality in science, but rather a shift to a more realistic understanding—to a different model of rationality. Indeed, this shift from a model of rationality that searches for determinate rules to one that emphasises the role of exemplars and judgemental interpretation is a theme that pervades all of Kuhn's thinking. It is a view that picks up on Michael Polanyi's strong emphasis on the tacit knowledge of the scientist—knowledge acquired in the practice of science, which cannot be formulated explicitly in propositions and rules.[39]

Importantly, for Bernstein, the real character of rationality in the sciences in general—but especially in theory choice—is closer to the tradition of practical reason than to the image of *epistēmē*.[40] MacIntyre puts it this way:

> Objective rationality is therefore to be found not in rule-following, but in rule-transcending, in knowing how and when to put rules and principles to work and when not to. Consider how practical reasoning of this kind is taught, whether it is the practical reasoning of generals, of judges in a common law tradition, or surgeons or of natural scientists. Because there is no set of rules specifying necessary and sufficient conditions for large areas of such practices, the skills of practical reasoning are communicated only partly by precepts but much more by case-histories and precedents. Moreover the precepts cannot be understood except in terms of their application in the case histories; and the development of the precepts cannot be understood in terms of the history of both precepts and case histories.[41]

As the new framework achieves dominance, it becomes the normal science of the next generation.

Kuhn subsequently acknowledged that his earlier description of scientific revolutions involved some rhetorical exaggeration. Paradigmatic changes during scientific revolutions do not imply total discontinuities in scientific debate. In this later account, scientific development is characterised by overlapping and interpenetrating paradigms, some of which can be incommensurable. Paradigms do not replace each other suddenly; rather they achieve dominance in a long process of intellectual competition. Nevertheless, Kuhn's stress on the role of normative judgements in scientific controversies—and sociological factors such as authority, hierarchy and reference groups—remains intact, along with a mistrust of the role of cognitive factors as determinants of scientific behaviour.[42] Because it is a social process, scientific research is heavily dependent on the norms and ideals underpinning society in general and the norms embedded in inter-subjective communication in particular.

Reflecting on the above literature, Kincaid has suggested that good science requires at least the following evidential virtues—though he acknowledges that they are abstract and simplistic and admit multiple interpretations:

- falsifiability as the first line of empirical adequacy
- empirical adequacy—the more predictive success the better
- wide scope—predicting a wide variety of different kinds of phenomena
- coherence with the best information from other sciences
- fruitfulness in terms of a past track record and a future promise
- objectivity.

Kincaid goes on to stress the importance of fair tests, independent tests and cross tests. Given what has already been said, we might baulk at the possibility of achieving objectivity, but at a practical level this seems a useful suggestion—particularly in respect of normal science—as long as we do not get carried away with its status as 'the method' to the exclusion of other lists or with the knowledge status of the results.

Austrian-born Paul Feyerabend (1924–94) goes further than Kuhn and Kincaid. He points out that the physical sciences—the usual exemplars of scientific practice—have not advanced in a manner consistent with the canon of the strict methodologists, including those of Popper. Rather, he believes that progress has depended on a willingness to breach those canons. In part, this is because he sees normal science as a process of indoctrination;[43] and, because science cannot be grounded philosophically in any convincing way, he warns us expressly that scientific findings are no more than beliefs that should not be privileged over other beliefs. Indeed, there is a substantial anthropological literature arguing that the religious stories and beliefs of other cultures are no less rational than our own scientific beliefs—making good sense of experience to the members of those cultures. It is simply that the frames of reference, the paradigms and the tools available differ significantly. It is the height of ethnocentric intellectual arrogance to suggest otherwise. In this regard, Shweder tells us:

> A remarkable feature of the entities of religious thought is that they are thought to be external, objective, and real. But it seems to me, it is precisely that feature that marks a point of strong resemblance with scientific concepts, for one of the features of scientific thinking is that 'representations' of reality are typically treated as though they were real, and unseen ideas and constructs are not only used to help interpret what is seen but are presumed to exist externally, behind or within that small piece of reality that can be seen.[44]

Nevertheless, Feyerabend believes that scientists should test their perceptions—seeing this willingness as the difference between science and non-science, though these beliefs are no less culturally, socio-politically and historically conditioned.[45] He also draws our attention to the ways in which scientific communities can become closed, rigid and intolerant of new ideas, even though science is often seen as the very model of openness. It is an important part of the argument that will be advanced in Chapter 8 that the community of neoclassical economists has become such a closed group.

The fact that the creation of scientific knowledge is a social process has an important corollary. There are power relationships within any scientific community, as within any other community. Those power relationships, associated with such things as prestigious professorships, the editorship of journals, the referring of papers, participation in funding and appointment committees and positions within the broader community, can have a big influence on the acceptance or rejection of particular theories. And, of course, scientists are no more virtuous than the rest of us. American social scientist and methodologist Donald Campbell (1916–96) described this social construction of knowledge as a quasi-conspiratorial social negotiation involving ambiguity, equivocality and discretionary judgement.[46] This group identification can suppress intra-group disagreement, while exacerbating disagreements between groups and restricting the flow of information and people between them.[47]

Let me reiterate that there is significant agreement on some essential points among these critics of the nineteenth-century image of science. They are all anti-positivist. Strict justification cannot be achieved. In particular, we cannot stand outside our current language and structure of thought. Ultimate justification is not achievable; neither is inquiry free of presuppositions. Consequently, the belief that scientific knowledge is an accurate representation of reality has had to be abandoned. As Rorty put it: 'We understand knowledge when we understand the social justification of belief, and thus have no need to view it as accuracy of representation.'[48]

It is also clear that any explanation is an explanation from a particular partial point of view—an attempt to reduce the unfamiliar to the more familiar—so that there can be multiple, even inconsistent explanations. All such explanations are tentative.[49] All theories involve abstraction from the complexity of the world and any particular theory highlights particular attributes only. It is an extraordinary leap of faith to believe that any particular point of view can capture successfully the essence of any phenomenon.

In particular, Rorty tells us that the attempt to isolate science from non-science through the use of words such as 'objectivity', 'rigour' and 'method' assumes that scientific success can be explained in terms of discovering the language of nature. Galileo—in claiming that the book of nature was written in the language of mathematics—meant that mathematics worked because that was the way things really were.[50] For Rorty, this was simply a bad metaphor; rather, Galileo's reductionist mathematical vocabulary just happened to work—something that lacked a metaphysical, epistemological or transcendental explanation.[51] Consequently, for Rorty, the moral that seventeenth-century philosophers should have drawn from Galileo's success was that scientific breakthroughs were not so much a matter of deciding which of various alternative hypotheses were true but of finding the right jargon in which to frame hypotheses in the first place.[52] What is clear is that the extent to which our mathematical vocabulary matches that of nature—whether nature can reasonably be described as having a vocabulary—will always remain problematic.

It follows that empirical sciences cannot claim an essential grasp of reality and, as a result, a privileged status in the human conversation. It also follows that economics, sociology, political science or even philosophy cannot claim to be objective and rational in a way that moral philosophy, aesthetics and poetry are not.[53] In all cases, justification is a search for persuasive arguments—a fully social phenomenon—not a transaction between the inquirer and reality. In this connection, Peirce[54] referred to the 'indefinite Community of Investigators', while Mead[55] spoke of the 'Community of Universal Discourse'. As we will see in Chapter 7, these concepts have much in common with Habermas's ideal speech conditions. When it comes to matters of the basic structures of society and major issues of public policy, this community is to be found in the ordinary citizens of the society—not in some intellectual elite who would be the equivalent of Plato's guardians.

The real problem lies with us and the excessive faith we want to place in scientific knowledge—including knowledge about economics—and the faith we want to place in its practitioners, and in their capacity to free us from anxiety. As Gadamer tells us, '[T]he problem of our society is that the longing of the citizenry for orientation and normative patterns invests the expert with an exaggerated authority. Modern society expects him to provide a substitute for past moral and political orientations.'[56]

Further, he says that philosophical hermeneutics 'corrects the peculiar falsehood of modern consciousness: the idolatry of scientific method and of the anonymous authority of the sciences and it vindicates again the noblest task of the citizen—decision-making according to one's own responsibility—instead of conceding that task to the expert'.[57]

The above difficulties in grounding rationality and science undermine any sharp distinction between science, philosophy and any other critical inquiry—undermining the special status that we have hitherto attached to science. They also point to our inability to insulate scientific inquiry from the need for practical reason, for judgement and even wisdom. As German critical rationalist philosopher Hans Albert tells us, '[T]he problem of adequate criteria is a very general problem. It is to be found in every field of social activity—in every kind of problem-solving activity; in law, morals, politics, literature, the arts, etc—and not merely in the enterprise of acquiring knowledge in science.'[58]

The Particular Difficulties of the Social 'Sciences'

Theorists have often sought to differentiate the social disciplines from the natural sciences on the grounds that the latter are more objective. Indeed, an invidious comparison is often made between the social disciplines and the natural sciences. This follows from a tendency to idealise the natural sciences and to see Newtonian physics as the exemplar of scientific practice. It is then assumed that the production of universal laws characterises the natural sciences in general—but this is far from being true.[59] Such a sweeping generalisation does not do justice

to the diversity of scientific practice in the natural sciences or to the variety of criteria of success negotiated within those diverse fields.[60] Simple law-like behaviour and predictability are elusive in the natural sciences also—though in the natural sciences it is possible more often to get away with simple idealisations, to isolate a system and to treat its properties as context independent.[61] In any event—as the above account makes clear—the broad claims of the natural sciences to objectivity—in the sense advanced by the Enlightenment tradition—cannot be sustained.

Nevertheless, there are particular difficulties with the social disciplines, which add to the above problems, and which are reflected in unease about their status. The result has been the development of a separate theoretical discussion of the philosophy of the social sciences, which can be quite esoteric. This discussion is at pains to distinguish itself from the positivism criticised earlier—though there are still unreformed positivists in economics. William Outhwaite categorises this discourse into three schools—involving realist, hermeneutic and pragmatic perspectives—though there appears to be significant overlap between them.[62] Nevertheless, the main issue separating these perspectives is the extent to which any social discipline can describe a social reality independent of the observer and her or his description of it. This discourse overlaps with that in the natural sciences described earlier. Critical realism—following Roy Bhaskar—is possibly the current dominant school. It agrees that a distinction is to be made between the natural and the social sciences, that the latter do not operate in the same way as the former and cannot be studied with the same methods, and that social life is constructed continually through practice.[63] Nevertheless, in neglecting the limitations of language, they attempt 'to privilege a concept of the real that can be definitely discovered, described and activated under definable conditions'.[64] In this, they appear to be too optimistic. As educationalist and methodologist John Schostak explains, symbolic representation—including through language—can never be the full measure of the 'real'.[65] There is something missing of the 'real' in any representation that we cannot recover, however much we try to tame it. Schostak suggests that for critical realism to be useful, it has to deal successfully with representation in all its possible articulations, and with the emergence of understanding as acts of creative imagination shared through discourse. This is why I lean towards the pragmatic and hermeneutical schools.

None of the above positions suggest that we should not try to understand the social world. The disagreement is about the extent to which we are likely to succeed and the confidence with which we are prepared to apply the resulting insights. No one is claiming that in any particular investigation there is a single, ultimately true theory that is accessible to us. Nor can we ever fully escape the language with which we describe the social system. In short, the 'TRUTH' about society is not available to us.

For example, Kincaid, who describes himself as a realist—believing the idea that things exist and act independently of our descriptions—claims that because there is no simple logic of science we cannot evaluate social science by looking at simple formal traits. At the same time, he believes that good social science cannot be ruled out on a priori conceptual grounds. Rather, he claims we have to look in detail at the methods used and the kinds of evidence adduced. Importantly, he concludes that large parts of the social disciplines have failed to produce such good science.[66] He goes on to claim that the philosophy of science can contribute to the study of society only if it eschews a priori armchair theorising in favour of a philosophy tied intimately to the real practice of social science research. In respect of that social science practice, Fiske and Shweder tell us:

> It is obvious that social science is not a single integrated discipline; rather it is a collectivity of endeavours sometimes working cooperatively, sometimes borrowing from each other, and only occasionally collaborating in joint enterprises. It is a range of disciplines and methodologies, above and beyond the somewhat anachronistic categories in university catalogs.[67]

Kincaid agrees that the social disciplines employ methods that are not found anywhere in the natural sciences.[68] Nevertheless, he claims that the social disciplines can be good science by the standards of scientific adequacy of the natural sciences—describing basic patterns found in nature—but only by meeting those standards. This is because he believes that human beings are part of the natural order and are amenable to scientific understanding. This, he declares, is simply an extension of an Enlightenment tenet. Given our critique of the Enlightenment, this is hardly a persuasive argument. Furthermore, he believes that behind the diverse methods of the natural sciences there is a common core of 'scientific rationality', which the social disciplines sometimes share.[69] Importantly, he believes that social science is distinct from psychology—with its own domain of inquiry largely to do with understanding large-scale social structures—and in the process rejects the methodological individualism of much of the social disciplines. Interestingly, Kincaid goes on to define those scientific standards in terms of 'scientific virtues'—virtues promoting confirmation and those promoting explanation—standards that deny that scientific justification can be reduced to a certain method. It should already be clear that Kincaid agrees with Rorty and that methods do vary across the sciences and do not provide a foolproof, mechanical basis for choosing theories. Nor does Kincaid believe all is well with social research. Nevertheless and confusingly, Kincaid appears to believe that there is something special about science, that, in effect, it possesses a privileged form of justification—a belief I have already discounted.

Kincaid's belief that human beings are part of the natural order goes to the heart of the problem of social inquiry. This is a belief that we must reject as being much too strong. In effect, Kincaid seeks to defeat the dichotomy made in our vocabulary between the natural and the social—a vocabulary he uses while denying its import. While the phenomena studied in the natural sciences could have an existence independent of the concepts used to describe them, this might not be true very often, if at all, of the social disciplines.[70] Rather, the social disciplines are concerned with human beings who—as we saw in Chapter 2—construct their social reality, defining themselves in symbolic forms with shared understandings of the world, which they use to structure their actions.[71] Consequently, it is not the way the world is, but the way we conceptualise it, that influences our actions.[72]

This is the reason why leading Canadian political philosopher Charles Taylor makes a distinction between human 'behaviour' and human 'action', in which the former is caused by forces over which the individual has no control—analogous to the forces of nature—and the latter results from that person's intentions. He then points out that the language describing human conduct is mainly an intentional one and it is about human action rather than human behaviour. It is the language of reasons and not of causes. This is important because—as we have seen already—the interpretation of any phenomenon depends on the language available to us, bringing with it particular theoretical entailments. The meaning of everyday behaviour and even the very fabric of society are woven into our ordinary vocabulary.[73] It is also clear that the meaning we attach to human actions depends on the particular circumstances with which we are dealing. Importantly, social structures and institutions play a large role in determining our actions. Secord seeks to clarify the situation, telling us that while social structures have real effects, they are different from natural structures in that they do not exist independently of our conceptions; nevertheless, they precede the individual. Such 'structures preceded the entrance of individuals into society, and individuals act within them as a medium'.[74] This is a view I endorsed in Chapter 2.

Additionally—as has been pointed out already—language, including the language used in the social disciplines, is inherently metaphorical. Similarly, the interpretation of any text and of any situation is dependent largely on historically situated conventions. Gergen draws our attention to the way in which the particular literary figures used dominate the process of interpretation.[75] He reminds us that, once a particular metaphor is selected, it restrains what else can be said. The root metaphors differ across the social disciplines, providing different perspectives—ideologies even—which are difficult to reconcile.[76] These stories—these definitions of ourselves—reflect to some extent the stories that social researchers tell. Our stories, therefore—our language games—cannot be objective or normatively neutral, as we will see in greater detail in the next chapter. While this is also true of the natural sciences, there is almost a qualitative difference in the extent to which these respective disciplines can aspire to objectivity. One further consequence is that generalisations in the social disciplines are generally narrow in scope.[77] Nagel suggests:

> [The] conclusions reached by controlled study of sample data drawn from one society are not likely to be valid for a sample obtained from another society. Unlike the laws of physics and chemistry, generalisations in the social sciences therefore have at best only a severely restricted scope, limited to social phenomena occurring during a relatively brief historical epoch within special institutional settings.[78]

Similarly, Gergen tells us that there are few patterns of human action that are not subject to significant alteration, while cultural anthropologist Roy D'Andrade records that the different fields of science have different canons of generalisation.[79] While researchers aspire to tell integrative stories, it could be simply inappropriate for social researchers to seek to emulate the natural sciences in an attempt to derive 'fundamental general laws' describing human conduct. Cronbach argues that this particular idealisation of scientific research—the development of general lasting laws on the model of parts of physics[80] —is not achievable in the social disciplines.[81] It might also not be achievable in much of the natural sciences. Nor is there any good reason to expect a unity of method across the social disciplines. On the contrary, Fiske tells us that such knowledge is fragmented, composed of multiple discrete parcels—a consequence of the different objects of inquiry and different methods of knowing. As a result, these bodies of knowledge are likely to always remain separate.[82] In particular, generalisations and theories in the social disciplines are rarely abandoned because most conceptual statements in those disciplines are formulated in such a way that they cannot be falsified. Fiske suggests that, in part, some of these difficulties arise because of too high a level of aspiration on the part of the social researcher.

All of this suggests that a strong onus lies with the theorist intent on developing systems of interrelated generalisations in a particular area of human activity to demonstrate that such generalisations do exist and then to delineate their scope. Consequently, the question arises as to whether neoclassical economics has discharged that obligation. I think not. As Ormerod tells us, the idea that people respond to economic incentives could be a universal generalisation, but the strength of any response to any particular set of incentives is emphatically not universal; it depends on the social, institutional and historical context. Human beings are not compelled to act by social 'forces' in the same deterministic way that natural phenomena respond to natural forces. Weber suggested therefore that the natural sciences were concerned with *erklären* or explaining focused on causality, while the social disciplines were concerned with *verstehen* or understanding. Such things as meaning, intention, ideas, values and emotions were, according to Descartes, non-things and were beyond the reach of the mechanical sciences.[83]

One approach used in an attempt to get around this problem is to consider reasons as causes. While Weber agreed that there was a logical distinction between natural and social reality, he did not believe that these differences required different scientific methods. He believed that uniqueness and historicity were features of natural as well as social phenomena. In any event, with his positivist, rationalist bent, Weber sought a rigorous method that would enable claims made about the social world to be subjected to empirical validation. While Weber accepted that no conceptual system could do full justice to the complexity of particular social phenomena, the tool he adopted for this purpose was the concept of an 'ideal type'—an idea used also by Mill and his contemporaries. This idea—a reflection of the perfectionism and transcendentalism embedded in Western thought and in particular the positivism popular at the time—is the conceptual source of the idealisation of the market in economics. An ideal type is an analytical construct, a rationalised reconstruction, a stereotype, a fiction even, deliberately exaggerating what are thought to be typical actions to produce a coherent whole in an attempt to get to the essence of a social reality—assuming in the process that there is such an essence to be got at. As such, it looks suspiciously like an attempt to revive Plato's forms in the context of the social disciplines. The ideal type was to be derived inductively from historical reality, though it would never correspond with reality. Importantly, Weber thought this tool could be applied only to social behaviour that was rational and goal oriented, which he believed was increasingly dominating Western society. In this regard, it is important to remember that Weber conceived of four different orientations towards social action—instrumentally rational, value rational, affective and traditional—though these categories were not intended to provide an overall classification. As we will see in the next chapter, the rational, instrumental nature of much economic activity is open to devastating criticism. In these circumstances—on the basis of Weber's own qualification—it can hardly be assumed to apply to economics.

Furthermore, the technique is open to misinterpretation resulting from the common metaphysical assumption that 'scientific laws' are authoritative—that is, that they determine the way the world is (that scientific generalisations, 'laws', are causal agents) rather than being simply descriptions of the way the world is. In the absence of a god—conceived of as a lawmaker, dictating the laws of nature and of human conduct in the way that the Enlightenment and Smith had assumed—it is hard to imagine where any authoritative force could come from. No one these days, however, thinks that the invisible hand of the market is the hand of God. Perhaps, given Weber's restriction of this method to the analysis of rational social action, it is rationality that is to provide this authoritative force. If so, it will just not do. To claim that the world is inherently rational or even mathematical, as the Pythagoreans thought, is only to postpone the question momentarily, as well as to overlook the problematic nature of those concepts. What gives rationality or mathematics an authoritative force? In any event, the critique of rationalism and mathematics in Chapter 5 undermines all such pretensions. Additionally, the work of the Nobel Prize-winning economists Simon, Daniel Kahneman and Vernon Smith on our cognitive limitations has undermined it at the empirical level. The fact that scientific laws do not have authoritative force has another important implication: the natural and social worlds are not, in principle, ultimately explicable.

If, on the other hand, one assumes that social laws are simply attempts at describing the way the social world is, the meaning to be ascribed to any such 'laws' based on unrealistic idealisations is problematic. While it might be interesting to some people to speculate about how people might behave if they were entirely economic beings, the value of such speculation and their 'tendency laws' to policy decision is far from certain when we all know that the assumption is false. Such idealisation is a highly reductionist strategy, with its origins in ancient Greek atomism, which attempts to reduce physical reality to fundamental and identical particles. One can complain justly that economic systems cannot be dissected in this fashion. Weber was not aware of the difficulties later theorists found in modelling interdependent complex systems. They are not open to this reductive strategy. Importantly, the idea that the factors left out can be added back in to form a more complete description—for example, the idea that economic analysis deals with 'tendency laws'—assumes that such entities are separable in the first place and are independent. They might not be if, for example, we are dealing with non-linear dynamic systems.[84] If they are not independent and it is improbable that they would be, such influences cannot simply be added together. Complex or non-linear dynamics could produce multiple possible solutions, while even very small changes in initial conditions could produce drastic changes in outcomes.

What this means is that human behaviour is not describable by simple deterministic models. Such reductionism has a systematic bias in that it ignores or over-simplifies the importance of the context of the system being studied.[85] This simplification of the context 'also often legislates higher-level systems out of existence or leaves no way of describing inter-systemic phenomena appropriately'.[86] Indeed, 'assumptions that appear benign at such an individual level may be dangerous over-simplifications when viewed from a higher level'.[87] This is, of course, what we find with Margaret Thatcher's claim that there is no such thing as society and with the methodological individualism practised by economics. It is this reductionism and methodological individualism that leads directly to the modelling of society as if it is based on self-serving individuals.

I have already drawn attention to the fact that this modelling is not a neutral strategy, and have expressed concern about the potential impact of such modelling on society itself. This concern leads me to question whether methodological individualism is a legitimate, albeit potentially dangerous, analytical strategy or simply a cloak disguising the ideological prejudices embedded in neoclassical economic analysis. If our study is intended to influence our policy decisions—and if there are reasons to believe that there are higher-level social structures that impact on our social problems—we are honour bound to study them. Additionally, the conclusions drawn from such simplifying assumptions could simply be the artefacts of those assumptions with little or no connection with the phenomena that we are supposed to be studying.

A further problem surrounds how to choose the ideal type—what is to sit within the system to be examined and what sits outside as the 'context'. This is hardly a normatively neutral exercise and it is a problem for which no persuasive answer has been given. A further and fundamental question surrounds whether such ideal types lead to generalisations that are, in fact, empirically falsifiable. Given what was said above, they certainly cannot be verified. We will return to this topic in Chapter 8 when we discuss the content of economics more directly. It is important in the interim to remember that while Weber was a positivist, he never intended these ideal types to be used as normative ideals. For Weber, any understanding of causation in the social disciplines is a result of 'an interpretative understanding of social action and involves an explanation of relevant antecedent phenomena as meaning-complexes'.[88] This seems a far cry from the deterministic, mechanical modelling of neoclassical economics.

In 1953, American economist Milton Friedman (1912–2006) offered a radical and highly influential new defence of economic idealisation in *The Methodology of Positive Economics*. Friedman accepted that experience reflected the complex influences of numerous causes and therefore could support numerous interpretations. This is consistent with the position taken here. Friedman believed that it was possible to subject our policy beliefs to empirical test and that the role of economic theory was to provide a system of generalisations able to generate predictions that could be checked against experience. Because no decisive disproof was possible of any hypothesis, however, we should have confidence only in those hypotheses that survived many tests and performed consistently better than the alternatives. Friedman was interested only in empirically meaningful and testable hypotheses as an engine of analysis for the problem at hand, rather than as a description of reality. For Friedman, the reality of a hypothesis was simply irrelevant. He claims that 'the more significant the theory, the more unrealistic the assumptions…To be important a hypothesis must be descriptively false in its assumptions…the relevant question to ask about the "assumptions" of a theory is not whether they are descriptively "realistic", for they never are.'[89]

To most of us this seems transparent nonsense—a further *ad hoc* rationalisation to defend the indefensible. Perhaps, however, he was just confused, as claimed by leading institutional economist Geoffrey Hodgson[90] and applied economist Daniel Bromley.[91] Hodgson points out that this position is not only theoretically incoherent; it has not been adopted in practice.[92] Hodgson draws a distinction between different kinds of assumptions: negligibility, domain and heuristic. Negligibility is where some factor will have a negligible impact on the result; domain assumptions specify the domain in which the theory is applicable; and heuristic assumptions are simplifying assumptions made in the early stages of a theory to allow successive approximations. Hodgson argues that Friedman is talking about negligibility assumptions and that it is not true that such assumptions are descriptively false, only that they have a negligible influence on the phenomenon being explained and consequently can safely be disregarded. Clearly, the core assumptions of neoclassical economics are not ones leaving out factors that have a negligible influence, but are truly descriptively false. This does matter.

Of course, Friedman's claims could be defended on the instrumental ground that the truth of a theory is irrelevant and that all that matters is the accuracy of the resulting prediction. Surely, however, the objective of such studies is not simply to make predictions—desirable though that might be—but rather to provide credible explanations? This is the generally accepted position in the philosophy of science. This instrumental approach would eliminate explanation and falsification from science and that should be the end of the matter. Friedman does not apply this criterion consistently in his own work. Rather, he uses Popper's falsification criterion in the case of the maximisation hypothesis. He neglects, however, to provide any relevant evidence for his claims and asserts that a failure of critics to develop any coherent, self-consistent alternative provides evidence of the worth of the maximisation idea. In any event, it is extremely doubtful that this approach has, in fact, led to successful prediction. Indeed, given the complex nature of economic systems and the sensitivity of non-linear models to initial conditions, the very possibility of making reliable predictions is being undermined.

German philosopher Wilhelm Dilthey (1833–1911) goes further than Weber, contrasting *verstehen* with *erklären* and suggesting that natural and social reality are different kinds of reality requiring different investigative methods—a position more in line with the position taken here.[93] British sociologist Anthony Giddens describes this aspect of the social disciplines as a 'double hermeneutic':

> The theory-laden character of observation-statements in natural sciences entails that the meaning of scientific concepts is tied to the meaning of other terms in a theoretical network; moving between theories or paradigms involves hermeneutic tasks. The social sciences, however,

imply not only this single level of hermeneutic problems, involved in the theoretical meta-language, but also a 'double hermeneutic', because social-scientific theories concern a 'pre-interpreted' world of lay meanings. There is a two-way connection between the language of social science, and ordinary language. The former cannot ignore the categories used by laymen in the practical organization of social life; but on the other hand, the concepts of social science may be taken over and applied by laymen as elements of their conduct. Rather than treating the latter as something to be avoided or minimised as far as possible, as inimical to the interests of 'prediction', we should understand it as integral to the subject–subject relation involved the social sciences.[94]

There has been a broad recognition that a proper understanding of the social disciplines requires an appreciation of the hermeneutical dimension of them. In fact, there is a convergence between the insights of the hermeneutical tradition and the insights derived from the pragmatism that is influencing the philosophy of science outlined above. As Gadamer tells us:

> When Aristotle, in the sixth book of the *Nichomachean Ethics*, distinguishes the manner of practical knowledge…from theoretical and technical knowledge, he expresses, in my opinion, one of the greatest truths by which the Greeks throw light on the 'scientific' mystification of modern society of specialisation. In addition, the scientific character of practical philosophy is, as far as I can see, the only methodological model for self-understanding of the human sciences if they are to be liberated from the spurious narrowing imposed by the model of the natural sciences.[95]

For Aristotle, there were three intellectual virtues: *epistēmē*, *phronēsis* and *techne*. As we have already seen, *epistēmē* is the kind of certain geometric knowledge to which the natural sciences aspire. *Phronēsis* is the kind of practical wisdom we all use in the expert social practice and moral judgements we make in day-to-day life; this was, for Aristotle, the most important of the intellectual virtues.[96] *Techne* is technical knowledge or technology. For Aristotle—as for Toulmin, Gadamer, Mary Hesse and Bent Flyvbjerg—it is *phronēsis* that provides the appropriate methodological model for the social sciences. From this perspective, the natural and social sciences are simply different intellectual ventures. In short, not only have the social sciences—including economics—not achieved practical success in providing certain predictive epistemic theory, they cannot in principle aspire to that certain geometric knowledge of *epistēmē*. Importantly, it is a view that denies that knowledge of human activity can ever be universal and context-independent in the same way as knowledge in the natural sciences. As Flyvbjerg—following Dreyfus—argues, 'a theory which makes possible explanation and prediction, requires that the concrete context of everyday human activity be excluded, but this very exclusion of context makes explanation and prediction impossible'.[97]

The actors in a concrete situation will not necessarily conceive of any action in the same way that any attempt at a context-free definition of a social action based on abstract rules or laws might do. Importantly, context-dependence does not imply a more complex form of determinism but an open, contingent relationship between context, action and interpretation. Consequently, it is not meaningful to speak of theory in the natural science sense in the social disciplines. We will return to the ontological consequences of context and openness for neoclassical economics in Chapter 8. This limitation of the disciplines is no real failing, as *epistēmē* in turn cannot provide the reflective analysis of values that is at the heart of political, economic and cultural life. In this spirit and consistent with Toulmin, Flyvbjerg calls for the social sciences to be restored to their classical position as practical intellectual activities, clarifying the problems, risks and possibilities involved in social and political praxis.

Bernstein and prominent American economist Deirdre McCloskey tell us that part of the problem arises from the English word 'science' and the distinctions we English speakers make between the natural sciences, the social sciences and the humanities. In contrast, in German, a distinction is made between the natural sciences and the moral sciences only. The consequence has been that English speakers tend to think of the social sciences as natural sciences concerned with individuals in their social relations, on the assumption that the social sciences differ in degree but not in kind from the natural sciences. In contrast, German speakers have a much greater tendency to think of the social disciplines as moral sciences, sharing essential characteristics with the humanities. McCloskey goes on to advocate the adoption of the word 'discipline' to describe these social investigations.

From this perspective, the sciences should be seen as a confederation of enterprises, with methods and patterns of explanation to meet their own distinct problems—not the varied parts of a single, comprehensive, 'unified science'.[98] The Platonic image of a single, formal type of knowledge is replaced by a picture of enterprises that are always in flux and whose methods of inquiry are adapted to the nature of the case. Importantly, the belief that we can start again by cutting ourselves off from inherited ideas is as illusory as is the hope for a comprehensive system of theories. The hope for certainty and clarity in theory has to be balanced with the impossibility of avoiding uncertainty and ambiguity in practice. We need to reappropriate the reasonable, tolerant, but neglected legacy of humanism more than we need to preserve the systematic, perfectionist legacy of the exact sciences. In particular, formal calculative rationality can no longer be the only measure of intellectual adequacy; one must also evaluate all practical matters by their human 'reasonableness'. Consequently, for Toulmin:

> [T]he charms of logical rigour must now be unlearned. The task is not to build new, more comprehensive systems of theory with universal and timeless relevance, but to limit the scope of even the best-framed theories, and fight the intellectual reductionism that became entrenched during the ascendancy of rationalism. It calls for more subdisciplinary, transdisciplinary, and multidisciplinary reasoning.[99]

In particular, Toulmin believes that biology provides less constricting analogies for thinking about social relations than does physics. In the organic world, diversity and differentiation are the rule and not the exception. The universality of physical theories is rare. In this spirit, Wimsatt recommends that, in studying human behaviour, we should use a variety of models and approaches in the hope that we can thereby detect and correct for biases, special assumptions and the artefacts of any one approach.[100] This perspective sees science as being like other human investigations employing a variety of heuristics that, while not guaranteeing success, is the best we can do. A reductionist, mathematical deductive heuristic is only one possible approach to such modelling. While I am not rejecting the mechanistic modelling of neoclassical economics in its entirety, I am cautioning that it provides only one limited perspective, which could well be mistaken, and there might be more fruitful metaphors. Importantly, it is up to the advocates of reductionism and mathematical deduction to demonstrate its usefulness—particularly as a policy tool—to a justifiably sceptical audience. Furthermore, rather than clinging stubbornly to physics envy and the illusion of certainty provided by what appears to be a degenerating research strategy, economists should learn to embrace pluralism for the richness of the insights it can provide. In particular, economists should open themselves more fully to the possibility of explanation at various levels of organisational complexity throughout the economic system and not stick stubbornly to a reductionist story.

It is within such a framework that American anthropologist Barbara Frankel—drawing on Bateson and Mead—suggests that it might not be forces and objects that are central to human action but rather the information and messages that define the social context and order behaviour within those contexts.[101] She argues, in particular, that there is a danger of confusing biological individuals with social persons—leading to an inability to deal conceptually with contexts and meanings—as opposed to objects and forces. She suggests, therefore, that it might be more appropriate to consider the selves studied by the social disciplines as the sum of an individual's achieved and ascribed social roles, as nodes in a network of communications, avoiding the distraction of biological boundaries. Consequently, she suggests that we need to take seriously 'the notion of social persons created by and existing only within systems of interaction, and as bounded, not by the skins of biological individuals, but by contextual boundaries that may be…of indefinite extent'.[102]

One consequence of the positivist approach to the social sciences and the associated attempt to appropriate the prestige associated with the natural sciences has been to suppress political and moral discourse, to confer a privileged position on the *status quo* and on the professional expert with a capacity for judgement based on the unsustainable claim to technical expertise, neutrality and impartiality. All of this should lead us to be wary—as leading American legal theorist Grant Gilmore (1910–82) advises—of abstract and impersonal values, of universal solutions and of logical imperatives[103] within economics, the law and social life more generally. We should also be wary of grand theory, sacred rules and mystical absolutes that have little connection to reality—especially since we have been taught to be wary of such claims in our spiritual life. As legal historian Morton Horwitz confirms, the belief in the explanatory possibility of general laws capable of making predictive statements in the social sciences has plummeted: 'The result has been a dramatic turn towards highly specific "thick description" in which narrative and stories purport to substitute for traditional general theories…a complex, multi-factored interdependent world has lost confidence in single-factor "chains of causation" that were embedded in most nineteenth-century explanatory theories.'[104]

In this spirit, English economist Edward Fullbrook recently argued for pluralism among the knowledge narratives with which we organised and interpreted experience, each of which would offer a different view of the object of inquiry.[105] This is because all representations—even the most sophisticated and comprehensive of scientific narratives—involve a radical, stylised and somewhat arbitrary simplification of reality, a choice among an infinite number of possible perspectives or conceptual frameworks. Such a choice rests ultimately on the explanatory usefulness of the narrative and the entities it connects. Fullbrook cites American-born quantum physicist David Bohm in support:

> What is called for is not an *integration* of thought, or a kind of imposed unity, for any such imposed view would itself be merely another fragment. Rather, all our different ways of thinking are to be considered as different ways of looking at the one reality, each with some domain in which it is clear and adequate. One may indeed compare a theory to a particular view of some object. Each view gives an appearance of the object in some aspect. The whole object is not perceived in any one view but, rather, it is grasped only *implicitly* as that single reality which is shown in all these views.[106]

Any such perspective brings with it a system for classifying the empirical domain, which in turn limits possible descriptions, possible facts, possible questions and possible stories and thus uniquely circumscribes our possible understanding of reality. In particular, the meaning of any concept depends on the framework within which it appears. Viewing a domain from a new perspective brings with it the possibility of new dimensions of understanding. Fullbrook goes on to distinguish between closed narratives such as those of Newtonian mechanics and neoclassical economics and open narratives such as those of evolution, which admit indeterminacy arising from chance, contingency, choice, uncertainty, randomness and spontaneity. In the process, he challenges the hegemony of such closed narratives and the hostility they exhibit to 'alien' and open narratives. Rather, he argues that a plurality of narratives enriches our understanding and is essential to the advancement of knowledge.

It might be thought that a rejection of the search for general criteria for judging theories poses problems when it comes to judging economic theories.[107] The undermining of the pretensions of science should not, however, detract us from the task of reasonable judgement in research. It seems that we just have to learn to live with the understanding that all knowledge is a social and linguistic construct, and that this applies with particular force to the social disciplines. Recognition of these difficulties does not justify the proposition that empirical tests are unnecessary. The fact that we are unable to guarantee the truth of a proposition—fulfilling utopian demands of the rationalists—does not absolve us from attempting to develop the best methods we can, even in the absence of an absolute criteria for 'best'. In particular, it provides no excuse for a failure to take falsification seriously or to subject our theoretical speculative narratives to serious examination. On the contrary, it should provide a good reason to take these tasks and narrative pluralism much more seriously. The awareness of the limitations of one's tools and how best to use them does not provide an excuse for using them badly—or not using them at all—but rather points to the need to develop the ability to employ them skilfully and honestly. Nor does it license a sloppy use of statistical inference within economic research—a practice that McCloskey has documented.

Of course, it is a standard critique of neoclassical economics that it has abandoned realistic assumptions and has insulated its core beliefs from empirical testing, and does not meet the canons of any reasonable methodology. We will discuss these implications for economics in greater detail in Chapter 8.

Summary

Summing up, it can be concluded that the claim that science has a privileged epistemological status in virtue of its empirical basis cannot be sustained. Rather, scientific and other inquiry uses much the same approach—a conclusion that applies in particular to normative reasoning. Against this background, the next chapter will turn to the examination of two interrelated issues—the distinction that has been made between positive and normative theorising, and the status of economics—before going on to consider the suggestion that economists should study moral philosophy.

ENDNOTES

[1] Medieval saying attributed to Aristotle, apparently derived from a passage in the *Nicomachean Ethics*.
[2] Oakeshott 1962.
[3] Rorty 1991.
[4] Kincaid 1996.
[5] Levine 1986.
[6] Polanyi 1946, p. 34.
[7] Nagel 1961.
[8] Winch 1970.
[9] Secord 1986.
[10] Davies 2004b.
[11] Davies 2007.
[12] Turner 1987.
[13] Swartz 1995.
[14] Blaug 1980. This story draws heavily on Blaug's account, supplemented by the other references cited.
[15] Webb 1995.
[16] Crotty 1998.
[17] Webb 1995.
[18] Kincaid 1996.
[19] Fiske 1986, p. 2.
[20] Fiske and Shweder 1986.
[21] Blaug 1980.
[22] Kincaid 1996.
[23] Crotty 1998, p. 64.
[24] Ibid.
[25] Ibid.
[26] Kincaid 1996.
[27] Bernstein 1983.
[28] Bernstein 1983, pp. 24–5.
[29] Hanson 1958.
[30] Popper 1959, pp. 278–81.
[31] Ibid., p. 111.
[32] Blaug 1998.
[33] Kuhn 1970.
[34] Crotty 1998.
[35] Kuhn 1977, p. 234.
[36] Rorty 1980.
[37] Bernstein 1983.
[38] Kuhn 1970.
[39] Bernstein 1983.
[40] Ibid.
[41] Cited in Bernstein 1983, p. 57.
[42] Blaug's account emphasises the extent to which Kuhn backed away from his earlier position, but this is not a shared view.
[43] Feyerabend 1993.

44 Shweder 1986, p. 172.
45 Crotty 1998.
46 Campbell 1986.
47 Wimsatt 1986.
48 Rorty 1980, p. 170.
49 Webb 1995.
50 Rorty 1980.
51 Ibid.
52 Ibid.
53 Phillips 1986.
54 Peirce 1934.
55 Mead 1934.
56 Gadamer 1975a, p. 312.
57 Ibid., p. 316.
58 Albert 1987, p. 79.
59 Secord 1986.
60 Richter 1986.
61 Wimsatt 1986.
62 Outhwaite 1987.
63 Schostak 2002.
64 Ibid., pp. 2–3.
65 Ibid.
66 Kincaid 1996.
67 Fiske and Shweder 1986, pp. 369–70.
68 Kincaid 1996.
69 Ibid., p. xv.
70 Winch 1958.
71 Bernstein 1983.
72 Wimsatt 1986.
73 Secord 1986.
74 Ibid., p. 215.
75 Gergen 1986.
76 Shweder 1986.
77 Fiske and Shweder 1986.
78 Nagel 1961, p. 459.
79 D'Andrade 1986.
80 Converse 1986.
81 Fiske and Shweder 1986.
82 Fiske 1986.
83 Fiske and Shweder 1986.
84 Richter 1986.
85 Wimsatt 1986.
86 Ibid., pp. 301–2.
87 Ibid., p. 305.
88 Crotty 1998, p. 69.
89 Friedman 1966, p. 14.
90 Hodgson 1988.
91 Bromley 1990.
92 Hodgson 1988.
93 Crotty 1998.

[94] Giddens 1977, p. 12.

[95] Bernstein 1983, p. 39.

[96] Flyvbjerg 2001.

[97] Ibid., p. 40.

[98] Toulmin 1992.

[99] Toulmin 1990, p. 193.

[100] Wimsatt 1986.

[101] Frankel 1986.

[102] Ibid., p. 360.

[103] Gilmore 1974.

[104] Horwitz 1992, pp. vi–viii.

[105] Fullbrook 2007.

[106] Bohm 1983, cited in ibid.

[107] Backhouse 1992.

Chapter 7: What, Then, Can We Say of the Status of Economics?

> I think that Aristotle was profoundly right in holding that ethics is concerned with how to live and with human happiness, and also profoundly right in holding that this sort of knowledge ['practical knowledge'] is different from theoretical knowledge. A view of knowledge that acknowledges that the sphere of knowledge is wider than the sphere of 'science' seems to me to be a cultural necessity if we are to arrive at a sane and human view of ourselves or of science.
> — Hilary Putnam[1]

Introduction

In the previous two chapters, we looked at the critique that has developed of the Enlightenment project and the implication of that critique for the status of science in general. That critique challenges also the right of reason and philosophy to be the final arbitrators of moral issues.[2] The Enlightenment's utopian search for *epistēmē* in moral, political, economic, legal and social theory more generally has failed and will continue to fail. It is now time to turn towards a more detailed application of those ideas to economics. This is necessary because most practising economists retain positivist methodological beliefs that philosophers have long since abandoned.[3] As we have seen above, no science and particularly no social discipline can claim to produce absolute knowledge. Rather, the insights of any conversation, of any story, of any discipline, are forever subject to revision. Economics has sought to appropriate the prestige attached in modern societies to the natural sciences because of their success in the past several centuries in unravelling some of the mysteries of the natural world. Accordingly, we saw the claim in Chapter 1 that economics is the universal grammar of the social sciences—or, as some would say, the queen of the social sciences. A little later, I will have something to say about the attempt of economics to appropriate the particular language of physics. For the moment, however, let us concentrate on the distinction that economists claim can be made between positive and normative theorising.

The Distinction Between Positive and Normative Theorising, Particularly in Economics

The attempt of Enlightenment philosophers to give a naturalistic, individualistic, 'scientific' and universal account of our moral codes was recounted above. Intertwined was the attempt to insulate that account from any divine authority, while at the same time trying to base those codes on empirical observation of human nature. The natural-law tradition—so central to Locke's justification of his social-contract theory—became increasingly secularised over several centuries. The effect of those attempts was merely to justify existing moral and political arrangements. Since then, much social thought has been preoccupied with finding a method that will either determine values objectively or avoid questions about values altogether.[4]

Notwithstanding the ambitions of Hobbes and Locke and their successors to found our moral judgements on science, recent social scientists have generally made a distinction between science and normative theorising. As a result, it is often claimed that value judgements lack the objective validity of science, and science must, as a methodological ideal, be kept free from them.[5] Similarly, economists have usually drawn a distinction between positive and normative economics. It has, of course, been admitted readily that the application of the 'positive' science of economics to real public policy problems is a normative issue. This—somewhat deceptively—usually took the form of suggesting that it was in the choice of ends that the normative issue arose, while positive economics could safely address the best way of achieving those specified ends. The fact that ends and means are usually intertwined escaped notice.

It should already be clear to the reader from the account in previous chapters that the idea of a value-free social discipline is not possible. All social knowledge and moral narratives are stories told from a particular normative perspective, employing language imbued with normative values. As Webb tells us, '[T]here is no human action of any importance which does not become imbued with moral and normative significance and hence develops an abstract and symbolic dimension.'[6]

The distinction between the positive and the normative is usually traced to Hume, who is taken to have held that there is a watertight distinction to be made between the realm of facts and the realm of values:

> I have always remark'd, that the author proceeds for some time in the ordinary way of reasoning, and establishes the being of a God, or makes observations concerning human affairs; when of a sudden I am surpriz'd to find, that instead of the usual copulation of propositions, *is*, and *is not*, I meet with no proposition that is not connected with an *ought*, or an *ought not*. This change is imperceptible, but is, however, of the last consequence. For as this *ought* or *ought not*, expresses some new relation of affirmation, 'tis necessary that it should be observ'd and explain'd; and at the same time that a reason should be given for what seems altogether inconceivable, how this new relation can be a deduction from others, which are entirely different from it. But as authors do not commonly use this precaution, I shall presume to recommend it to the readers.[7]

In economics, the distinction was picked up by Nassau Senior and Mill,[8] and was subsequently endorsed by Weber[9] and Robbins.[10] As such, it formed part of the process by which economics shed any overt moral, historical and institutional concerns and was transformed into a mathematical discipline. This transformation reflected the growing influence of positivism with its view that true scientific knowledge was divorced from metaphysical beliefs. As already pointed out, it reflected also the growing prestige of Newtonian physics and the desire of economists to emulate what they saw as the archetypical science. Accordingly, it was claimed that economics as a positive science could treat economic processes in isolation from their social environment, narrowing the scope of the discipline significantly.[11] In this formulation, the 'art' of policy formulation was considered to rest in the establishment of attainable policy goals, while the 'science' of political economy furnished the economic frameworks by which the actions of economic actors pursuing their self-interest ensured the attainment of the desired ends. As institutionalist Wesley Mitchell (1874–1948) told us in 1918, however, this move served an important ideological purpose: 'No one can read the Austrian writers, whose general scheme was similar to Jevons', without feeling that they are interested in developing the concert of the maximising of utility largely because they thought it answered Marx's socialistic critique of modern economic organisation.'[12]

Typically and more recently, Richard Lipsey and Colin Harbury made the distinction between positive and normative economics in their introductory textbook.[13]

Macintyre points out that this distinction between facts and values relies on the Enlightenment's dismantling of the Aristotelian teleological tradition of the medieval world, so that it becomes possible to conceive of the individual as prior to and independent of social roles. In contrast, in the medieval world, the argument that a 'ought' could not be deduced from an 'is' was clearly wrong,[14] and remained clearly wrong in any world where socially defined roles continued to exist.[15] Such socially defined and enforced roles carrying normative obligations are, however, an irreducible feature of any real social system, including our own.

The distinction can be traced to the Cartesian mind–body dualism in which facts are said to belong to the 'objective' realm of the body, whereas 'values' are said to belong to the subjective realm of the mind.[16] More recently, the distinction is to be found in the positivist view of science, which considers that all statements other than those that are empirical, logical or mathematical are without content—are nonsense. The idea that economics—while being a scientific discipline—is also a moral discourse is inconsistent with this demand and the latter idea had to be ditched.

Under the influence of Max Weber and the logical positivists, this distinction was transformed into a dualism between facts and values. Only judgements relating to the regularities of empirical phenomena were said to be either true or false, while normative judgements could not be considered in this way—being incapable of objective truth and objective warrant—or could not be considered at all, being left to individual judgement. Carnap, for example, called all non-scientific problems a confusion of pseudo-problems, claiming that all 'statements belonging to Metaphysics, regulative Ethics, and [metaphysical] Epistemology have this defect, are in fact unverifiable and, therefore, unscientific. In the Viennese Circle, we are accustomed to describe such statements as nonsense.'[17]

As Rorty points out, this is effectively a demand that the only language that is cognitively meaningful should resemble the language of physics. Despite the silliness of the claim, it held sway for many years and has come to seem like conventional wisdom within economics. It is also wrong—and, according to leading American philosopher Hilary Putnam, profoundly wrong, being self-refuting! Explanatory theories do not occupy a privileged epistemological position compared with normative theories.[18] Such claims rest on untenable arguments and over-inflated dichotomies.[19] The idea of an absolute dichotomy between 'facts' and 'values' depends on a strict dichotomy, applying to all judgements, between 'analytical' judgements—which are tautological or true by virtue of their meaning—and 'synthetic' judgements, which are subject to empirical falsification (terms borrowed from Kant). In reality, very few things are black or white.

Both these claims provided the foundations for logical positivism, ignoring Kant's own claim that the principles of mathematics were synthetic and analytical. Indeed, Kant also held that moral judgements could be justified rationally—his moral philosophy being an attempt to do so. Putnam goes on to argue that the fact–value dichotomy has corrupted our ethical reasoning and our descriptions of the world. Further, he disputes whether Hume would have approved of the way in which his advice has been used in an attempt 'to expel *ethics* from the domain of knowledge', because he was an important ethical thinker himself.[20] Putnam also tells us that the original positivist view of a 'fact' was of something that could be certified by mere observation or a report of a sensory experience. As we have seen earlier, however, this view of fact has been discredited thoroughly. Further, the key philosophical terms used by logical positivists—'cognitively meaningful' and 'nonsense'—are not observational terms, theoretical terms or logical/mathematical terms, and yet these are the only kinds of terms that they are prepared to allow in their language of science. They are, therefore, being internally inconsistent. In any event, Quine showed to the satisfaction of most philosophers that scientific statements could not ever be neatly separated into 'conventions' and 'facts', and that the idea was a hopeless muddle:

> The lore of our fathers is a fabric of sentences. In our hands it develops and changes, through more or less arbitrary and deliberate revisions and additions of our own, more or less directly occasioned by the continuing stimulation of our sense organs. It is a pale grey lore, black with fact and white with convention. But I have found no substantial reasons for concluding that there are any quite black threads in it, or any white ones.[21]

Facts and values are deeply entangled throughout our vocabulary. As we have seen in Chapter 6, normative and aesthetic judgements are essential to science itself, being the 'good reasons' used to justify empirical belief. In any event, little in the social disciplines meets Weber's test of universality. On the other hand, many value judgements do meet the criteria specified by Weber: a shared method and adequate data. They are, therefore, in Weber's terms, 'scientific'. What Weber failed to appreciate was that the terms used in the social disciplines were invariably ethically coloured—including in his own description of his 'ideal types'. It could, however, be preferable to speak of the 'justifiability' of a proposition, rather than to use the honorific 'scientific'. It is the shared standards for such truth and knowledge claims that are important, but these standards are determined socially—including, as we have already seen, among the scientific community. What is seen as true or scientifically justified is the result of an organised and contingent consensus among an intellectual or scientific community. Consequently, a normative claim is just as susceptible to justification as any empirical or theoretical claim. The consequence of this line of argument is that the conceptual distinction between positive and normative serves no convincing intellectual purpose, while serving to privilege a particular type of discourse—a political tactic in the broad sweep of discourse.

Science is a learning process, a social process, which develops in some subcultures, and is characterised by the acceptance of an ethic—a strong value system.[22] Knowledge of the social system is an essential part of the social system itself. Consequently, objectivity—in the sense of investigating a world that is unchanged by the investigation of it—is also not achievable. The social disciplines do not merely investigate the world; they simultaneously help create the world that they are investigating. At this point, it is appropriate to recall the point made in Chapter 1 and again in Chapter 6 that the stories we tell and the vocabulary we use create our understanding of who we are and how we should act. What scientific discourse creates becomes a problem of ethical choice. Even the epistemological content of science has an ethical component. Under these circumstances, the concept of a value-free science is untenable.

Leading Swedish economist Gunnar Myrdal (1917–92)—consistent with the constructionist view outlined in Chapter 2—endorsed this point of view:

> Throughout the book [*The Political Element in the Development of Political Theory*] there lurks the idea that when all metaphysical elements are radically cut away, a healthy body of positive economic theory will remain, which is altogether independent of valuations…This implicit belief in the existence of a body of scientific knowledge acquired independently of all valuations is, as I now see it, naïve empiricism. Facts do not organise themselves into concepts and theories just by being looked at; indeed, except within the framework of concepts and theories, there are no scientific facts but only chaos. There is an inescapable a priori element in all scientific work. Questions must be asked before answers can be given. The questions are all expressions of our interest in the world; they are at bottom valuations. Valuations are thus necessarily involved already at the stage when we observe facts and carry on theoretical analysis and not only at the stage when we draw political inferences from facts and valuations.[23]

Valuations are critical to the determination of facts and to all stages of inquiry. Consequently, value commitments are inevitable in the social disciplines. In particular, every social discipline carries an implicit definition of what it is to be human, to provide a focus for its research and to distinguish its field from those of the logician, physicist or biologist.[24] There are, however, no grounds for deciding what is an acceptable definition. It follows that the argument that neoclassical economics is a formal system—which merely explores the implications of its assumptions, the idealisations on which it is based—is not convincing. No one develops such a system for pure pleasure, but to provide a guide to policy decisions or as a justification of their ideological beliefs. Additionally, the assumptions themselves incorporate normative valuations. Furthermore, the social disciplines are moral disciplines by the very nature of the problems they deal with. Scarcity, conflict, inequality, domination, exploitation and war necessarily create problems for a stable and legitimate social order.

In any event, 'social science' is part of the Enlightenment tradition that instrumentalises nature and is now tending to instrumentalise human society itself. The claim for the value neutrality of science—particularly social science—is simply another highly questionable aspect of modernity. For Rorty also, the distinction between facts and values can be sustained only if there is a value-free vocabulary that renders sets of 'factual' statements commensurable.[25] There is, however, no such vocabulary. He argues that in choosing Galileo's vocabulary as a model, science and philosophy have confused its apparent lack of metaphysical comfort and moral significance with the fact that it worked within a particular narrow range. Consequently, the positivists sought to eliminate subjective elements by avoiding terms that could not be linked definitionally to the terms denoting primary qualities in Galileo's and Newton's vocabularies. This is the seventeenth-century myth of nature's own vocabulary—the idea that only a certain vocabulary is suitable for describing human beings or human societies and that it is the only vocabulary in which they can be understood. For Rorty, therefore, the issue between those who seek an objective, value-free, truly scientific social science and those who think it should be acknowledged as something more hermeneutical is not a disagreement about 'method' but a disagreement about the sort of terminology to be used in moral and political reflection.[26] To say that something is better understood in one vocabulary than another is simply a claim that a description in the preferred vocabulary is more useful for a particular purpose.

The growth of scientific and quasi-scientific knowledge has not been as beneficial socially as the Enlightenment imagined it would. The ethos of scientific rationality has consistently undermined and eroded the particular, the local, the implicit and the traditional in the name of individual human emancipation.[27] As scientific knowledge and technical expertise have grown ever more specialised, scientific experts are often able to wield power and authority through their monopolisation of esoteric knowledge and the prestige that this knowledge brings. This is the very criticism I have made of economists throughout this book. Additionally, the uncritical pursuit of social scientific knowledge works to reinforce the existing powers in society that fund that research.[28]

The common thread in this critique is the realisation that the social disciplines have an intrinsic connection with the moral and political life of society.[29] While the social scientist has an obligation to view reality as dispassionately as possible, our perceptions of reality and our assumptions about it are radically moral. There is no neutral platform of pure science utterly free from value commitments. Rather, social science is a product of the development of a particular kind of society and its lexicon. The development of Enlightenment economics clearly took place in parallel with the development of the market system and served to justify that system morally and scientifically. Nowhere is that connection more closely observable than in the period of the ideological conflict between capitalism and communism, when economics was deployed as a 'scientific' justification for the capitalist system.

Consequently, there is a growing body of opinion that again sees social disciplines and economics in particular as moral inquiries. Furthermore, the particular idealisations on which neoclassical economics is based are themselves based on particular ideological commitments, particularly individualism. The distinction becomes even less convincing when placed alongside the real public policy questions on which economists provide advice. Inevitably, they involve leading normative questions. The nature of property rights developed by a society clearly involves normative choices. Pareto-optimality—the major criteria for policy choice used by economists—is dependent on, and biased in favour of, the existing distribution of power, wealth and property rights, and consequently is not normatively neutral. Likewise, the choice of the goal of maximising the value of output is a normative one. Importantly, the price structure itself is not neutral. It is a function of the distribution of income, wealth and power.[30] The question of the regulation of unfair conduct is also a normative one, and the arguments used in that discourse are normative. Indeed, the advocacy of economic efficiency as the general goal of public policy is plainly a moral choice.

Importantly, the policy world is also one in which the distinction between ends and means quickly breaks down. While the distinction could have served to draw attention to the normative content of policy advice, in practice it has been used to camouflage the moral judgements being made by economists and the normative presuppositions of the market system—behind the cloak of alleged scientific objectivity. Consequently, while the idea and ideal of value neutrality persists, the confidence put in it is misplaced.

Among prominent contemporary economists, Daniel Hausman and Michael McPherson agree that the simple picture of the economist providing value-free technical information does not fit the economist who is asked for advice.[31] They summarise that economists should care about moral questions for at least the following four reasons.

1. Behaviour, and hence economic outcomes, is influenced by the moral values of economic agents. Economists rarely describe moral commitments without evaluating them, and they affect that morality by how they describe it. They should, therefore, think about the morality that should be accepted, as well as the morality that is, in fact, accepted in society.

2. Standard welfare economics rests on strong and contestable moral presuppositions. The standard definition of a social optimum compares social alternatives exclusively in terms of their outcomes—rather than the rightness of their procedures—and identifies the goodness of outcomes with satisfaction of individual preferences. These commitments are neither neutral nor uncontroversial. Consequently, they question the moral basis of the concern with efficiency, and whether it is any less controversial than the moral commitments that lie behind equity.

3. Politicians and non-economists talking about welfare employ concepts that do not translate easily into the language of standard economic theory. Ideas of fairness, opportunity, freedom and rights are more important in policy making than individual preference rankings. Equating welfare with the satisfaction of preferences—which could be short-sighted or ill-informed—begs questions of justified paternalism. They question the

quality of a world in which our humanity is always under the control of rational calculation.

4. In practice, positive and normative concerns are often intermingled in policy advice.

Hausman and McPherson point out that economics embodies a commitment to a certain mode of modelling and to a normative theory of prudence. The theory of rationality is already a part of the theory of morality. The view of rationality that economists endorse—utility theory—might not even be compatible with moral behaviour, and does not provide a rich enough picture of individual choice to permit one to discuss the character, causes and consequences of moral behaviour. As Saul says, 'If you confuse self-interest with ethics, you stumble into a false rationality— instrumentalism—in which ethics is meant to be profitable.'[32]

The Questionable Status of Economics within the Human Conversation

This account has already rejected the proposition that there can be such a thing as positive economics. Economics—particularly its application to public policy choices—is inherently normative. The systematic investigation of social phenomena—including economic phenomena—cannot be decried simply because it is normative. It is, however, a lot more difficult than it appeared to Enlightenment philosophers. At best, economics is a normative science, but given the false connotations of the word 'science' in English, it might be better to rename it a normative discipline. The dominant school of economics—neoclassical economics—has involved the application of a particular metaphor to social affairs. This, in itself, is legitimate. There is no other way of proceeding. The Newtonian metaphor is, however, only one among possibly countless numbers of such metaphors, and it might simply be an inappropriate one to use. After all, it is no longer fashionable within physics and that is where it came from. It also follows from the earlier argument that there are no final criteria for determining its worth. The criteria that are used in practice include its simplicity, its usefulness and its elegance—but our understanding of these cannot be tied down. They also are matters of human invention. It is, consequently, up to the advocates of the use of the Newtonian metaphor in economics to convince the rest of us of the worth of their project, independent of the 'truth' claims that were simply assumed by the Enlightenment.

In the spirit of this criticism, McCloskey claims that economics fits poorly within the hypothetical-deductive model of science and that its methodological theory has never been coherent. She recommends that economists turn from such positivism and recognise that what they do is to persuade.[33] She argues that all economists use rhetorical devices such as analogies and appeals to authority as thoroughly as poets and preachers—though with less understanding of why.

There is a danger, however, that a hermeneutical approach to economic analysis could be used to encourage the uncritical acceptance of modern economics.[34] The hermeneutical approach would not oppose the call for much greater empirical testing of economic theories. The falsification criterion is central to the coherence test applauded earlier. While still a minority view within the economics profession, the hermeneutical approach is being taken seriously by some. For example, economists Arjo Klamer and McCloskey[35] claim that economists have begun to see that their talk is rhetorical—an honest argument directed at an audience. This does not warrant a casual indifference to truth as newly understood. Consequently, they question what constitutes economic knowledge. In so doing, they point to specific influential papers as examples: one in the rhetoric of the hypothetical-deductive model of science, but which looks more like a charming metaphor; and another in the rhetoric of empirical finding, but which looks like a reading of history. Furthermore, prior convictions appear to have a large effect on the econometric results of normal economics. They question the point of publishing one's prior convictions dressed up as findings. They go on to argue that 'all conversations are rhetorical' and to recommend 'a rhetorically sophisticated culture for economists, following Richard Rorty in which neither the priests nor the physicists nor the poets nor the Party were thought of as more "rational" or more "scientific" or "deeper" than one another'.[36] They suggest, however, that being a good conversationalist asks for more than following some method. It asks for goodness. Presumably this means serious adherence to the norms of the scientific subculture, including the subjection of claims to serious and honest examination.

In the same spirit, American historian of economic thought Robert Heilbroner (1919–2005) reminded us that for Smith, rhetoric—the art of speaking effectively—was the rock on which economics stood.[37] He sympathises with McCloskey's attack on the pretentious scientism in which economists couch their mutual persuasions. He sees such scientism as dangerous, in that it conceals, or minimises, the elements of judgement and moral valuation that are an intrinsic part of economics. Indeed, for Heilbroner, economics is ideological, by which he means an earnest and sincere effort to explain society as its ideologists perceive it—an effort to speak the truth at all costs: 'What is "ideological" about such an effort is not its hypocrisy but its absence of historical perspective, its failure to perceive that its pronouncements are a belief system, conditioned like all belief systems by the political and social premises of the social order.'[38]

From this perspective, economics is intrinsically normative and directive in that it embodies the constitutive beliefs of its parent society. These beliefs are intrinsically political, in part the result of the self-justifying intentions of their spokespeople. It is also because all societies presuppose structures of subordination and superordination, of cooperation and conflict-resolution and of the justification and use of power. Consequently, all systems of social thought must contain that political character, knowingly and explicitly, or unknowingly and in disguise.

Of course, many economists dismiss methodological questions on the grounds that all the effort to determine whether economics is a science or not has never advanced economics in any practical sense.[39] This is not a tenable position in this inquiry. In practice, economists do pronounce with apparent authority on policy issues. What is the source of that authority?

Can Moral Philosophy Assist Economists in Providing Policy Advice?

The above critique of modernity calls into question the claim that moral and legal reasoning could imitate geometrical forms of argument. As indicated above, this particular idealisation of human rationality—this attempt to legislate how we are to think so as to achieve certainty, to privilege a particular class of stories and story-tellers—has been subject to quite destructive criticism. Contemporary philosopher Christopher Cherniak concludes as a result that 'the pervasively and tacitly assumed conception of rationality in philosophy is so idealised that it cannot apply in any interesting way to actual human beings'.[40]

In the face of these philosophical and methodological conclusions, the extent to which economists can have anything special to say on public policy development as a result of their 'economic expertise' is deeply problematic.

It is, however, at this point that we encounter the superficially helpful suggestion that economists should turn to the study of moral philosophy if they are to offer relevant policy advice. This turn to moral philosophy is, however, no turn at all. It is where economists have been all along—albeit disguised behind mathematical jargon. They seem to have forgotten that Smith, their hero, was a moral philosopher who considered his *Theory of Moral Sentiments* his greatest work. Indeed, neoclassical economics is inherently utilitarian and hedonistic. An appeal from economics to utilitarianism is therefore no more than an appeal from Caesar to Caesar. It is simply a further appeal to the Enlightenment's failed search for *epistēmē* in social, political and moral theorising.

The suggestion assumes that moral philosophy can produce rational answers to the moral questions raised by public policy questions, but it is that very concept of rationality that is in question. In any event, this search for basic principles of ethical action has run into the sand. The metaphysical and teleological superstructures that held the medieval and classical worlds together were dismantled by the Enlightenment project, which began as a rejection of religion as the guarantor of legitimacy and meaning. That project's search for a replacement collapsed and left a vacuum. As MacIntyre concludes, '[I]n spite of the efforts of three centuries of moral philosophy and one of sociology, [we] lack any coherent, rationally defensible statement of a liberal individualist point of view.'[41] The project has privatised all sources of meaning and belief, ensuring that no other tradition can assert itself as the sole claimant of a shared and public conception of good.[42] Saul makes a similar point: 'There is an ever-growing difference between theory and practice—that is, between theories of ethics and the ethical reality we know and understand. The result has been…the irrelevance of much of ethical theory to the ethical lives that people are actually striving to lead.'[43]

Importantly, why should we attach more weight to the pronouncements of philosophers on moral issues than those of other people?[44] There is little reason to believe that the academic practice of moral philosophy has any privileged authority to determine the style and method of thinking on moral matters, what the serious problems are and how they should be characterised.[45] The normative assumption underlying this form of justification is never justified. Apparently, we are somehow required by reason to accept certain basic moral injunctions; but where reason acquires this power to compel is never explained, it is simply assumed. This is a major problem:

> Again and again over the last 2,500 years we have been subjected to the assertion that reason alone allows us to identify and use ethics. The intention has often been good. But the effect each time has been to turn ethics into a creature of reason…It is this assumption about intellectual form which is central to distancing ethics from real use.[46]

Despite their high claims, however, moral philosophers do not start from a blank slate when they begin their system building. They start from an impression of the everyday social reality embodied in culture, language and tradition. For example, at the end of the day, Rawls seeks to justify the norms that he thinks are the critical ones in *his* society and to legislate them. As Saul points out, however, his procedure—which identifies justice with fairness and defines a person's good as the successful execution of a rational plan of life—is embarrassing in its naïvety.[47] Similarly, Yale philosophical theologian Nicholas Wolterstorff—noting that Rawls is trying to resolve the conflict in the American tradition between freedom and equality—questions how one could reasonably expect to extract principles from that American culture that could resolve that conflict.[48] Many other philosophers, including Nozick, could be accused of similar naïvety. In Nozick's case, the fundamental premise that we are born with certain intrinsic rights, which override all other considerations, is simply not true. That is only something that some of us say in a particular cultural environment. The consequence was that at the end of his life Nozick was left wondering why what he thought worked in theory did not work in practice.

For his part, Habermas rejects the idea of value-free inquiry, and instead advances a critical dialectic-hermeneutic approach to social and moral theorising.[49] He distinguishes between practical and technical instrumental knowledge, seeing the practical as the sphere of fully human activity—knowledge of which can be reached only by open human discourse. He believes that there is a crisis of legitimacy in the contemporary capitalist world arising from the fundamental conditions of capitalist societies and the social-welfare responsibilities of mass democracies. While this is a continuing problem for political and social discourse—as political and social theorists have always recognised—this particular crisis lies at the heart of the popular dissatisfaction with economic fundamentalist policy prescriptions. Habermas, however, retains his faith in rational discourse, believing that norms and institutions can be justified through rational discourse and consensus linked to the intention of a good and true life. For Habermas, legitimacy rests on rational justification. He therefore searches for the ideal speech conditions under which rational consensus can be achieved through unrestrained universal discourse. The ideal speech community, he postulates, can then provide a critical standard against which to judge the consensuses reached in practice. In this he is attempting, like Rawls, to define an ideal situation in which agreement can occur. Habermas and Rawls value freedom, rationality, equality and knowledge as essential preconditions for achieving consensus and valid moral principles.

Since we do not live in such a world, we cannot know what would command agreement, and consequently what ethical principles to recommend.[50] Both accounts, however, are important in reminding us that such judgements, to be legitimate, must rest on social consensus. They point to the fundamental importance of maintaining the health of our democratic traditions and institutions in the hope of approaching a basis on which we can all accept the legitimacy of the government's normative decisions. Let us face it, however: our public political discourse is in disarray. In particular, our federal parliament has degenerated into a farce devoted to the manipulation of the electorate, with Question Time a circus involving childish point scoring on all sides. Worse, ill-conceived, rapidly drafted complex legislation is rammed through the parliament with the minimum of examination. We deserve better! More broadly still, dishonesty in public discourse, the manipulative exploitation of the public's fears for political advantage, the demonising of political opponents or other individuals and groups and using public funds to finance political propaganda all threaten our traditions and institutions. As Hitler, Goebbels and Stalin taught us, such conduct is part of a slippery slope that ends in tyranny and death camps.

Accordingly, we need to look to the quality of our public discourse and the real reform of our democratic institutions. I believe, for example, that there is a strong case for a constitutional bill of rights. We should also limit the present excessive power of the prime minister and the Executive. An elected presidency might make sense in providing an additional check to the accumulation of excessive power by the prime minister, as would fixed terms for both houses of parliament and proportional representation in the House of Representatives. In addition, we need to increase the accountability of ministerial staffers. Other highly desirable changes include an independent speaker in the house, a greatly strengthened committee system in the house, senate scrutiny of appointments to the courts and statutory bodies and the restoration of some autonomy and balance to the Australian Public Service. Re-establishing an independent Public Service Board and restoring tenure and appeal rights at senior levels would help the last. In addition, we need to find some way to better balance the influence of central coordinating agencies over other departments. This could involve, in particular, a reduction in the size and influence of the Department of Prime Minister and Cabinet so that it operates more as a coordinating agency rather than as a super department second-guessing and overseeing all others. Similar concerns apply to the excessive influence of the Departments of Treasury and Finance and Administration. Accountants make good servants but poor masters.

Finally, as a community, we have to stop our governments using public funds for party-political advertising. Such conduct is of questionable morality as is systematic pork-barrelling in marginal electorates.

This democratic need is reinforced by the realisation that in practice there are different and incompatible schools in moral and political philosophy, each claiming rational justification.[51] Moral and political justifications take many different forms and people give many different justifications for these judgements. It follows that moral disagreements are the essence of political debate. These conflicting moral and political traditions are embedded in our moral vocabulary, culture and tradition: '[W]e live with the inheritance of not only one, but a number of well integrated moralities. Aristotelianism, primitive Christian simplicity, the puritan ethic, the aristocratic ethic of consumption and the traditions of democracy and socialism have all left a mark on our moral vocabulary.'[52]

Weber made a similar point when he claimed that modern people lived in a world of warring gods, presiding over highly organised but incompatible value systems. The extraordinarily powerful demands of kinship, economics, politics, art, love and science are inconsistent.[53] Indeed, Steven Tipson points out that such moral ideas change their meanings and social usage over time within all cultures.[54]

These incompatible traditions—when taken with the Enlightenment's privatisation of morality—mean that moral values are now often taken to be a matter for individual choice. The practical result is that arguments alone can give no definitive answer to moral questions, and all such philosophers do is disguise the answers they want to give as the verdict of philosophical inquiry.

Thus, 'expert' policy advisers are in a position to pick their school of moral thought to suit their rhetorical and ideological purposes, hiding their choice behind a cloud of impressive rhetoric. Hausman and McPherson warn us also of the many dimensions of moral appraisal and against reducing these many dimensions to one or two.[55] In practice, however, moral discourse seems to be afflicted with a very bad dose of reductionism.

This appeal to moral theory leads to a reliance on theoretical stories to explain moral values rather than real reflection on experience. At the heart of many such theoretical accounts remains the Enlightenment idea that social life is logically secondary to an unconstrained non-social life in which what people do is a matter of their individual 'natural' drives and choices. This psychological vocabulary presupposes an established web of social and moral relationships.[56] Moral justifications are always justifications to somebody who accepts the relevant standard.[57]

Indeed, MacIntyre[58] points out that contemporary moral philosophy is characterised by radical disagreement, interminable arguments and incommensurable premises. There is no rational way of securing moral agreement in our culture. We have competing and conflicting theories. For example, there are deontological theories such as those of Rawls, Nozick and Gerwith, which focus on the individual and usually take duty or rights as the basis of morality. We also have teleological theories, which judge actions on the basis of their consequences alone. From this teleological perspective, we can know whether something is right only if one knows the fundamental aims or ends that our activities are to promote.

The arguments MacIntyre cites are logically consistent, but their premises are such that there is no way of weighing their respective claims.[59] These premises employ quite different normative concepts, so that their claims are of different kinds. Furthermore, there is no established way of deciding between these claims in our society. The invocation of one premise against another is pure assertion and counter-assertion. The different conceptually incommensurable premises of rival arguments can be traced easily to a wide variety of historical origins, but we should not underestimate the complexity of the history and ancestry of such arguments. We need to recognise that the various concepts that inform our moral discourse were originally at home in larger totalities of theory and practice in which they enjoyed a role and function supplied by a context of which they have now been deprived.

This has led MacIntyre to complain that moral philosophy is often written as though the history of the subject were of only secondary and incidental importance. Some philosophers have even written as if moral concepts were timeless, limited, unchanging, determinate species of concept necessarily having the same features throughout their history. The history of ethics demonstrates, however, that moral concepts change as social life changes. For example, the list of virtues in the *Nicomachean Ethics* reflects what Aristotle takes to be the code of a gentleman in contemporary Greek society.[60] To understand a concept is always to learn the grammar that controls the use of such words and so to grasp the role of the concept in language and social life. There are, however, continuities as well as breaks in the history of moral concepts. The complexity is increased because philosophical inquiry itself plays a part in changing moral concepts.

Consequently, it is not clear that an investigation of how a concept is used will yield one clear and consistent account. Furthermore, if part of our ethical knowledge is tacit—as argued in Chapter 2—it might not even be possible to articulate the concepts successfully. Moreover, the current state of moral philosophy involves a whole range of interconnected, different views. The parties to these different views will not agree that they can be settled by empirical inquiry into the way in which evaluative concepts are really used. The ordinary use of moral concepts could on occasions be confused or even perverted through the influence of misleading philosophical theory. For MacIntyre, therefore, it is important for us to discover the narratives we inhabit, recognising that competing groups inhabit incommensurable universes of discourse.[61]

For his part, Rorty questions whether we already possess the moral vocabulary necessary to determine whether we are doing justice to others.[62] He argues that since Kant and Bentham, moral philosophy has identified moral perfection with doing justice to others, taking for granted that we already possess the necessary vocabulary. From this perspective, the problem is to split the difference between Kant and Bentham— between the categorical imperative and the utilitarian principle as formulations of 'the moral law'. This reduction of morality to the moral law has twin roots in the Christian and scientific traditions. On the one side, it is an attempt to update and make respectable the Judaeo-Christian idea that all the laws and the prophets can be summed up in respect for one's fellow humans. On the other hand, it is an attempt to secularise ethics by imitating Galileo's secularisation of cosmology, finding nice, elegant little formulae with which to predict what will happen. Consequently, when Aristotelians, Kierkegaardian Christians, Marxists or Nietzscheans argue that there is more to moral philosophy than that—that we might not yet know the words that will permit us to deal justly with our fellows—they are said to confuse morality with something else, something religious or aesthetic or ideological. When philosophers protest that what is needed is not rules that synthesise the utilitarian principles and the categorical imperative but rather a morally sensitive vocabulary, they are seen as doing something rather odd and 'literary', not to be confused with moral theory.

For Rorty, the difficult moral cases are ones in which we grope for the correct words to describe the situation, not ones in which we are torn between the demands of two principles. The fiction of real moral and political questions being resolved by finding the morally relevant features of the situation—those that can be described in the vocabulary in which classical moral principles are stated—should not be taken seriously. We should not think of our distinctive moral status as being 'grounded' in our possession of mind, language, culture, feeling, intentionality, textuality or anything else. These numinous ideas are simply declarations of our awareness that we are members of a moral community, phrased in pseudo-explanatory jargon. This awareness is something that cannot be further 'grounded'; it is simply taking a certain point of view on our fellow humans. It is the ability to wield complex and sensitive moral vocabularies that counts as moral sophistication. What makes the modern West morally advanced is not a clear vision of objective moral truths but its sense that we are creating morality—a moral text—rather than discovering nature's own moral vocabulary. What needs to be emphasised is that the moral vocabulary does not stand alone, but, in any culture, is supplemented greatly by endless narratives, which aim to explain the way in which the vocabulary should be used.

This emphasis on the existing moral vocabularies stands as a healthy correction to the Platonic system-building tendencies of Western rationalism. Indeed, Wolterstorff argues that we must carry on politics without a foundation. There is no neutral or coherent set of principles—no single story—that can adjudicate such conflicts as that between freedom and equality. Rather, Wolterstorff seeks a unity that emerges from dialogue in a society characterised by religious, moral and philosophical pluralism.[63] In this same spirit, American developmental psychologist Norma Haan looks to the construction of an empirically based, consensual theory of everyday morality.[64] This morality of everyday life is not a capacity that resides exclusively in individuals; it is social exchange in itself. For Haan, several Platonic ideas have obscured the simpler features of everyday morality. For example, it is assumed that for a moral theory to be adequate, it should provide clear and absolute guidance for all the important problems of living. Consequently, formulations of everyday morality have usually been depreciated as being relativistic and inferior.

In the spirit of Toulmin, Haan argues that such absolute claims attract human beings because they seem to deliver the security of moral clarity. Associated with this is an assumption that we can know a complete morality only when it is presented by a higher authority or by morally elite figures. The consequence of this way of thinking is that leaders can then employ morality and manipulate guilt as an instrument of political control. People's deep commitments to their various groups make them highly vulnerable and responsive to this form of manipulation. Leaders' public judgements of moral merit quell the efforts of the disadvantaged to promote their own good: those of lower status are guilty, intrinsically unworthy and have not earned the right to expect more. For Haan, however, everyday morality has no source other than the experience and agreements of people themselves. She therefore questions whether moralities must be in the form of complete, formalised systems, rather than the more proximate forms that emerge from the details of human interchange. In such a morality of everyday life, specialists are not needed. Under the influence of Piaget's work, Haan believes that the mind is active, rational and constructivist, and that morality must, therefore, be inductive and creative rather than compliant and rule deductive. She questions whether it is realistic to consider 'moral character' as a fixed faculty; rather, she sees moral responsiveness as a sensitivity and skill in social interaction. This would seem to require an ability to access the appropriate social text.[65] In this connection, psychology is moving towards the explicit recognition that humans are thoroughgoing social beings from birth and that infants are far less egocentric than previously thought.

When social interaction is taken as the pivotal feature of morality, a different view of moral processes, decisions, guidelines and individual capacities emerges. Moral dialogues occur continuously as major or minor events throughout the life of every person. People have a clear and strong expectation of engaging in moral dialogue as a means of organising the patterns of social thought and interchange. Consequently, moral dialogue can be regarded as the prime moral structure. The question of why people are willing to consider others' moral claims has some empirical answers. Haan[66] considers that people are willing to consider the moral claims of others for the following interrelated, empirical reasons:

- the need to conserve our view of ourselves as moral
- the mismatch between the moral person one thinks one is and the immoral person one is afraid one has been
- enlightened self-interest
- integrity among people, a matter of good faith.

This interactive view puts citizens and society in the difficult role of working constantly to achieve moral agreements. In order to be moral, people must really and authentically participate in building the morality they endorse and use. In particular, for Haan, a just society cannot exist without an interactive morality requiring equitable participation. The more remote justice is from the real experience of people, the less sensible it is for them to accept society as morally legitimated. This is a position very close to that advanced by Habermas—shorn of its Platonic tendencies. It also has much in common with the evolutionary account of the development of moral order advanced in Chapter 2. It is not, however, a position that rejects critical analysis, but it gives far greater weight to other forms of prophetic proclamation.

Conclusion

Earlier I argued that self-interest was not the fundamental ordering principle operating in society. This was in response to the argument from many economists that social norms and social groups could be explained as a result of a voluntary contract between self-interested individuals who made a rational calculation that cooperation was in their long-term interest. Rather it was claimed that human beings have always been social animals drawing their identity from their social relations and from their culture. Consequently, neither the self nor society had explanatory priority. As a result, the methodological individualism inherent in the social contract idea could not be sustained. It was also argued that our moral and legal infrastructures were essential to the social and economic system—the economic system being seen as a subsystem of the social system. An evolutionary account was given of the development of that social system. The neglect of the social underpinnings of economic activity by contemporary economists is surprising given the weight of earlier discussion. An account was provided in the previous chapter of the various ways in which that relationship has been described.

Chapter 4 developed a critique of the foundations of economic fundamentalism, examining a number of closely interrelated themes. The chapter has examined, firstly, the historical emergence of the intellectual basis of modernity and economic fundamentalism, recounting the waning of the medieval idea—inherited from Aristotle through Aquinas—that human beings are social and political beings necessarily involved in a network of social relations. This view was replaced by what was termed the natural-law outlook, in which the divine underpinnings of the inherited idea of natural law were gradually secularised. This was a trend associated with the developments of science and a desire to find a scientific and increasingly more natural explanation of the social order. Therefore, appeals to reason and nature—both increasingly divinised—provided a source of meaning and justification as comprehensive as the religion they had replaced. Social-contract theory emerged to provide a Newtonian and individualistic account of the social and political system. Gradually, the concept of contract replaced law and custom as the source of law and social obligations. Locke's account—with its emphasis on pre-social property rights—was particularly agreeable to the propertied classes. While the various theories recounted did not add up to a coherent whole, they reflected the Enlightenment's ambition to produce a secular, naturalist and rational justification for our moral allegiances and social arrangements.

Economics is the inheritor of this tradition of scientific discourse. This leads directly to the question of what kind of discourse is economics. Is economics a positive science or is it a moral discourse? Notwithstanding the ambitions of Hobbes and Locke and their successors to found our moral institutions on science, in the past century economists have generally made a distinction between positive and normative economics—a distinction traced to Hume's distinction between facts and values. Normative economics involved the application of the positive science of economics to policy problems in which the choice of ends was seen as normative, with positive economics addressing the best way of achieving those ends. It has been argued that it is a mistake to think that explanatory theories occupy a privileged epistemological position compared with normative theories. There is no value-free vocabulary. It was concluded, therefore, that the distinction between positive and normative economics could not be sustained, and that economics was a moral discipline.

The question then arises as to what can be said about the status of economics as a science. It is clear that the positivist pretensions of science—in which scientific progress is viewed as the inclusion of more and more phenomena under natural laws of greater and greater generality—have themselves been undermined. While there is not complete agreement among critics of the positivist view of science, there is broad agreement on essential points. The belief that scientific knowledge is an accurate representation of 'reality' needs to be abandoned. Accuracy of representation is not achievable. Rather, science is a social practice in which knowledge is constructed socially to produce coherence—a social practice that in the physical sciences has just happened to work so far. Consequently, the empirical sciences cannot claim an essential grasp of reality and thus a privileged status.

This is no minor quibble but a fundamental attack on the whole Enlightenment project. What is involved is a decisive break in our world-view. In particular, the Newtonian mechanistic world-view—which has dominated Western thought since the sixteenth century—has been undermined along with any sense of objective certainty in the physical sciences or the political-cultural sphere. As a consequence, we have to live with a profound sense of historical relativism and the belief that there can be no overarching absolute principle that can reconcile all the relativities of human thought and experience. In particular, the possibility of demonstrating the truth of ethical propositions has been undermined. This critique has also undermined the credibility of much economic theorising, particularly its use—at a high level of abstraction—to support arguments for a minimalist government, arguments that have their origins with Locke.

Within the economics profession there are those who are taking this hermeneutical view of science and economics seriously. Others have sought refuge in moral philosophy as a means of supporting their policy recommendations. As might be expected from the critique of rationalism, moral philosophy is itself in disarray. In any event, it is where economists have been all along. Furthermore, the idea that we already possess the moral vocabulary necessary for determining whether we are doing justice for others is disputed. It is the ability to wield a sophisticated moral vocabulary that counts, along with the awareness that we are creating—rather than discovering—morality.

It is against this background of deep scepticism about the claims of economics to moral neutrality that I turn in the next chapter to critique the content of mainstream economic theorising—or what is known as neoclassical economics.

ENDNOTES

[1] Putnam 1978.

[2] Seligman 1992.

[3] de Lavoie 1990.

[4] Horwitz 1992.

[5] Phillips 1986, p. 37.

[6] Webb 1995, p. 29.

[7] Hume 1978, pp. 469–70.

[8] Blaug 1980.

[9] Weber 1949.

[10] Robbins 1932.

[11] Lowe 1965. See also Alvey 1999.

[12] Mitchell 1918, cited in Meszaros 1995.

[13] Lipsey and Harbury 1988.

[14] MacIntyre 1981.

[15] Of course, it could be responded that this does not undermine Hume's logical point, as the concept of a social role involves a hidden moral premise. This response does not, however, deal with the practical implications of MacIntyre's point. People are involved in social roles with socially defined moral responsibilities and to designate the role is also to designate the responsibilities.

[16] Bush 1991.

[17] Carnap 1934, p. 22.

[18] Phillips 1986.

[19] Putnam 2002.

[20] Ibid., p. 20.

[21] Quine 1963, p. 405.

[22] Boulding 1970.

[23] Myrdal 1953, cited in Stark 1971, p. 66.

[24] Haan et al. 1983.

[25] Rorty 1980.

[26] Ibid.

[27] Toulmin 1990.

[28] Haan et al. 1983.

[29] Ibid.

[30] Samuels 1980.

[31] Hausman and McPherson 1996.

[32] Saul 2001.

[33] McCloskey 1994.

[34] Blaug 1980.

[35] Klamer and McCloskey 1988. See also Samuels 1990 and de Lavoie 1990.

[36] Klamer and McCloskey 1988, p. 32.

[37] Ibid., pp. 38–40.

38 Heilbroner 1990, p. 109.
39 Hoover 1995, p. 715.
40 Cherniak 1986, p. 5.
41 MacIntyre 1981.
42 Gascoigne 1994a.
43 Saul 2001 citing Tierney ????, p. 85.
44 Kennedy 1981.
45 Gaita 1991.
46 Saul 2001, pp. 90–1.
47 Ibid.
48 Wolterstorff 1995, cited in Hauerwas 2002.
49 Phillips 1986.
50 Habermas 1998.
51 Hausman and McPherson 1996.
52 MacIntyre 1966, p. 266.
53 Weber 1958.
54 Tipson 2002.
55 Hausman and McPherson 1996.
56 MacIntyre 1981, pp. 17–18.
57 MacIntyre 1966, p. 49.
58 MacIntyre 1981.
59 Ibid.
60 MacIntyre 1966.
61 Hauerwas 2002.
62 Rorty, Richard, Haan et al. 1983.
63 Wolterstorff 1995.
64 Haan et al. 1983.
65 Lacan 1991.
66 Haan et al. 1983, p. 238.

Chapter 8: The Critique of Neoclassical Economics and its Influence on Policy Decisions

Adam's Smith's invisible hand may be invisible because, like the Emperor's new clothes, it simply isn't there; or if it is there, it is too palsied to be relied upon...But let us be quite clear about the epistemological basis of the neoclassical proposition: It is not a deductive proposition...The neoclassical synthesis was put forward as dogma, an article of faith.
— Joseph Stiglitz[1]

Hitherto men have constantly made up for themselves a false conception about themselves, about what they are and what they ought to be. They have arranged their relationships according to their ideas of God or normal man, etc. The phantoms of their brains have gained the mastery over them. They, the creators, have bowed down before their creatures. Let us liberate them from the chimeras, the ideas, dogmas, imaginary beings under the yoke of which they are pining away.
— Karl Marx[2]

Where Are We Going?

Until now, I have confined my account to a critique of the historical, philosophical and scientific foundations of economic fundamentalism, pointing to general concerns about the practical value of economic theorising and the tradition of political and moral theorising of which it forms part. It is now time to turn more directly to the content of that theorising and its impact on economic policy. In this chapter, I propose firstly to make some further preliminary remarks about the influence of mainstream economics on economic policy settings. I then propose to draw attention to the long-running critique of neoclassical economics and the tendency of economists to run up the shutters in defence of their 'normal science'. The account will then turn to the nature of the knowledge that is involved in public policy making and the stubborn search for *epistēmē* rather than for practical wisdom among policy advisers. The account will then move to a description of the consequences of that search for *epistēmē* in the form of the idealisations and unrealistic assumptions of neoclassical economics. These are falsely supposed to result in an analytical situation analogous to the experimental situations of the natural sciences.

We will then take a brief diversion into the normative consequences of that idealisation—the fact that the idealisations assumed have become normative ideals. We will then return to a more detailed description of those flawed assumptions and their implications for faith in unregulated markets. From there, we will move to the formal ontological critique of neoclassical economics, which brings together the above ideas. In the absence of a secure theoretical foundation for economic policy making and the irrelevance of recent dabbling in game theory, I will describe briefly the appreciative justification for competitive markets that the above theoretical story is supposed to underpin. We will then move to the absence of a convincing growth theory in neoclassical economics and then to a brief description of alternative approaches to economic analysis. The chapter ends by drawing attention to proposals for the reform of economic teaching.

Mainstream Economics

It is important to note as a first step that mainstream economics is divided into two streams of theorising: macro and microeconomics. Macroeconomics is the study of the behaviour of the economy as a whole. It studies such things as aggregate trends in national income, unemployment and inflation. Microeconomics takes a bottom-up view of economic activity, abstracting from the institutional framework within which the economy operates and attempting to study the demand for goods and services, the formation of prices and the allocation of resources. It provides one of the central intellectual underpinnings for economic fundamentalism and its worship of markets.

Economic fundamentalism has influenced macro and micro policy—for example, influencing the willingness of governments to run budget deficits and to finance infrastructure investment through borrowings, the degree of independence given to monetary authorities, the policy emphasis given to monetary stability over full employment and the heed paid to the views of the financial industry and financial journalists on policy settings more generally. Perhaps the most pernicious recent influence of economic fundamentalism in Australia has been in the area of microeconomic policy, where it has motivated a wholesale restructuring of our institutional arrangements under the mantra of microeconomic reform.

The mainstream economist might ask what I am complaining about given that the Australian economy has been performing very well lately. It is important to acknowledge the enormous economic growth and improvement in material living standards achieved in developed countries and some developing countries in living memory and more broadly since medieval times. Economic fundamentalists are quick to attribute our recent good performance to the impact of their favourite microeconomic reforms. The current Secretary to the Treasury, Ken Henry, recently claimed that this much better performance was due overwhelmingly to the numerous economic reforms that were implemented progressively in response to the policy failures of the 1970s.[3] Henry points in particular to what he believes to have been the importance of flexible labour markets. He goes on to suggest that reforming the supply side of the economy will remain an enduring feature of Treasury advice. The question that these claims gloss over is whether Australians and their families want to be the servants of 'the supply side of the economy', and whether the claimed benefits of flexibility translate into real improvements in social welfare—properly conceived and measured. Furthermore, are any so-called efficiency benefits more important to Australians than fairness, stability and leisure?

There have been other things going on that have probably been much more influential, including the biggest mineral boom in our history. In the past 50 years, we have witnessed the extraordinary growth of Japan, South Korea, Taiwan and more recently China and India. As these countries are the major markets for our commodity exports, Australia has benefited enormously from that growth. Along with the rest of the Western world, Australia has also witnessed extraordinary change in educational attainment, health standards and the movement of women into the paid workforce. In addition, we have witnessed extraordinary technological changes in recent decades.

Then there has been the relatively successful record of the Reserve Bank in managing monetary policy after the Keating recession of the early 1990s, which finally killed the inflationary psychology of the previous two decades. That relative success in the face of its limited policy instruments has enabled low inflation and continued growth despite, in particular, the Asian meltdown. In addition, there have been positive influences from the numerous recent pragmatic departures from economic fundamentalist policy prescriptions; and there has been some benefit from the progressive removal of tariff protection in encouraging a more competitive economic environment. Those tariff policies were, however, particularly badly designed in the first place—being entitlement policies directed towards import replacement rather than export-driven growth. Their failure was inevitable given the lack of even a minimum commitment to strategic planning or enforceable industry investment commitments. The consequence was the development of production capabilities that lacked internationally competitive scale and were unsustainable in the long run.

In short, in my view, our recent good economic growth results from a complex of factors and good luck, and cannot be sheeted home solely or primarily to economic 'reform'.

That relatively good growth record has helped blind us to the costs involved in specific policies—particularly the costs of increased economic insecurity throughout the community, the increased intensity in our working lives, the heavy environmental costs and the uneven distribution of the benefits, often as a result of the abuse of market power, but also as a result of the reluctance of governments to invest in public goods. Recent research has demonstrated that most Australians want a reversion to regular working hours.[4] Further, while it is a cause for rejoicing, it is questionable whether Australia's current relatively low unemployment rate is a record low. More significantly, little attention is paid to the particularly tight definition of unemployment used in the headline unemployment rate—a definition that conceals the true level of unemployment and underemployment.

Our recent relatively good record has also blinded us to the opportunities that have been forgone as a result of our under investment in infrastructure and education and our reluctance to embrace more active and effective innovation and industry policies. Preferring the mantra of the level playing field, recent Australian governments have refused steadfastly to learn from history and, in particular, the recent strong growth of the Asian Tigers and a number of smaller European countries. That history has demonstrated the benefits of more effective coordination of economic activity through a partnership between the public and private sectors. Rather, we have pursued a utopian dream of separating roles and trying to perfect markets in the image of the neoclassical idealisation of those markets under the positivist illusion that doing so will maximise welfare—instead of the more sensible, practical task of learning how to compete and prosper in the very imperfect, fallible world of contemporary, oligopolistic, mercantilist capitalism with high levels of coordination by the State.

Let me emphasise the point. Policies that would optimise resource allocation in the perfect, static, predictable, mechanical, fantasy world of neoclassical economics have little to do with competing successfully or maximising real welfare in the very imperfect, uncertain, dynamic, oligopolistic and somewhat dishonest, manipulative and thuggish real world. Furthermore, self-flagellation over past policy failures—including industry-policy failures—provides no substitute for serious policy analysis and policy learning. In a world of Knightian uncertainty, such failures are inevitable and are to be planned for and learned from, not commiserated over. Relatively rich though we might be, why would we not want to improve real general welfare still further? Why would we be satisfied with crude national income and growth estimates as a measure of real welfare? And why would we not want to share that good fortune nationally and internationally? In this regard, Donald Horne warned us in 1964 against the complacency that our good fortune had bred—a warning we have largely failed to heed. I have already expressed my concern about the increasingly selfish nature of our society and the associated adulation of consumption, wealth and selfishness legitimised by economic fundamentalism and the excessive focus on economic values at the cost of other, more important values. It is no accident that *Business Sunday* has replaced *Divine Service* on our Sunday television sets.

The Long-Running Critique of Neoclassical Economics and its Limited Relevance to Policy

Notwithstanding its dominance as an economic policy tool, neoclassical economics has been the subject of devastating criticism from leading economists directed at its scientific standing, its lack of methodological rigour, its lack of empirical testing, its unnatural fascination with mathematical formalism, the grossly unrealistic and normative nature of its assumptions and the irrelevance of its conclusions for policy analysis. Even Alfred Marshall (1842–1924), an astute mathematician and leading microeconomist, expressed considerable reservations about the use of mathematics in economics. Hayek, a member of the Austrian school and an opponent of neoclassical economics, complained in 1945 that:

> [M]any of the current disputes with regard to both economic theory and economic policy have their common origin in a misconception about the nature of the economic problem of society. This misconception in turn is due to an erroneous transfer to social phenomena of the habits of thought we have developed in dealing with the phenomena of nature.[5]

He went on to criticise the scientific standing of economics in his Nobel Prize acceptance speech in 1974, warning us that market processes were so complex that the knowledge of them by economists was incomplete and virtually impossible to measure.

> While in the physical sciences it is generally assumed, probably with good reason, that any important factor which determines the observed events will itself be directly observable and measurable, in the study of such complex phenomena as the market, which depend on the actions of many individuals, all the circumstances which will determine the outcome of a process…will hardly ever be fully known or measurable.[6]

Hayek also warns us against a strong tendency in the social disciplines to focus exclusively on factors that are measurable—arbitrarily excluding factors that are not measurable. One important policy consequence of this focus on the easily measurable is the current obsession with growth in national production to the detriment of better measures of human welfare. The focus on growth in production has helped blind economists to the broader criticism of the capitalist system and its effects from the environmental and anti-globalism movements and from Marxists. Nevertheless—and somewhat inconsistently—Hayek remains the darling of economic fundamentalists because of his advocacy of a minimalist state arising primarily from his fear of political tyranny. This inconsistency reflects the inconsistency between the two primary sources of economic fundamentalism: libertarian political philosophy and neoclassical economics.

Similarly, another Nobel Prize-winning economist, Wassily Leontief, told us in 1983:

Not having been subject from the outset to the harsh discipline of systematic fact finding…economists developed a nearly irresistible predilection for deductive reasoning. As a matter of fact, many entered the field after specialising in pure or applied mathematics. Page after page of professional economic journals are filled with mathematical formulas leading the reader from sets of more or less plausible but entirely arbitrary assumptions to precisely stated but irrelevant theoretical conclusions.[7]

In fact, Leontief made numerous attacks on the poverty of a priori theorising in economics, and on the neglect of adequate statistical work.

Similarly, in his Nobel Prize lecture in 1991, Ronald Coase criticised in particular what he saw as the narrow focus in economics on market-price determination—a criticism that is relevant particularly to the fundamental theorems of welfare economics. Coase claimed:

The concentration on the determination of prices has led to a narrowing of focus which has had as a result the neglect of other aspects of the economic system. Sometimes, indeed, it seems as though economists conceive of their subject as being concerned only with the pricing system and that anything outside this is considered as no part of their business. What is studied is a system which lives in the minds of economists but not on earth. I have called the result 'blackboard economics'. The firm and the market appear by name but they lack any substance. The firm in mainstream economic theory has often been described as a 'black box'. And so it is. This is very extraordinary given that most resources in a modern economic system are employed within firms, with how these resources are used dependent on administrative decisions and not directly on the operation of a market. Consequently, the efficiency of the economic system depends to a very considerable extent on how these organisations conduct their affairs, particularly, of course, the modern corporation. Even more surprising, given their interest in the pricing system, is the neglect of the market or more specifically the institutional arrangements which govern the process of exchange. As these institutional arrangements determine to a large extent what is produced, what we have is a very incomplete theory.[8]

More recently, Coase confirmed: 'Economics, over the years, has become more and more abstract and divorced from events in the real world. Economists, by and large, do not study the workings of the actual economic system. They theorise about it.'[9]

Of course, Coase is too kind to neoclassical economics: because neoclassical economics largely ignores the role of the corporation, it does not have an adequate account of price formation. Ironically, Coase can also be accused of the above sins. Despite recent discussion of transaction costs, moral hazards and information asymmetries, mainstream economics on the whole makes do with a primitive reductionist view of the firm, ignoring the vast differences in their sizes and disparate goals, assuming that they are profit maximisers. Apart from recent contributions from new institutionalists—a movement within neoclassical economics focusing on transaction costs—this view largely ignores the internal organisation of firms, the practical difficulties of coordination and assumes that they are run as if they had a single owner. It is assumed that firms choose between different inputs in a manner analogous to consumer choice.[10] This simply lacks credibility.

In the same spirit, leading contemporary economic methodologist Mark Blaug told us in 1997:

> Modern economics is sick. Economics has increasingly become an intellectual game played for its own sake and not for its practical consequences for understanding the economic world. Economists have converted the subject matter into a sort of social mathematics in which analytical rigour is everything and practical relevance is nothing...Economics was once condemned as 'the dismal science' but the dismal science of yesterday was a lot less dismal than the soporific scholasticism of today.[11]

In short, the conceptual foundation of neoclassical economics and economic fundamentalism is a shambles. If it were not for its institutional momentum and ideological usefulness it would long ago have been abandoned.

The consequence for Blaug is that we now understand less of how real markets work than did Smith or even Leon Walras (1834–1910). Consistent with Leontief and Coase, he suggests that the real trouble is a belief among economists—going back to Ricardo—that economics is essentially a deductive science in which economic behaviour is inferred on the basis of some assumptions about motivations and some stylised facts about prevailing institutions, suppressing the temptation to ask whether these are realistic assumptions or accurately chosen facts. Contemporary economic teaching and the associated textbooks reinforce this focus. Whereas economics consists of a plurality of conversations, most of today's textbooks are dogmatic, one-dimensional and neoclassical, crowding out other and more fruitful forms of analysis.[12]

The Mainstream Reaction to this Torrent of Criticism

These criticisms are not new. They are echoes of criticisms that were directed against political economy, Ricardo and Mill and then neoclassical economics from its beginnings with Walras, William Jevons (1835–82) and Carl Menger (1840–1921). These criticisms came in particular from the German and English historical schools in the nineteenth and early twentieth centuries. These schools attacked the claimed universalism and abstract scientism of these economic schools, seeing economic phenomena as dependent on their historical, social and institutional context. They therefore saw the study of economic phenomena as a normative, historical and social discipline. The transition from classical to neoclassical economics brought a new mathematical formalism and the abandonment of interest in the institutional and historical underpinnings of the market system—and an intensification of the belief in the ahistorical, scientific and value-free nature of economic discourse. While neoclassical economics exercised a strong influence from its beginnings, it was only in the post-World War II period that it established itself finally as the dominant school across the profession. These criticisms have failed to dent the enthusiasm that economic fundamentalists and economists more generally have for that school. Rather, the response to the torrent of criticism has been to reassert belief in the hard core of the neoclassical research program—acceptance of which is now mandatory for any 'true' economist.[13]

None of this would matter if economics were merely an academic game for theorists fascinated by the intellectual beauty of their formal systems. Very few, however, study economics as an intellectual game. Rather economists are looking for insights into how to manage economic affairs. That is what they claim to have found. Consequently, this descent into scientism and scholasticism is simply not good enough. By default, neoclassical economics now provides the underlying political legitimisation for our market system and for the drift to the political Right to which I drew attention in Chapter 1. Consequently, it is unreasonable for economists to ignore the fundamental flaws in the dominant school of economics—flaws that give a false view of how the economy really operates—as if they are of little account. Paradoxically, the criticism has inspired many economists to argue more strongly for action to perfect markets—and in particular for the removal of social constraints such as minimum wages—rather than to criticise their fundamental theoretical framework.

Nor is it good enough for economists to say that, while neoclassical economics could be flawed, it is up to the critic to provide a better account—particularly when there are competing perspectives struggling to get attention from mainstream economists and policy makers, and when dissenters are purged from the profession and the policy discourse. This is a scandalous attitude given the frequently realised potential for economic advisers to ruin the lives of their fellow citizens—particularly the most vulnerable. Why shouldn't economists want to have a better understanding of the operation of the economic system? Why wouldn't we want to have a better understanding of the sources of human welfare and happiness and to reflect that better understanding in our policy decisions?

Importantly, what mainstream economists generally mean by a better account is another set of mechanical, deterministic, linear equations that will not disturb their mechanical, deterministic world. Indeed, the desire for closure and certainty and an abhorrence of open, indeterminate systems probably accounts for some of the continuing attraction of neoclassical economics and its Newtonian metaphor. In any event, as Phillip Ball reminded us recently, the tenets of neoclassical economics—which are the starting points for economic training—are gross caricatures that have hardened into rigid dogma. '[N]eoclassical theory is such an elaborate contrivance that there is too much at stake to abandon it.'[14] Nevertheless, Ormerod believes that what is required is the reconstruction of economic theory virtually from scratch[15] —a reconstruction that abandons the core assumptions of neoclassical economics and its Newtonian metaphor. Furthermore, Australian political economist Evan Jones has suggested that the past century of economic conceptualisation has been a complete waste of time. Mainstream economics has simply failed as a predictive and explanatory research program.[16]

What we are confronting here is the struggle between an increasingly discredited but entrenched 'normal science' with its particular ideological baggage, and new economic paradigms offering fresh and hopefully more realistic and more fruitful insights. These insights could involve elements of the neoclassical program but those elements will be useful only in a significantly different conceptual framework. As Kuhn has warned us—and as Galileo's experience demonstrates—such struggles are not easily resolved, involving as they do significant threats to the intellectual, social and political standing of existing mainstream economists. In addition, it is hard to give up ways of thinking that have been central to one's professional life; and no one wants to be told that they have wasted their lives talking rubbish. The result is that abandoning such false beliefs requires something akin to a religious conversion. For most economists, this vehement criticism of their paradigm has led to a hardening of their commitment to the mainstream story, and a continuing search for *ad hoc* rationalisations to justify that continuing commitment.

The Newtonian metaphor at the heart of neoclassical economics has a particularly destructive consequence for economic fundamentalism, which is usually overlooked. It commits the theorist to viewing the person as reactive to and dependent on inputs from the environment. It stands in direct contradiction to the views of the libertarian philosophers, who stress the individual's autonomy.[17] There is, therefore, a fundamental conceptual inconsistency at the very heart of the economic fundamentalist project.

Furthermore, in its physical form, the Newtonian metaphor presupposed the existence of a prior harmony established by God, and its import into economics via Smith and Walras involved the assumption of a continuation of some pre-established balance. The mechanical model cannot explain the emergence of a spontaneous order, but presupposes it.[18]

Economic Policy and *Epistēmē*

Classical economists claimed they had discovered nature's socio-economic laws—that is, universal laws of nature with the same status as those of physics. They assumed also that what was 'natural' was also good.[19] This moral assumption persists throughout economics. It is assumed implicitly that the capitalist market system is 'natural' and therefore good—despite the fact that the capitalist system is clearly a social and historical artefact. As we have already seen, this silly assumption flows from the Enlightenment's attempt to secularise God, along with the medieval concept of natural law, combined with an attempt to avoid moral responsibility for our institutions and conduct. Therefore, it is taken for granted by economists and economic policy analysts that economic policy analysis involves the search for—and the application of—unqualified, authoritative, universal, scientific laws and principles capable of providing unique, definitive and good answers to our policy questions.[20] As we saw earlier, this approach to policy analysis—this resort to *epistēmē*—has deep roots extending back beyond the Enlightenment to Christian transcendentalism and then to the central doctrine in Plato's philosophy: his 'Theory of Forms'. This transcendentalism was revived and reinforced by the Enlightenment's search for certain, ahistorical, positive knowledge. Aristotle warned us, however, that not all knowledge was of this type—nor could we have this theoretical certainty in every field. He made a distinction between *epistēmē*—or theoretical grasp—and *phronēsis*—or practical wisdom. In particular, Aristotle argued that the good had no universal form and, consequently, judgements about what was good for society and the individual had always to respect the detailed circumstances of the particular case.

Practical knowledge does not require a prior grasp of definitions, general principles and axioms, as in the realm of theory. Rather, it depends on accumulated experience of particular situations and this practical experience leads to a kind of wisdom— *phronēsis*— different from the abstract stories of theoretical science. Practical knowledge differs from *epistēmē* in that it is concrete, temporal and presumptive and might not hold true universally but only typically. Importantly, it involves judgement or wisdom. In contrast, theoretical statements can make universal claims that hold true at any time or place only if they are as idealised as the axioms or theorems of Greek geometry. At best, very little, if any, knowledge is capable of approaching the exacting demands required of *epistēmē*. Conservative political philosopher Oakeshott shared Aristotle's emphasis on *phronēsis* in his later works, in which he was highly critical of utopian rationalist projects in politics and stressed the importance of tradition and the practical knowledge it gives us.[21] This emphasis is reinforced by Michael Polanyi's insight that most of the knowledge by which we get by in the world is tacit, rather than consciously known, and is acquired through experience.[22] One important consequence is that what counts as convincing evidence in practical matters differs from what counts in *epistēmē*. In particular, it legitimises reliance in policy analysis on accumulated experience, policy learning and anecdotal information rather than reliance on theoretical arguments.

Consequently, any reform of contemporary policy analysis needs to acknowledge that public policy decisions involve *phronēsis* rather than *epistēmē*. Despite the many warnings above, it is Plato's dream of *epistēmē*—as revived by the Enlightenment—that is privileged in contemporary economic policy debates in the form of the theoretical speculative stories of neoclassical economics, whereas the practical economic learning of the business person, consumer and policy administrator is dismissed arrogantly as anecdotal, unscientific and irrelevant.

Idealisation in Neoclassical Economics

This contemporary search for *epistēmē* in neoclassical economics involves a series of 'idealisations' of the economic agent and the setting in which 'he' operates. As we saw above, the particular idealisations were driven by a desire to describe human beings and their interactions as if they were a deterministic, mechanical system characterised by equilibrium—by the Newtonian metaphor. Smith was a great admirer of Newton and his moral analysis is thoroughly Newtonian and carries over into his understanding of self-interest as it appears in his economic analysis. Therefore, Smith, in the *Wealth of Nations*, speaks of the price of commodities 'gravitating towards the natural price'.[23] More broadly, those Newtonian tendencies dominated physics, which came increasingly to provide the model for science in general. The marginalist movement pioneered by Walras, Jevons and Menger in the nineteenth century strengthened these tendencies in economics, which were strengthened still further by the post-World War II fascination with formalism. All three claimed specifically that economics—as an exact universal natural science—resembled classical mechanics, involving a calculus of the natural 'forces' of pleasure and pain.[24] This reflected the utilitarian inheritance of neoclassical economics as well as the desire of economists to emulate the mathematical formalism of physics, which they saw as the archetypical science, whose prestige they wished to share. Although Phillip Mirowski distinguishes the physics that Walras relied on from that of Newton, he nevertheless objects strongly to the resulting mechanical nature of neoclassical economic reasoning.[25] He traces at some length the powerful influence of physics on Walras and his colleagues, criticising them for their misunderstanding of that physics and their misapplication of the associated equations to economics. Despite Mirowski's minor reservations, there can be little doubt that general equilibrium theory is fundamentally Newtonian in concept. For example, Jevons claimed in 1871 that 'the theory of Economy…presents a close analogy to the science of Statical Mechanics, and the laws of Exchange are found to resemble the laws of Equilibrium of the lever as determined by the principle of virtual velocities'.[26]

This adoption of the equations of physics and the renaming of the relevant variables to give them an economic meaning was criticised by Mirowski in the following terms:

> The most curious aspect of this program to make economics more rigorous and more scientific is that not one neoclassical economist in over one hundred years has seen fit to discuss the appropriateness or inappropriateness of the adoption of the mathematical metaphor of energy in a pre-relativistic gravitational field in order to discuss the preferences and price formation of transactors in the marketplace.[27]

As Clark points out—following Guy Routh—these developments are intended also to support their political views. Asserting—on the basis of scientific credentials—that the economy is an equilibrium system regulated by nature in the same way as the solar system lends weight to the claim that such an economy exists in harmony and is best left to itself without government intervention. There were, however, non-mainstream economists who objected strongly to this identification.[28] Knight argued as long ago as 1935 that any reconstruction of economics had to reject this mechanical analogy.[29]

Within this mechanical framework, *Homo economicus*—economic man—created originally by classical economics, is a reductionist attempt to obtain an idealised creature defined by economic motives only—a machine for making decisions, an atomistic economic billiard ball on which economic 'forces' act, which at the same time remains perfectly 'rational'. This contradiction in terms is made only remotely credible by the instrumental mechanical understanding of rationality employed. This understanding is itself an unjustified and misleading idealisation to which we will return shortly. *Ceteris paribus*—the assumption of other things being equal—is then invoked on the unsafe reductionist assumption that this isolates successfully the influence of other phenomena. In the case of interdependent complex phenomena, it is now clear that this is far from true.

Importantly, Weber also believed that no conceptual system could do full justice to the complexity of social phenomena. Nevertheless, he believed that his methodology would enable claims made about the social world to be subjected to rigorous empirical verification, provided this tool was applied only to rational and goal-oriented behaviour. These idealisations were thought, falsely, to provide economics with an analytical situation analogous to those involved in the control of excluded variables in experimental situations in the natural sciences. Among the heroic simplifying assumptions used in neoclassical economics are assumptions derived from classical economics—those of rational behaviour and consistent preferences. The claim that economic behaviour is so governed has allowed economists—drawing on Pareto—to claim that economics is the science of logical actions and of rational choice. Unfortunately, for mainstream economics, the empirical evidence shows that the preferences of real people are not consistent—that is, they are not transitive—and this undermines the claim.[30]

There is a deeper, more hidden motive for this idealisation. Acknowledging any diversity among economic agents further undermines the mathematical tractability of the analysis and has to be avoided at all costs.[31] This 'ideal' type is obtained by stripping out most of the ethical, religious, altruistic and other motives of real human beings.[32] The other idealisations are those involved in the setting, in particular, of the postulation of perfect competition, perfect information, complete markets and resource mobility. The particular idealisations have been subject to enormous criticism and it is a moot point whether the regularities detected by this procedure are artefacts of real economic affairs or of the analytical system. I hold the latter interpretation.

This approach to economics did not originate with Weber or Pareto. For example, John R. McCulloch (1789–1864), the leader of the Ricardian school after Ricardo, in his *Principles of Political Economy* published in 1825, gave an early defence of this practice.[33] Interestingly, McCulloch was trying to deal with objections to what he claimed to have been political economy's 'best established conclusions'.[34] Nevertheless, he thought that the conclusions of political economy applied only in the majority of cases, because special circumstances could differentiate particular cases. Even so, McCulloch believed that those conclusions were an appropriate basis for government policy decisions. In practice therefore, McCulloch avoided dealing with those objections. Mill, in turn, did the same, while drawing attention to the practical men who objected to what they believed to be the inappropriate conclusions that economists drew from invented assumptions. Mill rejected those objections on the basis that while Euclid's 'laws' were also true only in the abstract, they were, nonetheless, useful. He claimed that all 'phenomena of society are phenomena of human nature, generated by the action of outward circumstances upon masses of human beings; and if, therefore, the phenomena of human thought, feeling, and action are subject to fixed laws, the phenomena of society cannot but conform to fixed laws'.[35]

While aspiring to exactness, Mill nevertheless drew a distinction between exact sciences such as astronomy and inexact sciences such as the moral sciences, which he saw as lacking the necessary information. While Mill claimed to have a richer conception of human beings than Bentham, it nevertheless involved a deterministic view little different from Bentham's.[36] Any placidity in human nature operated in the longer term. Mill also drew a distinction between general and specific causes and—going further than McCulloch—believed that the causes operating in political economy were laws of human nature, something he believed the individual could check for themselves by introspection. Consequently, he argued that political economy was an abstract and aprioristic science such as geometry. For him, economic conclusions—which are derived from assumptions that resemble real circumstances—are true in the abstract and express tendencies present in human behaviour. These 'truths' are applicable in practice when the influences of the neglected effects are added. Of course, these universal truths were said to be manifest most completely in Britain—the most advanced industrial country in the world. Importantly, however, Mill did not extend these claims to the distribution of production—this, in his view, being subject to the laws and customs of mankind.

Marx went further again, postulating a hierarchy of factors, believing that his law of value represented the deepest essence of society. These increasing levels of abstraction have an important consequence. Whereas for McCulloch the conclusions of political economy were generally valid, for Mill they were laws of human nature, while with Marx we finally arrived at something even more abstract: a Platonic form. Of course, neither Mill's abstract truth nor Marx's deepest essence was open to empirical falsification. Ironically, for those on the Right, it is this Platonic form— articulated most strongly by Marx—that unconsciously underpins economic fundamentalism and much neoclassical economic theorising.

The positivist movement associated with the Vienna Circle in the 1920s and 1930s strengthened these positivist tendencies in economics. For his part, Pareto sought also to develop a scientific economics based on what he thought were natural phenomena based on natural laws independent of social institutions and using an analogy with mechanics and the concept of general equilibrium. Nevertheless, Pareto was conscious of the limits of pure economics and saw a need to add back into the analysis the factors left out by these idealisations before one could make predictions about real phenomena, and before these analyses could be applied in the world. He also thought that the applied scientist should turn to other disciplines for those other analyses.[37] That was the reason why he turned to the study of sociology. Pareto tells us, for example, 'In order to judge whether customs protection is harmful to people, we need help not only from political economy but also from all those sciences which in their totality constitute that branch of human knowledge called social science.'[38]

The contemporary economist feels no such need before offering policy advice. Indeed, there is no greater insult for mainstream economists than to describe someone as a sociologist.[39] There is little doubt, therefore, that Pareto would have rejected the particular positivist use that economists now make of Pareto-optimality and the economic imperialism of many economists.

If we are going to use economic analysis as a framework to erect hurdles to policy initiatives, we have to have a great deal of confidence in that analysis. The confidence that is currently placed in the mainstream framework is, however, mistaken. That framework should be replaced by a framework demonstrating relevance to the continuing transformation of the economy and to the achievement of real improvements in social welfare—particularly among the disadvantaged. In this regard, it seems bizarre to look for regularities in human conduct by grossly exaggerating one aspect of the apparent reality, and then to claim that this exaggeration represents a simplification rather than a distortion. I doubt this is a fair description of what the natural sciences seek to do. In a scientific experiment, one can hold all other things as being equal through careful experimental design. In the social disciplines, in a non-experimental environment, it seems a wild leap of faith to assume that an idealisation enables one to ignore possible interactions with other influences. This reductionism is a fundamental mistake, as it is highly likely that when we are dealing with human beings we are dealing with non-linear dynamic systems; and if we are, such influences cannot simply be added together. It is an approach that also legislates higher-level systems out of existence. In any event, the uncorrupted layperson's complaints that the neoclassical assumptions and the conclusions drawn from them are unrealistic are simply dismissed—usually with a sneer.

The Normative Use of Neoclassical Economic Idealisations

Part of our problem arises because it is too easy to slip unconsciously between very different understandings of the word 'ideal' and to end up believing that—with Hirshleifer, Becker, Posner and Thatcher— the true nature of human beings is being described by *Homo economicus*. Similarly, it is too easy to make a similar slip in respect of the idealisation of the situation. What was justified initially as being a helpful analytical tool to get around some of the complexities of human behaviour has ended up being used as a normative ideal. Without a doubt, the most important policy sleight of hand in the neoclassical story—its reversal of the onus of proof—is a consequence of these idealisations. In neoclassical economics therefore we have an idealisation of 'THE MARKET'—another of Plato's forms and the god of economic fundamentalists. It is then easy to further assume that the market system is the ideal form of economic organisation and, for the true believers, the ideal form of social organisation. What Weber justified as idealisations to illustrate only one aspect of social phenomena and to enable empirical investigations have been turned into a normative ideal contrary to his intention and to good sense. This slide has been assisted by the fact—as we saw in the previous chapter—that it is simply not possible to separate the positive from the normative. All the talk about positive economics serves only as a smoke screen to hide the fact that economics is legislating one form of social organisation. One particular result is that most government action is now categorised by economists as intervention in market processes, which has to be justified in terms of the neoclassical idealisations and the associated theology, rather than as collective action furthering collective goals.

Market failure

Of course, economists usually admit that the transactional situations we all face in daily life could be different from those assumed in their idealisation, but they leave it to us to demonstrate that those differences matter in the context of their particular flawed conceptual framework; that they result in 'market failures' and that government correction is less costly than maintaining the status quo. In the absence of any convincing empirical confirmation of the validity of this form of modelling, this reversal of the onus of proof—this demand that policy activists demonstrate that real markets are not perfect before they can act—is inconsistent with any reasonable interpretation of good scientific practice. This tactic also places the policy activist in an impossible position because, in the absence of action, it is impossible to demonstrate the benefits of any particular action or even the costs. It is also impossible to know what the economy—or particular sectors of the economy—will look like if there were complete and perfectly competitive efficient markets and free trade.

One further important effect of this search for market failures is that it endorses tacitly the above flawed conceptual framework. The result is a theoretical discussion couched in neoclassical terms even where the activists reject that neoclassical framework. It is like trying to persuade the Pope that birth control or abortion may be permissible in certain cases when one rejects the theological and authority claims of the Catholic Church. These concerns are amplified when economists and libertarians apply these flawed simplistic concepts to political systems and voting patterns as if they were economic phenomena and start talking about the dangers of 'government failure'. This is just pseudo-scientific nonsense—a very limited rediscovery of the concept of original sin. We all know that human beings are fallible, have questionable motives and make mistakes—but to refuse to do anything on the ground that we could be wrong is not prudence; it is simple cowardice.

The Flawed Assumptions of Neoclassical Economic Idealisation

Atomism

Among the flawed assumptions of neoclassical economics is its reliance on methodological individualism as its 'official' methodology. This is a research stratagem imported from Greek atomism via Descartes—with his atomistic system and mechanical rules—and then the individualistic political theorising of Hobbes and Locke. In those stories, explanation was to be located in the actions of individual actors interacting in a mechanical fashion rather than in the complex organic interplay of social institutions, groups and individuals. As we saw in Chapter 5, the emerging dominance of theoretical reasoning in political and moral theorising through the Enlightenment marked a sharp discontinuity with the practical approach to political and moral reasoning that had been derived from Aristotle and which characterised the medieval world. One important element in this transformation was the abandonment of forms of explanation based on organic metaphors and the emergence of a mechanical Newtonian metaphor as the dominant form of explanation. This atomism is an essential feature of this form of explanation, in which causal relationships are seen as being analogous to the forces operating in the movement of the planets or in classical mechanics, with individuals taking the place of the planets or of billiard balls and interacting in a mechanical fashion. As we saw in Chapter 5, however, the Newtonian mechanistic world-view has been undermined. Newtonian physics has been completely discredited as an answer to any fundamental question about the nature of the world.

Physics has come to understand reality not in terms of atomism—of discrete particles that can be described independently of all others—but as a complete network, the most basic elements of which are not entities or substances, but relationships. The properties of things are no longer seen as being fixed absolutely with respect to some unchanging background; rather, they arise from interactions and relationships.[40] This abandonment of Newtonianism within its parent discipline should cause economists to pause and wonder whether the Newtonian metaphor provides an adequate master narrative for economics. Having stressed the fundamental importance of our social relationships and our socially constructed moral codes in Chapters 2 and 7, I don't believe methodological individualism can deal adequately with these continuing social relationships.

In any event, Kincaid warns us that individualism is a fuzzy doctrine: 'Sometimes it makes ontological claims, for example, that social entities do not act independently of their parts. Other individualists put the issue in terms of knowledge: we can capture all social explanations in individualistic terms or no social explanation is complete or confirmed without individualist mechanisms.'[41]

Kincaid argues that the debate about holism and individualism is primarily an empirical issue about how to explain society. The upshot for Kincaid is that individualism is seriously misguided: 'When individualism is interesting, it is implausible; when it is plausible, it is uninteresting.'[42] It should already be clear from Chapter 2 that the claim that methodological individualism provides the exclusive proper explanatory strategy in the social disciplines is deeply flawed. It mistakes the biological entity for the complete human. To use a modern metaphor, it mistakes a discrete piece of hardware for the whole system, forgetting that the 'software' is an open social construct and that together they form part of a large network. In the spirit of narrative pluralism, this does not mean that methodological individualism might not be useful in some instances. It is up to the analyst using that assumption to demonstrate its usefulness and the 'validity' of the results. The Enlightenment tradition from Descartes and Locke onwards to contemporary mainstream economics has just assumed this question away. In economics, this strategy assumes that all individual choices are self-serving and promote individual welfare. Not only does it fail to acknowledge the social constraints on choice, it fails to confront the possibility of mistaken choices and the normative consequences of that possibility. In those cases, one could always respond that people should bear the consequences of their mistaken choices. This, however, is a normative judgement that is open to question and is something economists claim not to be making. It is also a judgement with which the rest of us might disagree—though not necessarily all the time. There is a dynamic element in choices as people learn over time what is important to them in the changing circumstances of their lives. Mistakes are an important part of that learning process.

Individual preferences again

The empty concept of revealed preferences is—as we have already seen, and as Sen confirms—simply 'a robust piece of evasion'[43] to avoid a serious examination of the formation and nature of 'preferences'. This is to preserve the ideological usefulness, analytical structure and mathematical tractability of mainstream analysis. Sen calls this theory and the associated rational-choice theory a remarkably mute theory. This is because it explains behaviour in terms of preferences, which in turn are defined only by behaviour. This circular reasoning has no explanatory power. It does, however, require consistency in choice—but that is something that is not observed in practice. Furthermore, there is much evidence, including in economics, to show that in practice people's choices are often not selfish. For most of us, this would seem to undermine the whole idea. Sen goes on to argue that, while choices based on sympathy for others could perhaps be accommodated in mainstream models, choices that are made on the basis of moral commitments are counter-preferential and cannot be so accommodated. Of course, this is something that most of us knew already, even if we did not know the jargon in which the argument is expressed. At most, only some choices are made on the basis of their contribution to personal welfare. As Sen points out, this conclusion is particularly important in respect of the provision of public goods and in work motivation. In the latter case, it would be impossible to run any organisation entirely on the basis of personal incentives—and they have necessarily to rely on moral commitments and social cohesion in order to operate at all.

Rational choices and optimisation

The above critique undermines the normative instrumental view of rationality used in mainstream economics.[44] This was a view of rationality that was rejected firmly in Chapter 5. Human judgement cannot be reduced to static optimisation. People do often act in a self-interested fashion, but it can be rational to do things that are not in one's personal interests. Indeed, it is normal to do so. It can be rational to make choices in accordance with moral values and it is normal to do so. It can also be rational to disregard the consequences in making choices. Some things are just not done and some things have to be done regardless. Some economists might respond to these arguments by making a distinction between short-term and long-term self-interest, and then try to accommodate our moral commitments to those long-term interests. Really, this is just further consequentialism and, as we saw in Chapter 7, it is an attempt to legislate a particular moral theory that is part of the same tradition of moral reasoning as mainstream economics. In that regard, it is now obvious that our moral principles cannot be reduced to a single conceptual system and that the moral rules that regulate life in contemporary Western society derive from several incompatible historical sources augmented constantly by contemporary cultural influences. These in turn are different from those operating in other societies. Consequently, the appeal to long-term interests is simply further evasion. One could play that game forever; but the average punter should just decline to play.

Nevertheless, mainstream economists continue to claim that economic agents in their choices optimise the benefits to be derived and that it is only rational to do so. Behavioural economists have, however, demonstrated successfully that everyday human economic behaviour is not consistent with this claim. This demonstration undermines much of the associated analysis. In particular, real human beings simply lack the cognitive abilities to maximise the benefits from their choices. Furthermore, the contexts within which we make decisions are such that optimisation—either *ex anti* or *ex post*—is simply not possible. This brings us back to the realisation that human choices involve a dynamic process relying on practical wisdom based on experience, learning about opportunities and tastes and balancing different attainable goals—rather than a crude optimisation process.

Among economists, this realisation has led to a long discussion of 'bounded rationality' and of 'satisficing'—concepts associated with Kalneman and Simon, more dissident Nobel Prize winners. For example, Tversky and Kalneman make a distinction between intuitive judgements and deliberative decisions, demonstrating that even statistical experts make systematic errors in their intuitive probability-based judgements.[45] Even significant research decisions are guided by flawed intuitions. Tversky and Kalneman have undermined the proposition that choices involving risk are made on the basis of a rational analysis of the risks involved. Their prospect theory describes how such choices are made in practice involving a two-stage process: editing and evaluation. In editing, possible outcomes are ordered following some heuristic, choosing a reference point against which to evaluate the possible outcomes. In the evaluation phase, people choose an outcome with the highest utility based on the potential outcomes and their respective probabilities. Importantly, the way people frame an outcome subjectively in their mind affects the utility they expect or receive. What is more, it has been demonstrated empirically that people not only consider the value they receive, but the value received by others.

Similarly, Simon pointed out during a long career beginning with his first book in 1947 that real people have only limited abilities to formulate and solve complex problems. In particular, we have only limited abilities to acquire, process, retrieve and transmit information. In addition, we often have conflicting aims and frequently our goals and the means to achieve them are interrelated and cannot be separated. Furthermore, it is simply impossible to make a logical search though the myriad options open to us, and their consequences. Consequently, we use heuristics or rules of thumb and our emotions as well as logical analysis in our decision making. Any attempt to optimise in practice just leads to confusion. Therefore, we make decisions that are satisfactory rather than optimal. The 'normal science' of economics has tried to maintain its framework by introducing the concepts of search, deliberation and time costs into the decision-making process and claiming as a result that satisficing is effectively the same as optimising. In doing so, mainstream economists have trivialised Simon's devastating theoretical insights in the interests of their research program. To my mind, these are very different worlds and the above attempt to maintain the neoclassical framework is just another form of evasion.

Pareto-optimality and welfare

Neoclassical economics goes on to claim that, subject to a broad range of assumptions, a competitive market will allocate resources between competing uses in an optimal fashion. This is the contemporary version of Smith's belief in the 'invisible hand of the market'. Smith believed that God had so arranged creation and human affairs that self-interest balanced by sympathy for our fellow humans would produce the best of all possible worlds. Now, in the absence of God, mainstream economists would have us believe that the rational choices of the individual, exercised in perfectly competitive markets with perfect information and mobility of resources, will have the same effect. This idea of the theoretical primacy of competition and markets is developed in first-year microeconomic courses as an extension of the 'laws of supply and demand' and the properties of market equilibrium.

This scheme draws on utilitarianism's search for the 'greatest happiness of the greatest number' to propose that the consumer is motivated to purchase goods by the 'utility' she or he derives from it—a reflection of her or his preferences. Then it is claimed that with competition in demand, the benefit or utility received by the individual consuming the last unit of goods—for example, an apple—equals the price she or he is willing to pay. Similarly, with competition in supply, it is claimed the resource cost to produce that last apple equals the price the producer receives. Voluntary exchange between the producer and consumers in a market-clearing auction will then yield a set of prices that equates the marginal benefit of each commodity with its marginal cost. This has the practical effect of assuming out of existence the problems for the achievement of the greatest happiness that result from the existing socio-economic order and its power relationships. To the limited extent that these problems are recognised, they are seen as constraints on preferences that disappear into the background. At one stage, it was hoped that utility might be measured and thus provide an objective measure of the benefit derived. This quickly proved an illusion, leading ultimately to the development of the empty concept of revealed preferences. As we saw earlier, this means that people buy only what they prefer and they prefer what they buy; and, as it turns out, they are not logically consistent in those purchases.[46]

There are even further technical problems with this most basic of models in the marginalist movement.[47] The model assumes that supply and demand curves are continuous and well behaved, but that is not necessarily the case. Prices can also be resistant to change. In any event, can this model be operationalised? The most damaging criticism of these models is that they impose impossible computational demands on individuals and firms. Real people cannot be making production and purchasing decisions on the basis of such computations. Consequently, in the real world prices cannot be established in this manner except in the crudest possible sense. The result is that it seems likely that the marginalism implicit in the model is an artefact of the analytical system rather than an accurate description of real behaviour. The whole model appears to exaggerate the influence of pricing signals on economic decisions, reducing all other influences to 'costs', however difficult it might be to attribute a monetary value to those costs. Nevertheless, these concerns are generally ignored.

The first fundamental law of welfare economics is then derived by generalising from such single-commodity models to general equilibrium of the economy, abstracting from much detail. This involves the unrealistic assumptions of optimisation in all other markets and independence from them. We are then told that under very restrictive and unrealistic assumptions, a competitive market equilibrium is 'Pareto-efficient' or 'Pareto-optimal' or 'socially optimal'—where Pareto-optimality is defined as that state in which it is impossible to improve the welfare of some members of society without reducing the welfare of others. In practice, those restrictive assumptions are quickly forgotten.

Although superficially attractive as a definition of maximum welfare, Pareto-optimality is more than deeply flawed; it is simply not true. As Blaug writes: 'Pareto welfare economics…achieves a stringent and positivist definition of the social optimum in as much as Pareto-optimality is defined with respect to an initial distribution of income. The practical relevance of this achievement for policy is nil.'[48]

Bromley is among the many other economists who have attacked the scientific objectivity of Pareto-optimality as a decision rule in policy analysis, seeing it as being inconsistent and incoherent with no special claim to legitimacy.[49] The claim that economic efficiency is an objective measure of objective scientists is simply wrong. Warren Samuels, for his part, has described in some detail the large number of normative assumptions underpinning the definition, showing that the concept of Pareto-optimality necessarily involves moral judgements about the existing distribution of wealth and power and the legal system, which enforces ownership rights.[50] Its imposition as a decision rule in economic policy making—the requirement that 'economic efficiency' ought to be the decision rule for collective decision making—is also a normative choice.[51] In short, it is nothing but a pseudo-scientific defence of the economic and social *status quo*.

This approach also prohibits interpersonal utility comparisons on the ground that there is no 'scientific' method for doing so, that interpersonal utility comparisons involve normative judgements and on the principle of consumer sovereignty. The fact that the principle of consumer sovereignty is itself a normative judgement and that we make such interpersonal comparisons every day seems to have passed the economics profession by. In doing so, it contravenes a fundamental insight of the marginal movement in economics: the everyday experience of declining marginal utility—that is, the experience that the benefit derived by any consumer from one unit of consumption declines as the total amount of that consumer's consumption increases.[52] It is possible, therefore, in practice, to improve welfare by taking from the rich and giving to the poor—regardless of what Pareto's disciples might claim.

Furthermore, this measure of welfare depends on the subjective judgements of individual consumers and producers; however, we all know from painful experience that not all subjective choices are welfare enhancing—and those exceptions are very important. Furthermore, as is readily conceded by most economists, the price system does not operate as an adequate signalling system for public goods or for goods where there are either positive or negative spill-overs. Those prices never reflect their real social and economic worth and cost. Importantly, while this is a well-recognised phenomenon within mainstream theorising, we give almost no policy attention to the negative externalities associated with advertising. The subjective willingness of individuals to pay for many advertised goods does not necessarily reflect their contribution to welfare.

Finally, in practice, beyond a minimum level, real people do not judge their well-being in absolute terms. Rather, we judge our subjective welfare by comparing ourselves with each other—particularly those in our immediate social circle. The net result is that in a world in which there are differences in individual welfare, there is never an occasion when it is not possible to improve our subjective welfare by redistributing income. Nevertheless, the search for efficiency is usually—and unreasonably—considered by mainstream economists to be the best available decision rule in the circumstances. In contrast—in concert with Blaug and Bromley—I argue that these fundamental flaws mean that Pareto-optimality is not a legitimate decision rule in public policy. Its continued use reflects an improper unwillingness on the part of policy advisers to undertake the messy, non-algorithmic task of judging the likely real welfare consequences of possible actions. This does not mean that welfare improvement is unimportant, only that this is not the way to judge it.

Of course, these criticisms are well known to mainstream economists, but they tend to pass over them in embarrassed silence as they press on with their normal science. The consequences for their normative prescriptions are simply ignored. A cynic might conclude that the whole idea of Pareto-optimality was invented to deflect a strong conclusion from marginalist theory in favour of redistribution to the poor.

General equilibrium

The strongest version of the contemporary economist's faith in competitive markets is the concept of general equilibrium—the core concept of neoclassical economics, that best of all possible worlds. The idea of a social equilibrium dates back to Smith's moral theorising, but the direct application of the idea to neoclassical economics originates with Walras. In its modern form it dates from the mathematical modelling of Arrow and Gerard Debreu in the 1950s. One cannot but wonder whether this particular development resulted from a need to find a 'scientific' justification for the claimed superiority of the capitalist system in the face of the ideological challenge posed by communism at that time. In any event, it follows from Kurt Gödel's work on mathematical logic that no such formal logical system can be self-contained and consequently such systems cannot contain within themselves the rules for their application.[53] Nevertheless, the basic idea in its present form is that the prices, consumption, production and distribution of all goods and services in an economy are interrelated, with a change in the price of one product affecting all others. Another way of saying the same thing is that the economy is composed of a set of interrelated markets. Of course, this simply ignores the large part of the economy that is not in the market sector and the social determinants of the operation of the market sector.

In a 'perfectly competitive economy', it is claimed, the economy operates so that at a unique set of prices there exists equilibrium of production and consumption that is Pareto-optimal and in which there are no under-utilised resources. That assumption of perfect competition involves the idea that no economic agent has sufficient market power to affect the price paid for goods or services—that is, they are too small to affect the price. While it is central to the whole framework, this is clearly not true. Huge multinational corporations that have very considerable and enduring market power dominate modern economies. They also enjoy massive increasing returns to scale and scope, rather than the diminishing returns assumed in this theory.

In any event, leading British economist Joan Robinson (1903–83) argued in the *Impossibility of Competition* that there was a logical contradiction in the basic conception of competition as a state of equilibrium.[54] The tendencies for competition to make markets imperfect through product differentiation, towards oligopoly in the presence of economies of scale and for excess capacity to lead to collusion are all rooted deeply in the very nature of the competitive system. As a result, she strongly doubted that it was proper to treat competition as a normal equilibrium state. Further, she was a very strong critic of the value of this formalism and its 'thicket of algebra'.[55]

Nothing has really changed to undermine this early critique. Rather, it has been repeated regularly since that time. There has been a recent tendency for economists to claim that the potential for firms to enter a market guards us against the exploitation of market power. As entry into markets dominated by one or more large companies can be very costly, however, this claim simply lacks credibility. Similarly, Nicholas Georgescu-Roegen criticised the economic value of such general equilibrium modelling and even its value as a mathematical exercise: 'There are endeavours that now pass for the most desirable kind of economic contributions although they are just plain mathematical exercises, not only without any economic substance but also without any mathematical value.'[56]

In his more recent critique, Ormerod calls the model a travesty of reality, singling out the assumption of a 'continuum of traders', meaning an infinity of infinity of traders—an absurd mathematical assumption necessary for the solution of the equations in the model.[57] In any event, this formal system drastically over-simplifies the complexity encountered in real economies and abstracts from their differing institutional frameworks. In addition, firms in all their complexity do not appear in this model. Furthermore, it is simply assumed that the price system exists and that economic agents are simply price takers without any real freedom of choice. To get over this difficulty, the fantasy was invented of an auctioneer who would set prices but would disallow trade until equilibrium was achieved. In practice, however, people do buy and sell at prices that would not clear the market. Any such trade could undermine the possibility of any convergence towards equilibrium. Furthermore, any auctioneer—and economic agents more generally—faces a task that is a computational impossibility. The whole idea is just more nonsense.

Importantly, it is far from clear whether the model will result in a single stable unique equilibrium.[58] Rather, multiple equilibria could exist and could be path dependent. This possibility alone undermines the generality of the policy conclusions of the mainstream model and opens the possibility of successful coordination by governments.[59] Furthermore, it is not clear how these prices and resource allocations are arrived at or whether, in the event of a shock, the economy will converge back to the same equilibrium. As we have seen, the theory involves the standard assumptions that economic agents are rational, that there are no externalities, that information is perfect and that there is a complete set of markets. The theory also requires consumer preferences to be subject to diminishing marginal utility and that there be no economies of scale. As we have seen, these assumptions are just not credible.

Much of the normal science in neoclassical economics therefore involves trying to relax these assumptions while retaining the fundamental conclusion of the Pareto-optimality of markets and the proposition that they will clear. None of this can deal successfully with the consequences of introducing uncertainty into the model. David Newbery and Stiglitz have shown that, in an uncertain world, a competitive equilibrium is in general not a Pareto-optimum. The real world is an uncertain world. This undermines the whole point of the model, except in extremely restrictive conditions.[60]

The attempt to relax the assumptions of the neoclassical framework looks like medieval scholasticism and is a waste of time. In this respect, Stiglitz sees 'the pervasiveness and persistence of unemployment' as the 'critical experiment which should lead to the rejection of the basic equilibrium model which [depending on how you view it] either predicts or assumes full employment'.[61]

The general theory of the second-best

Further, a powerful neoclassical qualification to the use of neoclassical economics as a policy tool—the 'General Theory of the Second-Best', which questions whether any incremental move towards the market idealisation will, in practice, produce an improvement in social welfare (still defined in positivist terms)—is ignored as being incapable of application in practice. Lipsey and Kelvin Lancaster have, however, demonstrated convincingly that all violations of the assumptions of the general equilibrium model would have to be removed in order to be confident that any move towards the market idealisation would lead to increased welfare.[62] Indeed, Lipsey confirms that Pareto and Paul Samuelson had a similar insight.[63] It follows that one cannot assume the contrary in practice. As we saw above, market failures are pervasive in the real economy—or, as Lipsey says, the proportion of economic space affected by distortions is close to 100 per cent.

Furthermore, there are no general policy rules that can be applied to piecemeal improvements. This undermines the policy usefulness of the whole idea of market failures.

Information economics

Information economists have unpicked the information assumptions underlying the fundamental theorem of welfare economics—undermining the long-standing presumption that markets are necessarily efficient. They have shown—using conventional analysis—that where information is costly, which it almost always is, appropriate government intervention could make everyone better off.[64] This alone undermines the standard presumption in contemporary policy discourse against government action. This has the effect of confirming the view that market failures are pervasive in real economies—further undermining the policy relevance of the whole framework. Nowhere are the insights of information economics more important than in respect of financial markets—a central mechanism for the allocation of resources in capitalist economies. Stiglitz argues from a mainstream and information theoretical perspective that since financial markets are concerned essentially with the production, use and processing of information, they are somewhat different from other markets: 'Market failures are likely to be more pervasive in [financial] markets; and…there exist forms of government intervention that will not only make these markets function better but will also improve the performance of the economy.'[65]

For example, given the casino-like atmosphere in stock markets, the prevalence of information cascades, misinformation, insider trading, booms and busts and downright fraud, how anyone can think that capital raising in these markets will maximise welfare is beyond me. If, however, financial markets are not efficient in the neoclassical sense, there is little prospect that the rest of the economy could ever be efficient either. Of course, some might claim that regardless of their short-term deficiencies, financial markets are efficient in the long run, but that is more evasion, as there can be little doubt that the short run does matter in the allocation of resources by these markets.

The separation of efficiency from distribution

One of the consequences of the neoclassical framework is that economists usually claim that issues to do with economic efficiency can be separated from distributional issues. This separation is used to justify their focus on efficiency issues and on the importance of economic growth in policy discourse—leaving it to governments to deal with distributional issues in a somewhat *ad hoc* and illegitimate manner. Stiglitz has, however, also undermined the practical usefulness of that distinction: 'Government cannot and does not rely on lump-sum taxes as a basis of redistribution…One of the central consequences of the second fundamental welfare theorem was the ability to separate efficiency issues from distribution issues. In the absence of lump-sum taxes, this separation is not possible.'[66]

The practical consequence is that measures that are claimed to promote efficiency will inevitably have distributional impacts, while measures to promote equity will have efficiency impacts. This lack of separation complicates greatly the task of economic management. This complication has, however, usually been overlooked in the recent priority given to efficiency in the optimistic hope that the benefits of greater efficiency will somehow trickle down to the underprivileged. In any event, this inability to separate efficiency and distribution effects further undermines Pareto-optimality as a minimal measure of welfare.

It should be noted that because of its idealisation of the market and its absurd assumptions, neoclassical economics has almost nothing useful to say about the achievement of efficiency—defined in any realistic fashion—in real economies.

Game theory

In an attempt to bolster its shabby claims to credibility, mainstream economics has taken to playing games based on simple optimisation assumptions comparable with those of neoclassical economics but with uncertainty of outcomes thrown in—claiming that this is a scientific procedure akin to the natural sciences and that it throws light on how real humans behave. As Frank Stilwell confirms, game theory has shown that the focus in mainstream economics on rational individuals is internally inconsistent and descriptively inaccurate. What it really demonstrates is that real people—even in highly artificial games—tend to behave in an altruistic way, assuming that other people are guided by social norms. It has, therefore, strengthened the critique of neoclassical economics.[67]

The Formal Ontological Critique of Neoclassical Economics

Throughout this book and especially in the above chapter, I have been highly critical of the positive image of science that still pervades economics and the associated Newtonian metaphor. Similarly, in drawing attention to the historical emergence of the capitalist system and its institutions, I have been questioning the ahistorical nature of economic analysis and the ahistorical human nature it claims to investigate. Additionally, I have been critical of the narrow mathematical formalism of the neoclassical program and the fictional assumptions it employs to maintain the mathematical tractability of its analysis. In this, I am joining distinguished economic company, as we saw earlier in this chapter. Despite such objections, the use of mathematics has become the unifying feature of the neoclassical program and that modelling is often employed for its own sake—rather than for the light it is believed to throw on economic phenomena.[68] This formalism results from the unfounded belief that mathematical methods are an essential part of the scientific method—a belief derived from classical physics and ultimately from Pythagoras via Plato and the Enlightenment. It is also an essential part of the illusion that neoclassical economics is a positive rather than a normative discipline. It is simply assumed that these methods can be applied irrespective of the nature of the domain being studied. As we saw earlier, however, the use of this method cannot be equated with 'science' in general.

Lawson, a critical realist, makes the same point in the language of ontology—that is: the study of the nature and structure of being, of the nature of what exists and, in the particular case, of the nature of social reality. To transfer mathematical deduction and the Newtonian metaphor successfully from classical physics to economics requires both domains to share underlying ontological characteristics—that is, that they are special cases of the same general thing. It is this sharing of characteristics that can allow parallel forms of analysis. Clark expands this point by suggesting that there are two types of analogy that involve shared characteristics that are used in this transfer. In the first, the formal structure of the model must correspond in some way with the phenomena being explained. In the second, the shared characteristics involve a material analogy—as in the assertion of a uniform invariant human nature.

Human economic behaviour does not, however, share characteristics with the physical entities of classical physics. They are very different things, not special cases of the same general thing. Lawson calls their confusion the abductionist fallacy. As Clark points out: 'Societies are not natural phenomena ruled by natural laws, nor created by natural forces. They are the creation of humans, as are their institutions, culture and history.'[69] Consequently, mathematical deduction is not a tool that is appropriate for the use to which it is being put.

To reiterate, there is a mismatch in most cases between the nature of social and economic phenomena and the nature and structure of reality presupposed by mathematical deductive modelling and its world-view. Furthermore, Lawson points out that the occurrence of event regularities of the sort that can be analysed scientifically by mathematical modelling are rare even in the natural realm—being restricted mostly to well-controlled experiments. Mathematical deductive modelling as an explanatory form or structure requires a closed, self-contained, atomistic, deterministic system that allows the deduction of consequences or predictions. This follows from Hume's conception of causality as constant conjunctions of brute, atomistic events in which 'same cause, same effect' applies everywhere.[70] In this view, causal laws are empirical regularities that are reducible to sequences of events and those events to experiences.[71] These are essential features of the particular explanatory form. Such atomistic entities are required to have separate, independent and invariable properties. This is not true of human beings, who are active agents in an open, complex world. In this world, there are no constant conjunctions among events and we cannot rely on empirical generalisations as law-like statements.[72]

Adolph Lowe drew attention to this fundamental objection to neoclassical modelling as long ago as 1935, when he argued that neoclassical economics rested on a highly questionable conception of mechanistic rationality and the constancy and uniformity of individual behaviour.[73] Interestingly, Lowe points out that even the laws of supply and demand involve adjustments of a much more complex nature than proposed in the mechanics of a pendulum, which do no more than maintain a preordained equilibrium.

He therefore rejected the idea of uniform economic laws, including the so-called laws of supply and demand. As he claimed, '[T]here are today no reliable laws of economic behaviour on which prediction can be based.'[74] Similarly, Knight—also in 1935—criticised the mechanical analogy in economics, and in particular the idea that the motive causing an economic action was understood as a force, similar to that idea in classical mechanics. That idea in mechanics—as well as having been discredited—was also criticised by March and Heinrich Hertz as being metaphysical. It acquired respectability only because in mechanics it was experimentally reproducible, not because it provided any ultimate explanation of mechanical behaviour. That experimental reproducibility is not true, however, for economic preferences.

Lowe, in his 1965 book *On Economic Knowledge*, develops his early critique into a formal argument with similarities to Knight's and Lawson's. Like them, he questions whether the logical structure of economic systems can be defined properly in mechanical terms. Lowe finds three features that are cornerstones of classical mechanics, which do not match those of real economic systems: the atomistic hypothesis; the mode of behaviour of these 'atoms'—what he calls the extremum principle, the economic equivalent of a force, the universal action directives operating in economic affairs, maximisation and minimisation; and a conservation hypothesis in which market processes are understood in terms of the conservation of energy in a closed system. As in Newtonian mechanics, the atomised entities of neoclassical economics are entirely independent and entirely reactive in a predictable manner to the forces acting on them with no independent freedom of movement. This simply denies human agency; and this feature of mathematical deduction requires economists to specify their theories in terms of atomised entities that are isolated so that only a few factors bear on phenomena, and to produce constant and invariable responses to given conditions so that event regularities are guaranteed. In such a closed system, event regularities occur in a causal sequence.

Economic 'idealisation' is, then, falsely supposed to produce a situation analogous to the experimental situations in the natural sciences, which attempt to close the system and to prevent any interference with the operation of the mechanism under study. Explanation, however, requires a move from phenomena at one level to underlying causal conditions. In experimental conditions in the natural sciences, most event regularities are restricted by experimental control so that the workings of specific intrinsically stable causal mechanisms are isolated from the effects of countervailing factors. The purpose of experimentation in a controlled environment is to identify empirically an underlying causal mechanism—not to produce event regularities for its own sake. It must also be assumed that the powers attributed to agents must always be exercised in non-experimental situations and in the given ways, regardless of the real outcome. This is so in the experimental situations used in the natural sciences: the underlying causal relationships identified by any experiment also operate in a predictable way in non-experimental situations and the event regularities produced relate to an underlying empirical causal relationship.

Such isolated event regularities in the social disciplines are rare because aspects of social systems are not static, but are open and intrinsically dynamic, involving a multitude of shifting causes. Such social systems exist in a constant state of becoming, exhibiting emergent properties and causal power dependent on human agency and practice but not reducible to that agency and practice, and dependent on internal relationships with other social entities. We are all involved in a very large number of different and changing, relatively stable social positions or roles that are independent of the individuals occupying them and which influence what we can do. These roles involve rights and obligations with normative force only and are related in turn to other roles occupied by other individuals with their different rights and obligations. Our reactions to social situations are related internally and are highly context specific, with primary importance probably attaching to the relations between roles rather than between people. Nevertheless, human beings possess intentionality or agency: they are not just passive reactors to the environment but are forward looking and make variable choices. Lawson argues that individuals form their longer-term goals in terms of the enduring, highly abstract aspects of society with the intention of adapting those plans to the specific contexts they encounter in action through life. They are therefore involved in the emergence of a sense of identity of the individual—the autographical narrative of the individual. Lawson warns us also against treating the features of social reality that are rather abstract as though they are concrete, and of mistaking the particular for the general. As we saw in Chapter 2, such social behaviour involves a skilled performance that is not reducible to analytical rationality involving the simple application of rules, but involves the transcendence of rationality by intuitive, experience-based, situational behaviour. In short, social entities are not invariable in behaviour, they are not atomistic and they are not reducible to a representative agent. Indeed, because of the way in which the social structure and human agency depend on each other—but are not reducible to each other—methodological individualism is not a tenable position in social theorising: 'Mainstream economics continually falls back on states of affairs, etc, that could not possibly come about.'[75]

In any event, in economics, the fictions assumed are not employed as a means of isolating the influence of other phenomena so as to identify an underlying causal relationship that explains how the surface phenomena was produced, but as essential preconditions to the mathematical deductive form of analysis and to the generation of the results. At the same time, abstractions such as representative agents and preferences are treated as if they are concrete and can successfully isolate the real phenomena of interest from other influences. Because of the above interdependencies, it is highly unlikely that social behaviour can be manipulated in any useful way by the experimental researcher. In short, Weber's qualified justification for his idealisations is misconceived.

To summarise, the closed atomistic and deterministic system of deductive mathematical modelling—this modern manifestation of a priori reasoning in economics—cannot, in general, fit the open, non-deterministic and non-atomistic social world. This lack of fit renders mathematics an inappropriate tool in the study of most economic and social phenomena; and this is the reason why this sort of modelling has been unsuccessful. It simply lacks the ability to illuminate most of the social realm. This is what Aristotle effectively told us 2,300 years ago. This is the fundamental reason why it is illegitimate to use this form of modelling and the associated Pareto-optimality decision rule in policy analysis. In addition, Lawson sees these methods as a barrier to true progress in economics—preventing us from uncovering any real causal relationships in economic phenomena. Although not excluding entirely the possibility of using mathematical deductive methods, Lawson is pessimistic about the prospects of their successful use. Consistent with the views expressed in Chapter 6, he calls for a pluralistic and interdisciplinary approach to economic analysis, but one involving a critical reflection on the ontological assumptions being used.

The Appreciative Justification for Competitive Markets and its Association with Lockean Political Theorising

In the absence of convincing empirical support for the neoclassical framework—an impossible task given the above ontological criticism—mainstream economists have usually taken the much stronger performance of capitalist economies compared with socialist economies as broad justification for their emphasis on market-based competition. Of course, very few people today are prepared to advocate the bureaucratic stupidity that was central to the command economies of the Soviet era. Nor is anyone denying that competition suitably channelled by cultural and legal norms plays a role in capitalist economies in sharpening the performance of firms. Is competition, however, the only thing that is important to capitalism? And, since capitalism is not a monolithic system, which capitalist system are we talking about? Why not, for example, imitate Denmark, a capitalist country that is very prosperous and has a comprehensive welfare state? Why pick the mean-spirited social policies of the contemporary United States? If one is to copy the United States, why not copy its active industry and innovation policies? Better still, why not pick the best of everyone's experience? Complacently satisfied with economic fundamentalism, we do not devote anything like sufficient resources to studying what other people do—or how the world is changing. Experience does not support the adoption of pure-market policies. As Ormerod points out, free-market policies are contrary to the whole of economic history since the Industrial Revolution:

> With the possible exception of the first wave of industrialisation in Britain, every country which has moved into the strong sustained growth which distinguishes industrial, or post industrial, societies from every other society in human history, has done so in outright violation of pure, free-market principles.

> Markets, competition and entrepreneurship are all very important, but by themselves they are not enough. Infant industries—even when they have become industrial giants—have sheltered behind tariff barriers; government subsidies have been widespread; there has been active state intervention in the economy; and, perhaps most important of all, successful companies have exercised power and control over their markets.[76]

Indeed, this is true of the whole of economic history.

The evolutionary and information schools of economics see this stronger performance as a reflection of the restlessness of capitalist economies—seeing economic growth as being driven not by market equilibrium but by the lack of such equilibrium. Market imperfections such as knowledge asymmetries, knowledge spill-overs, monopolies and disequilibrium could drive innovation and economic growth.[77] The stronger economic performance of capitalist economies might be due, therefore, not to a lack of government coordination, but to the combination of largely decentralised decision making and incentives and particular forms of government coordination involving strategic positioning, a very broad interpretation of market imperfections, strong investment in social capital and knowledge creation, social mobility and social risk sharing.

Despite these powerful objections, unregulated markets continue to be seen by economic fundamentalists, mainstream economists and many contemporary policy makers as the general rule, the natural state of affairs and the normative ideal, which real markets should emulate. As we have already seen, contemporary economic analysis then perceives government action as an intervention in the market, which has to be justified as a correction that will move the real situation towards that idealised state. This approach erects a sharp dichotomy between the public and private spheres—spheres separated by sharp boundaries enclosing distinct roles, which the above alternative approach denies. This dichotomisation, with its sharp separation of roles, has more to do with our rationalist heritage and with Lockean political philosophy than with the more nuanced relationships and permeable boundaries we encounter in practice. Importantly, different societies conceptualise these relationships differently, suggesting that these are culturally determined distinctions rather than universal principles. These distinctions also reflect our reductionism, which makes it difficult to conceptualise higher levels of organisation, collective purposes and coordinating roles.

This strategy produces an essentialist view of the State, which effectively excludes governments from any role in coordinating economic activity or redistributing income or risks—beyond providing a limited number of public goods such as maintaining property rights, enforcing contracts and maintaining public order—a position inconsistent with long historical practice. Economists in central agencies then act as Plato's authoritarian guardians in enforcing this questionable approach to policy analysis, with non-acceptance of this framework seen as irrational and not deserving respect. Of course, this stance conveniently ignores the unequal structural impacts of the macroeconomic instruments welded by central agencies and the Reserve Bank.

Economics and Economic Growth

Because of the static heritage of mainstream economics, it is a commonplace that mainstream economics lacks a convincing explanation of growth and dynamic change within an economy. Mainstream economics typically treats the growth of knowledge as a matter that is independent of the economic system—an assumption that is transparently false. This is not because economists do not recognise the central role of the growth of knowledge in economic development, but rather because they have been unable to incorporate this insight successfully into their mainstream models. The growth of knowledge is simply not a mechanical process. Though many have tried, it is not possible to simply add a new parameter for knowledge to a production function to get a sensible growth model.[78] The very idea of an aggregate production function that combines such disparate activities as cleaning shoes and building hydrogen bombs seems incoherent. The 'Cambridge Capital Theory Controversies' have undermined the logical coherence of the concept by showing the insurmountable theoretical problems involved in measuring capital. It follows that the concept of an aggregate production function is unhelpful, as is the empirical work based on it.[79] In this regard, Lipsey tells us: 'I have slowly come to accept that models of growth that use aggregate production functions and stationary equilibrium concepts, whether in the neoclassical tradition or the new growth tradition, offer only limited assistance in studying long term economic growth.'[80]

As much policy analysis is about economic growth, this lack of a convincing explanation of growth is something of an embarrassment to the profession. Similarly, the long-term strategic economic development decisions that confront governments—and which involve significant uncertainty—do not lend themselves to the mechanical method of mainstream economics. As George Shackle (1903–92) demonstrated convincingly, the future that flows from any particular decision is unknowable, involving as it does an infinite exponential cascade of different possible futures—undermining the possibility of any calculable probability analysis and consequently of any so-called rational analysis.[81] Therefore, the future is uncertain and any strategic positioning requires practical judgement.

In the absence of a successful growth theory, mainstream economists have been forced to rely on a wide range of statistical analyses to try to identify the significant influences underpinning economic growth, but such studies involve formidable conceptual and data issues. It is clear, however, that growth is not just about the accumulation of physical capital. These statistical studies are tending to provide empirical support for the importance of such things as innovation, knowledge, education and skills in the growth process. This reflects a strong consensus that innovation and technological development have underpinned economic development. Consequently, it is clear that comparative advantage is not simply a matter of natural endowments but can be created. Indeed, economic development is a contingent, path-dependent process and often occurs in clusters. As a result, developed countries throughout the world are placing increasing emphasis on these factors in their economic policies. It is also clear from Weber and North that economic development is heavily dependent on the complex of institutions and beliefs that underpin high trust and initiative in society. This is now seen as a major factor explaining the uneven nature of economic development throughout the world. The existence of mechanisms sharing risk and uncertainty in social and economic life could well be important to economic development.

New and Revived Schools of Economics

A number of relatively new and revitalised schools of economic analysis are attempting in complementary ways to address the fundamental inadequacy of the conventional conceptual framework. As indicated above, the information school has—contrary to the conventional assumption of perfect information—pointed to the costliness of information, to its asymmetrical distribution and to the inadequacy of pricing signals for coordinating economic activity in the real world. Revised institutionalist and sociological approaches are seeking to explain more fully how economic behaviour occurs in a complex web of social relationships and institutional arrangements, which vary from society to society and which exhibit features of historical contingency and path dependency. The effect is to undermine the belief that there is a universal model of the capitalist system that we can aspire to imitate. In this regard, the 'National Systems of Innovation' approach to innovation studies emphasises that innovation by firms cannot be understood in terms of decisions at the firm level and emphasises the role of the complex interactions between the firm and its economic and social environment in promoting innovation. This approach draws attention to the importance of country-specific institutional arrangements for innovation, technological development and economic performance more generally. Similarly, political economy schools point to the pervasive presence of power relationships in the economic system—and the impossibility of isolating the two influences. Of course, the impacts of those complex power relationships are not open to simple modelling, least of all by neoclassical models.

Importantly, the evolutionary school denies that the social and economic world is a machine. Furthermore, it has abandoned the idealisation of the market, methodological individualism, Pareto-optimality, the concepts of market failure and the Newtonian metaphor in favour of the biological metaphor of a living system. In such an interdependent system, the behaviour of the system in aggregate cannot be deduced by simple extrapolation from the behaviour of typical individuals. Rather, it is the result of complex interactions throughout the system—a system that learns and adapts.[82] Furthermore, it means that there is also macroeconomic behaviour that cannot be traced to microeconomic foundations. Consequently—and contrary to Thatcher—there is such a thing as society,[83] something the rest of us knew already.

What this all means is that the evolutionary school has abandoned the Enlightenment's utopian dream of reorganising society on the basis of a priori reasoning. This represents a historically important paradigm shift, and a return to an earlier and more fruitful master narrative. It also denies the possibility in practice of achieving an optimal allocation of resources. Consequently, Ormerod tells us:

> The behaviour of the system may well be quite different from what might be anticipated from extrapolation of the model of [the] behaviour of individuals. Individual behaviour does not take place in isolation. On the contrary, there are impacts on the behaviour of other individuals, which in turn cause feedbacks elsewhere in the system, and so on and so forth. Behaviour is altogether too complex to be captured by a mechanistic approach.[84]

Instead, the evolutionary approach sees the economy as an emergent complex, interdependent system subject to positive feedback, uncertainty, path dependency and historical contingency. The last two teach us that history matters in economic development. Ormerod, citing mathematician Henri Poincaré, tells us: 'The distinguishing feature of chaotic systems is that their behaviour is impossible to predict in the long run, a property which cannot be encompassed by a view of the world which regards it as an enormous machine.'[85]

There has therefore been a great increase in interest in chaotic and non-linear systems in the natural sciences. Importantly, in such systems, the connection between the size of an event and the magnitude of its effects is no longer simple or linear. Small initial differences can lead to enormous differences in outcomes and, consequently, outcomes are extremely difficult to predict or control. For example, although such systems might remain stable in a wide range of circumstances, the presence of tipping points could lead to wholesale changes of behaviour. This has led Ormerod to emphasise that 'unpredictability is an inherent part of the processes that underlie a very wide range of economic and social phenomena'.[86] In contrast with mainstream economic analysis, it employs a very sophisticated form of mathematical analysis made available only recently through the development of chaos and complexity theory.

This perspective is not open to the reductionist modelling employed in mainstream economics, or to simple prediction. Nevertheless, it employs simulations to compare theoretical speculations with real-world data. For example, its simulation of the growth and decline of business firms has successfully shown patterns that are encountered in experience. Interestingly, the evolutionary and institutional economists are generating new growth models that dispense with the neoclassical assumptions and which are proving to be consistent with real data. Similarly, such modelling is capable of generating the main characteristics of movements in unemployment over time, in volatile financial markets and in the clustering that results from the geographical location decisions of businesses.[87] As Michael Porter has already told us, there could be good sense in trying to seed cluster development.[88] Such modelling can also throw light on the impact of random decisions on the selection of new technologies. In respect of the latter, it follows clearly that government support to get new products to market quickly is well justified. Indeed, the evolutionary perspective fits well with organisational theory, with its emphasis on the strategic interdependence between firms, uncertainty, asymmetrical information and increasing returns.[89] Nevertheless, this form of modelling cannot finally escape the ontological objections raised by Lawson, as it also is inherently deterministic. While it could illustrate phenomena that occur in practice, it cannot provide adequate causal explanations. That does not apply, however, to non-mathematical forms of evolutionary theorising, which seem to offer significant promise.

An evolutionary perspective—although not discounting the above insights into the inability of prices to capture fully the social costs and benefits of economic activity—draws particular attention to the experimental nature of all economic institutions, policy decisions and policy structures. Additionally, in the presence of uncertainty, decisions can be made only on the basis of guesswork, and economic agents and decision makers learn as they proceed, groping towards better outcomes and arrangements. In particular, such uncertainty can result from the path-dependent nature of innovation, where things are learned sequentially as experience accumulates through time, where the range of choice defies analysis or where the situation is ill defined. This approach therefore places great store on the capacity and willingness of economic agents to experiment and absorb knowledge and experience and—contrary to the recent emphasis on rationalisation—on the value of redundancy and variety.

This situation, contrary to Hayek, does not reduce the policy maker to impotency. It does require *phronēsis* or practical wisdom. It should lead to a far stronger emphasis on learning from international experience and from policy experience more generally. Policy development should, therefore, wherever possible, rest on experience, including the tacit learning of market participants, with all the contingencies that this involves rather than on the reductionist analysis of conventional theorising. Importantly, this perspective denies the conventional assumption that returns to investment—adjusted for risk—tend to equalise in practice. It points to areas of investment that will potentially deliver greater benefits than others. This is a policy approach that fits well with the recent East Asian, European and US experiences with their strong emphasis on the creation of comparative advantage through innovation.

Consistent with the above, Lipsey, Ken Carlaw and Clifford Bekar argue that the long-term growth that has raised our living standards to undreamed of levels has been driven by technological revolutions that have periodically transformed the West's economic, social and political landscape in the past 10,000 years and allowed the West to become, until recently, the world's only dominant technological force.[90] They point to a series of technological revolutions, from the domestication of plants and animals, through writing and printing, to the factory system, the dynamo and information and communications technology (ICT). Because of their widespread effects throughout the economy, these general-purpose technologies have driven economic growth in the past 10,000 years. Importantly, they suggest that the development of such technologies has sped up in recent centuries and that this provides a point of strategic policy leverage. They therefore suggest that policy makers should pay particular attention to the development and diffusion of technologies with these general-purpose characteristics, and in particular to ICT, nanotechnology and biotechnology.

Bromley, an 'old' institutionalist, draws attention to the important distinction between the institutional framework within which day-to-day economic decisions are made and those day-to-day decisions themselves. He reminds us that the market is simply the artefact of a large number of prior collective actions. The market cannot, therefore, logically constrain other collective actions.[91] Nevertheless, Bromley counsels particular care in making institutional change. I would also counsel particular care in making significant organisational changes with widespread impacts. Because it sets the framework for economic activity in general, and the distribution of its benefits, institutional and significant organisational changes should not be treated as if they are simple welfare-enhancing transactions. It is in that context—and with a firm recognition of the gross limitations of the concept of economic efficiency—that many of the changes made in the name of microeconomic reform should have been considered. What was required was not simply a trite assertion that competition was inevitably good because it promoted efficiency, which in turn promoted welfare, but a historically informed analysis of the purposes served by those institutions and arrangements, and a more realistic assessment of the real welfare consequences of change. In short, we deserved more from our political leaders and policy advisers.

It should by now be clear that economics, Lockean political philosophy and their advocates can claim no privileged position in public discourse, standing in judgement of the public's collective policy wishes and of government action.

The Reform of Economic Teaching

In Australia, only a few universities teach alternative economic perspectives or try to place economic behaviour in its historical and institutional setting. This is true also of economics teaching world-wide. The widespread criticism of mainstream economics and of the extreme policy agendas of economic fundamentalists have led to calls for the reform of economic teaching, including by economics students in France, Britain, the United States and Australia. Students at Cambridge University have called for an opening up of economics. They wish to encourage debate on contemporary economics and have criticised the monopolisation of the discipline by a single mode of reasoning.[92] They complain that the content of the discipline's major journals, its faculties and its courses all point in this one direction. They doubt, like the analysis above, the general applicability of this formal approach to understanding economic phenomena and call for the foundations of the mainstream approach to be debated openly along with competing approaches. In particular, they believe that the *status quo* is damaging to students who are taught the 'tools' of mainstream economics without learning the domain of their applicability. They believe this situation is harmful to society in that it is holding back a deeper knowledge of economic phenomena and is denying the possibility of more fruitful policy approaches. It is also inhibiting the funding of alternative research approaches. Consequently, they advocate pluralism in economic research, calling not merely for its tolerance but for its flourishing. To this, I say Amen!

I therefore suggest that the teaching of economics should be changed so that the core content of undergraduate courses consists of the philosophy of the social disciplines, the history of economic thought, contemporary schools of economic thought—and then, and only then, more detailed study of particular schools. This should be complemented by a resumption of the study of economic history and the history of approaches to economic policy problems.

ENDNOTES

1 Stiglitz 1991, p. 14.
2 Marx and Engels 1970.
3 Henry 2007.
4 van Wanrooy 2007, cited in Sydney Morning Herald 2007.
5 Hayek (1945, p. 520), cited in Lowe 1965, p. 103.
6 Hayek 1974.
7 Leontief 1983, p. 2.
8 Coase 1991.
9 Coase 1999.
10 Shubik 1970.
11 Blaug 1997, p. 3.
12 Klamer et al. 2007.
13 Hodgson 1993.
14 Ball 2006.
15 Ormerod 2006.
16 Lawson 2003.
17 Hollis 1977.
18 Koslowski 1983.
19 Hodgson 1993.
20 Jonsen and Toulmin 1988.
21 Oakeshott 1962.
22 Polanyi 1946.
23 Smith 1776, Book 1, Ch. 7.
24 Lowe 1965. See also Clark 1992.
25 Mirowski 1989.
26 Jevons 1871, Preface.
27 Mirowski 1989, p. 103.
28 Clark 1992.
29 Knight 1935.
30 Loomes 1991, cited in Ormerod 1994.
31 Hodgson 1993.
32 Guala 1998.
33 Hamminga and de Marchi 1994. This brief account draws on the historical account given by these authors.
34 Cited in ibid., p. 20.
35 Mill 1874, p. 608.
36 Clark 1992.
37 Gaula 1998.
38 Pareto ????, cited in Gaula 1998, p. 40.
39 Ormerod 1994.

[40] Smolin 1998.

[41] Kincaid 1996, p. 7.

[42] Ibid., pp. 12–13.

[43] Sen 1977, p. 323.

[44] Let us be clear, it is a normative view as well as being a false factual claim. It tells how we are supposed to behave—and anyone who does not behave 'rationally' is criticised as being deficient.

[45] http://en.wikipedia.org/wiki/Daniel_Kahneman

[46] Knight 1935. See also Koslowski 1983.

[47] Keen 2006.

[48] Blaug 1992, p. 49.

[49] Bromley 1990.

[50] Samuels 1972.

[51] Bromley 1990.

[52] This is, of course, not true in every instance, as the rich derive considerable satisfaction from conspicuous consumption. That conspicuous consumption poses considerable difficulties for the theory. In any event, that satisfaction provides us with no persuasive reason to assign moral priority to such consumption.

[53] http://www.miskatonic.org/godel.html

[54] Robinson 1954.

[55] Ibid., cited in Omerod 1994, p. 42.

[56] Georgescu-Roegen 1979.

[57] Ormerod 1994.

[58] Ibid.

[59] Ibid.

[60] Ibid.

[61] Stiglitz ????, p. 21.

[62] Ormerod 1994.

[63] Lipsey 2007.

[64] See http://www.econlib.org/library/Enc/Information.html for a quick summary by Joseph Stiglitz.

[65] Stiglitz 1993.

[66] Ibid., p. 29.

[67] Stilwell 2002.

[68] Lawson 2003.

[69] Clark 1992, p. 174.

[70] Ozel 2002.

[71] Bhaskar 1998.

[72] Ozel 2002.

[73] Lowe 1935. See also http://en.wikipedia.org/wiki/Adolph_Lowe

[74] Lowe 1969.

[75] Lawson 2003, p. 19.

[76] Ormerod 1994, p. 63.

[77] DISR 1998.

[78] Lamberton, Don 1993, Personal communication.

[79] McCombie 2006.

[80] Lipsey 2005.

[81] Shackle 1961.

[82] Ormerod 1998.

[83] Ormerod 1994.

[84] Ibid., p. 37.

[85] Ibid., p. 40.

[86] Ormerod 1998, p. xii.
[87] Ormerod 1994 and 1998.
[88] Porter 1979.
[89] DISR 1998.
[90] Lipsey et al. 2005.
[91] Bromley 2006.
[92] The Cambridge 27 2001.

Chapter 9: The Doctrine of Freedom of Contract

Thou shalt not take the name of the Lord thy God in vain; for the Lord will not hold him guiltless that taketh His name in vain.
— Exodus 20

But governments do not limit their concern with contracts to a simple enforcement. They take upon themselves to determine what contracts are fit to be enforced...There are promises by which it is not for the public good that persons should have the power of binding themselves.
— J. S. Mill[1]

Few who consider dispassionately the facts of social history will be disposed to deny that the exploitation of the weak by the powerful, organised for purposes of economic gain, buttressed by imposing systems of law, and screened by decorous draperies of virtuous sentiment and resounding rhetoric, has been a permanent feature in the life of most communities that the world has yet seen.
— R. H. Tawney[2]

Introduction

Contract law is one of the fundamental institutions that underpin the market system. It is not often understood that the religious and governmental regulations that underpin agreements have a very long history. Therefore, it is not often realised that the above quotation from the Ten Commandments refers not to the uttering of obscenities, but to the process of oath taking in ancient Israel, which—among other things—helped enforce contractual arrangements. A rigid view of contract law in the form of the doctrine of freedom of contract is a central element in economic fundamentalist rhetoric. It is desirable, therefore, for critics of economic fundamentalism to equip themselves with some understanding of the origins of this doctrine and how it emerged and then declined as part of the nineteenth-century view of social theory and *laissez-faire* economic doctrine. Our account now turns to an examination of the emergence of classical contract law towards the end of the nineteenth century in England and the United States. It will be shown that the doctrine has its origins in the breakdown of medieval ideas regulating social and economic life and the emergence of social contract ideas as a basis for explaining social order and for justifying the property rights of the elite. Natural law, the natural lawyers and the gradual secularising of that tradition also heavily influenced the growth of the doctrine. Consequently, my account parallels the earlier account of the rise of social contract ideas. As we saw then, many philosophers and economists used the concept of a contract as their fundamental explanatory device in explaining or justifying social order. The doctrine of freedom of contract is therefore central to the conceptual framework within which economists and, in particular, economic fundamentalists operate.

The development of common law and the associated growth of contract law in England and the United States parallel the rise of capitalist society and its adherence to social-contract theory.[3] That law was influenced heavily by the Enlightenment and by its natural-law outlook while English judgements and theorists continued to exercise considerable influence in the United States after the War of Independence.[4]

Chapter 4 pointed to the gradual breakdown in the medieval idea that people owed a wide range of social and religious duties. In that medieval world, relationships were largely customary, but law backed that custom. Indeed, law, custom and morality are not distinguished clearly. In particular, while there were some elements of bargaining and free choice in economic life, that freedom was constrained severely by ethical ideas, which ensured that economic relationships occurred in ways that were thought to be fair and just. The notions of a just price and a just wage were central to medieval economic thought.[5] Custom and law imposed a duty on those exercising authority to enforce those just prices and wages. Any bargain in which one party obviously gained more advantage than the other and used his power to the full was regarded as usurious. Similarly, no one doubted that everybody was entitled to subsistence. As a result, there were repeated attempts to impose price controls on staple items as well as to regulate wages. Until the end of the fifteenth century, all lending at interest was, in theory, prohibited. A sale in which there was a defect in either quantity or quality was sinful and was void. A seller was obliged to reveal a secret flaw in the product being sold. In this world, the doctrine of *caveat emptor*—the companion to the doctrine of freedom of contract—had no standing, while the possession of property involved temporary custodianship and carried duties as well as rights.[6]

The system of justice included the King's tribunals and local and special courts in which administrative and judicial functions were blended. These functions included a wide range of regulations controlling trade and ensuring an open market, a fair price and good quality. These arrangements became even more formalised as market towns succeeded fairs. As ecclesiastical authority broke down, the secular realm—particularly the Crown—took a larger and larger role in maintaining these fair-trading regulations. By the end of the sixteenth century, the system of justice was shared between the common law, the courts of custom, the liberties of the towns and special tribunals. Importantly, customary law had not yet emerged as the common law.

The above attitudes towards the regulation of economic activities were associated with a view of the law as a body of essentially fixed doctrine, derived from divine and natural law, and to be applied in order to achieve a fair result in particular cases.[7] As a consequence, judges in England, and later in the American states, conceived of their role as merely discovering and applying pre-existing legal rules. This brought with it a strict conception of precedent in which judicial innovation was not permissible. At the same time, statute was conceived of largely as an expression of custom.

With the gradual breakdown of these ideas, the lords and freeholders came to question to some extent the legitimacy and privileges of the Crown and of government more generally. They also began to see themselves as the owners of the land they occupied, while at the same time ideas about the ownership of property become more absolute. Similarly, ideas about freedom also became more absolute. The breakdown of central government during the Civil Wars (1642–51) also disorganised the system of market control, which had come to depend on national authority.[8] That authority to regulate economic life never completely recovered even though the supervision of an expanding trade and commerce was maintained with decreasing effectiveness until well past the Restoration (in 1660).

As recounted in Chapter 4, these changes made it easier for the propertied elite to see civil society as based on a social contract, rather than socially defined moral obligations backed by divine law. Unlike the traditional natural law, natural-rights theories were based on conflict between the individual and the State. As the basis of legal obligation was redefined in terms of popular sovereignty and contract, the natural-law foundations of common-law rules began to disintegrate.[9] By the eighteenth century, political theorists and men more generally thought of their relationships with each other, and the State, in contractual terms in which a key role was assigned to individual choice.

With this came a growing perception that judges did not merely discover law, they made it. Therefore, judges began to gradually feel free to disregard earlier precedent and to make law consistent with the prevailing contractual ideology. There developed, as a result, a close connection between liberal economic ideas and the rule of law as it came to be understood after 1688. In this regard, the idea that the law should be regular, certain and subject to interpretation by independent judges is not normatively neutral, but has a powerful value content—valuing individual freedom and free choice above some other values such as equity. Nor is the rule of law normatively neutral because by promoting procedural justice it enables the shrewd, the calculating and the wealthy to manipulate its forms to their advantage.[10]

English common law gained its supremacy over the prerogatives of the Crown largely through the efforts of Sir Edward Coke (1552–1634).[11] Coke was opposed to what he saw as the usurping of power by the King, and appealed to the common law as a traditional barrier to the interference by government with the economic and other freedoms of the individual.[12] In the process, Coke distorted and misinterpreted the past common-law tradition to make it seem more strongly favourable to economic liberalism than it was in fact. In particular, the doctrine of *caveat emptor* had no ancient ancestry. It was Coke who helped establish it by setting it down in his treatises on law.[13] Lord Mansfield, Chief Justice of the King's Bench from 1756 to 1788, was another economic liberal, who did much to consolidate and develop commercial law. During his tenure, the overthrow of the traditional role of the courts in regulating the equity of agreements began in earnest.

Mansfield's conception of a general jurisdiction of commercial law—which emphasised its claimed universal character and its supposed correspondence with natural reason—had an overwhelming influence in the United States. This involved a new stress on the functionality and rationality of the legal rules free from every local peculiarity, and brought with it a growing distinction between morality and the law. Horwitz,[14] in particular, notes the influence of a new utilitarianism in nineteenth-century US law in general and in the erosion of concern for the fairness of contracts in that country. What was involved was a change in the moral conception underlying contract in which the express contract became paramount. Horwitz also notes the influence of a new alliance between the mercantile classes and the legal profession—firstly in trying to subvert the influence of equity and of juries on commercial cases, and ultimately in moulding legal doctrine to accommodate commercial interests. This growth in commercial law also reflected the increasing complexity of economic transactions.

While there had never been an overt principle of fairness in the common law of contracts, lawyers of the seventeenth and eighteenth centuries were not indifferent to such concerns. There were signs of a broad principle of good faith emerging in the common law of contracts in the late eighteenth century—a development that ultimately came to naught. This could have been because jury control over damages rendered it unnecessary to strive for such a substantive doctrine. For Atiyah, it was the jury that bridged the gap between morality and the law.[15] In any event, grossly unfair contracts were liable to be upset in chancery, and it was in chancery that the greater part of contract litigation took place.

Chancery was the second of two different traditions in English legal practice. Equity consisted originally of a body of rules and procedures that grew up separately from the common law and were administered in different courts. From the time of Edward II or earlier, the chancellor and his officials—later the Court of Chancery—as 'keeper of the King's conscience', could give equitable relief where the common-law courts might provide no remedy. The chancellors until the appointment of Sir Thomas Moore in 1529 were churchmen. With the rationalisation of legal practice, the common law and equity are now merged and administered by a single set of courts almost everywhere. While the merger of law and equity is usually portrayed as a rationalisation of civil procedure, for Horwitz, it represents the final and complete emasculation of equity as an independent source of legal standards.[16]

As the law moved increasingly to recognise the generality of the binding nature of contracts, they began to be seen as being about promises, wills and intentions and not about particular relationships and particular transactions. The rationalisation of the common law was influenced by a new legal literature looking for legal principles based on rational first principles. Further, there was a particularly close relationship between law, economics and the social sciences in the first 40 years of the nineteenth century. The economic ideas that influenced the development of the common law were those of the classical economists between 1776 and 1870. While they assumed that the law must provide for the enforcement of contract, they gave little thought to why the enforcement of contracts was not itself a form of government intervention.[17]

Laissez-faire principles might well have had more influence on judges—and judge-made law—than on the other organs of the State. Atiyah makes much of the emphasis on principle in Victorian life and on its tendency to become more absolute.[18] The rise of formalism in the law, particularly in the United States, played a role in this attitude. This formalism—the attempt to place the law under the rubric of science—was a further development of the rationalism noted earlier. It involved a belief that all law was based on abstract legal doctrines and principles, which could be deduced from precedents, and that there was only one correct way of deciding a case. The formalists aspired to create formal general theories that would provide uniformity, certainty and predicability in legal arrangements and which would distinguish sharply between law and morals.[19]

This formalism served to reinforce the recently developed law of contract by giving the impression that the principles of the law of contract were inexorable deductions drawn from neutral principles. Within this framework, it was the market that supplied the so-called neutral principles, free from all political influence. This attempt to separate law from politics has been a central aspiration of the American legal profession in particular.[20] It served the interests of the legal profession to represent the law as an objective, neutral, apolitical and scientific system. This encouraged a search for fixed principles that would govern a large number of cases without too close an inquiry into the facts. As a consequence, every law not fitting the pattern of the free market was defined simply as being outside the law of contract, as some other exceptional body of rules: company law, factory legislation, building laws, sanitary laws and so on. Such statutes were excluded from the emerging conceptual scheme of a general law of contract based on free-market principles—the classical theory of contract. Nevertheless, Atiyah cautions that legal writers, in commenting on the influence of *caveat emptor* and *laissez-faire*, attribute a much greater significance to particular legal cases than is warranted by the practice of the courts more generally. Nevertheless, the effect of these changes in values was to reshape the legal system to the benefit of business and to the detriment of less powerful groups. The selection of 'leading cases' and the dismissal of the 'anomalous' were clearly influenced by the ideological commitments of the system builders.

Ironically, while the nineteenth century was the very heyday of sanctity of contract and of *laissez-faire*, it was also the period when Britain was creating its modern machinery of government. Despite the widespread support for free markets, the role of government and of government regulation expanded greatly. Atiyah comments that one of the main inhibitors of such government regulation had been ignorance of the social evils associated with rapid population growth, industrialisation and urbanisation, and of how to deal with them.[21] The growth of a professional bureaucracy—and the activities of royal commissioners and parliamentary select committees—overcame this ignorance and led to much legislative and regulatory activity. Many of the participants—who started as disciples of Smith and Ricardo, and as firm believers in individualism and self-reliance—were converted by their inquiries into zealous public servants demanding more legislation, better enforcement and more administrative staff.

This enormous change in the character and quantity of legislation had a profound impact on the very idea of a contract-based society. With the growth in increasingly sophisticated legislative activity, the courts abandoned overt law-making activity. Atiyah argues, therefore, that by 1870, the influence of individualism had largely broken down, and had been replaced by a different order in which control, regulation, licensing and institutional arrangements had become the dominant mode of social organisation.

Atiyah also qualified his account of the dominance of the doctrine of freedom of contract by suggesting that English judges were stronger in doing justice in a pragmatic fashion than in providing theoretical justifications for their decisions. In addition, the weight of earlier tradition was influential in particular cases. As a result, *laissez-faire* and the doctrine of freedom of contract had a much greater influence on contract law in the United States than in England. Gilmore attributes this to the influence of 'the great systems-builders' seeking to develop self-contained and logically consistent systems of rules and doctrines.[22] Gilmore also speculates that the Puritan ethic was somehow involved, noting the moral fervour with which judges insisted on the performance of contractual obligations. For Horwitz,[23] nineteenth-century US judges professed a contractual ideology that was instrumental in promoting economic development and *laissez-faire*, in being hostile to legislative or administrative regulation. Moreover, the idea of property as a pre-political Lockean natural right—not created by law—remained at the centre of American legal thought.[24]

Under this influence, the US Supreme Court in 1905[25] elevated the principle of freedom of contract to the level of a sacred constitutional principle. In the common law in England, however, the tide was about to turn. Even in the United States, the dominance of the doctrine of freedom of contract was short-lived. The US Supreme Court decision of 1905 provoked a progressive reaction and fundamental attacks on this form of legal thought. With these attacks came a breakdown in these absolute concepts of property and contract.

In England, the idea of *caveat emptor* did not long survive the growth in consumption of manufactured goods and the reality that people did rely on their suppliers when it came to the quality of the goods they supplied. For example, in *Piggott v. Stratton* in 1859, Lord Campbell and the Lords Justice of Appeal ruled that 'the business of life could not be conducted if it were required that men should anticipate and expressly guard against the wily devices to which the deceitful may resort'.[26]

From the 1860s onwards, the English courts started to limit the application of the principle of *caveat emptor*. Consequently, some inquiry by the courts into the facts was needed from this date onwards. In 1884, in *Foakes v. Beer*, the House of Lords started to move back towards the idea of fairness in an exchange and away from the idea that a bare agreement was always binding. At the same time, the idea of freedom of contract was itself subject to increasing political challenge, particularly with the expansion in franchise. This involved a significant shift in political thinking—a shift that occurred in England and the United States. For example, in the 1880s, George Bernard Shaw opposed the appeal to free contract, free competition, free trade and *laissez-faire* against the regulatory activities of the State.[27]

Similarly, philosopher T. H. Green set out to challenge the primacy of freedom of contract in his *Liberal Legislation and Freedom of Contract*: 'To uphold the sanctity of contracts is doubtless a prime business of government, but it is no less its business to provide against contracts being made, which from the helplessness of one of the parties to them, instead of being a security for freedom becomes an instrument of disguised oppression.'[28]

Joseph Chamberlain in 1885 also criticised the faith that had been placed in freedom of contract for the best part of the nineteenth century:

> The great problem of our civilisation is still unresolved. We have to account for and to grapple with the mass of misery and destitution in our midst, co-existent as it is with the evidence of abundant wealth and teeming prosperity. It is a problem which some men would set aside by reference to the eternal laws of supply and demand, to the necessity of

freedom of contract, and to the sanctity of every private right of property. But gentlemen, these phrases are the convenient cant of selfish wealth.[29]

Increasingly, the common law and legislation interfered with that freedom of contract and with the principle of *caveat emptor*. The effect was to narrow significantly the field of activity over which freedom of contract and contract law held sway. This change is perhaps marked most clearly by the passage in England in 1893 of the *Sale of Goods Act*, dealing with such matters as title, quiet possession, freedom from encumbrances, correspondence with description, merchantable quality, fitness for purpose and sales by sample. This legislation was adopted virtually unchanged by every Australian state and territory.[30]

It is clear, therefore, that the idea of freedom of contract as an absolute ideal gained credibility and influence in the nineteenth century but was eclipsed by the end of the century as the practical consequences of reliance on this principle began to be realised and began to offend the sense of justice of the bulk of the population.

Surely it is now clear that property and contract are not natural rights but social and legal artefacts, or even 'techniques'. Atiyah argues that there is much about the modern world that suggests an affinity with some of the older traditions and suggests that, at least in England, the law is returning to these traditions. This is a theme that arose in Chapter 4 with Toulmin's suggestion that there is a need to return to the humanism characterised by Erasmus and away from the dogmatism of the Enlightenment.[31]

Some Reflections on the Doctrine of Freedom of Contract

As indicated above, the doctrine of freedom of contract was the central doctrine of the classical contract law that came to full development in the last half of the nineteenth century. The very idea of a general law of contract is part and parcel of the same positivist era. This law was the creation of judges and thesis writers influenced by social-contract ideas dating back to Locke, by classical economic thought and the associated ideology of voluntariness. Among legal theorists of the late nineteenth century, the law of contract was the archetypical branch of what was conceived of as legal 'science'. This involved an attempt to systematise the various doctrines and decisions of the courts to do with contract issues into a consistent and logical theory in which the legal rules were to be deduced from general concepts such as property.

The classical view of contract involved a process of abstraction, generalisation and systemisation in an attempt to create a unitary theory that was thought to be free of moral valuations and could therefore be described appropriately as a science. This development formed part of the more general attempt to substitute scientific discourse for moral discourse at a time when the traditional religious underpinnings of moral values were coming under increasing attack with the decline in formal, traditional religious belief. There was, therefore, an attempt to distinguish between what was conceived of as public law and contract or private law—law that individuals legislated for themselves. This distinction between public and private law was part of the Enlightenment's attempt to separate the public from the private realm in political and legal theory. Central to this conception of contract was the idea that contract obligations arose from the wills of the individuals concerned, and not as a result of a socially and historically constructed legal institution. It has much in common with the Lockean idea of property as a pre-social natural right. Indeed, the obligation to fulfil promises—central to classical contract law—was at its heart a Lockean natural law, but a natural law increasingly bereft of its metaphysical foundations.

In retrospect, this development could be seen as a process of reification—a manifestation of an excessively legalistic mentality in which legal rules and universal abstractions acquired sanctified status and became absolutes. What was also involved was an attempt to claim that the rule of law provided norms independently of politics. There is a close connection between this ideal of a rule of law and not of men and *laissez-faire* ideas. It was assumed that rules fixed and known beforehand would make it possible for economic actors to foresee how the courts would use their coercive powers and would allow those economic actors to plan their activities effectively. Hayek made much of these ideas in his defence of the market system.[32] They involve an underlying assumption that predictability is associated with generality. It is also a view that conceives of courts as enforcers of rules rather than as settlers of disputes. This is a view that also conceives of judges as rulers on the truth—a view that encourages the adversarial approach of common-law courts. From this rule-based point of view, any movement away from the strict enforcement of rules towards multi-dimensional standards such as fairness is to be deplored. Herein lies the source of the conflict between equity as it had been developed in earlier times and classical contract law. The nineteenth-century desire for uniformity, certainty and predictability could not be reconciled with the discretionary element implicit in equity. Herein also lies the source of the reluctance to inquire too closely into the particularities of the subject matter of an agreement, the circumstances of its making, the expectations of the parties and especially of the outcomes realised. In practice, what came to be important in contracts was the written document as interpreted by the courts in a highly literalist manner, independent of any substantive inquiry of the parties (the parole evidence rule precluded such inquiry into the circumstances surrounding written contracts). All of this involved a commitment to a rigid and mechanical decision rule, to be implemented in a mechanical manner—a replica of the determinism of Newtonian physics.

This view of contract law has increasingly foundered on the evidence of experience. Too rigid an enforcement of contracts on the basis of freedom of contract led to what were recognised clearly as unjust outcomes. Legislatures and, over time, the courts themselves did not tolerate these. As a matter of practical politics, legislatures everywhere moved to legislate and regulate to remove the grosser abuses of the contract system. These measures have not been confined to simply addressing issues associated with contract formation but have been concerned increasingly with the substantive outcomes of contractual arrangements. Therefore, contract law came to be robbed systematically by legislatures of much of its subject matter. As a consequence, pure contract law has ceased to occupy so central a position in the economic system.

Among legal theorists, it was recognised increasingly that the refusal to inquire into the circumstances surrounding a contract was obviously inconsistent with the will theory on which classical contract theory rested.[33] This in turn led to the replacement of the will theory with the development of the objective theory of contract—a theory that acknowledged openly that contracts were enforced for reasons of public policy. It has come to be recognised—particularly in the work of the theorists of the American realist school—that classical contract theory is neither neutral nor natural; it is instead a historically contingent social and legal construct.[34]

In consequence, the very idea of contract law as a neutral system has had to be abandoned. Rather, all valuations at law are moral choices. Contract law—and decisions in particular cases—involves a balancing of conflicting social values, not a deduction from consistent scientific principles. This realisation has posed an overwhelming challenge to deductive legal reasoning, as it is impossible to reason down from very general principles to particular decisions. Furthermore, this viewpoint leads directly to a good deal of scepticism about the practicality of general rules of the kind Hayek advocated.[35] It also became clear that classical contract law conferred a privileged position on the *status quo*, the intelligent and the powerful.

Even the ideology of voluntariness has come under attack. The first point to be made in this regard is that methodological individualism in economic and moral theorising does not necessarily lead to any justification for a policy of self-reliance, however much the two are confused in practice. Secondly, it is obvious that individuals are frequently not the best judges of their own interests. In any event, individual interests are often subordinated to social and political goals, including in the law of contracts. It has been pointed out also that markets are to some extent coercive. Consequently, the problem is to decide what forms of coercion are to be regarded as legitimate.

The ideology of voluntariness has been seen to provide the more powerful party to a contract a freedom of manipulation and motivation, a freedom from any onus of articulation and a freedom from any other legal duties that cannot be fitted under the rubric of contract as promise.[36] Consequently, there has been a growing reluctance to concede to big business the right to dictate contract terms to less powerful parties—particularly consumers—through standard-form contracts. Equally, there is a problem of deciding to what extent deception and concealment of information in contractual negotiations are also to be regarded as legitimate.

More generally, having acknowledged that contracts are enforced for reasons of public policy, and that contracts involve a balancing of conflicting value choices, the idea that contracts should always be enforced is open to question. This is what has happened as a result of legislative action and as a consequence of judicial enlargement of the law of contract and various equitable doctrines. Adding to the confusion has been the realisation that the grounds for equitable intervention in the enforcement of contracts cannot be fitted under a unified doctrine or theory. The law is not in fact static. Judges are required frequently to rule on novel situations requiring departure from precedent. In such cases, even perfect knowledge of precedent and other case law applying to the situation will not protect the subject of litigation. In these cases, the judge retrospectively rules certain conduct to be contrary to law—that law being the decision just made. In practice, one can conduct oneself in accordance with the law only to find out some time later that when a judge considers that conduct it is ruled to be contrary to the law. Only at that point does the conduct become, retrospectively, contrary to law. No degree of knowledge or foresight can prepare someone for a judgement such as this.

As Joseph Schumpeter pointed out, it is inevitable that the creative destruction inherent in capitalism will create new situations. The destructive and creative impulses of capitalism create novel situations requiring novel judicial treatments. If judges were not free to create novel legal pronouncements, commercial activity would move progressively beyond the influence of law. While precedent binds judges, if they were not free to rule creatively in novel situations the law would ossify.

Equity is always available as a remedy in a court of law, even though equity is distinct from law. Being governed by vague maxims rather than strict rules—and gifted with great flexibility with regard to remedies—equity has been criticised by many legal scholars and practising jurists as too unpredictable to be relied on to produce the proper result. Nonetheless, all lawyers within the common-law tradition are examined in equity during their training, and equitable arguments are always available to litigants. It is the reputation of equity as soft, vague and unpredictable that prevents it from occupying a similar place of renown as the law proper. Only a brave barrister will resort to an equitable argument in place of a legal one, despite vast quantities of case law recording successful equitable arguments.

All of these influences have led to a period of confusion in contract theory. Here in Australia there has been a growing acceptance of the objective theory of contract at the very time that theorists in the United States detect a process of doctrinal disintegration. There, it has been perceived increasingly that contract law—as modified by the various equitable doctrines—involves a complex of diffused principles.[37] Even the idea of—and a need for—a general law of contracts as a uniform body of rules has been questioned.[38]

Some theorists such as Gilmore predict the death of contract and its collapse into the law of torts.[39] While it might be going too far to suggest that a uniform law of civil obligations might emerge, there is certainly an increasing recognition of an obligation of good faith and a development in the direction of a duty of care in contractual arrangements. The former is not as radical as some of its opponents might like to suggest. For example, the German civil code has had such an obligation for more than a century and a doctrine of good faith is now firmly entrenched in the US Uniform Commercial Code and in the Restatement of Contract. More generally, contract theorists such as Atiyah[40] and Ian Macneil[41] have questioned whether contracts should be seen as a legal mechanism for establishing long-term business relationships, rather than the risk-allocation mechanisms that economists have conceived them to be. This point of view emphasises the relational element involved in any commercial arrangement that is not a simple one-off exchange transaction. Atiyah,[42] for example, sees contractual obligations arising primarily from the reliance one party places on another, while Macneil stresses the fact that all longer-term contracts are incomplete. It is simply not possible, in practice, to anticipate all the possible eventualities and risks involved in a continuing commercial relationship. Macneil sees the solution to this incompleteness as involving the development of intermediate contract norms to govern the continuing relationship. This is consistent with empirical evidence of real commercial behaviour, particularly between large companies where the existence of a valued long-term relationship induces companies to resolve difficulties that occur in the relationship without reference to the written agreements between them, and without reference to the courts.

The Recent Fair-Trading Debate in Australia

These debates in eighteenth and nineteenth-century England and the United States have had their parallels in other jurisdictions that share the common-law tradition, including Australia—most recently, in the fair-trading debate that occurred at the federal level between 1974 and 1997. That debate arose out of continuing complaints from the small-business sector regarding the conduct of big business towards small business. It revolved around a series of proposals aimed at effectively broadening, by statute, the Equitable Doctrine of Unconscionability—the doctrine that carried the remnant of the medieval concern for fairness in trade and contracts, and which permitted courts to decline to enforce contractual arrangements. As we saw above, while the remit of contract law diminished progressively in the past two centuries, the Equitable Doctrine of Unconscionability within contract law had been progressively emasculated—being restricted to tightly defined procedural issues. Consequently, the proposals at the heart of the fair-trading debate challenged directly the classical doctrine of freedom of contract.

Lack of space prevents me dealing with the movement away from the doctrine of freedom of contract in the Australian states through detailed legislation covering such matters as weights and measures, sale of goods, safety and hire-purchase legislation. In particular, attention will not be directed at the New South Wales *Contract Review Act 1980*, which authorised the NSW courts to rewrite unfair contracts or to refuse to enforce them. Rather, attention will be directed to Commonwealth legislation intended to apply broadly to all trade and commerce. Nor will a detailed account be given of the constitutional limitations that confine the application of that legislation.

The first Commonwealth trade practices legislation was the *Australian Industries Preservation Act 1906*, which was inspired by US antitrust laws. The act proved ineffective, being subjected to a successful High Court challenge in 1910 and a successful Privy Council challenge in 1912. Similar state legislation was also rendered ineffective. The second major attempt was the *Trade Practices Act 1965–71*, which took a limited approach, influenced by the UK's *Restrictive Trade Practices Act of 1956* rather than the broad prohibitions of the US law. It established a process of registration and adjudication of the lawfulness of a practice by an administrative tribunal. This act and related successors were criticised as being inefficient, slow and costly and because examinable agreements or practices remained operative until restrained by the tribunal.[43]

The *Trade Practices Act 1974* was the third major attempt to introduce effective general trade practices legislation in Australia:

> Restrictive trade practices have long been rife in Australia. Most of them are undesirable and have served the interests of the parties engaged in them, irrespective of whether those interests coincide with the interests of Australians generally. These practices cause prices to be maintained at artificially high levels. They enable particular enterprises or groups of enterprises to attain positions of economic dominance which are then susceptible to abuse; they interfere with the interplay of competitive forces which are the foundation of any market economy; they allow discriminatory action against small businesses, exploitation of consumers and feather bedding of industries…The consumer needs protection by law and this Bill will provide such protection.[44]

The *Trade Practices Act 1974* involved a substantial statutory interference in freedom of contract. Not only was it intended to promote economic efficiency, it was intended to promote fairness in competition and in dealings between businesses and between businesses and consumers, and to promote honesty in the provision of information. The inference to be drawn was that in enacting this legislation, the government and parliament had accepted that market forces left to themselves would not produce either just or economically satisfactory outcomes.

Since the enactment of that legislation in 1974, there have been at least 18 major reports or proposals to amend the act to strengthen the regulation of unfair business practices. The most influential of these inquiries was the Fair Trading Inquiry by the House of Representatives Standing Committee on Industry, Science and Technology (the Reid Committee).[45] The Reid Committee tabled a bipartisan report, *Finding a Balance Towards Fair Trading in Australia*, in the House of Representatives in May 1997. It concluded that concerns about unfair conduct towards small business were justified and should be addressed urgently. To this end, the report made wide-ranging recommendations to induce behavioural change on the part of big business towards small business and to provide adequate means of redress. In summary, the recommendations covered:

- major amendments of the *Trade Practices Act 1974* prohibiting unfair conduct in trade or commerce
- Commonwealth facilitation of uniform state and territory retail tenancy legislation and a retail tenancy code backed by the *Trade Practices Act 1974*
- generic franchising legislation
- representative actions by the Trade Practices Commission in respect of Part IV of the *Trade Practices Act*
- a range of measures regarding the financial sector's treatment of small business
- mandatory pre-trial mediation of unfair conduct disputes
- an educational campaign for small-business entrants.

The committee believed that an inequality of power in commercial transactions was the underlying cause of the unfair business conduct raised with it. The result was a bias in business dealings in favour of powerful companies with the financial resources to engage in lengthy litigation. This left small-business people open to arbitrary or opportunistic conduct with an associated economic and social cost. The committee pointed also to a lack of adequate research into small-business failures in Australia, and to an absence of any formal research in evidence tendered to the committee. Nevertheless, the anecdotal evidence provided by the numerous small-business people convinced the committee that unscrupulous conduct of big business towards small business was a serious problem causing significant economic and social damage. The committee was conscious that in a competitive economic environment many businesses would fail, but that awareness did not exclude the need to examine the causes of failure—and action to alleviate its adverse consequences.

While acknowledging the inadequacies of the previous regulatory control regime, the committee was strongly critical of the efforts of the Australian Competition and Consumer Commission (ACCC) in relation to small-business disputes. It believed that there was a need to establish a body of precedent under proposed new provisions in the *Trade Practices Act 1974* as quickly as practicable.

The strength and breadth of the committee's report came as a surprise to many observers, including small-business representatives. It ran directly counter to the rhetoric of deregulation that had surrounded much recent public policy debate, including the rhetoric contained in its own terms of reference. As could be expected, small-business representatives welcomed the committee's report warmly, while big-business representatives were much more reserved. Typical of the critical reactions was an editorial in the *Australian Financial Review* on 26 June 1997, which attacked the report as naïve, claiming that economic competition was desirably deliberate and ruthless. The editorial also claimed that requiring fair conduct from banks or large shopping centre managers in dealing with their clients and tenants would be a restriction on their ability to compete and that small businesses would suffer as a result. For its part, the Property Council of Australia commissioned economic consultancy firm Access Economics to produce a so-called 'independent' response. Their document, *Tipping the Balance?*,[46] which focused on retail tenancy issues, claimed the Reid report was not consistent with its terms of reference in that it would promote 'sub-optimal economic outcomes' as well as increasing the regulatory burden on retail businesses. Additionally, the Reid report was said to be internally inconsistent and to have paid scant regard to hard data on retail-industry performance. *Tipping the Balance?* criticised the Reid report's reliance on anecdotal evidence from small-business operators and small-business groups and from competing expert witnesses. Of course, the claim to independence lacks credibility, given that the Property Council was paying. Rather, *Tipping the Balance?* provides an example of the partisan use made of economic analysis in public policy debate. It also provides an example of the demands made by economists generally that the forms of analysis used in public policy debate be confined to formal economic analysis relating to economic efficiency, as they define it, and that the direct experience of those involved in markets be disregarded.

Prominent economic fundamentalist P. P. McGuinness claimed that the Reid Committee's report relied on emotion, prejudice and a desire to cater to the voters.[47] This reflects an elitist contempt for the political process typical of many economic fundamentalists. McGuinness claimed that the report was a classic case of an attempt to enrol political power and anti-competitive regulation in the cause of ripping off consumers. This one-sided application of capture theory also appears typical of economic fundamentalism: only economic fundamentalists can be trusted to present views untainted by self-interest—a view peculiarly inconsistent with their own theories. It also attempts to exploit the Enlightenment's depreciation of the role of emotions in human judgement.

On the other side, Professor Andrew Terry argued in the *Australian Financial Review* on 27 June 1997 that the committee's recommendations would not damage the economy, but would lead to a much needed extension and clarification of the law. The chief executive of the Council of Small Business Organisations in Australia, Rob Bastian, dismissed big-business concerns about uncertainty as 'crap', pointing to the uncertainty that had previously confronted hundreds of thousands of small businesses.[48]

Press reports claimed that the government had been subjected to heavy lobbying by several business groups strongly opposed to the committee's proposals to adopt a new Section 51AA banning unfair conduct. The Treasury and the Department of Industry, Science and Technology were also reported to have been opposed. On the other hand, there was said to be support from coalition backbenchers.[49] Interestingly, a significant proportion of the government's backbench had experience with small business, including members of the Reid Committee.

On 11 July 1997, the Minister for Small Business, Geoff Prosser, who was hostile to the committee's recommendations, was forced to resign his portfolio after weeks of political controversy because of a perceived conflict of interest on these issues. Prosser was replaced by one of the government's most experienced and effective politicians, Peter Reith, whose portfolio, Workplace Relations, acquired responsibility for small-business matters. This represented a significant upgrading in the importance of the small-business portfolio.

The government responded to the committee's report in a statement by Reith to the House of Representatives, 'New Deal: Fair deal—giving small business a fair go', on 30 September 1997. As far as the rhetoric of the statement was concerned, the minister said:

> Make no mistake about it, this Federal Coalition Government, this Prime Minister, and this Minister, is [sic] pro-small business, and proud of it…This response on fair trading policy…is the strongest message ever sent from Canberra to Australia's small business community that they now have a national Government that has listened, has understood and has acted.[50]

The minister announced that the government would act on the recommendations of each of the seven areas of reform identified by the committee: unfair conduct, retail tenancy, franchising, misuse of market power, small-business finance, access to justice and education. Nevertheless, while claiming full credit, the government did not implement the committee's recommendations in full. The minister said that, in a number of important respects, the government response had gone further than the committee's recommendations, particularly in the area of effective enforcement of fair-trading issues by the ACCC. In summary, the government action involved:

- a new provision in the *Trade Practices Act* to give small business genuine access to protection against unconscionable conduct
- a new provision that would allow industry-designed codes of practice, in whole or part, to be underpinned legally and made mandatory under the *Trade Practices Act* and enforced as breaches of that act
- a new provision that would allow the ACCC to take representative action on behalf of small business for misuse of market power by big business
- a new provision that would give small-business interests equal importance to consumer interests when appointments were made to the ACCC
- a directive to the ACCC under the *Trade Practices Act 1974* requiring the ACCC to enforce small-business legal rights against unfair business conduct. The government also provided funding to enable test cases to be undertaken.

In respect to the first of these, the new provision extended the existing common-law doctrine of unconscionability by mirroring the legal rights available to consumers under the existing Section 51AB and incorporating most of the matter included in the committee's proposed Clause 51AA. Importantly, however, the government legislation persisted with the term 'unconscionable conduct' rather than 'unfair conduct' proposed by the committee. The committee had recommended that the term 'unconscionable conduct' be replaced with a term without its limiting legal entailments and proposed the term 'unfair' as covering all the circumstances that would be covered by the terms 'unconscionable', 'harsh' and 'oppressive'. The government's bill also dropped the terms 'harshness of the result' from the matters that the courts could take into account. Importantly, the new provision was also limited to transactions under $1 million and publicly listed companies were excluded from instigating action under the provision. This limit was subsequently raised to $3 million and is currently being increased to $10 million. In addition, a new provision is being added to include the use of a unilateral right to alter a contract as one of the matters the court can have regard to. Perhaps the most important recommendation that survived the government's consideration of the Reid Committee's proposals was the requirement that corporations covered by the section were effectively required to act in good faith.

While the committee recommended clearly that the law should be extended to cover procedural and substantive circumstances, it was unclear to what extent the government's legislation achieved that widening. The government's response, therefore—which, in other respects, was very much in the spirit of the committee's recommendations—fudged the central issue in the inquiry, and limited the application of the changes to unconscionability to relatively small transactions. Consequently, it will be necessary to await the reaction of the courts over time to the new clauses before it is clear how extensive the change has been. In this regard, Bob Baxt recently criticised the ACCC for its failure to bring more meaningful unconscionability cases to the courts in the past five years.[51]

Throughout this debate, the issues remained essentially the same: whether, and to what extent, the Commonwealth should legislate to regulate unfair conduct by big business towards small business. Similarly, the arguments used throughout changed in style only, not in content. The debate also exhibited the tendency for public policy to follow a path of incremental change, which the early Charles Lindblom advocated as the best form of policy development.[52] It exhibits also the entrenched power of big-business groups that the less optimistic late Lindblom feared would forever provide a barrier to more radical change.[53] It is also unusual among contemporary policy debates in that, for the most part, it finds big and small-business lobby groups on different sides of the debate. Governments had sought to chart a course through two powerful business lobbies—advancing two different conceptions of justice—neither of which governments wished to offend. Consequently, throughout the debate, governments of both persuasions conceded as little to the pressure of small-business groups as they could get away with at the time.

The debate also provides a good illustration of the entrenched power of economic methodologies and values as the dominant evaluative considerations used in contemporary policy debates. Big business used the rhetoric of classical contract law—along with the contemporary economic rationalist rhetoric of minimum effective regulation—as the means of deflecting the political pressure. Indeed, the debate has been conducted almost entirely under this rubric. For example, during the Blunt Committee Inquiry in 1979, in commenting on a proposal from the Law Council of Australia for a general prohibition of harsh, unconscionable or unfair conduct, the Blunt Committee expressed the view that the *Trade Practices Act 1974* was directed primarily at enhancing competition and should not deal with the 'moral' issues involved in business conduct.[54] The Business Council of Australia endorsed this view in its submission to the Reid Inquiry.[55] The claim is, of course, unsustainable. It is a view that relies directly on the positivist separation of law and morals—a separation that is largely discredited. In the particular case, protecting competition—as the *Trade Practices Act 1974* does in some of its sections—is not an end in itself. It is done because of the belief that competition enhances economic outcomes and that in turn enhances human welfare. That is, it is done for moral reasons—economic efficiency being one of the intermediate moral values served by that Act. Competition is seen also as producing fairer economic outcomes, as enhancing equity. Consequently, the competition provisions of the Act are intended to enhance welfare and fairness. Conduct that directly reduces welfare or fairness can hardly be thought to be consistent with the aims of that Act. Even the Blunt Committee acknowledged that competition laws operated directly on business conduct and accepted that the Act's thrust against anti-competitive conduct was tempered to some extent to protect small business and to promote fairness.[56] This should come as no surprise as this is what the minister said when introducing the legislation in the first place. The Act was intended to enhance competition and protect against unscrupulous conduct.

There is some similarity between the position of the Business Council of Australia and Posner's economic theory of the law, in which the law is seen as serving wealth maximisation.[57] Of course, the law to which he refers is judge-made law, which he considers morally superior to statute law, which tends to depart from his efficiency norm.[58] Posner's theory is, in fact, an extreme manifestation of the economic fundamentalism of the Chicago school. It is such a transparently impoverished account of justice—running in the face of our contemporary moral vocabulary—that it warrants little serious consideration. For Posner, suffering is irrelevant to his conception of justice unless it is accompanied by a capacity to pay. It equates justice with economic efficiency, but an economic efficiency that is defined purely in terms of wealth maximisation. It is clearly intended to be a descriptive and a normative theory. It is a theory that attaches importance to freedom of choice, but only to the positive rights and values intrinsic to capitalism, the protection of private property rights, promise keeping and freedom of contract—those rights and obligations that are also central to Locke's social-contract theory.

The Blunt Committee went on to define 'desirable economic performance' specifically in terms of 'economic efficiency'—a concept that it took to be the equivalent of Pareto-optimality. The Blunt Committee acknowledged—in a footnote only—some limitations of this concept, but its analysis remained unaffected by that acknowledgement, a deficiency shared by subsequent references to 'economic efficiency' throughout this debate, and in recent public policy debate more generally. Similarly, the Business Council of Australia's submission to the Reid Inquiry mounts a standard economic argument based on Pareto-optimality: that there should be 'regulatory intervention' only when 'economic efficiency' is lessened by distortions in a market—interventions that hinder the movement of resources to their most valuable and efficient use, and where the benefits of that intervention outweigh the costs. It went on to suggest that this calculus is one that should properly be performed by the Productivity

Commission, the successor body to the Industry Commission, an organisation believed popularly to be committed to economic fundamentalism.

Throughout the debate, the Trade Practices Commission and its successor—the ACCC—consistently argued that economic efficiency would be enhanced by action directed against unconscionable conduct in commercial transactions. Similarly, small-business groups responded with theoretical arguments to the effect that economic efficiency would be enhanced by legislation of the type they had proposed. There seems little recognition of the fact that mainstream economics has little to say about productive and dynamic efficiency.

Similarly, the Treasury responded with concerns about the impact of regulatory action on transaction costs throughout the economy. It went on to argue that there were two primary reasons for government intervention: market failure and equity/fairness. As we saw earlier, this use of the word 'intervention' is not neutral, as it implies interference in the normal, or even the ideal, state of affairs—an interference that has to be justified. The implication is that the normal or ideal is an unregulated market. It carries with it a commitment to the minimalist account of the role of the State derived from Locke. Treasury agreed, however, that inadequate information, high transaction costs and substantial market power might give rise to a 'market failure'. This failure can result in efficient small businesses being discouraged from entering the market or being forced out of business, thereby producing a sub-optimal allocation of the community's resources. Treasury also acknowledged that unfair business conduct could lead to other social costs, such as increased bankruptcies and social dislocation. It was concerned, however, that general legislative action to deal with these issues—and associated equity considerations—could have adverse consequences on business certainty and the competitive process. In relation to the economic arguments, neither the relevant departments nor the big-business lobby paid any serious attention to 'distributional' or equity issues. In the case of the Treasury, the existence of equity concerns is acknowledged briefly, but not discussed. There seems to be no recognition that, in practice, it is impossible to separate efficiency from distribution issues, however much economists like the conceptual distinction. More broadly, the word justice is never uttered.

In Chapter 3, attention was directed in particular to the role of trust in promoting social and economic interaction. In the language of neoclassical economics, however, trust and similar values—loyalty or truthfulness—are called 'externalities'.[59] The very language seems to marginalise their importance even though technically they are called externalities only because they are external to the price system—those areas in which the price system fails to operate. In a climate in which the importance of externalities is discounted, there is a danger that the importance of those moral values will be forgotten. This is relevant particularly to contracts in contemporary society that rely on informal constraints to ensure that parties will act honourably when unforeseen circumstances arise during the course of contracts, which, in practice, are necessarily incomplete.

The dangers associated with a transaction depend not only on the nature of that transaction, but with the trading environment of which it is a part. Consequently, opportunistic behaviour on the part of one party to a transaction or a contract can increase risks attached to all transactions and the costs of doing business generally. Consequently, the moral and legal sanctions that reduce opportunistic conduct also reduce transaction costs generally. In particular, they can have the effect of infusing trading confidence into transactions that are characterised by costly information and power asymmetries. Moral standards and a complementary legal framework provide infrastructure fundamental to the efficiency of the market system—our moral and legal institutions are an essential part of the capital of the economic system. As Arrow has noted, a lack of mutual trust is among the properties of many societies whose economic development is backward. This argument runs directly counter to Treasury's claim that unfair trading laws could raise transaction costs generally.

Such social demands can be expressed through the internalised demands of conscience or they can be embodied in formal legal rules. Reliance on the more informal demands of conscience could well have efficiency benefits in some situations because of their adaptability to different circumstances. The calculation involved in the application of rigid rules could well be dysfunctional if cooperative attitudes—with their positive spill-over effects—are undermined. It follows that an exploitative business culture is likely to be less efficient than one in which there is a greater degree of give and take. A number of specific studies have looked at the role played by social convention in helping to sustain collaborative relationships—even where recourse to the courts might have been preferred. In particular, Stewart Macauley researched non-contractual relations in the manufacturing industry in Wisconsin in 1963.[60] He found that business people often preferred to rely on a person's word in a letter, a handshake or common honesty and decency—even when the transaction involved exposure to serious risks—rather than seek professional legal advice and protect themselves with a tightly worded contract. Macauley discovered that in some cases, business people considered that recourse to legalism in relationship-building indicated a lack of trust, turning a cooperative venture into an antagonistic horse-trade. Any weakening of the social and moral sanctions promoting such give and take could well increase the need for the codification of such standards through law.

The potential exists for significant conflict between the internalised social demands of conscience and the social demands expressed through formal legal rules, particularly in a litigious culture. Lacking extensive experience of the rigid application of the formal rules of contract law, inexperienced small-business operators are likely to expect that standards of conscience will govern—or at least moderate—the business relationships they enter into. Further complicating this situation is the likelihood that unscrupulous businesses will exploit these expectations in contract negotiations so as to impose harsh contract terms. Of course, unscrupulous businesses have been known to lie about their intentions in order to obtain the agreement of the other party.

It is argued, therefore, that such competition as is permitted is the servant of our fundamental social values, not the determinant of our values. In particular, it is those fundamental values that define what is meant by social welfare. Consequently, such fundamental values as fairness or justice in social relationships are not to be conditioned by more instrumental values such as competition. Competition must therefore always remain bounded; the question that then has to be decided is to what extent? What is also evident is that the debate cannot be settled on the basis of theoretical arguments based on mainstream economic analysis or current moral theories based on individualistic premises. It involves the complex empirical issue of whether, in practice, unregulated markets can produce efficient or equitable outcomes. It appears to be an economic issue that can be answered only by experience—by experimentation. Economic categories do not, however, cover all the possible issues adequately. Some forms of behaviour are simply considered wrong, regardless of the consequences. Consequently, resolution of the question involves the application of practical moral wisdom and can be mediated only by the political process.

Curiously, it appears that we are unable to come to terms with the meanings of the words 'unconscionable' and 'unfair', while being obliged to pretend that all legal words should have an objective and identifiable meaning available to all. Of course, most people will not have heard of the word 'unconscionable', let alone how the courts have used it in recent times. This stands in marked contrast with the word 'fair', which is used daily by everyone in our society.

There is a particular irony about the closing phases of this debate as well. At a time when small-business groups were pressing strongly for justice in their dealings with large businesses—pointing in particular to oppressive terms and conditions of contractual arrangements, to the unilateral alterations of terms and conditions and to unfair terminations of long-term contractual arrangements—these same lobby groups were also opposing unfair dismissal laws intended to protect employees from similar unfair conduct by small-business employers.

The next chapter will turn to a more general reflection on the long journey we have shared together.

ENDNOTES

[1] Mill 1994, p. 162.

[2] Tawney 1926, pp. 252–3.

[3] Horwitz 1974.

[4] Horwitz 1977.

[5] Tawney 1926, p. 157.

[6] Hamilton 1931, p. 1133.

[7] Horwitz 1977. Horwitz's comment is applied to eighteenth-century America, but the context makes it clear that it applies with equal force to England in an earlier period.

[8] Hamilton 1931.

[9] Horwitz 1977.

[10] Horwitz 1977b.

[11] Encyclopaedia Britannica 1981, p. 825.

[12] Viner 1960.

[13] Hamilton 1931.

[14] Horwitz 1977.

[15] Atiyah 1979. In this account of the rise of the doctrine of freedom of contract, I have drawn heavily on Atiyah.

[16] Horwitz 1977.

[17] Atiyah 1979.

[18] Ibid.

[19] Horwitz 1992.

[20] Horwitz 1977.

[21] Atiyah 1979.

[22] Gilmore 1974.

[23] Horwitz 1977.

[24] Horwitz 1992.

[25] Ibid., citing *Lochner v. New York*.

[26] Atiyah 1979, p. 478.

[27] Ibid.

[28] Ibid., p. 585.

[29] Ibid., p. 587.

[30] Taperell et al. 1978.

[31] Toulmin 1990.

[32] Hayek 1973.

[33] Horwitz 1972.

[34] Ibid.

[35] Hayek 1973.

[36] Lucke 1987, pp. 173–5.

[37] See Mason and Gageler 1987 and Horwitz 1992.

[38] Atiyah 1986.

[39] Gilmore 1974.

[40] Atiyah 1986.

[41] Macneil 1980.

[42] Atiyah 1986.

[43] Government of Australia 1976.

[44] Commonwealth of Australia 1973, pp. 1013–14.

[45] Government of Australia 1997.

[46] Access Economics 1997.

[47] McGuinness 1997.

48 Abernethy 1997.

49 Burton and Murphy 1997.

50 Reith 1997, p. 1.

51 Baxt 2007.

52 Lindblom 1977.

53 Lindblom 1982.

54 Government of Australia 1979. In the event, the committee considered that a law prohibiting 'unfair' business conduct was going further and was not compatible with the provisions of Part IV of the Act. The committee felt, however, that there was great merit in exposing the proposal to debate and discussion and considered it a worthwhile area for the government to keep under active examination.

55 Business Council of Australia 1997.

56 Blunt Committee 1979.

57 Posner 1981.

58 Campbell 1988.

59 Arrow 1974.

60 Macaulay 1963.

Chapter 10: Some Normative Reflections

Man's fate will forever elude the attempts of his intellect to understand it...The quest for the laws which will explain the riddle of human behaviour leads us not towards the truth but towards the illusion of certainty, which is our curse.
— Grant Gilmore[1]

The love of money is the root of all evils...Warn those who are rich in the world's goods that they are not to look down on other people; and not to set their hopes on money...Tell them they are to do good, and to be rich in good works, to be generous and willing to share—this is the way they can save up a good capital sum for the future if they want to make sure of the only life that is real.
— St Paul[2]

Reiteration

This book has—like Gilmore above—been highly critical of the 'abstract impersonal values, the universal solutions and the logical imperatives' being relied on by contemporary governments and international economic organisations to formulate economic policy.[3] Human knowledge narratives—including economic theories—like human laws, should not be seen as mystical absolutes but as tentative and imperfect social constructs, open to challenge and change. In particular, economic and social theories and laws—like the classical law of contract—cannot be understood independently of their social and historical contexts, and of the traditions of thought of which they form part.[4] Therefore, the rise and the subsequent fall of the doctrine of freedom of contract—recounted in the previous chapter—has much to do with the rise and the subsequent disintegration of the nineteenth-century concept of explanation in the natural and social disciplines. That doctrine and the associated forms of explanation lie at the heart of economic fundamentalism.

Nineteenth and twentieth-century social theory—in the tradition of Descartes, Hobbes and Locke—sought to find general laws of society modelled on the natural sciences, just as Spencer, Marx and numerous others sought to find general laws of history and social progress. Classical contract law in its fully mature state—as exemplified in Langdell's casebook of contract law towards the end of the nineteenth century—was an abstraction from which all the particularities of person and subject had been removed.[5] Indeed, for theorists such as Langdell (1826–1906), law was a science and his casebook was an attempt to select and classify all the important contract cases ever decided, and to determine what he thought to be the small number of logically consistent and self-contained principles and doctrines that lay beneath those cases. For classical contract law, there was only one true, universal and unchanging rule of law—what Gilmore[6] calls a 'mystical absolute' or a 'logician's dream of heaven'. This view of contract law had a close intellectual and historical relationship with *laissez-faire* economics and with the free market of classical and neoclassical economic theory.

This 'positive' tendency of the social disciplines and of law had its origins in the Enlightenment project, enjoyed a renaissance in the 1920s and 1930s and persists in economics to this day. Elsewhere, as such authorities as Horwitz, Toulmin, Rorty and Lyotard tell us, belief in the possibility of general laws capable of making explanatory or predictive statements in the social disciplines has plummeted: 'The result has been a dramatic turn towards highly specific "thick description" in which narrative and stories purport to substitute for traditional general theories.'[7]

We should therefore be wary of the seductions of grand theories, sacred rules and idealisations that have a problematic connection to the 'reality' they purport to describe.

In Chapters 5, 6 and 7, the privileged epistemological status of scientific reasoning was seriously challenged along with the separation between fact and value as the basis of value-free social disciplines. This challenge has been associated with a growing understanding of the contingency of the categories and frames of reference employed in the social disciplines, along with a growing awareness that knowledge is itself constructed socially. There has also been a growing understanding of the world as complex, multi-factored and interdependent. This, in turn, has led to a loss of faith in the single-factor chains of causation that were embedded in most nineteenth-century explanatory theories.[8]

This critique also points to the collapse of the philosophical dualisms that have characterised all forms of theoretical debate since the Enlightenment. The representative schemes of our language cannot sustain these efforts to formulate categories that are mutually exclusive and final. This insight led, for example, to Dewey's refusal to accept a deep chasm between 'principled' and 'results-oriented' ethics and jurisprudence, and to neo-pragmatism's rejection of the choice between deontological and utilitarian moral theory.[9] These developments have tended to undermine the hope of finding rational ethical foundations for our social, political and economic arrangements and, with it, the special right of philosophers and other theorists to preach about those arrangements. For Dewey, James and Peirce, truth 'was not to be found in the abstract logic of ideas, but in their practical consequences. There were no absolute or a priori truths, only workable and unworkable hypotheses.'[10] The very idea that human reason could discover immutable metaphysical principles that could explain the true nature of reality was an illusion. This, of course, undermines faith in all forms of dogmatism—and dogmatic explanatory schemes—including absolute property rights, absolute human rights, absolute markets and absolute rules more generally.

Among American legal theorists of the progressive and realist schools, the challenge to nineteenth-century legal orthodoxy—with its scientific pretensions rooted in natural rights, individualism and absolute property rights—involved a fundamental re-examination of the idea of a rule of law independent of politics and the idea of a 'self-regulating, competitive market economy presided over by a neutral, impartial, and decentralised "night-watchman" state...Classical legal thought and contract law was neither neutral, nor necessary, but was instead a historically contingent and socially created system of thought.'[11]

This attack questioned the dichotomy between the State and the market, between ends and means, between procedure and substance and between public and private law. The last dichotomy was a central feature of classical contract thought, with its will theory of contract. Over time, it came to be recognised that the institution of contract was itself subordinate to social and political goals. The market, property rights and the law more generally were social creations—products of social and political struggle. Importantly, there was no privileged category of economic relations that could be regarded as voluntary.[12] Rather, property was a delegation of coercive state power to individuals, while the market was an organised form of coercion of the weak by the strong. The Lockean idea of natural property rights helped to disguise the coercive nature of these institutions. Since there was no such thing as a completely voluntary market, there could be no completely normatively neutral market because rules were needed to regulate that coercion. Of particular relevance to this book are the rules that regulate the coercive enforcement of contracts by the State.

These developments in American legal thought—influenced by American pragmatism—and the claim that truth was not to be found in the abstract logic of ideas, but in their practical consequences, also called into question the claim that legal reasoning could imitate geometrical forms of argument. Such deductive reasoning suppressed the moral or political choices that were inevitable between possible inferences in long chains of reasoning. Likewise, deductive reasoning—by assuming contradictory postulates—could produce radically different ethical systems. In any event, such forms of reasoning have themselves come under sustained attack. Mathematicians and geometers had come to understand that geometries were formal logical systems based on arbitrary assumptions whose only essential attributes were self-consistency, with no necessary connection to reality. Similarly, it was possible to invent different logics such as the different non-Euclidean geometries. Consequently, there are no universal laws of logic attributable to the universe or to human reason; they are merely human conventions, valued only for their usefulness. Similarly, mathematics was simply a humanly devised tool with no connection to any metaphysical or theological absolutes. All logical and mathematical reasoning is purely tautological—the elaboration of implications contained in the definition used, according to problematic, socially created, formal systems of thought. This critique of logic and mathematics undercuts all pretensions to a priori and absolute knowledge. There was no such thing as abstract reason and impartial legal or any other theory. Moral beliefs and social preferences were prior to reason, and we needed to be conscious of the philosophical assumptions underlying our actions.

Within the American legal profession, objective contract theory—and legal theory more generally—has been recognised as 'Euclidean', proceeding deductively from what are claimed to be 'self-evident truths' about the judicial process. Many of the a priori assumptions of traditional legal theory are, however, themselves subject to significant attack. For Jerome Frank, the legal profession manipulated abstract concepts to construct a façade of certainty and absolute rationality over a confused legal process.[13] Such positivist legal theory—and positivist social science—suppresses political and moral discourse by appropriating the prestige associated with the natural sciences and conferring a privileged position on the *status quo* and on the professional expert—be it a judge or social scientist—with a capacity for judgement based on claimed technical expertise, neutrality and impartiality. It is also reflected in the increasing professionalisation and credentialism of political, social and academic discourse and the need for such professionals to justify their prestige and influence. Such 'scholasticisms' were merely escapes and delusions. In practice, judges shared and implemented their personal standards, the moral standards of the legal profession or the moral standards of those members of society they admired, with the reasons given for judgements being rationalisations that manipulated the language of precedents to produce the desired result. All of this should sound familiar to critics of economic fundamentalism.

The rejection of the possibility of demonstrating the truth of ethical propositions has left such moral ideas without a convincing theoretical basis. This does not in itself undermine the fundamental significance of such ideas for the stability of society. Paradoxically, the declining faith in the expertise, neutrality and impartiality of experts has led—in the United States in particular—to a reinvigorated emphasis on proceduralism within political theorising and the law. It is, however, a proceduralism that, imitating the alleged neutrality of the market, is biased in favour of the existing distribution of wealth, power and privilege, and which refuses to look at substantial outcomes of legal and market processes. Indeed, the market system is proceduralism writ large. In the case of the equitable doctrine of unconscionability within Australia, it has been seen that, while there has been a steady increase in concern about procedural unconscionability, there has been a considerable reluctance to extend the doctrine formally to cover substantive issues.

More broadly, with such theories as Rawls' 'Theory of Justice' and Habermas's ideal speech conditions, there has been a major theoretical effort to revive social-contract theory and procedural accounts of justice. These reflect a desire to accommodate the positivist claim that values were incapable of objective determination—a claim that assumed a privileged epistemological status for scientific knowledge. Hart and Sacks therefore make the claim that:

> These institutionalised procedures and [the] constitutive arrangements establishing them are obviously more fundamental than the substantive arrangements in the structure of society...The principle of institutional settlement expresses the judgment that decisions which are duly arrived at as [a] result of duly established procedures of this kind ought to be accepted as binding upon the whole of society unless and until they are duly changed.[14]

We see a similar attempt in the use of economic concepts to model politics. Consensus theorists attempted to achieve the same accommodation with the positivists by trying to locate social and political norms in widely shared customs and conventions. The extent to which there are such widely shared norms—or even underlying shared norms—remains, however, problematic. It could simply be that values conflicting with the interests of the economic and political elites are suppressed. Others have sought to return to a natural-law tradition or to some form of Aristotelianism. The attempt to find a rational, ethical foundation for our social, political and legal systems remains hotly contested. As our discussion in Chapter 7 indicates, it is ever likely to remain so. This general lack of agreement has, however, the effect of undermining the credibility of our moral and philosophical theorists and of this form of theorising.

Joseph Hutchison sees dangers in four intellectual 'cults', which infect such attempts at theorising: a cult of scepticism holding that all beliefs, with the possible exception of scientific discoveries, are simply matters of opinion; a cult maintaining that only the present is meaningful; a scientism that assumes that empirical knowledge is the answer to all human problems; and, finally, an anti-intellectualism that downgrades the intellect and raises the human will to a position of primacy.[15] Consistent with the account given by Rorty and Toulmin, the first three cults flow directly from the Enlightenment project. The radical scepticism of the Enlightenment has, however, undermined its own project: there is nothing of which we can be absolutely certain, and there is no way of avoiding belief as the ground of our moral values or anything else. As for the fourth cult, this seems to be a well-justified reaction to the arrogance and dogmatism of past intellectual optimism and pretension.

The total social environment could be too complex—and the human mind too limited—for us to understand fully the scope and operation of our social activities, a view with echoes in Hayek,[16] Habermas[17] and Arthur.[18] Abstract ethical theories are simply a historical, cultural phenomenon, the progressive invention of humans striving to deal with the uncertainties of day-to-day life, the mystery of human existence and to give themselves some purpose. They can do so only from within a paradigm—or, as MacIntyre would prefer, from within a tradition.[19] As such, they are only a limited part of a much broader human conversation.

Development

The above marks a profound loss of confidence in scientific rationalism and in the associated moral speculation that dates from the Enlightenment. It points squarely to the normative basis of such speculation. Consequently, it also challenges the application of that speculation—particularly economic speculation—to public policy problems. Economic speculation in its Newtonian guise is simply one way, among many possible ways, of speaking about the social world. It heralds a search for alternative ways of talking about, and trying to make sense of, the world and its bewildering confusions—as a source of existential comfort and as a guide to actions. In the face of this confusion, however—and our inability to firmly ground our speculations—public policy formulation has to be seen as an experiment in which the criteria for success and the evaluative vocabulary are cultural artefacts—inventions of the human heart and mind.

Speaking within the Protestant tradition, leading American theologian Reinhold Niebuhr (1892–1971) shared this loss of confidence. For him, there was simply not enough intelligence to conduct the intricate affairs of a complex civilisation, though he believed initially that intelligent analysis and experimentation could help overcome social evils. He believed also in the incommensurability of individual and group morality. Like James, Niebuhr was convinced of the indeterminateness of the universe and the relativity of all human knowledge:

> God, though revealed, remains veiled; His thoughts are not our thoughts, nor His ways our ways. The worship of such a God leads to contrition; not merely to a contrite recognition of the conscious sins of pride and arrogance which the human spirit commits, but to a sense of guilt for the inevitable and inescapable pride involved in every human enterprise.[20]

For Niebuhr, as for a majority of the population including me, God exists, and consequently, absolute truth exists. This provides an absolute basis for human hope and morality. God's transcendence, however, places that truth beyond our reach. Consequently, God's absolute truth can never become fully our truth, nor can we know how much we possess. This should come as no surprise, as Sidharta Gautama (the Buddha) warned us 2500 years ago to stop speculating about absolutes. The human search for knowledge is necessarily tainted by self-interest. Consequently, the truth we know is necessarily personal and limited. Nevertheless, we continually proclaim our personal truths as universal in the vain belief or hope that we are masters of the universe. The Enlightenment merely succeeded in displacing the Christian vision of God—as creator, redeemer and sanctifier—from the centre of the universe. It replaced this vision first with a more limited and non-Christian, anthropomorphic, masculine vision of God as a rule-maker, and then, in turn, with man within nature and, for some true believers, with humans as the servants of 'THE MARKET'. Surely in this age, the idea of men, let alone their artefacts—markets—being at the centre of the universe is bizarre. Furthermore, the idea of nature as the ultimate ground of all being is not much of a god around which to build a life or a moral discourse.

The Enlightenment's assumption that the universe is rational and benevolent is fundamentally wrong. The price of freedom, of change and of progress is finitude, failure, uncertainty, decay and sin. At best, the universe provides a partially stable background against which we make our play and narrate our stories, including the stories of our own lives. All too often, the social worlds in which we create our knowledge narratives are dominated by power, selfishness and passion. In this climate, the scientific tradition and economic thinking all too often become the tools of the dominant social group. 'No society and no social group can ever escape the vicious circle of the sin which aggravates human insecurity in seeking to overcome it. All societies and individuals must therefore remain under the judgment and the doom of God.'[21]

Consequently, Niebuhr rejected faith in progress, pointing out that necessarily selfish groups dominated societies and that scientific knowledge, popular education or universal Christian love could not end group conflict.[22] Belief in human progress and scientific achievement were the height of sinful pride and led unavoidably to disastrous failure. The greatest intelligence and the noblest ideals inevitably led humans to set themselves above God's teachings. Only a profound humility before a transcendent God—which acknowledged our finiteness—and limited vision could help alleviate much social oppression. Of course, this critique of human dogmatism extends to dogmatic absolutist claims within Christianity itself. Consequently, for Niebuhr:

> [T]here is no historical reality, whether it be the church or government, whether it be the reason of wise men or specialists, which is not involved in the flux and relativity of human existence; which is not subject to error and sin, and which is not tempted to exaggerate its errors and sins when they are made immune to criticism.[23]

If the 'Children of Light' were ever to establish a humane and stable society, they had to abandon excessive faith in the goodness and rationality of humanity and recognise human sinfulness and self-interest. This vision was attainable only on the basis of revelation. I would not limit that revelation to the canonical texts of the Bible but would extend it to that revelation of the divine mystery in other religious traditions . This view does not lead to any reinstatement of natural law, certainly not to any assertion of absolute human rights, let alone absolute property, or to the reinstatement of some form of Aristotelian virtue, however much the moral vocabulary derived from those traditions might continue to figure in social and political discourse. Rather, it leads to a humble journeying, an uncertain search for the right and the good. It is always uncertain; it is always a groping. Dogmatism has therefore to be forsworn as we can see only a partial and distorted vision of the kingdom. The kingdom that can be grasped is not the kingdom. Reality always falls short of the kingdom, though it is an image of the kingdom that inspires a striving for newness of life.

In summary, Niebuhr added to pragmatic and relativistic social theory a profound appreciation of human evil, an appreciation founded in his Christian tradition, but absent from Enlightenment optimism. This optimism was, however, an illusion. Marxism was distinguished from liberalism only by sharper and more specific schemes for identifying and providing an elite with power. This critique of Marxism's particular claim to certain knowledge of the end towards which history must move—and its associated willingness to sacrifice every value to that end—applies with equal force to alternative pretensions about the end of history and to any absolutist faith in markets and freedom of contract. Importantly, for Daniel Boorstin:

> To say that a society can or ought to be 'unified' by some total philosophical system—whether a Summa Theologica, a Calvin's Institute or Marx's Capital—is to commit oneself to an aristocratic concept of knowledge: let the elite know the theories and values of the society: they will know and preserve for all the rest.[24]

Such elitism was the very reverse of the intellectual humility that Niebuhr called for. Of course, the acceptance of a relativist position can all too easily lead to an acceptance of the political and economic arrangements of the current dominant state—the United States—as the norm.[25] The particular danger for us is that the American anti-statist tradition that dates from Locke—and which was encouraged by secularised American Calvinism and by Spencer's social Darwinism—will become the moral standard by which we should judge our institutional and organisational arrangements.

Consistent with Niebuhr, Stackhouse[26] advances a biblical covenantal view of justice, supplementing the Catholic model of 'subsidiary' with 'fairness as equity'. As we saw in Chapter 4, the idea of covenant comes from the social and religious history of the ancient Middle East, where divine authority was invoked as a witness to morally binding agreements. The Old Testament related how this '"basic", "mutual", oath-bound creation of responsible relationships'[27] was recognised to be a close analogy of the way in which God related to humanity and a model of how we should relate to each other under God. It involves also a revelation of the nature of a just, merciful God who engages directly in the formation and sustainment of righteous living in community. This justice of a covenanting God is pre-given in that it is constituted by a standard and ultimate end that humans do not make; it is unfinished in that the standards of right and wrong, good and evil are neither fully recognised nor completely fulfilled in this life. Thus, the deontological right and the teleological good must be fulfilled and joined for full justice. Stackhouse recognises, however, as does moral philosophy more generally, that a tension exists between these two views of justice, which has not been reconciled.

As was shown in Chapter 4, the development of the idea of a social contract was influenced by those Old Testament covenant ideas. A fuller understanding of the implication of those ideas was, however, lost in Locke's appeal to the natural-law rights and in deism's limited vision of God as a rule giver. This covenant view leads directly to the rights of humans to develop religious, educational, social and political organisations to exemplify their best vision of the ultimate good and how it is related to what is right. It recognises, however, that an individualistic understanding of human rights provides only a partial understanding, for it fails to recognise that humans are inevitably relational beings, called to live in groups and to assume associated responsibilities. Freedom and rights are best used to fulfil responsibilities in interpersonal and civil life. Consequently, Stackhouse sees contract theories among those who see no need for a higher moral law or greater purpose—and for whom morality consists of whatever is agreed—as a degeneration of the covenantal idea and the greatest temptation in the West.[28] Rather, 'the full actualisation of the right and the good in our inner lives, in our human relationships, and in the matrices of social life cannot be attained on humanistic grounds alone but…a divine initiative must be taken'.[29]

The social-contract tradition involved a progressive impoverishment of the covenant idea with the progressive secularisation and impoverishment of the natural-law ideas that underpinned Locke's account and resulted, *inter alia*, in the reification of the concept of freedom of contract. It is, however, degeneration implicit in Locke's appeal to a natural law assessable by human reason. It was only late in the day that we came to realise that the appeal to nature involved in that process of secularisation effectively removed the moral content of the tradition. In contrast, Stackhouse's covenantal account of justice would lead directly to a relational view of the law of contract such as that advanced by Macneil—a view concerned far more with the substantive outcomes of contractual relationships, which recognised a substantial duty of care on the part of the parties towards each other.

Of course, none of this means that I believe we should accept direction on particular moral issues from self-righteous, authoritarian churchmen—in fancy dress or otherwise—who claim to mediate between God and the rest of us. It should be clear also that I have little sympathy for Calvinism with its claims of divine election—in either its traditional or secular forms. For non-believers also there should be little attraction in the residual transcendentalism in Western epistemology, moral and political philosophy and science. There could also be an understandable reluctance to accept any moral guidance from the above overtly theological traditions, particularly when they are in conflict. Nevertheless, at a practical level, non-believers might be prepared to see them as particular distillations of human experience and as legitimate contributions to moral and political discourse and to the application of the practical reasoning and wisdom that Aristotle advocated. Overt theological insights are not the only or necessarily the most important source of moral insights in contemporary society. We are the inheritors of a long political and moral history and we would be unwise to disregard that history and its lessons, particularly in respect of our willingness to exploit our compatriots in the name of high principle. In addition, we are the beneficiaries of an extraordinarily active popular discourse on the human condition—all of which can contribute to our moral understanding. In that sense, religious authorities are not the only, or necessarily the most important, source of revelation in contemporary secular society. After all, Bob Geldof and Bono are among the great prophets of our age, challenging individual and communal indifference to Third-World suffering, particularly in Africa.

Economics as a Secular Religion

Importantly, the Enlightenment's search for rational principles as a secular alternative to traditional religious authority and beliefs to justify our moral decisions is itself a religious search, serving the same dogmatic and legitimating functions of what Bergson calls static religion.[30] Economics claims to provide that secular justification for many contemporary policy choices. As a result, economics threatens to become the dominant rationalist and fundamentalist religion of contemporary capitalist society and of the emerging global civilisation. This threat is aided by its attempt to appropriate the prestige associated with the natural sciences. Importantly, it is easy to slip between the uses of individualism as an analytical tool to a promotion of individualism as a normative ideal. This religion is of particular appeal to business and political elites because it tends to legitimise greed, love of money and power. It is leading to the commercialisation of all human activity, while aiding the atomisation and privatisation of competing values and groups. It has elevated money beyond a convenience to the means of salvation and the source of meaning, values and security, turning it, and the mechanism for acquiring it, into idols.[31]

Economists—the prophets and priests of this new religion—preach about and have a major impact on public policy and our institutional arrangements. Economics therefore provides an alternative faith tradition, complete with values, ideas of welfare and of progress—usually defined in terms of quantitative economic indicators, which dominate public discourse and which seek to reshape our institutions and organisations.[32] With their influence on government, economists are the new theocracy, the contemporary manifestation of Plato's guardians. In particular, the economic theologian's rhetoric resembles contemporary process theology. In this school, although God will possess the classic attributes of omnipotence (all power), omniscience (all knowledge) and omnipresence (present everywhere), He does not yet possess them in full. Such a theology offers considerable comfort to the economic theologian, explaining the dislocation, pain and disorientation that are the results of transitions from economic heterodoxy to free markets. THE MARKET is becoming more like Yahweh of the Old Testament: not just one superior deity contending with others, but the Supreme Deity, the only true God, whose reign must now be accepted universally and who allows no rivals. There is no conceivable limit to THE MARKET's inexorable ability to convert creation into commodities. In the church of THE MARKET, everything—no matter how sacred—eventually becomes a commodity. This radical de-sacralising dramatically alters the human relationship to land, water, air and space. Indeed, human beings themselves start to become commodities as well. This comprehensive wisdom of THE MARKET is something that, in the past, only the gods knew. In ancient times, seers entered a trance and informed anxious seekers of the mood of the gods and whether the time was auspicious for particular enterprises. Today, the financial media are the diviners and seers of THE MARKET's moods, the high priests of its mysteries. THE MARKET has become the most formidable rival to traditional religions, not least because it is rarely recognised as a religion. The contradictions between the world-views of traditional religion and the world-view of THE MARKET religion are so basic that no compromise seems possible.

This critique has much in common with the critique of 'autonomous technology' developed by Jacques Ellul[33] and by Langdon Winner and Weber's critique of the 'iron cage of reason'.[34] For Ellul, la technique is sacred in our society. No social, human or spiritual fact in the modern world is so important. It transforms everything it touches—including the socio-politico-religious software that runs the system—into a machine. It is the pattern of organisation, the rationalisation of society, beyond the willingness of anyone to accept responsibility. Technical means have become ends in themselves. This attack is directed particularly against the technocrats to whom we have handed over our ethical responsibilities.

In the process of implementing their utopian vision, a narrow technological and theocratic elite is in the process of redefining the evaluative methodology for social action, our social goals, our social institutions and who we think we are.

Efficient ordering is the only principle of the ever-expanding and irreversible rule of technique. It is the unconscious response to every challenge and is being extended to all areas of life. Means are remade into ends as we are committed increasingly to continually improved means to ends that are examined only poorly. Of particular concern to Winner are the changes that have taken place in ordinary language, traditional social institutions, earlier kinds of artefacts, human identity, personality and conduct. Efficiency, speed, precise measurement, rationality, productivity and technical improvement have all become ends in themselves and are applied obsessively to areas of life from which they had previously been excluded. In particular, efficiency has become a more general value—the universal principle for all intelligent conduct. It is not that such instrumental values are themselves perverse, but the fact that they have escaped from their proper sphere.

Technique refuses to tolerate competing moral judgements, excluding them from its field in favour of its own technical morality. Consequently, human beings have become objects—no longer choosing agents, but devices for recording the results obtained by various techniques. Decisions are no longer to be made on the basis of complex and human motives, but only in favour of the technique that gives maximum efficiency. In the process, the qualitative becomes quantitative and every stage of human activity is forced to submit to mathematical calculations. Whatever cannot be expressed numerically is to be eliminated. All the technical devices of education, propaganda, amusement, sport and religion are mobilised to convince us to be content with our condition of mechanical, mindless 'mass man', and to exterminate the deviant and the idiosyncratic.

In particular, technique forms the very substance of economic thought. Technical economic analysis has been substituted for political economy and its concern with the moral structure of economic activity. In seeking to grasp, but also to modify, it is no mere instrument but possesses its own force. This technical orientation is evident particularly in the application of mathematics and statistical techniques to economics. In the economic sphere, as in others, the technicians form a closed fraternity with their own esoteric vocabulary from which the layperson is excluded.

Technique involves the progressive dehumanisation of the economic sphere in which the abstract concept of *Homo economicus* becomes real. Not only has the entire human being been absorbed into the economic network validating the producing–consuming parts of the human, the other facets have been progressively devalued. Consequently, all values have been reduced to money values. The whole of human life has become a function of economic technique. This is particularly so in respect of work.

Politics in turn becomes an arena for contention among rival techniques. The consequence is the progressive suppression of ideological and moral barriers to technical progress. In this environment, the conflict of propaganda takes the place of the debate of ideas. Technique permits public discussion only of those ideas that are in substantial agreement with the values created by a technical civilisation. This technical economy is anti-democratic and a form of slavery. Despite all the talk about freedom and popular sovereignty, people are unable to exert any genuine influence on the direction of the economy, and their votes count for very little.

For technique, there is there no mystery, no taboo and no rules outside itself. Because people cannot live without a sense of the secret, or the sacred, they have created for themselves a new religion of a rational and technical order. Since the religious object is that which is worshipped uncritically, technology has become the new god. Technique has become the essential mystery. For the technician in particular, technique is the locus of the sacred, an abstract idol and the reason for living. Without technique they would find themselves poor, alone, naked and stripped of all pretensions. They would no longer be the heroes, geniuses or even 'archangels'. Technique is thus the god that brings salvation.

These technological influences—these economic influences—have become so much part of everyday life that they have become virtually invisible. For Ellul and Winner, there can be no human autonomy in the face of technical autonomy; people have lost their roles as active, directing agents:

> Each individual lives with procedures, rules, processes, institutions, and material devices that are not of his making but powerfully shape what he does. It is scarcely even imaginable what it would mean for each of us to make decisions about the vast array of sociotechnical circumstances that enter our experience.[35]

Consequently, technical rationality and modernisation pose a particular and significant challenge to liberalism. They are incompatible with the central notion that justifies the practice of liberal politics: the idea of responsible, responsive, representative government. In the technocratic understanding, the real activity of governing can have no place for mass participation. All of the crucial decisions, plans and actions are simply beyond their comprehension. This technological society is not governable. Rather, the ideal is of a self-directing and self-maintaining system, requiring no human direction. This is true even of the means of analysis itself—the meaning of 'rationality' having been distorted and corrupted by these technocratic tendencies. For Ellul, 'Every intervention of technique is, in effect, a reduction of facts, forces, phenomena, means, and instruments to the schema of logic.' Similarly for Weber, 'The fate of our time is characterised by rationalisation and intellectualisation and, above all by the "disenchantment of the world".'[36]

The price for this rationalisation is the loss of freedom. It is ironic that the libertarians' search for increased human autonomy ends, in practice, in the loss of the value that they claim to hold dearest.

The Need for Intellectual Humility

The critique developed in this book of rationality and of deductive reasoning does not question the need to use concepts to bring some order to experience. There is nowhere else to go. Rather, it questions the practical use of concepts that are so general, at such a level of abstraction, that they lose touch with empirical reality. This is particularly so when they are conceived of as absolutes. In such circumstances, their application as a guide to action is inherently problematic and ideological. The perspective to be drawn from pragmatism—and from Niebuhr and Stackhouse in particular—should make us wary of such God-like pretensions and cause us to become more aware of the need for humility about our limited abilities, our intellectual techniques, our intellectual speculations and our real policy decisions.[37] Absolute truth is not available to us. All truth, as we know it, is constructed socially and is subject to revision—sometimes radically.

The substantial judgements involved in public policy development are moral rather than technical. It is the quality of our moral judgements, the sensitivity of our moral vocabulary and stories—rather than the quality of our economic logic—that is the crucial element in public decision making. Judgement needs to be informed by a moral sensitivity to the needs of others, wide learning, deep reflection, wide consultation and by wide experience of the practical world. We therefore need to acknowledge that it is not so much the lack of technical knowledge that inhibits government policy as it is the dominant moral values that shape what it is possible to think and do.

We need to be particularly wary when it comes to postulating this or that as an overarching moral principle with priority over all other values. Despite pretensions to the contrary, economics does not and cannot provide the moral equivalent of a unified field theory—an equivalent of the physicists' Holy Grail, which can be invoked to justify collective action directed by government. For example, there is no ideal form of social or economic organisation against which to measure real organisations; the forms of organisation used in the private sector do not provide an ideal form or vocabulary that must be emulated. Social evolution, like biological evolution, does not lead to optimal outcomes, only satisfactory ones.

Of particular note is the prevalent tendency to fasten onto particular ideological interpretations of human rights and of liberty, to make them into absolutes and then to use those interpretations to exclude collective action based on other values. We have tended to elevate individualism, freedom of contract and economic efficiency above values that point to mutual interdependency and responsibility for our neighbours. Such humility should make us more conscious of the needs and claims of others in contrast with our own needs and claims. It should make us more conscious that we frequently lack the knowledge for sound decisions, and of the need to consult widely, to proceed carefully, to be willing to experiment and to change direction. Humility should also make us aware of the pretensions of 'rationality' and of the need to accord emotions and values a legitimate role in decision making.

We should be more careful about such abstractions as 'the economy', 'the market' and particularly 'the labour market'. In the practical policy debate, the fact that these are abstractions has long been forgotten—the dancers have become the servants of the steps. We should also be more careful about the division of people and their social groups into rigid categories. Rather, we should admit that is it difficult to unscramble all the influences that bear on real people in all their relationships.

This critique should also serve as a reminder to avoid seeing the complex issues we confront in the world through simple dichotomies. Unfortunately, most policy debate occurs at a simplistic, markets-are-good/governments-are-bad level. Rather, as Popper recommends, in the search for knowledge, every source, every suggestion is welcome, while all are open to critical examination. Qualitatively and quantitatively, by far the most important source of our knowledge—apart from inborn knowledge—is tradition.[38]

In particular, the current distinction made in public debate between the public and the private sectors is overdrawn. We quickly forget that what we are really talking about are real, interdependent groups of people engaged in complex interrelationships, involving different and complex organisational structures and in a bewildering variety of activities and exchanges. Governance is a necessary part of all of these activities. It is only the types of governance that are in question. This is a question that cannot be answered on the basis of a priori reasoning. Collective action is a necessary part of any complex society and the government is a legitimate organ of that collective action. Limitations on government action are not to be established on the basis of abstract a priori reasoning but on the basis of experimentation within the framework of a political tradition—a tradition incorporating much practical wisdom and learning.

Complexity

As has been shown, current Australian public policy debate is constrained heavily by a belief on the part of many participants that there is some acceptable theoretical basis for determining the role of the government, or that such a basis is attainable. The very language of the discussion contains this belief. An artificial dichotomy has been envisaged between the market and the State, which fails to recognise the interdependencies within our economic system and the role of the State and the social system more generally in underpinning economic activity. It is a dichotomy based on an idealised conception of markets that is grounded neither in fact nor in credible economic theory.

The claims of neoclassical economics to intellectual rigour are also subject to innumerable challenges at a more detailed level. In response to these detailed attacks, many economists have insisted that critics provide an alternative theory. In doing so, they have not realised that metaphors play the key role in theory formation. Consequently, they have not understood the extent to which their economic thinking has been bounded by the Newtonian metaphor, and by their search for natural laws of the economy analogous with those of mechanics. They have assumed that economic phenomena can be treated as if they are natural phenomena, caused by natural forces, and not social phenomena, the result of social invention and institutions. Running through the history of this economic thought is a persistent effort to evade responsibility for the outcomes of the economic system—a responsibility that would have to be faced were the idea of natural law to be abandoned. In the process, economic theory has been emptied of its historical and social elements. Nor has economics faced up to the normative judgements involved in the choice of metaphors and the extent to which they can serve to legitimate the existing social order and the privilege of the commercial and policy elites.

Since the Enlightenment, the physical sciences and the reductionist method have established priority over other ways of knowing because of their ability to produce reproducible results, accurate predictions and plausible explanations. This form of mastery is, however, unlikely to be achieved of systems as complex as the social and the economic. In any event, given human freedom of action, there is no prior reason to believe that society will exhibit the types of natural regularities seen in the physical sciences.

Part of a search for a better understanding must be the recognition that we are part of an indivisible totality that we—in all our complexity and diversity—have a share in creating, in partnership with our ancestors. Important support is given to a new holistic approach to economic speculation by the new science of complexity. Complexity is not simply a new reductionist model, but a new way of looking at the world, which attempts to deal with the interconnectedness, interdependence and non-linearity of systems.[39] Such a complex system cannot be understood through reductionism, as the whole is greater than the sum of its parts. Real complex systems cannot be modelled successfully mathematically because of the extraordinary difficulty of the mathematics involved, and the radical differences that small differences in initial states can make. Furthermore, there is a mismatch between the ontology assumed by mathematics and the ontology of social systems. The way ahead is not through the reductionist approach and a more refined Newtonian model. There is a fundamental mismatch between our predominant ways of thinking about reality derived from the Enlightenment's scientific tradition and the nature of reality in a complex social system.[40]

Arthur has argued that the alternative to the Newtonian model is Taoist. It involves the recognition that there is no inherent order underlying economic phenomena. Consequently, our economic institutions are matters for social choice; and we have to learn to live with the relativism and circularity that this involves. As Arthur explains, 'The world is a matter of patterns that change, that partly repeat, but never quite repeat, that are always new and different.'[41] There is no perfect system to be discovered, no magic word that will remove our responsibility for each other and ourselves. This involves abandoning the idealisation of THE MARKET that is at the heart of economic fundamentalism.

What this means for policy is that there is no one correct approach to policy or to organisational arrangements. Just as biological organisms have evolved a bewildering variety of systems, it is reasonable to expect a wide variety of approaches in social organisations. Such variety is not to be despised; rather it is to be valued as it could reflect subtle or even coarse differences in the environment or a degree of 'indifference' between approaches. Secondly, complexity in environmental circumstances could be so great as to defy analysis. It is not possible in principle to list in order of importance the influences affecting a complex system. History cannot be ignored. It shapes the evolution of a complex system and, consequently, a complex system cannot be understood in isolation from its history. Similarly, the state of 'fitness' of an organisation cannot be determined by reference to crude reductionist criteria, but could, perhaps, be reflected in broad measures of confidence and happiness, which reflect some common judgement.

The 'organisational capital' of such a system is not primarily in its physical endowments but in the complex network of relationships formed within that system and the knowledge held within that network. Our evolved institutional arrangements—ethical rules, legal rules, conventional ways of behaving and popular culture—are all part of the organisational capital of our system, are critical to the effectiveness of the system, cannot be ignored and need constantly to be renewed. Such values assume critical importance. One of the features of complex systems is that they emerge at the edge of order and chaos.

Consequently, they can be highly unstable. Fundamental changes in the values and rules that underpin our society—of the type advocated by economic fundamentalists and, to some extent, implemented in Australia in recent times—could therefore have unforeseen and radical implications that we will all regret.

An inability to deduce an appropriate theoretical framework does not, however, reduce us to impotence. It does mean that there is no alternative to experimentation. Nor are the criteria to be applied in assessing those experiments written in the heavens. Therefore, a balanced approach would not be one that rules some classes of government action as inadmissible on theoretical grounds, nor would it suggest that all possible government action would be beneficial. The experiments need not be all ours. Rather the way ahead should be characterised by a more careful examination of the models and approaches used elsewhere, and a more careful examination of the policy problem. Effective policy design has often been seriously inhibited by too much ideology, with too little attention to the practical problems of policy implementation and behavioural change.

In framing practical policy, the important question is 'What works?' The question cannot, however, be asked in isolation from our moral, religious and political traditions. The answer is to be found more in experimentation backed by empirical investigation of the consequences than in theoretical knowledge, a priori reasoning and high-level abstraction. It involves substantive moral judgements and moral sensitivity, not formal logic. It follows that the policy development process should properly be seen as pragmatic, eclectic and political. We should acknowledge that public policy decisions legitimately involve balanced judgements involving potentially conflicting criteria—not a departure from a postulated market ideal for 'illegitimate' social and political reasons. It should encourage a much closer examination of the environment, a much closer examination of policy approaches that others have employed along with an assessment of their impacts and a willingness to engage in careful experimentation in the full knowledge that we will, from time to time, make mistakes. We also need to recognise the limitations of past policy development processes and to commit ourselves to changing those processes.

While structures are very important, their effectiveness—and the effectiveness of public and private networks—depends ultimately on trust. Economic fundamentalism has neglected the essential contribution that moral conduct makes to the capitalist system and to our governance structures. Many economists have no concept of history and of the delicately constructed social fabric, which makes the difference between workable and unworkable market economies. Nor do they have an adequate understanding of the complex motivations that bind individuals into functioning organisations and effective economies. Sound business ethics—and moral conduct more generally—are an essential part of the social infrastructure. That moral conduct cannot, however, be reduced simply to compliance with rules; rather it requires an aspiration towards virtue. The codified law established the minimum standards of behaviour required of citizens before social sanctions were applied, not the optimal standards for the good life.

Final Thoughts

For Robert Bellah et al. in *The Good Society*, social science and policy analysis have not taken the place of public philosophy but, instead, have regrettably strengthened the notion that our problems are technical, rather than moral and political. In this, they echo the critique developed by Ellul and Winner. In particular, they are concerned about the erosion of trust in the political system and public institutions that results from the current emphasis on Lockean individualism and the associated economic theorising with its emphasis on efficiency. It threatens to undermine our democracy. In their words:

> If policy elites stand outside the world of citizens, designing social policies evaluated in terms of outcomes, efficiency, or costs and benefits, as they define them, they short-circuit the democratic process, and this is so whether they believe that people are essentially 'interest maximisers' or even that they are motivated in part by 'values'. Politics under these circumstances becomes the art of image manipulation by expert media managers.[42]

The consequence is a gross abuse of power that eats at the heart of the liberal tradition.

No society can survive without stable moral traditions and social conventions backed up by effective means of coercion. The prevailing scepticism about the possibility of establishing any moral principle as true or valid beyond reasonable doubt troubles some with the theoretical thought that as a consequence we are unable to identify the difference between might and right.[43] This search for *epistēmē* in moral matters was, however, always an illusion. At a practical level—the level of practical wisdom or *phronēsis* —we nevertheless possess a highly developed moral vocabulary and a long political tradition, both of which provide a source of stability. This represents the social and moral capital of our civilisation. Brennan and Buchanan[44] have, however, argued that there is now a widely sensed deterioration in the social, intellectual and philosophical capital of Western civil order. Hirsch had a similar sense of foreboding, believing that an excessive reliance on self-interest as the fundamental social organising principle would undermine the basis of the market system itself:

> In brief, the principle of self-interest is incomplete as a social organising principle. It operates effectively only in tandem with some supporting social principle. This fundamental characteristic of economic liberalism,

which was largely taken for granted by Smith and Mill in their different ways, has been lost sight of by its modern protagonists...The attempt has been made to erect an increasingly explicit social organisation without a supporting social morality...In this way, the foundations of the market system have been weakened, while its general behavioural norm of acting on the criterion of self-interest has won ever-widening acceptance.[45]

The fear is that in acting on the precepts of economic fundamentalism modern governments have participated in changes in the institutional structures of their societies that could weaken the matrix of social rules on which their economic systems depend. For their part, Nancy Foulbre and Thomas Weisskopf argue that the care and nurture of human capital has always been difficult and expensive, and that the erosion of family and community solidarity imposes enormous costs—costs that are reflected in inefficient and unsuccessful educational efforts, high crime rates and a social atmosphere of anxiety and resentment.[46] Such forebodings are, however, as old as civilisation itself. They could reflect the prevailing uncertainty about the foundations of our moral values as well as the intuition that civilisation is always under threat from what used to be called human sinfulness.

It is at this point that it is wise to recall that it is the control of our greed that represents one of the prime victories of culture over 'animality'. If this is so, it is greed that also represents one of the prime threats to our civilisation; economic fundamentalism is an ideology that attempts to justify that greed. In particular, it promotes selfishness and materialism. Even for the non-religious, however, the acquisition of personal wealth and power is not a satisfactory basis for self-definition. Consequently, economic fundamentalism is a significant threat to our civilisation. Its application to public decisions cannot be reconciled with the ethical import of our cultural heritage, with its Christian underpinnings, its command to love God and to love one's neighbour as oneself. Nor can it be reconciled with other religious traditions, including Buddhism, with its calls for compassion and detachment. Taking something that is good—such as rational thought, or economic analysis, or markets, or human rights, or liberty, or law, or money, or consumption—and turning it into an absolute is the essence of a new idolatry.

ENDNOTES

[1] Gilmore 1974, p. xviii.

[2] St Paul, in 1 Timothy 6:10–19.

[3] Collins 1995.

[4] Horwitz 1992.

[5] Gilmore 1974.

[6] Ibid.

[7] Horwitz 1992, p. vi.

[8] Ibid., p. viii.

[9] Murphy 1990.

[10] Purcell 1973, p. 6.

[11] Horwitz 1992, pp. 4–6.

[12] Ibid.

[13] Purcell 1973.

[14] Hart and Sacks 1958, pp. 3–4.

[15] Purcell 1973.

[16] Frowen 1997.

[17] Habermas 1998.

[18] Waldrop 1992.

[19] MacIntyre 1981.

[20] Niebuhr 1965, p. 45.

[21] Ibid., p. 108.

[22] Niebuhr 1944.

[23] Ibid., pp. 70–1.

[24] Boorstin 1958, p. 168.

[25] Purcell 1973.

[26] Stackhouse 1999a.

[27] Ibid., p. 2.

[28] Ibid., p. 22.

[29] Ibid., p. 9.

[30] Bergson 1935.

[31] Stackhouse 1999b.

[32] This does not mean, of course, that all economists share this faith or that it is necessarily tied closely to an understanding of the discipline of economics. Nor does it mean that many economists lack high standards of integrity in their private lives or are not personally religious in the more traditional sense.

[33] Ellul 1964.

[34] Winner 1977. This work is largely a commentary on Ellul's *The Technological Society*.

[35] Ibid., p. 86.

[36] Ibid., p. 180.

[37] Etzioni (1988) takes a similar position.

[38] Popper, On the Sources of Knowledge and Ignorance.

[39] Waldrop 1992.

[40] Senge 1992a.

[41] Waldrop 1992, p. 330.

[42] Bellah et al. 1991, p. 293.

[43] Reiman 1990.

[44] Brennan and Buchanan 1985.

[45] Hirsch 1977.

[46] Foulbre and Weisskopf 1998.

Bibliography

Abbott, H. Porter 2002, *The Cambridge Introduction to Narrative*, Cambridge University Press, Cambridge.

Abernethy, Mark 1997, 'Full weight behind fair trading report', *Australian Financial Review*, 8 July 1997.

Access Economics 1997, *Tipping the Balance?*, July 1997, Canberra.

Adorno, T. W., Dahrendorf, Albert H., Habermas, J., Pilot, H. J. and Popper, K. R. 1976, *The Positivist Dispute in German Sociology*, Glyn Adey and David Frisby (trans.), Heinemann Educational Books, London.

Agassi, Joseph and Jarvie, Ian Charles (eds) 1987, title?, Martinus Nijhoff, Dordrechte.

Albert, Hans 1987, 'Science and the Search for Truth', in J. Agassi and I. C. Jarvie, title?, Martinus Nijhoff, Dordrechte.

Alvey, James E. 1999, 'A Short History of Economics as a Moral Science', *Journal of Markets and Morality*, Spring.

Amariglio, Jack, Resnick, Stephen and Wolff, Richard 1990, 'Division and Difference in the "Discipline" of Economics', *Critical Inquiry*, Autumn 1990.

Arestis, Philip, McCombie, John and Vickerman, Roger (eds) 2006, *Growth and Economic Development: Essays in honour of A.P. Thirlwall*.

Arrow, Kenneth J. 1974, *The Limits of Organization*, W. W. Norton & Company, New York.

Atiyah, P. S. 1979, *Rise and Fall of Freedom of Contract*, Clarendon Press, Oxford.

Atiyah, P. S. 1986, *Essays on Contract*, Clarendon Press, Oxford.

Australian Financial Review 2000, *Australian Financial Review*, Monday, 25 September 2000, p. 20.

Australian Financial Review 2003, *Australian Financial Review*, Monday, 10 February 2003, p. 62.

Australian Financial Review 2004, *Australian Financial Review*, 7 August 2004, p. 6.

Backhouse, Roger E. 1992, 'The Constructivist Critique of Economic Methodology', *Methodus*, June, pp. 65–82.

Ball, Phillip 2006, 'Baroque Fantasies of a Peculiar Science', *Post-Autistic Economics Review*, (40), 1 December 2006, p. 58, http://www.pae-con.net/PAEReview

Bannister, Robert C. 1979, *Social Darwinism*, Temple University Press, Philadelphia.

Barrett, William 1978, *The Illusion of Technique: A search for meaning in a technological civilization*, Anchor Press/Doubleday, New York.

Baxt, Robert 2007, 'Trade Practices proposals still fail to protect needy', *Australian Financial Review*, 6 July 2007, p. 66.

Becker, Garry 1981, *Treatise on the Family*, Harvard University Press, Cambridge, Mass.

Bellah, Robert 1967, 'Civil Religion in America', *Daedalus*, 96, Winter.

Bellah, Robert 1975, *The Broken Covenant: American civil religion in a time of trial*, Seabury Press, New York.

Bellah, Robert et al. 1991, *The Good Society*, Alfred A. Knopf, New York.

Ben-Ner, Avner and Putterman, Louis (eds) 1998, *Economics, Values and Organizations*, Cambridge University Press, Cambridge.

Berger, Peter L. and Luckmann, Thomas 1967,

Berger, Peter L. and Luckmann, Thomas 1971, *The Social Construction of Reality*, Penguin Books, London.

Bergson, H. 1935, *The Two Sources of Morality and Religion*, Macmillan, London.

Berkson, William 1987, 'Sceptical Rationalism, in Rationality: The critical view', in J. Agassi and I. C. Jarvie (eds), title?, Martinus Nijhoff, Dordrechte.

Bernstein, Richard J. 1983, *Beyond Objectivism and Relativism: Science, hermeneutics, and praxis*, Basil Blackwell, London.

Bhaskar, Roy 1998, *The Possibility of Naturalism: A Philosophical Critique of the Contemporary Human Sciences*, 2nd edition, Harvest Wheatsheaf, London.

Bita, Natasha 2002, 'The innocent for sale', *The Australian*, 5 September 2002, p. 9.

Blair, Tony 1997, Text of a message from the Prime Minister delivered by the British Ambassador to the Republic of Ireland, 31 May 1997.

Blaug, Mark 1992, *Methodology of Economics*, 2nd edition, Cambridge University Press, Cambridge.

Blaug, Mark 1997, 'Ugly Currents in Modern Economics', *Policy Options*, September.

Blaug, Mark 1998, 'The problems of Formalism', Interview with Mark Blaug, *Challenge*, May–June, http://www.btinternet.com/~pae_news/Blaug1.htm

Blunt Committee 1979

Bohm, David 1983, *Wholeness and the Implicate Order*, Routledge, London.

Boorstin, Daniel J. 1958, *The Americans*, Random House, New York.

Borger, Robert and Cioffi, Frank 1970, *Explanation in the Behavioural Sciences*, Cambridge University Press, Cambridge.

Boulding, Kenneth E. 1970, *Economics as Science*, McGraw-Hill, New York.

Brennan, Geoffrey and Buchanan, James M. 1985, *The Reason of Rules*, Cambridge University Press, Cambridge.

Bromley, Daniel W. 1990, 'The Ideology of Efficiency: Searching for a theory of policy analysis', *Journal of Environmental Economics and Management*, 19, pp. 86–107.

Bromley, Daniel W. 2005, *Why Economists Have No Theory of Public Policy: The triumph of analysis over explanation*, The Gosnell Lecture, Department of Economics, Rochester Institute of Technology, 7 April 2005.

Bromley, Daniel W. 2006, *Sufficient Reason: Volitional pragmatism and the meaning of economic institutions*, Princeton University Press, Princeton.

Brown, Harold I. 1988, *Rationality*, Routledge, London.

Bruner, J. 1987, 'Life as Narrative', *Social Research*, 54, pp. 1–17.

Burrow, J. W. 1966, *Evolution and Society: A study in Victorian social theory*, Cambridge University Press.

Burton, Tom and Murphy, Katharine 1997, 'Govt considers compromise on unfair conduct', *Australian Financial Review*, 22 September 1997.

Bush, Dale Paul 1991, 'Reflections on the Twenty-Fifth Anniversary of AFEE: Philosophical and methodological issues in institutional economics', *Journal of Economic Issues*, XXV, (2), June.

Business Council of Australia 1997, *Submission No. 119*, Reid Inquiry.

Campbell, Donald T. 1986, 'Science's Social System and the Problem of the Social Sciences', in D. W. Fiske and R. A. Shweder, *Pluralisms and Subjectivities*, University of Chicago Press, Chicago.

Campbell, K. 1981, *Final Report of the Committee of Inquiry into the Australian Financial System*, AGPS, Canberra.

Campbell, Lewis and Lowett, Benjamin 1987, *Plato's Republic*, Garland, New York.

Campbell, Tom 1988, *Justice*, Macmillan Education, London.

Carnap, Rudolf 1934, *The Unity of Science*, Kegan Paul, Trench Hubner, London.

Carrithers, Michael 1992, *Why Humans Have Cultures*, Oxford University Press, Oxford.

Carrithers, Michael, Collins, Steven and Lukes, Steven (eds) 1985, *The Category of the Person*, Cambridge University Press, Cambridge.

Carroll, John 2004, 'Coalition of the willing more than coincidence', *Australian Financial Review*, 23–28 December 2004, p. 66.

Carruthers, Mary J. 1990, *The Book of Memory*, Cambridge University Press, Cambridge.

Chapman, Simon 2004, *The Sydney Morning Herald*, 5 August 2004.

Chase, Phillip G. 1999, 'Symbolism as Reference and Symbolism as Culture', in R. Dunbar, C. Knight and C. Power (eds), *The Evolution of Culture*, Rutgers University Press, New Brunswick, NJ.

Cherniak, Christopher 1986, *Minimal Rationality*, MIT Press, Cambridge, Mass.

Churchland, Paul M. 1995, *The Engine of Reason, the Seat of the Soul*, MIT Press, Cambridge, Mass.

Clark, Charles Michael Andres 1992, *Economic Theory and Natural Philosophy*, E. Elgar, Hants.

Coase, Ronald H. 1991, *The Institutional Structure of Production*, http://nobel-prize.org/economics/laureates/1991/coase-lecture.html

Coase, Ronald H. 1999, 'The Task of the Society', Opening Address to the Annual Conference, 2(2), *Newsletter of the International Society for New Institutional Economics*, 1, (3–6), Fall 1999.

Colebatch, H. K. 1998, title?, Open University Press, Buckingham.

Coleman, James S. 1990, *Foundations of Social Theory*, The Belknap Press of Harvard University Press, Cambridge, Mass.

Collins, Ronald K. L. 1995, 'Foreword', in G. Gilmore 1995, *The Death of Contract*, 2nd edition, Ohio State University Press, Columbus.

Commonwealth of Australia 1973, *Parliamentary Debates, Senate*, vol. S57, 27 September 1973.

Converse, Phillip E. 1986, 'Generalization and the Social Psychology of "Other Worlds"', in D. W. Fiske and R. A. Shweder, *Pluralisms and Subjectivities*, University of Chicago Press, Chicago.

Conway, David 1987, *A Farewell to Marx*, Penguin, London.

Corcoran, Paul E. 1979, *Political Language and Rhetoric*, University of Queensland Press, St Lucia.

Cowherd, Raymond D. 1977, *Political Economists and the English Poor Laws*, Ohio University Press, Athens.

Cox, Harvey 1984, *Religion in the Secular City*.

Cox, Harvey 1999, 'When Mammon Is God', *Atlantic Monthly*, reprinted in *Australian Financial Review*, 30 April 1999.

Cox, Harvey 2002, 'Mammon and the Culture of the Market', in R. Madsen, W. M. Sullivan, A. Swidler and S. M. Tipson, *Meaning and Modernity: Religion, Polity, and Self*, University of California Press, Berkeley.

Crook, Clive 2007, 'Not easy for some to get ahead in the US', *Atlantic Monthly*, reprinted in *Australian Financial Review*, 6 July 2007.

Crotty, Michael 1998, *The Foundations of Social Research*, Allen & Unwin, St Leonards.

D'Andrade, Roy 1986, 'Three Scientific World Views', in D. W. Fiske and R. A. Shweder, *Pluralisms and Subjectivities*, University of Chicago Press, Chicago.

Davies, Paul 2004a, '2500 years on, the big question remains: how long is a piece of string theory?', *Sydney Morning Herald*, Wednesday, 25 February, p. 15.

Davies, Paul 2004b, 'Be warned, this could be the matrix', *Sydney Morning Herald*, 22 July, p. 11.

Davies, Paul 2004c, http://www.onlineopinion.com.au/view.asp?article=2035

Davies, Paul 2007, 'Laying down the laws', *New Scientist*, 30 June 2007, pp. 30–4.

de Botton, Alain 2004, *Status Anxiety*, Penguin Books, New York.

de Fontenelle, Bernard le Bovier 1686, *Plurality of Worlds*.

de Lavoie, Don 1990, *Economics and Hermeneutics*, Routledge, London.

Department of Industry, Science and Resources (DISR) 1998, 'A new economic paradigm', *Discussions of Science and Innovation*, 4, Canberra.

Dixon, Norman 1976, *On the Psychology of Military Incompetence*, Jonathan Cape, London.

Downie, R. S. 1972, *Roles and Values, An Introduction to Social Ethics*, Methuen & Co. Ltd, London.

Dunstan, G. R. 1974, *The Artifice of Ethics, The Moorhouse Lectures 1973*, SCM Press, London.

Durkheim, Emile 1993, *The Division of Labor in Society*, G. Simpson (trans.), The Free Press, New York.

Eckhardt, William 1989, title?, in R. Leger Sivard, *World Military Expenditures*, ???

Edgeworth, F. Y. 1881, *Mathematical Psychics, An Essay on the Application of Mathematics to the Moral Sciences*, Kegan Paul, London.

Eisenstadt, S. N. 1978, *Revolution and the Transformation of Societies: A comparative study of civilizations*, Free Press, New York.

Elias, Norbert 1994, *The Civilizing Process, The History of Manners and State Formation and Civilisation*, E. Jephott (trans.), Blackwell, Oxford.

Ellul, Jacques 1965, *The Technological Society*, Knopf, New York.

Elster, Jon 1989, *The Cement of Society*, Cambridge University Press, Cambridge.

Emmet, Dorothy 1966, *Rules, Roles and Relations*, Macmillan, London.

Encyclopaedia Britannica 1981, *Encyclopaedia Britannica*, 15th edition, vol. 4.

Etzioni, Amitai 1988, *The Moral Dimension, Towards a New Economics*, The Free Press, New York.

Feyerabend, P. 1993, *Against Method*, Verso, London.

Fiske, Donald W. 1986, 'Specificity of Method and Knowledge', in D. W. Fiske and R. A. Shweder, *Pluralisms and Subjectivities*, University of Chicago Press, Chicago.

Fiske, Donald W. and Shweder, Richard A. 1986, *Pluralisms and Subjectivities*, University of Chicago Press, Chicago.

Fleck, Ludwik 1979, *Genesis and Development of a Scientific Fact*, University of Chicago Press, Chicago.

Flyvbjerg, Bent 2001, *Making Social Science Matter*, Cambridge University Press, Cambridge.

Fortes, Meyer 1983, *Rules and the Emergence of Society*, Royal Anthropological Institute of Great Britain and Ireland, London.

Foulbre, N. and Weisskopf, T. N. 1998, 'Did Father Know Best?', in A. Ben-Ner and L. Putterman (eds), *Economics, Values and Organizations*, Cambridge University Press, Cambridge.

Frankel, Barbara 1986, title?, in D. W. Fiske and R. A. Shweder, *Pluralisms and Subjectivities*, University of Chicago Press, Chicago.

Frankfurt, H. 1992, 'On Bullshit', in R. J. Foglein (ed.), *Thirteen Questions in Ethics*, Harcourt Brace Jovanovich College Publishers, New York.

Fraser Institute year?, *The Fraser Institute at 30, A Retrospective*, http://www.fraserinstitute.ca/

Freud, Sigmund 1932, *Correspondence with Einstein*.

Friedman, Milton 1966, 'The Methodology of Positive Economics', *Essays In Positive Economics*, University of Chicago Press, Chicago.

Frisby, David and Sayer, Derek 1986, *Society*, Ellis Horwood and Tavistock Publications, London.

Frowen, Stephen F. 1997, *Hayek: Economist and social philosopher*, Macmillan, London.

Fukayama, Francis 1995, *Trust*, The Free Press, New York.

Fullbrook, Edward 2007, 'Narrative Pluralism', *Post-Autistic Economics Review*, 42, 18 May 2007, http://www.paecon.net/PAEReview

Gadamer, Hans-Georg 1975a, 'Hermeneutics and Social Science', *Cultural Hermeneutics*, 2.

Gadamer, Hans-Georg 1975b, *Truth and Method*, Seabury Press, New York.

Gaita, R. 1991, *Good and Evil: An absolute conception*, Macmillan, London.

Ganbmann, Heiner 1998, 'Economics and Sociology: Lowe and Mannheim on Cooperation in the Social Sciences', in H. Hagemann and H. D. Kurz, *Political Economics in Retrospect*, Edward Elgar, Cheltenham.

Gascoigne, Robert 1994a, 'Christian Faith and the Public Forum in a Pluralist Society', *Colloquium*, 26/2.

Gascoigne, Robert 1994b, 'Contemporary Culture and the Communication of the Gospel', *Plenaria*.

Gauthier, David 1977, 'The Social Contract as Ideology', *Philosophy and Public Affairs*, 6, (2), Winter, pp. 130–64.

Geeetz, Clifford 1966, 'Religion as a Cultural System', in M. Banton, *Anthropological Approaches to the Study of Religion*, Tavistock Publications, London.

Geertz, Clifford 1973, *Interpretation of Culture*, Basic Books, New York.

Geertz, Clifford 1975, 'On the nature of anthropological understanding', *American Scientist*, 63.

Geertz, Clifford 1979, 'From the Native's Point of View: On the Nature of Anthropological Understanding', in P. Rabinow and W. M. Sullivan, *Interpretive Social Science*, University of California Press, Berkeley.

Georgescu-Roegen, Nicholas 1979, 'Methods in Economic Science', *Journal of Economic Issues*, 13, (2), June.

Gergen, Kenneth J. 1985, 'Social Constructionist Inquiry: Context and Implications', in K. Gergen and K. E. Davis (eds), *The Social Construction of the Person*, Springer-Verlag, New York.

Gergen, Kenneth J. 1986, 'Correspondence Versus Autonomy', in D. W. Fiske and R. A. Shweder, *Pluralisms and Subjectivities*, University of Chicago Press, Chicago.

Gerth, Hans and Mills, C. Wright 1954, *Character and Social Structure*, Routledge & Kegan Paul, London.

Giddens, Anthony 1977, *Studies in Social and Political Theory*, Basic Books, New York.

Gilligan, Carol 1982, *In a Different Voice*, Harvard University Press, Cambridge, Mass.

Gilligan, Carol 1983, 'Do the Social Sciences have an adequate theory of Moral Development?', in N. Haan, R. N. Bellah, P. Rabinow and W. M. Sullivan (eds), *Social Science as Moral Inquiry*, Columbia University Press, New York.

Gilmore, Grant 1974, *The Death of Contract*, 2nd edition (1995), Ohio State University Press, Columbus.

Glover, Jonathan 1999, *Humanity, A Moral History of the Twentieth Century*, Yale University Press, New Haven.

Goodman, N. 1968, *Languages of Art*, Bobbs-Merrill, New York.

Goodwin, Brian 1997, *How the Leopard Changed its Spots*, Phoenix, London.

Goody, Esther N. (ed.) 1995, *Social Intelligence and Interaction: Expressions and implications of the social bias in human intelligence*, Cambridge University Press, Cambridge.

Gorski, P. S. 2002, 'Calvinism and Revolution', in R. Madsen, W. M. Sullivan, A. Swidler and S. M. Tipson, *Meaning and Modernity: Religion, Polity, and Self*, University of California Press, Berkeley.

Gough, J. W. 1936, *The Social Contract*, Clarendon Press, Oxford.

Government of Australia 1976, *Report of the Trade Practices Act Review Committee (Swanson Committee)*, August 1976, AGPS, Canberra.

Government of Australia 1979, *Small Business and the Trade Practices Act*, Trade Practices Consultative Committee, AGPS, Canberra.

Government of Australia 1997, *Finding a Balance Towards Fair Trading in Australia (The Reid Report)*, Report by the House of Representatives Standing Committee on Industry, Science and Technology, May 1997.

Granovetter, Mark 1991, 'The Social Construction of Economic Institutions', in A. Etzioni and P. R. Lawrence, *Socio Economics, Towards a New Synthesis*, M. E. Sharp, New York.

Granovetter, Mark 1992, *Economic Action and Social Structure: The problem of embeddedness*, in M. Granovetter and R. Swedberg, *The Sociology of Economic Life*, Westview Press, Boulder.

Gray, John 1998, *False Dawn, The Delusions of Global Capitalism*, The New Press, New York.

Grimes, Ken 2002, *New Scientist*, 13 April 2002.

Guala, F. 1998, 'Pareto on Idealization and the Method of Analysis-Synthesis', *Social Science Information*, 37, (1), Sage Publications, London, pp. 23–44.

Gutting, Gary 2003, *Michael Foucault*, http://plato.stanford.edu/entries/foucault/

Haan, Norma, Bellah, Robert N., Rabinow, Paul and Sullivan, William M. (eds) 1983, *Social Science as Moral Inquiry*, Columbia University Press, New York.

Habermas, Jurgen 1981, 'Modernity Versus Postmodernity', *New German Critique*, 22.

Habermas, Jurgen 1998, *On the Pragmatics of Communication*, MIT Press, Cambridge, Mass.

Hamilton, Clive and Denniss, Richard 2005, title?, Allen & Unwin, Crows Nest.

Hamilton, Garry G. 1994, 'Civilization and the Organization of Economics', *Handbook of Economic Sociology*, Princeton University Press, Princeton.

Hamilton, Walton H. 1931, 'The Ancient Maxim Caveat Emptor', *Yale Law Journal*, 40.

Hamminga, B. and de Marchi, N. (eds) 1994, *Idealization VI: Idealization in economics*, Rodopi, Amsterdam.

Hanson, N. 1958, *Patterns of Discovery*, Cambridge University Press, London.

Harre, R. 1985, 'The Language Game of Self-Ascription: A Note', in K. J. Gergen and K. E. Davis, *The Social Construction of the Person*, Springer-Verlag, New York.

Hart, H. and Sacks, A. 1958, *The Legal Process*, Harvard University Press.

Hauerwas, Stanley 2002, 'On being a Christian and an American', in R. Madsen, W. M. Sullivan, A. Swidler and S. M. Tipson, *Meaning and Modernity: Religion, Polity, and Self*, University of California Press, Berkeley.

Hausman, Daniel M. and McPherson, Michael S. 1996, *Economic Analysis and Moral Philosophy*, Cambridge University Press, Cambridge.

Hayek, Friedrich 1945, 'The Use of Knowledge in Society', *American Economic Review*, 35.

Hayek, Friedrich 1973, *Law, Legislation and Liberty, Volume 1, Rules and Order*, Chicago University Press, Chicago.

Hayek, Friedrich 1974, *The Pretence of Knowledge, Lecture to the Memory of Alfred Nobel*, http://nobelprize.org/nobel_prizes/economics/laureates/1974/hayek-lecture.html

Heilbroner, Robert L. 1986, *The Essential Adam Smith*, W. W. Norton & Company, New York.

Heilbroner, Robert L. 1990, 'Economics as Ideology', in W. J. Samuels (ed.), *Economics as Discourse*, Kluser Academic Publishers, Boston.

Henry, Ken 2007, *Achieving and Maintaining Full Employment*, Sir Roland Wilson Foundation Lecture, http://www.treasury.gov.au/documents/1296/RTF/Sir_Roland_Wilson_Foundation_Lecture.rtf

Hesse, Mary 1978, 'Theory and Value in the Social Sciences', in

Hilmer, F., Rayner, M. and Taperell, G. 1993, *National Competition Policy*, Report by the Independent Committee of Inquiry, AGPS, Canberra.

Hirsch, Fred 1977, *Social Limits to Growth*, Routledge & Kegan Paul, London.

Hirschman, Albert O. 1983, 'Morality and the Social Sciences: A Durable Tension', in N. Haan, R. N. Bellah, P. Rabinow and W. M. Sullivan (eds) 1983, *Social Science as Moral Inquiry*, Columbia University Press, New York.

Hirshleifer, Jack 1982, 'Evolutionary Models in Economics and Law: Cooperation versus Conflict Strategies', in R. O. Zerbe Jr and P. H. Rubin (eds), *Research in Law and Economics*, 4, p. 52.

Hirshleifer, Jack 1985, 'The Expanding Domain of Economics', *American Economic Review*, 75, (6), p. 53.

Hobbes, Thomas 1651 [1968], *Leviathan*, Pelican Classics, London.

Hobsbawm, E. J. 1990, *Industry and Empire*, Penguin, Harmondsworth.

Hobson, Peter 2002, *The Cradle of Thought*, Macmillan, London.

Hodgson, Geoffrey M. 1988, *Economics and Institutions*, Polity Press, Cambridge.

Hodgson, Geoffrey M. 1993, *Economics and Evolution: Bringing Life Back into Economics*, Polity Press, Cambridge.

Hollis, Martin 1977, *Models of Man*, Cambridge University Press, London.

Hollis, Martin 1985, 'Of Masks and Men', in M. Carrithers, S. Collins and S. Lukes (eds), *The Category of the Person*, Cambridge University Press, Cambridge.

Hollis, Martin and Nell, Edward 1975, *Rational Economic Man*, Cambridge University Press, Cambridge.

Hookway, C. and Pettit, P. 1978, *Action and Interpretation: Studies in the philosophy of the social sciences*, Cambridge University Press, Cambridge.

Hoover, Kevin D. 1995, 'Why Does Methodology Matter for Economics', *The Economic Journal*, 105.

Horton, Robin 1967, 'African Traditional Thought and Western Science', *Africa*, 37, pp. 50–71.

Horwitz, Morton J. 1974, 'The Historical Foundations of Modern Contract Law', *Harvard Law Review*, 87, (5), March, pp. 918–56.

Horwitz, Morton J. 1977a, *The Transformation of American Law, 1780–1860*, Harvard University Press, Cambridge.

Horwitz, Morton J. 1977b, *Yale Law Journal*, 86, pp. 561–4.

Horwitz, Morton J. 1992, *The Transformation of American Law 1870–1960*, Oxford University Press, New York.

Howell, David 2000, *The Edge of Now: New Questions for Democracy in the Network Age*, Macmillan.

htpp//www.spartacus.schoolnet.co.uk/PKluddites.htm

http://dspace.dial.pipex.com/town/terrace/adw03/c-eight/pitt/repress.htm#comb

http://dspace.dial.pipex.com/town/terrace/adw03/peel/poorlaw/attacks.htm

http://en.wikipedia.org/wiki/Adolph_Lowe

http://en.wikipedia.org/wiki/Causality

http://en.wikipedia.org/wiki/Daniel_Kahneman.html

http://en.wikipedia.org/wiki/General_equilibrium

http://en.wikipedia.org/wiki/Institutional_economics.html

http://www.cbc.ca/ideas/massey.html

http://www.econlib.org/library/Enc/Information.html

http://www.historyplace.com/worldhistory/famine/hunger.htm

http://www.miskatonic.org/godel.html

http://www.rootsweb.com/~irlker/famemig.html

http://www.vincentpeters.nl/triskelle/history/greatfaminepolitics.php?index=060.090.010

Hume, David 1878, *A Treatise on Human Nature: being an attempt to introduce the experimental method of reasoning into moral subjects and dialogues concerning natural religion*, Longmans Green, London.

Hume, David 1966, *Treatise of Human Nature*, Clarendon Press, London.

Hume, David 1978, *A Treatise of Human Nature*, Oxford.

Hume, David 1980, 'Social Contract', in E. Baker (ed.), *Essays by Locke, Hume and Rousseau*, Greenwood Press, Westport, Conn.

Humphrey, N. K. 1976, 'The social function of intellect', in P. P. G. Bateson and A. Hinde (eds), *Growing Points in Ethology*, Cambridge University Press, Cambridge.

Jevons, H. S. 1871, *The Theory of Political Economy*, London, Macmillan and Co.

Jones, Evan 2000, Economic Utopia and its Handmaidens, Unpublished manuscript.

Jonsen, A. R. and Toulmin, S. 1988, *The Abuse of Casuistry*, University of California Press, Berkeley.

Jordan, Kirrily and Stilwell, Frank 2007, *Who Gets What? Analysing Economic Inequality in Australia*, Cambridge University Press, Sydney.

Kanth, Rajani J. 1986, *Political Economy and Laissez-Faire*, Rowman & Littlefield, Totowa, NJ.

Kaye, Bruce 1994, 'The real issue in business ethics? Institutional ethics and the free market', *Australian Journal of Management*, June.

Keen, Steve 2001, *Debunking Economics: The Naked Emperor of the Social Sciences*, Pluto Press, Sydney.

Keen, Steve 2006,

Keesing, Roger M. 1981, *Cultural Anthropology, A Contemporary Perspective*, 2nd edition, Holt, Rinehart and Wilston, Fort Worth.

Kellner, Douglas 1988, 'Postmodernism as Social Theory: Some Challenges and Problems', *Theory, Culture & Society*, 5.

Kennedy, Ian 1981, *The Unmasking of Medicine*, George Allen and Unwin, London.

Key, Catherine A. and Aiello, Leslie C. 1999, title?, in R. Dunbar, C. Knight and C. Power (eds), *The Evolution of Culture*, Rutgers University Press, New Brunswick, NJ.

Keynes, J. M. 1926, *The End of Laissez-Faire*, The Hogarth Press, London.

Keynes, J. M. 1936, *The General Theory of Employment, Interest and Money*, Macmillan Cambridge University Press, Cambridge.

Kincaid, Harold 1996, *Philosophical Foundations of the Social Sciences*, Cambridge University Press, Cambridge.

Kinealy, Christine 2002, *The Great Irish Famine*, Palgrave, London.

Klamer, Arjo and McCloskey, Dierdre 1988, *The Consequences of Economic Rhetoric*, Cambridge University Press, Cambridge.

Klamer, Arjo, McCloskey, Dierdre and Zilias, Stephen 2007, 'Is There Life After Samuelson's Economics? Changing the Textbooks', *Post-Autistic Economic Review*, (42), 18 May 2007, http://www.paecon.net/PAEReview/

Kline, Morris 1980, *Mathematics: The Loss of Certainty*, Oxford University Press.

Knauft, Bruce M. 1996, *Genealogies for the Present in Cultural Anthropology*, Routledge, New York.

Knight, F. H. 1935, 'The Ethics of Competition and Other Essays', *Internal Journal of Ethics*, 45, (1), January, pp. 200–20.

Knodt, Eva M. 1995, 'Foreword', in N. Luhmann, *Social Systems*, Stanford University Press, Stanford.

Koslowski, Peter F. 1983, 'The Ethics of Capitalism', in S. Pejovic (ed.), *Philosophical and Economic Foundations of Capitalism*, Lexington Books, Lexington.

Kruskal, W. K. (ed.) 1982, *The Future of the Social Sciences*, University of Chicago Press, Chicago.

Krygier, M. 1996, 'The Sources of Civil Society', *Quadrant*, November.

Kuhn, T. S. 1970, *The Structure of Scientific Revolutions*, 2nd edition, University of Chicago Press, Chicago.

Kuhn, T. S. 1977, *The Essential Tension*, University of Chicago Press, Chicago.

Kung, Hans 1988, *Theology for the Third Millennium, An Ecumenical View*, Doubleday, New York.

Lacan, Jacques 1991, *Lacan and the Subject of Language*, E. Ragland-Sullivan and M. Bracher (eds), Routledge, New York.

Lakoff, G. and Johnson, M. 1980, *Metaphors We Live By*, University of Chicago Press, Chicago.

Landes, Elizabeth M. and Posner, Richard A. 1978, 'The Economics of the Baby Shortage', *Journal of Legal Studies*, 7.

Langmore, John and Quiggin, John 1994, *Work for All*, Melbourne University Press.

Lawrence, D. H. 1977, *The Complete Poems*, Penguin, Harmondsworth.

Lawson, Tony 2003, *Reorienting Economics*, Routledge, London.

Leontief, W. 1983, *Why Economics is Not Yet a Science*, Macmillan, London.

Lessnoff, Michael 1986, *Social Contract*, Macmillan, Basingstoke.

Levack, Brian P. 1987, *The Witch-Hunt in Early Modern Europe*, Longman, London.

Levine, Donald N. 1986, 'The Forms and Functions of Social Knowledge', in D. W. Fiske and R. A. Shweder, *Pluralisms and Subjectivities*, University of Chicago Press, Chicago.

Lewis, C. I. 1932, 'Alternative Systems of Logic', *Monist*, 42, October.

Lieberman, Philip 1998, *Eve Spoke*, Picador, London.

Lindblom, C. E. 1977, *Politics and Markets*, Basic Books, New York.

Lindblom, C. E. 1982, 'The Market as Prison', *The Journal of Politics*, 44, (2).

Lipsey, Richard 2005, *Home Page*, http://www.sfu.ca/~rlipsey/res.html

Lipsey, Richard 2007, 'Reflections on the General Theory of Second Best at its Golden Jubilee', *International Tax and Public Finance*, 14, (4), August.

Lipsey, Richard G. and Harbury, Colin 1988, *First Principles of Economics*, Weidenfeld Paperbacks, London.

Lipsey, Richard G., Bekar, Cliff and Carlaw, Kenneth 1998, 'What Requires Explanation?', in E. Helpman (ed.), *General Purpose Technologies and Economic Growth*, MIT Press, Cambridge, Mass.

Lipsey, Richard G., Carlaw, Kenneth I. and Bekar, Clifford T. 2005, *Economic Transformations, General Purpose Technologies and Long Term Economic growth*, Oxford University Press, Oxford.

Llewellyn, Karl N. 1931–32, 'What Price Contract', *Yale Law Journal*, (40), pp. 704–51.

Loomes, G. 1991.

Lowe, Adolph 1935, *Economics and Sociology*, George Allen and Unwin, London.

Lowe, Adolph 1965 [1977], *On Economic Knowledge*, M. E. Sharp Inc., New York.

Lowe, Adolph 1969, 'Towards a Science of Political Economy', in R. L. Heilbroner (ed.), *Economic Means and Social Ends*, Prentice-Hall, Eaglewood Cliffs.

Loy, David R. 1997, *The Religion of the Market*, www.bpf.org/tsangha/loy-market.html

Loy, David R. 2002, *A Buddhist History of the West*, State University of New York Press, New York.

Lucke, H. K. 1987, 'Good Faith and Contractual Performance', in P. D. Finn (ed.), *Essays on Contract*, The Law Book Company, North Ryde.

Lux, Kenneth 1990, *Adam Smith's Mistake, How a Moral Philosopher Invented Economics and Ended Morality*, Shambhala, Boston.

Lyotard, Jean-Francois 1984, *The Postmodern Condition: A Report on Knowledge*, University of Minnesota Press, Minneapolis.

Macaulay, Stewart 1963, 'Non-Contractual Relations in Business: A Preliminary Study', *American Sociological Review*, 28, (1), pp. 55–67.

MacIntyre, Alisdair 1966, *A Short History of Ethics*, Routledge and Kegan Paul, London.

MacIntyre, Alisdair 1981, *After Virtue*, 2nd edition (1985), Duckworth, London.

MacIntyre, Alisdair 1988, *Whose Justice? Which Rationality?*, Duckworth, London.

Macneil, Ian R. 1980, *The New Social Contract*, Yale University Press, New Haven.

Macpherson, C. B. 1964, *The Political Theory of Possessive Individualism: Hobbes to Locke*, Clarendon Press, Oxford.

Madsen, R., Sullivan, W. M., Swidler, A. and Tipson, S. M. 2002, *Meaning and Modernity: Religion, Polity, and Self*, University of California Press, Berkeley.

Mallery, John C., Hurwitz, Roger and Duffy, Gaven 1986, *Hermeneutics: From Textual Explication to Computer Understanding*, http://www.ai.mit.edu/people/jcma/papers/1986-ai-memo-871/me

Malthus, Thomas 1973, title?, in L. D. Abbott (ed.), *Masterworks of Economics, Volume 1*, McGraw-Hill.

Mandelbaum, D. G. (ed.) 1949, *Selected Writings of Edward Sapir*, University of California Press, Berkeley.

Mannheim, Karl 1936, *Ideology and Utopia*, Routledge, London.

Mansbridge, Jane 1998, 'Starting with Nothing', in A. Ben-Ner and L. Putterman (eds), *Economics, Values and Organizations*, Cambridge University Press, Cambridge.

Mantoux, Paul 1961, *The Industrial Revolution in the Eighteenth Century*, Macmillan, New York.

Markoff, J. and Montecinos, V. 1993, 'The Ubiquitous Rise of Economists', *Journal of Public Policy*, 13, (I), pp. 37–68.

Marsh, Ian 1994, 'The Development and Impact of Australia's "Think Tanks"', *Australian Journal of Management*, December.

Marty, Martin E. and Appleby, R. Scott (eds) 1993, *Fundamentalisms and Society, Reclaiming the Sciences, the Family and Education*, University of Chicago Press, Chicago.

Marx, Karl 1961, *Selected Writings in Sociology and Social Philosophy*, 2nd edition, Penguin, Harmondsworth.

Marx, Karl and Engels, Frederick 1970, *The German Ideology*, International, New York.

Mason, A. M. and Gageler, S. J. 1987, title?, in P. D. Finn (ed.), *Essays on Contract*, The Law Book Company, North Ryde.

McCloskey, D. N. 1994, *Knowledge and Persuasion in Economics*, Cambridge University Press, Cambridge.

McCombie, J. S. R. 2006, 'The Nature of Economic Growth and the Neoclassical Approach: More Questions Than Answers', in P. Arestis, J. McCombie and R. Vickerman (eds), *Growth and Economic Development: Essays in honour of A.P. Thirlwall*.

McGuinness, P. P. 1997, *Sydney Morning Herald*, 13 August 1997.

McIntyre, John 2005, 'The March of Progress', *Australian Financial Review*, 29 April, Review p. 1.

McKenna, Bernard 2005, 'Wisdom, Ethics and the Postmodern Organization', in D. Rooney, G. Hearn and A. Ninan 2005, *Handbook of the Knowledge Economy*, Edward Elgar, Cheltenham.

McPherson, Michael S. 1983, 'Want Formation, Morality, and Some "Interpretive" Aspects of Economic Inquiry', in N. Haan, R. N. Bellah, P. Rabinow and W. M. Sullivan (eds) 1983, *Social Science as Moral Inquiry*, Columbia University Press, New York.

Mead, George Herbert 1934, *Mind, Self and Society*, University of Chicago Press, Chicago.

Meek, Ronald L. 1977, *Smith, Marx and After*, Chapman & Hall, London.

Meszaros, Istvan 1995, *Beyond Capital*, Merlin Press, 3.2.1, www.marxists.org/archive/meszaros/works/beyond-capital/ch03-2.htm

Midgley, Mary 1984, 'Sex and Personal Identity, The Western Individualistic Tradition', *Encounter*, 63, (1), June.

Midgley, Mary 1994, *The Ethical Primate*, Routledge, London.

Miliband, Ralph 1969, *The State in Capitalist Society*, Weidenfeld and Nicolson, London.

Mill, John Stuart 1874, *A System of Logic, Ratiocinative and Induction*, 8th edition, Harper and Brothers, New York.

Mill, John Stuart 1962, *Utilitarianism*, New American Library, New York.

Mill, John Stuart 1994, *Principles of Political Economy*, Oxford University Press, Oxford.

Miller, J. G. 1984, 'Culture and the development of everyday social explanation', *Journal of Personality and Social Psychology*, 46, pp. 961–78.

Milton, J. R. 1998, 'Laws of Nature', in D. Garber and M. Ayers, *The Cambridge History of Seventeenth-Century Philosophy Volume 1*, Cambridge University Press, Cambridge.

Mirowski, Phillip 1989, *More Heat Than Light: Economics as Social Physics, Physics as Nature's Economics*, Cambridge University Press, Cambridge.

Mitchell, Wesley C. 1918,

Mokyr, Joel 2002, *The Gifts of Athena*, Princeton University Press, Princeton.

Morrice, David 1996, *Philosophy, Science and Ideology in Political Thought*, Macmillan, London.

Murphy, John P. 1990, *Pragmatism From Peirce to Davidson*, Westview Press, Boulder.

Murphy, Nancey 1996, *Beyond Liberalism and Fundamentalism*, Trinity Press International, Valley Forge.

Myrdal, Gunnar 1953, *The Political Element in the Development of Economic Theory*.

Nagel, Ernst 1961, *The Structure of Science*, Harcourt, Brace and World, New York.

Nagel, Ernst and Newman, James R. 1959, *Gödel's Proof*, Routledge and Kegan Paul, London.

Needham, Joseph 1947, *Science and Society in Ancient China, Conway Memorial Lecture*, Watts and Co., London.

Neville, J. W. 1997, 'Economic Rationalism: Social philosophy masquerading as economic science', *Background Paper No. 7*, The Australia Institute, Lyneham.

Niebuhr, Reinhold 1944, *The Children of Light and the Children of Darkness*, Charles Scribner's Sons, New York.

Niebuhr, Reinhold 1965, *Beyond Tragedy: Essays on the Christian Interpretation of History*, Nisbet, London.

Noble, William and Davidson, Iain 1996, *Human Evolution, Language and Mind*, Cambridge.

North, Douglass C. 1990, *Institutions, Institutional Change and Economic Performance*, Cambridge University Press.

North, Douglass C. 1998, title?, in A. Ben-Ner and L. Putterman (eds), *Economics, Values and Organizations*, Cambridge University Press, Cambridge.

Oakeshott, Michael 1962, *Rationalism in Politics and Other Essays*, Methuen, London.

Ong, Walter J. 1977, *Interfaces of the Word*, Cornell University Press, Ithaca.

Ormerod, Paul 1994, *The Death of Economics*, Faber and Faber, London.

Ormerod, Paul 1998, *Butterfly Economics*, Faber and Faber, London.

Ormerod, Paul 2001, 'Revisiting the Death of Economics', *World Economics*, 2, (2), April–June, p. 3.

Ormerod, Paul 2006, 'Shun the rational agent to rebuild economics', *Post-Autistic Economics Review*, (40), 1 December 2006, http://www.pae-con.net/PAEReview

Outhwaite, William 1987, *New Philosophies of Social Science*, Macmillan, Basingstoke.

Ozel, Huseyin 2002, 'Closing Open Systems: The "Double Hermeneutic" in Economics', *International Congress in Economics*, VI, Middle East Technical University.

Pareto, Vilfredo 1896 [1964], *Cours d' conomie politique*, Rougwe, Laussanne, reprinted in Oeuvere completes, vol. 1.

Parsons, Talcott 1949, *Essays in Sociological Theory: Pure and Applied*, Free Press, Glencoe, Ill.

Passmore, John 1967, *Logical Positivism, The Encyclopaedia of Philosophy*, Macmillan & Collier MacMillan, New York.

Passmore, John 1994, personal communication.

Peirce, Charles S. 1934, *Collected Papers, Volume 5*, Harvard University Press, Cambridge, Mass.

Penrose, Roger 1995, 'Consciousness involves non-computable ingredients', in J. Brockman (ed.), *The Third Culture*, Simon & Schuster, New York.

Philips, Helen 2006, 'Everyday fairytales', *New Scientist*, 7 October 2006.

Phillips, Derek L. 1986, *Towards a Just Social Order*, Princeton University Press, Princeton.

Pitt, William 1817, *Speeches of William Pitt, Volume 1*, London.

Plamenatz, John 1963 [1992], *Man and Society, Volume II, From Montesquieu to the Early Socialists*, Longman, Hartlow.

Plotkin, Henry 1994, *Darwin Machines and the Nature of Knowledge*, Harvard University Press, Cambridge, Mass.

Polanyi, Karl 1944, *The Great Transformation*, Rinehart, New York.

Polanyi, Karl 1957 [1992], 'The Economy as an Instituted Process', reprinted in M. Granovetter and R. Swedberg, *The Sociology of Economic Life*, Westview Press, Boulder.

Polanyi, Karl 1971, *The Great Transformation*, Beacon Press, Boston.

Polanyi, Michael 1946, *Science, Faith and Society*, Oxford University Press, Oxford.

Polanyi, Michael 1958, *Personal Knowledge, Towards a Post-Critical Philosophy*, Routledge & Kegan Paul, London.

Popper, K. R. date?, *On the Sources of Knowledge and Ignorance*,

Popper, K. R. 1959, *The Logic of Scientific Discovery*, Harper, New York.

Popper, K. R. 1962, *Conjectures and Refutations: The Growth of Scientific Knowledge*, Basic Books, New York.

Popper, K. R. 1974, *Unended Quest*, Fontana, London.

Porter, Michael E. 1979, 'On Competition', *Harvard Business Review*, Boston.

Posner, Richard 1981, *The Economics of Justice*, Harvard University Press, Cambridge, Mass.

Purcell, Edward A. Jr 1973, *The Crisis of Democratic Theory*, The University of Kentucky, Lexington.

Pusey, M. 1991, *Economic Rationalism in Canberra*, Cambridge University Press, Melbourne.

Putnam, Hilary 1978, *Meaning and the Moral Sciences*, Routledge & Kegan Paul, London.

Putnam, Hilary 2002, *The Collapse of the Fact/Value Dichotomy*, Harvard University Press, Cambridge, Mass.

Quiggin, John 1999, 'Rationalism and Rationality in Economics', *On Line Opinion*, www.onlineopinion.com.au

Quiggin, John 2002, http://johnquiggin.com/index.php/archives/2002/07/30/news-from-across-the-tasman/

Quine, W. V. 1963, 'Carnap and Logical Truth', in P. A. Schilpp (ed.), *The Philosophy of Rudolf Carnap*, Open Court, LaSalle, Ill.

Rabinow, Paul 1983, 'Humanism as Nihilism: The Bracketing of Truth and Seriousness in American Cultural Anthropology', in N. Haan, R. N. Bellah, P. Rabinow and W. M. Sullivan (eds), *Social Science as Moral Inquiry*, Columbia University Press, New York.

Rawlings, John 1999, *Derrida*, http://prelectur.stanford.edu/lecturers/derrida/

Rawls, John 1971, *A Theory of Justice*, Belknap Press, Cambridge, Mass.

Reid, Duncan 1993, 'So What's New With the New Paradigm?', *St Mark's Review*, Summer, Canberra.

Reiman, Jeffrey 1990, *Justice and Modern Moral Philosophy*, Yale University Press, New Haven.

Reith, Peter 1997, 'New Deal: Fair deal—giving small business a fair go', Statement by the Minister for Workplace Relations and Small Business, September 1997.

Rengger, N. J. 1995, *Political Theory, Modernity and Postmodernity*, Blackwell, Oxford.

Reynolds, Peter C. 1981, *On the Evolution of Human Behavior: The argument from animals to man*, University of California Press, Berkeley.

Richter, Frank M. 1986, 'Nonlinear Behaviour', in D. W. Fiske and R. A. Shweder, *Pluralisms and Subjectivities*, University of Chicago Press, Chicago.

Robbins, L. 1932, *An Essay on the Nature and Significance of Economic Science*, Macmillan, London.

Robbins, L. year?, *Theory of Economic Policy in English Classical Political Economy*.

Robinson, Joan 1954, 'The Impossibility of Competition', in L. H. Chamberlin (ed.), *Monopoly, Competition and their Regulation*, Macmillan, London.

Rorty, Richard 1979, *Philosophy and the Mirror of Nature*, Princeton University Press, Princeton.

Rorty, Richard 1980, *Philosophy and the Mirror of Nature*, Basil Blackwell, Oxford.

Rorty, Richard 1991, *Objectivity, Relativism and Truth, Philosophical Papers, Volume I*, Cambridge University Press, Cambridge.

Rosenberg, Alexander 1986, title?, in D. W. Fiske and R. A. Shweder, *Pluralisms and Subjectivities*, University of Chicago Press, Chicago.

Rothschild, Emma 2001, *Economic Sentiments: Adam Smith, Condorcet, and the Enlightenment*, Harvard University Press.

Rousseau, Jean-Jacques 1935, *The Social Contract and Discourses*, Dent & Dutton.

Ryan, Alan 1970, *The Philosophy of the Social Sciences*, Macmillan, London.

Sahlins, M. D. 1960, 'The Origin of Society', *Scientific American*, 203, (3), September, pp. 77–86.

Samuels, Warren J. (ed.) 1990, *Economics as Discourse*, Kluser Academic Publishers, Boston.

Samuels, Warren J. 1972, 'Welfare Economics, Power and Property', in G. Wunderlich and W. G. Gibson Jr (eds), *Perspectives of Property*, Pennsylvania State University.

Samuels, Warren J. 1980, 'Economics as science and its relation to policy: The example of free trade', *Journal of Economic Issues*, 14, March.

Sartre, Jean-Paul 1964, *The Words*, Braziller, New York.

Saul, John Ralston 2001, *On Equilibrium*, Penguin Books, Canada.

Schostak, John 2002, *Critiquing Critical Realism: A working paper*, ECER Conference, Portugal, http://www.enquirylearning.net/ELU/Issues/Research/Critical%20Realism.htm

Schumpeter, Joseph A. 1976, *Capitalism, Socialism and Democracy*, 5th edition, George Allen and Unwin, London.

Secord, Paul F. 1986, 'Explanation in the Social Sciences', in D. W. Fiske and R. A. Shweder, *Pluralisms and Subjectivities*, University of Chicago Press, Chicago.

Self, Peter 1999, *Rolling Back the Market: Economic dogma and political choice*, Macmillan Press, Houndmills, Hampshire.

Seligman, Adam B. 1992, *The Idea of Civil Society*, Princeton University Press, Princeton.

Sen, Amartya K. 1977, 'Rational Fools: A Critique of the Behavioural Foundations of Economic Theory', *Philosophy & Public Affairs*, 6, (4).

Sen, Amartya K. 1987, *On Ethics and Economics*, Blackwell, Oxford.

Senge, Peter 1992a, *The Fifth Discipline*, Century Business, London.

Senge, Peter 1992b, *The Fifth Discipline*, Random House, Milsons Point.

Senior, Nassau 1965, *An Outline of the Science of Political Economy*, Augustus M. Kelly, New York.

Service, Elman R. 1975, *Origins of the State and Civilization, The Process of Cultural Evolution*, W. W. Norton & Company, New York.

Shackle, G. L. S. 1961, *Decision, Order and Time in Human Affairs*, Cambridge University Press, Cambridge.

Shergold, Peter 2003, *Two Cheers for the Bureaucracy: Public Service, Political Advice and Network Governance*, Australian Public Service Commission Lunchtime Seminar, 13 June, www.pmc.gov.au/docs/Shergold1306.cfm

Shotter, John 1985, 'Social Accountability and Self Specification', in K. J. Gergen and K. E. Davis, *The Social Construction of the Person*, Springer-Verlag, New York.

Shubik, Martin 1970, 'A Curmudgeon's Guide to Microeconomics', *Journal of Economic Literature*, 8, (2), June.

Shweder, Richard A. 1986, 'Divergent Rationalities', in D. W. Fiske and R. A. Shweder, *Pluralisms and Subjectivities*, University of Chicago Press, Chicago.

Shweder, Richard A. and Miller, Joan G. 1985, 'The Social Construction of the Person: How is it Possible?', in K. J. Gergen and K. E. Davis, *The Social Construction of the Person*, Springer-Verlag, New York.

Simon, Herbert A. 1991, 'Organizations and Markets', *Journal of Economic Perspectives*, 5, (2), Spring, pp. 25–44.

Simons, Robert G. 1995, *Competing Gospels, Public Theology and Economic Theory*, E. J. Dwyer, Alexandria.

Smelser, Neil J. and Swedberg, Richard 1994, 'The Sociological Perspective on the Economy', in N. J. Smelser and R. Swedberg, 1994

Smith, Adam 1757 [1976], *Theory of Moral Sentiments*, Raphael and Macfie, Oxford, http://www.adamsmith.org/smith/tms/tms-index.htm

Smith, Adam 1776, *An Inquiry Into the Nature and Causes of the Wealth of Nations*, http://www.econlib.org/LIBRARY/Smith/smWN.html

Smolin, Lee 1998, *The Life of the Cosmos*, Phoenix, London.

Solomon, Robert C. and Higgins, Kathleen M. 1996, *A Short History of Philosophy*, Oxford University Press, New York.

Sophocles, *Antigone, The Thespian Plays*.

Soros, George 2002, *On Globalization*, Public Affairs, New York.

Spradley, James P. and McCurdy, 1994, *Conformity & Conflict, Readings in Cultural Anthropology*, 8th edition, Davis W. Harper Collins College Publishers, New York.

St Augustine [1972], *City of God*, Pelican Classics.

Stackhouse, Max L. 1999a, *Mutual Obligation as Covenantal Justice in a Global Era*, Paper Delivered at A Colloquium on Hard Choices, John XXIII College, The Australian National University, 29 September 1999.

Stackhouse, Max L. 1999b, *Public Theology in Global Perspective: A Reformed View*, 1st draft, Paper Delivered at A Colloquium on Hard Choices, John XXIII College, The Australian National University, 29 September 1999.

Stark, Werner 1962, *The Fundamental Forms of Social Thought*, Routledge and Kegan Paul, London.

Stark, Werner 1971, *The Sociology of Knowledge*, Routledge & Kegan Paul, London.

Stark, Werner 1976, *The Social Bond, Volume I, Antecedents of the Social Bond, The Phylogeny of Sociability*, Fordham University Press, New York.

Stark, Werner 1978, *The Social Bond, An Investigation into the Bases of Law-Abidingness, Volume II, Antecedents of the Social Bond, The Ontogeny of Sociality*, Fordham University Press, New York.

Stark, Werner 1983, *The Social Bond, Volume IV, Safeguards of the Social Bond, Ethos and Religion*, Fordham University Press, New York.

Stiglitz, J. E. 1991, 'The Invisible Hand and Modern Welfare Economics', in D. Vines and A. Stevenson (eds), *Information, Strategy and Public Policy*, Basil Blackwell, Glasgow.

Stiglitz, J. E. 1993, 'The Role of the State in Financial Markets', *Proceedings of the World Bank Annual Conference on Development Economics*.

Stiglitz, J. E. 2002a, 'Striking a Better Deal', *Australian Financial Review*, 17 May 2002, Review p. 2.

Stiglitz, J. E. 2002b, *Globalization and Its Discontents*, W. W. Norton & Company, New York.

Stiglitz, J. E. 2003, *The Roaring Nineties*, W. W. Norton & Company, New York.

Stiglitz, J. E. 2005, 'In Search of the Ethical Economy', *Australian Financial Review*, 18 November, Review p. 10.

Stilwell, Frank 2002, *Political Economy, The Contest of Economic Ideas*, Oxford University Press, South Melbourne.

Stobæus, Joannes, *Pythagorean Ethical Sentences*, http://www.sacred-texts.com/cla/gvp/gvp08.htm

Stone, J. 2000, 'Dollar could use less speculation', *Australian Financial Review*, Wednesday, 20 September, p. 25.

Sugden, Robert 1998, 'Normative Expectations', in A. Ben-Ner and L. Putterman (eds), *Economics, Values and Organizations*, Cambridge University Press, Cambridge.

Swartz, Norman 1995, 'A Neo-Human Perspective: Laws as Regularities', in F. Weinert (ed.), *Laws of Nature—Essays on the Philosophical, Scientific and Historical Dimensions*, Walter de Gruyter, New York.

Swidler, A. 2002, 'Saving the Self', in R. Madsen, W. M. Sullivan, A. Swidler and S. M. Tipson, *Meaning and Modernity: Religion, Polity, and Self*, University of California Press, Berkeley.

Sydney Morning Herald 2007, 'Millions Yearn for 9-to-5 Heyday', *Sydney Morning Herald*, 2 June 2007.

Taperell, G. Q., Vermeesch, R. B. and Harland, D. J. 1978, *Trade Practices and Consumer Protection*, 2nd edition, Butterworths, Sydney.

Tarnas, Richard 1991, *The Passion of the Western Mind*, Pimlico, London.

Tawney, R. H. 1926 [1938], *Religion and the Rise of Capitalism*, Pelican Books.

The Cambridge 27 2001, 'Opening Up Economics', *Post-Autistic Economics Newsletter*, (7), July, Article 1, http://www.btinternet.com/~pae_news/review/issue7.htm

Thompson, E. P. 1963 [1968], *The Making of the English Working Class*, Penguin Books, Harmondsworth.

Tierney, Nathan L. year?, *Imagination and Ethical Ideals*, ?.

Tillich, Paul 1963, *Systematic Theology Volume III*, University of Chicago Press, Chicago.

Tipson, S. M. 2002, 'Social Differentiation and Moral Pluralism', in R. Madsen, W. M. Sullivan, A. Swidler and S. M. Tipson, *Meaning and Modernity: Religion, Polity, and Self*, University of California Press, Berkeley.

Toulmin, Stephen Edelston 1958, *Uses of Argument*, Cambridge University Press, Cambridge.

Toulmin, Stephen Edelston 1972, *Human Understanding, Volume 1*, Princeton University Press, Princeton.

Toulmin, Stephen Edelston 1990, *Cosmopolis*, The Free Press, New York.

Tracey, David 1976, *Chicago University Lectures*.

Trichet, Jean-Claude 2004,

Turner, Jonathan H. 1987, 'Analytical Theorising', in A. Giddens and J. H. Turner (eds), *Social Theory Today*, Stanford University Press, Stanford.

van Wanrooy, B. 2007, *A Desire for 9 to 5: Australians' Preference for a Standard Working Week*.

Veblen, T. 1898, 'Why Economics is not an Evolutionary Science', *Quarterly Journal of Economics*, XIII.

Veblen, T. 1961, *The Place of Science in Modern Civilisation*, Russell Sage, New York.

Viner, Jacob 1960, 'The Intellectual History of Laissez-Faire', *Journal of Law and Economics*.

von Bruck, Michael 1986, *The Unity of Reality*, James V. Zeitz (trans.), Paulist Press, New York.

Voorhoeve, Alex 2003, http://www.philosophers.co.uk/cafe/phil_oct2003.htm

Waldrop, Mitchell 1992, *Complexity*, Viking, London.

Walker, E. Ronald 1943, *From Economic Theory to Policy*, University of Chicago Press, Chicago.

Webb, Keith 1995, *An Introduction to Problems in the Philosophy of Social Sciences*, Pinter, London.

Weber, Max 1930, *The Protestant Ethic and the Spirit of Capitalism*, Talcott Parsons (trans.), Unwin Paperbacks, London.

Weber, Max 1949, *The Methodology of the Social Sciences*, E. A. Shils and H. A. Finch (trans.), The Free Press.

Weber, Max 1958, 'Science as Vocation', in H. Gerth and C. Wright Mills (trans. and eds), *From Max Weber: Essays in Sociology*, Oxford University Press, New York.

Weber, Max 1978, *Economy and Society*, University of California Press, Berkeley.

Westphal, J. D. and Khanna, Poonam (forthcoming), 'Keeping Directors in Line: Social Distancing as a Control Mechanism in the Corporate Elite', *Administrative Science Quarterly*.

White, Stephen K. 1991, title?, Cambridge University Press, Cambridge.

Whitwell, G. 1986, *The Treasury Line*, Allen & Unwin, Sydney.

Whorf, B. L. 1967, *Language Thought and Reality*, J. Carroll (ed.), MIT Press, Cambridge, Mass.

Wicks, Robert 2004, *Nietzche*, http://plato.stanford.edu/entries/nietzsche/

Williams, Pamela 2004, 'Howard's legacy: an entrenched, hand-picked elite', *Australian Financial Review*, 16 July 2004, p. 1.

Williamson, Oliver E. 1994, 'Transaction Cost Economics and Organizational Theory', in N. J. Smelser and R. Swedberg, 1994

Wimsatt, William C. 1986, 'Heuristics and the Study of Human Behaviour', in D. W. Fiske and R. A. Shweder, *Pluralisms and Subjectivities*, University of Chicago Press, Chicago.

Winch, Peter 1958, *The Idea of a Social Science and its Relation to Philosophy*, Humanities Press, New York.

Winch, Peter 1970, 'Comment on Jarvie paper', in R. Borger and F. Cioffi, *Explanation in the Behavioural Sciences*, Cambridge University Press, Cambridge.

Winner, Langdon 1977, *Autonomous Technology, Technics-Out-of-Control as a Theme in Political Thought*, MIT Press, Cambridge, Mass.

Wittgenstein, Ludwig 1951, *Philosophical Investigations*.

Wittgenstein, Ludwig 1978, *Tractatus Logico-Philosophicus 4.0022*, D. F. Pears and B. F. McGuinness (trans), London.

Wolterstorff, Nicholas 1995, *From Presence to Practice: Mind, World, and Entitlement to Believe, Gifford Lectures*.

Woodham-Smith, C. 1992, *The Great Famine: Ireland 1845–1849*, Penguin Books, Harmondsworth.

Zippelius, R. 1986, 'Exclusion and shunning as legal and social sanctions', *Ethnology and Sociobiology*, 7, pp. 159–66.

www.ingramcontent.com/pod-product-compliance
Lightning Source LLC
Chambersburg PA
CBHW050038220326
41599CB00041B/7206